D0409118

Entry and Escape in Nazi Europe

RONALD WEBER

IVAN R. DEE
Lanham • Boulder • New York • Toronto • Plymouth, UK

Ivan R. Dee
A member of The Rowman & Littlefield Publishing Group, Inc.
4501 Forbes Boulevard, Suite 200, Lanham, Maryland 20706
http://www.ivanrdee.com

Estover Road, Plymouth PL6 7PY, United Kingdom

Distributed by National Book Network

British Library Cataloguing in Publication Information Available

Library of Congress Cataloging-in-Publication Data
Weber, Ronald, 1934–
    The Lisbon route : entry and escape in Nazi Europe / Ronald Weber.
      p. cm.
    Includes bibliographical references and index.
    ISBN 978-1-56663-876-0 (cloth : alk. paper) — ISBN 978-1-56663-892-0
(electronic)
    1. World War, 1939–1945—Portugal—Lisbon. 2. Exiles—Portugal—Lisbon—
History—20th century. 3. Immigrants—Portugal—Lisbon—History—20th
century. 4. Escapes—Portugal—Lisbon—History—20th century. 5. Neutrality—
Portugal—Lisbon—History—20th century. 6. Lisbon (Portugal)—History—20th
century. 7. Lisbon (Portugal)—Social life and customs—20th century. 8. Lisbon
(Portugal)—Biography. 9. World War, 1939–1945—Biography. 10. World War,
1939–1945—Social aspects—Portugal—Lisbon. I. Title.
    D763.P82L593 2011
    940.53086'9140946942—dc22

                                                                    2010047524

∞™ The paper used in this publication meets the minimum requirements of
American National Standard for Information Sciences—Permanence of Paper for
Printed Library Materials, ANSI/NISO Z39.48-1992.

Printed in the United States of America

For Pat, Liz, Andrea, and Kathy

CONTENTS

PREFACE

The script of Casablanca opens with a capsule account of Lisbon as the escape hatch from Nazi Europe:

A long shot of a revolving globe. As it revolves, lines of fleeing refugees are superimposed over it. Over this scene comes the voice of a narrator.

NARRATOR: With the coming of the Second World War, many eyes in imprisoned Europe turned hopefully, or desperately, toward the freedom of the Americas. Lisbon became the great embarkation point. But not everybody could get to Lisbon directly; and so, a tortuous, roundabout refugee trail sprang up.

After a map displays the circuitous Lisbon route of the film, the narrator checks off the main stops along the way: Paris to Marseille, across the Mediterranean to Oran, around the rim of Africa to Casablanca in French Morocco, and finally—after "wait in Casablanca, and wait, and wait and wait"—to Lisbon.

The Lisbon Route tells the story of refugees like *Casablanca*'s Ilsa and Victor Laszlo who fled to Lisbon in wartime, transforming the tranquil port city on the edge of the Continent into occupied Europe's last open door to freedom. The great bulk of refugees made a land journey to Portugal, and consequently it was in Lisbon rather than Casablanca where they often waited out their long delays. At the same time Lisbon offered escape from Europe, it allowed entry to it, and the following pages also trace the flow of figures who had reason to journey toward the war zone. Whether coming or going, I view those who took the Lisbon route against a background of the illuminated city they reached after the lights of Europe had largely gone out—a city, unlike the City of Light between the wars, that was a funnel to pass through more than a final destination. Those who reached Lisbon in World War II were a tribe of transients, and typically their experience of the city was narrowly bounded by immediate needs of food, shelter, and further transportation.

There was a sense in which the Lisbon of the Portuguese scarcely existed for the transients, and vice versa. An American magazine article in 1941, describing the refugee migration through Lisbon during its high period, held that "all the Portuguese people together with their dictator, virtually vanished from sight. The outside world couldn't see the Portuguese because they were temporarily eclipsed by the swarms of fugitives who descended upon Portugal after the collapse of France." Hugh Muir, a British journalist working in Lisbon during the war, wrote that the wave of refugees, diplomats, spies, and assorted others that washed over the city "left the Portuguese much as they were." Aside from workers in hotels and restaurants who could not avoid it, the "imported activity seemed to be unnoticed by most of the resident population."

Such comments put the divide between the transients and the Portuguese too starkly, yet they suggest the existence of an essentially separate city: the Lisbon of the displaced or those otherwise set in motion by the war. Of course, the city of the Portuguese could not be entirely ignored by the transients, and it is not in these pages. Portugal and the Portuguese provided the setting, the services, and most critically the shield of neutrality that allowed Lisbon to function as a gateway to and from the war. In later chapters I look at matters—diplomatic links with Britain; propaganda and spy warfare; the fate of Portugal's Atlantic islands; trade involvement with both the Allies and Axis—that challenged neutrality and so were of vital importance to the Portuguese and the transients alike. But my primary focus is on the experience of those who paused for long or short periods in the wartime city—as distilled in memoirs, diaries, letters, government reports, press accounts, articles, fiction, film, and theater—rather than on that of those, the willing or unwilling hosts, for whom it was home.

A geographical note: "Lisbon" as used here encompasses the beach communities of the Sun Coast, Sintra, and other nearby locales in Portugal, as it usually did for Lisbon's temporary residents. I also give attention to events and people in locations outside Portugal, mainly the cities of Bordeaux, Marseille, and Madrid, which were important way stations for many who took the Lisbon route.

Europe Following the Franco-German Armistice of June 1940

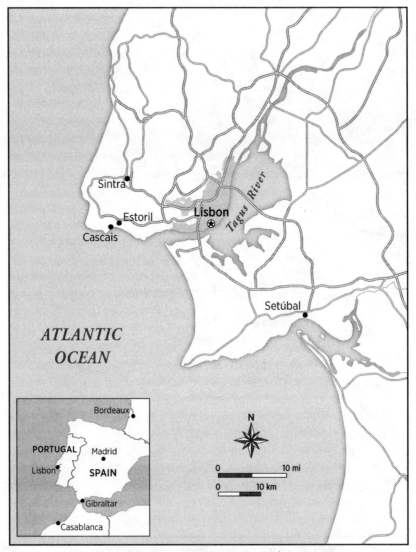

Lisbon, the Tagus River and Estuary, and Nearby Locales

1

HUB OF THE WESTERN UNIVERSE

> Lisbon at present is the hub of the western universe, and it
> must be the most fascinating place in the world.
>
> —*Irish Times*, October 23, 1941

Today Lisbon stands once more at the threshold of great events."
So began a lengthy article in the National Geographic magazine in
August 1941. In the illustrious past, adventurers had sailed from the Portuguese port city on the southwestern sliver of the Old World to claim new
lands and a world empire; now, in a new and radically reversed period of
prominence, Lisbon was on the receiving end of a great flood of refugees
escaping an Old World at war. Geography and Portugal's wartime neutrality had thrust the country's capital to international attention as Europe's last
open gateway of escape for victims of Nazi terror.

But there was irony here.

Refugees reached Lisbon after long and sometimes perilous journeys,
only to leave again as swiftly as possible. They were the new adventurers,
though of need rather than choice. Lisbon was still Europe; for nearly all
exiles the city was merely a transfer point to permanent resettlement in
Great Britain, North and South America, Africa, Asia, the Caribbean—to
anywhere that was not Europe.

Since they streamed in faster than they could be sent out by ship or air
transport, on freighters carrying Portuguese goods to Britain or America, or
on fishing boats willing for a price to take them through the Straits of Gibraltar to North Africa, the refugees formed in Lisbon a swelling bottleneck

of fretful humanity. The city freed them from war yet also stopped them in their tracks, with no more borders to cross, with only the open sea ahead and limited means of getting across. For weeks and months they waited, milling about in a no-man's-land between past and future. The Lisbon route was the way of freedom, but the holdup before the final journey to safety could seem a cruel twist of fate.

And there was further irony.

Lisbon in World War II was a way into Europe as well as a way out— a revolving door of no importance to refugees wanting only to get away but of high value to the warring powers. As an open city, Lisbon allowed figures from both sides—correspondents, diplomats, businessmen, military brass, secret agents, smugglers, exchanged internees, ordinary citizens—to come and go, as it did newspapers, magazines, films, mail, and cables.

And members of both sides could simply linger in the city, savoring sun-splashed days and brightly illuminated nights, ample food and drink, well-stocked stores, and the possibility of winning or losing a fortune at the gambling casino in nearby Estoril while rubbing shoulders with the enemy in a café or, equally unsettling, following his foursome on manicured golf links. New arrivals at the airport in Sintra, some fifteen miles from Lisbon, were invariably startled by its multinational character in the midst of war. Five airlines provided passenger service from Lisbon to Britain, Germany, Italy, Spain, and North Africa while sharing office space in the terminal and parking their planes side by side on the tarmac.

But given the course of the European war, with Germany in control of France and capable of pressuring Francisco Franco's fascist regime in Spain, Portugal's vast neighbor on the Iberian peninsula, could a country so small and weak maintain its neutrality? Would the Allies demand military access to the Continent through Lisbon or take over Portugal's strategically placed Atlantic islands of Cape Verde or the Azores, in either case forcing Germany to add the country to its list of victims? As the war waged on could Lisbon possibly hold out as occupied Europe's lone port of arrival and departure?

The *National Geographic* article raised doubts. "Before these lines appear in print," came a disclaimer at the start, "Portugal may be only a memory and Lisbon a ghost town of the Second World War." And in closing the article returned to the possibility of the virtually defenseless country of some six million soon coming under Nazi rule: "It is almost too much to hope that, after ravaging nine-tenths of the Continent, the dogs of war should stop at the Portuguese border."

★   ★   ★

The author of "Lisbon—Gateway to a Warring Europe," Harvey Klemmer, had reached the city by way of London, where the ex-newspaperman had served since 1938 as a publicist and speechwriter for American Ambassador Joseph P. Kennedy. His book about life in embattled Britain, *They'll Never Quit*, had just been published in the United States, the gritty resistance of the title leading to a plea for unlimited American economic and military support. Shortly before printing his Lisbon report, the *National Geographic* had carried "Everyday Life in Wartime England," an article drawn from the book.

In photos accompanying Klemmer's "Lisbon," only two depicted transients—passengers arriving on a Pan American Airways Clipper from New York; ticket-seekers jamming the airline's Lisbon's office—with the rest, many credited to Klemmer, merely local tourist snapshots. One of the unexpected pleasures of wartime Lisbon, Klemmer pointed out, was the freedom to take photographs when and where one wished. "I do not suppose," he wrote, "there is another city in Europe today where one may take pictures of such things as shipyards, factories, quays, and oil tanks. You can take anything you like in Portugal." (One photo accompanying the article, not taken by Klemmer, showed young boys parading down the broad Avenida da Liberdade, Lisbon's leafy version of the Champs-Elysées. The caption identified the boys as members of the "Youth Movement," a group created by the government to "promote physical fitness, form character, and inculcate respect for law and discipline." Left unremarked was that Portuguese Youth, formed in 1936, was a fascist-style organization modeled on Hitler Youth. The uniform of green shirt and khaki trousers included a leather belt, its large metal clasp branded with an S, which some believed stood for the Portuguese dictator António Salazar, and authorities said referred to Service.)

In Lisbon you could also read what you liked. International publications overflowed newsstands, Klemmer reported, with the displays seemingly devoid of emphasis or segregation, the vendors playing no favorites. "You could get," he noted, "the *London Daily Mail* and the *New York Times*; you can also get the *Deutsche Allgemeine Zeitung*, the *Lavora Fascista*, and the *Falangist Arriba*." The same was true of Paris newspapers published under German occupation. French refugees were startled when they saw such familiar papers as *Paris-Soir* or *Le Matin*, and startled again when they encountered the crude Nazi propaganda inside. (In Marseille an American aid worker was advised to buy *Paris-Soir* on grounds that "everything is in it, if you know how to read it properly. Read just the opposite of what is written, and you'll have the whole truth.")

Klemmer told of refugees jamming all Lisbon-area boardinghouses and hotel rooms while waiting for ships and planes to carry them away. With the United States the destination of choice, its consulate was inundated with applicants for visas. "If we could go out on the front steps and announce that everyone who wanted to could go to America," said a consular official, "I think we would get about 40,000." Klemmer learned that already seven thousand Americans had been evacuated from Lisbon, and those remaining were going home at a rate of about a hundred a week.

However gradual their rate of departure, American citizens ranked among the privileged few, with priority on American-owned overseas transport—though companies were required to honor previously purchased tickets of noncitizens on dates they came due. Other refugees roamed about the city, grasping at snatches of conversation, easy prey for rumor and deception:

> *There's a Basque fisherman who, for 20,000 escudos, will run passengers to North Africa.*

> *Have you heard about the Greek passenger ship, going to New York?*

> *My brother knows a man at the American Express; he says the Portuguese are going to put on another boat.*

> *My hotel porter says a Spanish freighter is in port, loading for South America.*

If they could somehow block out the plight of the refugees, new arrivals coming from suffering London, Klemmer among them, discovered in lush and colorful Lisbon "some half-forgotten splendor out of another life." They gaped at the lights, the strolling throngs, the automobile traffic, the displays in the windows. And in seaside Estoril they found a casino operating full blast, conversations conducted without censorship, beaches without mines or barbed wire. Still, never far from mind was Portugal's vulnerability.

The country had little military capability, giving rise to a standing joke among Germans and others in the country that Hitler could take Portugal with a telephone call—meaning that a powerful fifth column, already positioned in the country, would rise up; or that the government had a fascist leaning despite its neutrality; or simply that Germany's military might was so obviously superior that Portugal would not attempt resistance. The best to be said, Klemmer concluded, was that "the Portuguese have handled themselves well, thus far, in one of the most difficult situations with which any nation has even been confronted."

★   ★   ★

Klemmer's "Lisbon" bore the importance of appearing in a prominent magazine. But, in the summer of 1941, the article added mostly detail and texture to already familiar accounts in American, British, and other national publications about the surprising wartime importance of the small, poor, peripheral, but proud nation that was outside the war and hoping to remain so, yet found itself—as imagined by a columnist in the *Irish Times*, looking on from a similarly neutral nation—"the most fascinating place in the world." In December 1940, some nine months before Klemmer's report, the London *Times* cited war developments that "have brought Portugal into the glare of the international limelight." In the same month the *New York Times* reported that Portugal, "the last comparatively free country on the Continent of Europe," had war refugees flocking to its port city. Earlier, in October 1940, the London *Times* noted in an editorial that for more than three months refugees had been coming to Lisbon "by sea and land, by boat and bicycle, by train and on foot, from every country invaded or threatened by the Nazi scourge."

Earlier still, in July 1940, the *New York Times*' Lisbon correspondent, Alva E. Gaymon, wrote of an expanding refugee population in Lisbon that was increasing by the hundreds each day. The city was a "veritable bee hive" of activity. "From early morning until late at night taxis are running about in all directions. Cafés are open virtually all night and interpreters are at a premium." As a result of the refugee buildup, accommodations were nearly impossible to find in Lisbon or the nearby beach communities of Estoril, Monte Estoril, and Cascais. The consulates of the overseas countries that the refugees hoped to reach were swamped with work. In the same month of 1940 Lilian Mowrer related in *The New Yorker* a personal story of joining the flight through France to Lisbon, "the new and magic goal of the growing thousands of refugees." The refugees were a jumble of nationalities and backgrounds—she was the British-born wife of Edgar Ansel Mowrer, a notable American correspondent based in Paris—but shared a single goal: "All of them were headed for Lisbon, the port of good hope, from which they could escape from the Germans by Clipper, or ocean liner, or freighter, or tramp ship—anything that would take them away from a Europe that was rapidly becoming a prison."

The German blitzkrieg that had swept through the Low Countries and France in May 1940 had triggered a mass exodus of refugees fleeing south while under aerial assault by the Luftwaffe. Most of those overflowing the roads and rail stations were French, but there were also Belgians, Dutch, Luxembourgers, Central Europeans, and German refugees who had earlier fled to France and elsewhere—in all, some six to eight million people, with four million fleeing from the Paris region alone. Following the total collapse of France and the signing of the Franco-German armistice on June 22, the country was redrawn into zones—the most important splitting the nation into an occupied zone, which included Paris and the entire Atlantic coast, and a free zone with Vichy as seat of a puppet government and the aged Marshal Philippe Pétain as head of state—and many of the French, refugees in their own land, returned to their homes. For a million or more others, including tens of thousands of Jews and sizable numbers of American and British citizens who had been living or traveling in Europe, the great migration pressed on.

At the time of the armistice, the German military thrust into France along the Atlantic Coast had reached south to Bordeaux. Refugees still ahead of the Wehrmacht could head for Bayonne, Biarritz, St. Jean-de-Luz, and finally Hendaye on the border with Spain. The other main escape route was to the east, through unoccupied France to such centers as Toulouse, Nîmes, Avignon, and eventually Marseille on the Mediterranean. Despite its advantage as France's largest port and major link with North Africa, the old Roman city was now under Vichy authority and its shipping subject to the British sea blockade. As result, most of the refugees reaching Marseille used it as a preparation area for, so they hoped, a continued overland journey to the Spanish border at Cerbère.

Whether fleeing through occupied or unoccupied France or from Italy, by the summer of 1940 the final European goal for most refugees was Lisbon. Reaching it meant leaving France, crossing Spain, entering Portugal—a long, costly, often frightening three-stage journey further burdened by a gauntlet of bureaucrats and a maddening array of differing national demands for proper papers. A character in Erich Maria Remarque's acclaimed 1964 novel *The Night in Lisbon*—published while the literary lion of World War I was living in the United States—bitterly recalled the frenzied gathering of documents that faced World War II refugees trying to reach Portugal:

> Bordeaux. The Pyrenees. You feel out the border crossing. Retreat to Marseille. The battle to move sluggish hearts as the barbarian hordes come closer. Through it all the lunacy of bureaucracy gone wild. No residence permit, but no exit permit either. They won't let you stay

and they won't let you leave. Finally you get your exit permit, but your Spanish transit visa has meanwhile expired. You can't get another unless you have a Portuguese visa, and that's contingent on something else again. Which means that you have to start all over again—your days are spent waiting outside the consulates, those vestibules of heaven and hell! A vicious circle of madness!

Finally arriving in Lisbon meant only another trek to leave Europe behind completely, yet without arrival there was little hope of total escape. Other neutral nations not already overrun by the Nazis—Sweden, Switzerland, Spain—also offered sanctuary, but Lisbon alone had an Atlantic port for resettlement overseas and the vital land buffer of Spain between it and the Nazi war machine. The Lisbon route, as the Swiss writer Denis de Rougemont characterized it in his journal when he reached Portugal in August 1940, was the war's lifeline of freedom.

$$\star \quad \star \quad \star$$

Like Portugal, Spain had declared neutrality when the war broke out in September 1939. But whether the country would remain free of the war was, from the summer of 1940 onward, anyone's guess. Three years of civil war had left the Spanish economy in shambles. Food shortages were now such that the American embassy in Madrid used its own truck to haul in supplies from Portugal. Politically the civil war had drawn the Franco regime deeply within the German orbit, and when the European war began, and especially after the fall of France, Spain leaned heavily in the direction of the Third Reich. Refugees pushed as rapidly as possible through the country, wrote Lilian Mowrer, because "no one knew how soon Spain would drop the mask of neutrality or how quickly Portugal's independence would be threatened. It was this fear which kept us swiftly on the move."

There was ample reason to fear. Following a meeting of Hitler and Franco at Hendaye in October 1940—the second stop of the Führer's private train on a journey that included talks with Pétain and Mussolini—Spain signed a protocol with Germany that pledged entry into the war at some future point agreed upon by the two governments. Spain never carried through with the pact, though for the next two years joining the Axis powers remained Spanish policy, and collaboration between Madrid and Berlin was pursued on many fronts.

Nonetheless in the summer and early fall of 1940 Spain went its own way by liberally issuing transit visas to Jews and other refugees who also had Portuguese transit visas and some evidence of a final destination overseas.

It was clear the refugees were meant to keep moving through Spain; in the words of the foreign minister of the time, Jordana y Sousa, they were "passing through our country as light passes through a glass, leaving no trace." Spain wanted no trouble with Germany over the exiles, yet beyond the exclusion of fit men of military age together with some currency restrictions, the country kept its doors open to those with proper papers.

Those without were another matter. In a country as large as Spain many illegal entrants avoided detection, but those caught were usually imprisoned, often in harsh conditions, though for the most part they were not returned to occupied France. A possible explanation for not turning over illegals was concern expressed by British and American envoys in Madrid for the welfare of refugees—a concern perhaps aimed mainly at freeing an avenue of flight for servicemen who had escaped prisoner-of-war camps or had been shot down over German terrain and managed to reach Spain on their way to British territory in Gibraltar.

Portugal shared Spain's insistence that refugees move on to overseas destinations. Its economy was in good condition compared to its battered neighbor, and Salazar had no wish to play a vassal's role in a German-ordered Europe. But a country of Portugal's diminutive size was necessarily wary of a large influx of temporary residents. In November 1939 Portuguese consulates were instructed to get prior approval from Lisbon before issuing visas to various groups, among them stateless figures and Jews who had been expelled from their countries of origin. While anti-Semitism was not considered a feature of Salazar's government, anti-communism decidedly was, and the order also applied to Russian refugees.

Despite grave personal risk, one Portuguese consul found himself unable to follow the new regulation. From a distinguished family and a law graduate of the University of Coimbra, Portugal's oldest and most prestigious university, Aristides de Sousa Mendes was a career diplomat in Portugal's small but elite foreign service. His twin brother, César de Sousa Mendes, was likewise a diplomat and would occupy higher positions—he was ambassador to Sweden when, in Salazar's first government in 1932, he was called to Lisbon as foreign minister; but by 1929 Aristides de Sousa Mendes had climbed to the modest rank of consul general in Antwerp, Belgium. In 1938 he took up the same post in Bordeaux. The work at the time was undemanding, and Sousa Mendes along with his wife and a family of fourteen children lived placidly in a large apartment on the Quai Louis-XVIII, which also served as offices of the consulate.

With the German invasion of France and subsequent removal of the French government from Paris to Tours to Bordeaux, the consul suddenly found himself at the center of a storm of panic-stricken refugees. Among them was his nephew, the son of his brother César, whom Salazar had recently posted to Warsaw as ambassador. When the nephew reached Bordeaux he went at once to the consulate and found the offices "packed with refugees."

> They were dead tired, because they had spent days and nights in the street, on the stairs and finally in the offices. They could no longer relieve themselves or eat or drink, for fear of losing their place in the queue. That sometimes happened and caused scuffles. The refugees consequently looked haggard, and were no longer able to wash, comb their hair, shave or change their clothes. In most cases, anyway, the clothes they were wearing were the only ones they had.

All the Bordeaux consulates were under siege by refugees, but the Spanish and Portuguese consulates were typically, given the escape routes believed to be available through the neutral nations, the first ports of call. Those crammed together before the Portuguese consulate also may have heard stories of Sousa Mendes's sympathetic concern for refugees before the prior-approval order was handed down by the foreign ministry. In any case, the consulate was now overrun with requests for transit visas, and before issuing nearly all of them the consul was required to seek consent from Lisbon. When Sousa Mendes telegraphed Salazar for instructions on how to deal with the newly chaotic situation, he got a stern reply: follow the regulation. When shortly thereafter he sought visas for some thirty people, the government flatly refused. The requests had included permits for Rabbi Chaim Kruger and his family, with whom Sousa Mendes had struck up a friendship in Antwerp. Now in Bordeaux, the Krugers lodged in the consul's apartment while he pleaded their case with Lisbon.

At this point Sousa Mendes, acting from principle and conscience, chose to defy Lisbon. As his nephew recalled, he stepped outside the consulate and announced his decision to the massed gathering of refugees:

> My government has denied all applications for visas to any refugee. But I cannot allow these people to die. Many are Jews and our Constitution says that the religion or the politics of a foreigner shall not be used to deny him refuge in Portugal. I have decided to follow this principle. I am going to issue a visa to anyone who asks for it—regardless of whether or not he can pay. . . . Even if I am discharged, I can only act as a Christian, as my conscience tells me.

The consul then commanded a police officer protecting the consulate door, "You are no longer to prevent these people from seeing me. You are to merely maintain order."

On June 16, 1940, Sousa Mendes began his extraordinary rescue operation. With the help of Rabbi Kruger and some members of the Mendes family he began signing visa after visa, with no questions asked. To hurry the effort along he sent Kruger outside the consulate to collect the passports of Jews. "He was carrying fistfuls of passports," Kruger's son, Jacob, remembered of his father. "But the most extraordinary thing was that he was so engrossed in his task, so keen to act fast and save as many people as he could, that he went out into the street without his black jacket, without his hat and even without his skullcap—something I'd never seen him do before." Once the passports were brought to his desk, Sousa Mendes rapidly signed his name—the signature in time falling off from a flourishing "Aristides de Sousa Mendes" to simply "Mendes"—and a consular aid stamped them.

As news spread about what was occurring in the consulate, it was swamped all the more with refugees. For two additional days and nights the mass visa signing went on, allowing scores of refugees to begin the journey from Bordeaux to Lisbon. But the consul was not finished with his work. With the Franco-German armistice he traveled south to Bayonne, where a vice consul under his supervision was not following the same open visa policy. Once again Sousa Mendes set up an assembly-line operation, working from the consular office but also, in the recollection of some, authorizing visas in the street, his hotel, and his car.

Lisbon knew of the consul's defiance, and on June 24 he was instructed to leave his post in France and return to Portugal. But since the order had not yet been delivered to him, he made a final effort to assist refugees by signing more visas at the Spanish border and personally driving his car across the border with a group of refugees behind. "I'm the Portuguese consul," he announced to Spanish border guards. "These people are with me. They all have regular visas, as you can check for yourselves, so would you be so kind as to let them through?" After the guards did, Sousa Mendes returned to France and Bordeaux. German forces had now entered the city, but the consul, stripped of his powers, continued to receive refugees at his apartment. On July 8 he and his wife returned to Portugal. Salazar had already set in motion disciplinary action against him.

While Sousa Mendes's heroic work was brief, his period of official disgrace dragged on and on. The consul apparently believed he could quickly clear up matters by talking with Salazar, and sought an audience. It was never granted. During an investigation from August to October 1940, Sousa Mendes responded to a bill of indictment against him by, among other things, presenting an article from the daily newspaper *Diário de Notícias*—considered semi-official by many—praising Portugal's hospitality to refugees. While the investigation's verdict was that the consul should be demoted in rank but remain in the foreign service, Salazar's personal ruling suspended him for a year on half-pay, then forced him into permanent and financially crippling retirement.

★   ★   ★

Exiles fortunate enough to get transit visas from Bordeaux and other Portuguese consulates also needed entry visas to ultimate overseas destinations stamped in their passports, and for a time the consulates casually accepted permits to China, Siam, and the Belgian Congo despite the fact these countries lacked transport from Lisbon. Once holders of such questionable credentials reached Lisbon they could seek entry visas to the United States or other countries they actually intended to reach, their Portuguese transit visas regularly extended by the local police. Holders of legitimate overseas visas had only to contend with the frustrating shortage of further transport.

On June 21, 1940, an American press report told of three hundred Americans, most of them former residents in France, who were gathered in Biarritz, St. Jean-de-Luz, and other towns in occupied France's frontier area with Spain while awaiting an official dispatched from the embassy in Madrid to aid them in border crossing. They were hoping to reach Lisbon for passage to New York on weekly sailings of liners of the American Export Lines. Space on Pan American Airway's seaplane flights to New York, added the report, was already booked weeks ahead.

A report five days later said seventy Americans had crossed from occupied France into Spain and another four hundred to five hundred, including many well-known correspondents who had been posted in Europe, were still waiting in the southwestern corner of the country. Time was of the essence since German forces were expected to soon penetrate as far south as Bayonne. The road from St. Jean-de-Luz to Hendaye on the border was already solid with cars, some stranded without gasoline; refugees reaching Hendaye said they had "lived for the past three days almost entirely on lettuce." Once the Americans crossed over and reached the Spanish cities of San Sebastian or Bilbao, they would come under the authority of embassy officials—Madrid's condition for waiving their lack of Spanish transit visas— for their journey to Lisbon.

On July 1 the London press reported on a British contingent managing to cross into Spain just before Nazi troops reached Hendaye and raised the German flag. Those safely across in Spain told harrowing tales of traveling through France on lorries, bicycles, and French troop trains. All were now part of the refugee bottleneck of Lisbon, though for the time being they were being put up in comfortable quarters in the Royal British Club.

A lengthy report in the American press about the city's refugee buildup came from James Reston of the *New York Times* on December 15, 1940. Earlier, writing from London, Reston had tried to capture the overall enormity of the movement of refugees with a dispatch that began: "In the whole story of the world's confusion nothing is quite so tragic or so complicated as the desperate plight of Europe's refugees." His Lisbon story, thick with statistics, concentrated on the plight of those freed to the extent of reaching Portugal. It opened: "Another handful of that tragic horde of European refugees—twenty-seven children from Southern France and ten Jewish youngsters from Vienna—sailed for the United States tonight on the American Export liner *Excambion*, but eight thousand homeless and stateless persons still are waiting in Portugal to get away from the war zone." The exiles caught in the city were part of an original eleven thousand who had reached Lisbon by the end of August 1940, and they constituted a mere fraction of the many thousands hoping to follow them.

Jews holding passports from Poland, Germany, Belgium, and the Netherlands, Reston went on, made up 90 percent of the eight thousand, with fifteen hundred of them considered destitute. The latter could be seen circling through the cafés and squares of central Lisbon, searching for war information and trying to console one another, then at noon trekking up into the Lisbon hills for meals provided by the American Jewish Joint Distribution Committee, one of the local relief groups providing humanitarian aid. Later they flowed back to the docks to say goodbye to friends lucky enough to be leaving on ships. The wearisome routine would be repeated for weeks and months until they obtained permission to enter another country, and then turned up funds for getting there.

The Portuguese people were said to be unfailingly kind in providing housing and clothing, and the government had extended visas that allowed those already legally in the country to stay. In an effort to ease the blockage in Lisbon, refugees were now distributed in towns throughout the country. "These people," wrote Reston, "are being well treated by the Portuguese authorities, who have taken the general line that it is willing to help those refugees who already are here, but unwilling to establish a permanent refugee colony." The United States was also helping relieve the pressure by allowing its Lisbon consulate to provide refugees presently in Portugal with needed immigration papers for America rather than requiring they be sought from American consulates in countries of origin.

"Lisbon's Refugees Now Put at 8,000," read the headline on Reston's story. Such numbers attached to the uprooted, usually derived from data gathered by government officials or estimates by relief organizations, varied considerably in press and broadcast reports about wartime Lisbon. A seemingly extravagant Reuters wire-service story carried in August 1941—with attribution simply to "a summary today"—said that "since November, 1939, about two hundred thousand refugees have *sailed* from Lisbon," and "several thousand have also *left* by air." A house magazine of Pan American Airlines reported that between June and December 1940 more than eighty thousand refugees in the city needed overseas transportation.

Still today there is no consensus on the number of exiles who passed through Lisbon in the war years. An often cited historical study puts the figure at about 100,000, with nearly half coming in the year following the surrender of France. Other studies give the number of 200,000, while one estimates it as nearly a million, and yet another, supremely cautious, leaves it that "many refugees" moved through during the war. Numbers aside, what is certain is that, as the historian Michael S. Marrus wrote, beginning in the summer of 1940 "Lisbon soon became the refugee capital of Europe, the nerve center of various relief agencies and the principal port of embarkation on the European continent." The writer Arthur Koestler, who knew the Lisbon route by hard personal experience, said the same in a 1941 book: "Lisbon was the bottle-neck of Europe, the last open gate of a concentration camp extending over the greater part of the Continent's surface." And, in a grim metaphor, he repeated himself in the same work: "And the procession of despair went on and on, streaming through this last open port, Europe's gaping mouth, vomiting the contents of her poisoned stomach."

★   ★   ★

James Reston had gathered material on Lisbon's refugees while awaiting ship passage to Bermuda and on to the United States. A member of the *Times*' London bureau during the worst days of German bombing, he had survived the air war only to come down with a case of undulant fever that caused a return home. The usual way back was a flight from London to Lisbon, then transatlantic passage by ship or plane to New York. Reston's Lisbon report carried a local dateline, and if in fact it was transmitted by cable or radio from the city it would have passed under the eye of Portuguese censors. In the country's balancing act of wartime neutrality, they would strip it of anything that might annoy the warring sides or the Salazar government.

An obvious way of circumventing censorship was to have news written in Lisbon then carried to New York by passengers on Pan American flights, a method followed by Ralph Ingersoll, editor and founder of New York's *PM*, when he brought back with him dispatches by the Lisbon correspondent of the London *Times*, W. E. Lucas. Ingersoll both told of his stay in Lisbon and introduced Lucas's first story in the December 3, 1940, edition of the newspaper. "Berlin may be the most depressed, London the most inspiring city in Europe," Ingersoll began his report, set off by a box within Lucas's. "But Lisbon is the most extraordinary." He went on to depict the city in colorful detail as a place where

> American generals sleep in attics because they cannot get rooms in hotels. Where the fisherwomen still walk barefoot with their baskets on their heads—past the traffic lights that are so new and wonderful that crowds still stand and watch them change from red to green. . . . Lisbon, where they go to work at ten and stop at one to talk and sleep. Where at eleven they come out of their offices into the coffee shops to read the newspapers in which there is no news, because, if the papers printed any news, it might offend the Germans or the British.

Since censorship equally restricted what American readers knew about extraordinary Lisbon, while in the city Ingersoll had looked for someone to improve his newspaper's coverage, then coming from a Portuguese working for the United Press, and found him in Lucas. He was, said Ingersoll, American trained, had a wife born in Chicago, and knew well the current situation in Portugal from his position with the London *Times*. "I hope he can get further dispatches across the Atlantic by Clipper," Ingersoll added. "I cannot guarantee they will reach this country, but as long as they do, *PM* will print them."

Lucas's initial story concentrated on the sort of shocking refugee accounts heard in Lisbon from those who had fled through France and Spain. His second, carried in *PM* on December 4, sketched recent Portuguese history, then turned to the present with Europe's tragedy bringing "a fleeting though real excitement to Lisbon's streets and a startling prosperity to her people" at the same time it left them "surprised and not a little bewildered as the spotlight of international interest swung on them." Remaining pieces in the four-dispatch series dealt with Portugal's lack of military strength, with noting the excessive number of Germans seen on Lisbon streets ("What on earth can they do?"), and with Nazi propaganda inundating the country. On December 13 *PM* temporarily closed its focus on Lisbon with a two-page photo display of stranded refugees, the pictures taken by Eugene Tillinger, a French journalist and photographer who had been waiting months for a ship to the United States.

Another obvious way of getting around Portuguese censorship was for newsmen passing through Lisbon, as against those posted there, to wait for return to Britain or America before submitting work for publication. In so doing, less deadline-bound magazine journalists like Harvey Klemmer gained a distinct edge on newspaper colleagues. Among the earliest Lisbon stories in American magazines—it appeared more than a half-year before Klemmer's report—came from a newspaperman turned broadcaster, Eric Sevareid. Working in Paris with Edward R. Murrow's fledging CBS radio team when the war began, Sevareid had escaped the German advance with passage from Bordeaux to Britain aboard a small ship overloaded with refugees. In London he reported on the blitz, the work cut short when, like Reston, sickness caused his return to America. Lisbon would be his second escape point from the Continent.

Sevareid's "Lisbon—Escape Hatch of Europe" in *The Living Age* in January 1941 opened with his arrival on a British flying boat coming in over the "scrambled necklace of twinkling lights about Lisbon's superb harbor" and a feeling of immense relief at "this sight of the lamps of peace after fourteen months in war and darkness." A steward on the plane injected a dash of complexity into his mood by pointing out two other descending planes—one a Pan American seaplane from New York, the other a converted Nazi bomber, a Junkers 90, carrying passengers from Berlin.

Once on the ground, Sevareid turned back to his sense of relief by noting about Lisbon a "fragrance of Paris before the war." The hot working day over, Portuguese men, their wives customarily at home after dark, were emerging from steep narrow streets to sit and talk at cafés that spilled across sidewalks beneath gaudy neon signs. Sevareid's hotel was the elegant Palácio in Estoril, but here another complication arose when a nightcap in the bar brought the realization that "luck had tossed me into the espionage center of World War II." Lisbon might feel like Paris before the present war, but Estoril seemed to have more the atmosphere of Zurich before World War I. Hushed conversations went on throughout the hotel, where rooms were occupied by deposed statesmen of occupied countries, and a suite was said to be reserved for the former king of Romania, Carol II, currently in Spain and unable to reach Portugal. Portugal itself, Sevaried suspected, might soon come under the German heel.

This seemed a strong possibility when in the hotel lobby he spotted Biefurn, identified as the "sinister assistant" to the Gestapo's Heinrich Himmler, talking with Friedrich Sieburg, a former Paris correspondent for a German newspaper and now a high-ranking propagandist credited with perfecting fifth column tactics in countries on the Nazi invasion list. The implication of the meeting was that Portugal might now figure in the German agenda, the likelihood strengthened by Sieburg recently insinuating himself into Portuguese intellectual life with a flattering book about the country's colonial past and bright future.

If Sieburg's methods were sly, a German pilot's were literally out in the open—or so Sevareid learned one morning when a Junkers passenger plane on its way to Berlin passed alarmingly low over the Palácio. "We think it's to get us used to the swastika," a waiter observed when Sevareid asked why the pilot flew so off course. "The first time he did it, the visa line at your consulate grew much longer."

Mention of the visa throng drew Sevareid's attention to the exiles waiting in Lisbon to get to America, a number he placed at about twenty thousand. They were nervous, depressed, listless since Portugal had no new frontier to sneak or bribe their way across but an ocean that could be spanned only with a stamped visa. The young and harassed American vice consuls were gods for the refugees, their days given over to lining up at the consulate to learn if there was any change in their status. Some, knowing of the American draft, offered themselves as military volunteers—"a humorless joke to the harassed consuls." Still others carried money they had brought with them or won gambling at the Estoril casino in hope of spotting an American consul and initiating a conversation. "They have bribed their way across many borders," Sevareid wrote, "and cannot believe that money doesn't talk with American officials, too."

Finally, Sevareid concentrated on a specific refugee met by chance in the casino. A young German teacher and writer is recognized because, incredibly, he is wearing ill-fitting trousers Sevareid had given him while visiting a French concentration camp during his days as a newspaper reporter for the Paris *Herald*. Like other exiles, the young man is waiting in Lisbon for an overseas visa. Together the two leave the smoky casino for the Estoril beach, and here Sevareid mentions the presence of Friedrich Sieburg in the hotel. The young man's eyes flashed and he said, "Sieburg here? I think that means the kiss of death. Tomorrow I will make some acquaintances among the Portuguese fishermen who have boats in the harbor." (In his autobiography, Sevareid identified the young German as Ernst Adam and, after his remark about leaving on a fishing boat, had him reverse course and say, "No, I won't. Some time or other you have to stop this running and turn around. It may as well be here. There is no longer any room to be a neutral or a refugee.")

★   ★   ★

T. J. Hamilton's "Turbulent Gateway of a Europe on Fire" appeared in the *New York Times*' Sunday magazine two months after Eric Sevareid's article and echoed his sense of the wartime relief provided by Lisbon. "For a man without a country," Hamilton reported, "there could be no lovelier place to be in exile" than Lisbon. But in contrast to most published reports of the time, he largely concentrated on refugees who were sufficiently well off to take advantage of the city's pleasures. (A story in the newspaper just over a week before Hamilton's article noted that although "moneyed refugees" tossed about their funds at roulette and baccarat in the casino, the bulk of Portugal's refugees were "mostly incapable of self-support"; those "who are destitute get $1.20 weekly" as a handout from the government.) "Money is no object to these refugees," Hamilton pointed out.

> Many, particularly Belgians and Dutch, brought away fortunes in uncut diamonds, which they draw from manila envelopes in proof of their claims that they would not become public charges if admitted to the United States. Others, profiting from their own ingenuity and the general confusion as the Germans swept through France, managed to smuggle bar gold across frontiers where discovery would have meant immediate confiscation or perhaps arrest.

Yet while valuable possessions opened the way to luxury hotels, rented villas, and fine restaurants, getting beyond the city to permanent resettlement, and getting there quickly, could prove stubbornly difficult if not impossible. The United States and other countries had cut back on the number of refugees they would accept; and even with a precious overseas visa in hand, the westbound Clippers of Pan American Airlines averaged about thirty passengers on each flight while the small ships of the American Export Lines carried fewer than two hundred. Many of the limited places on ships and planes went to diplomats and others on official wartime business rather than to political and racial refugees.

Hamilton put the total number of refugees then caught in Lisbon at about five thousand. This was what was left of some ten thousand who had fled to Portugal in the first year of the war, a figure that included many returning Americans. Given the stubborn realities of getting overseas visas and then overseas transport, Hamilton believed the lingering five thousand were probably stuck in Portugal for the duration of the war. Still, any refugee who reached Portugal had to "rank among the darlings of the gods" since they were in a neutral country and could divert themselves with the delights of Lisbon, the Estoril casino, and the cocktail bars of the Sun Coast ("where else in Europe can you get a Martini made with English gin?"). Hamilton told of a French family who had fled to Portugal after learning they were on a Gestapo list to be sent to a concentration camp. In Estoril they occupied a bathing cabin next to some Nazi visitors, "and to see the two families sitting within a few feet of each other in the bright sunshine was an incredible demonstration of the difference neutral territory makes, although they found nothing to say to each other." Hamilton added:

> For these refugees, what was once a sizeable continent has now shrunk to this narrow strip of land along the coast. Here at the southwestern extremity of Europe they are safe for the moment from Hitler's divisions. But there is no way of knowing the Axis will not turn on defenseless Portugal, and the refugees think of nothing but further flight across the sea.

Yet for the time being there were no troops marching on Portuguese streets, there was no censorship of personal letters, and while the local press was tightly controlled, newspapers from New York, London, and Berlin were readily available. "All in all," Hamilton concluded, Lisbon is the "last refuge of sanity in Europe, where for the moment there are no problems."

For the Portuguese government, on the other hand, there was ongoing worry about fifth columnists together with an influx of Germans in the country with no apparent reason for being there. Hamilton relayed a story passed around among refugees of a lengthy discussion in a Lisbon bar one night about whether a German fifth column existed in the country. Finally, "one of the sturdy men at the next table arose and, with a stiff bow, said in English, 'You need not worry about the fifth column, we are already here.'" The government had bolstered the size of the secret police (known in the World War II period as the PVDE, the initials in Portuguese of the Police of Vigilance and State Defense) to keep an eye on the refugees, had moved about half of the five thousand into towns outside Lisbon, and required a police pass for anyone visiting Lisbon even for a day. The decision to scatter the refugees was, however, only partly a security matter. Grumbling provincial hotel owners who felt they were missing out on the lucrative refugee business had made it known they wanted their slice of the financial pie.

★   ★   ★

A month before Hamilton's account of Lisbon's prosperous refugees, *Fortune* magazine had mused on the same subject, though as glimpsed from the ultimate end of the escape route in America, in an article with the forthright title "Rich Refugees." Such exiles—or as they preferred to think of themselves, émigrés—bore no resemblance to the humble immigrants who had previously sailed past the Statue of Liberty. While still far fewer in number, the rich arrivals came not with a dream of making fortunes in America but with fortunes to preserve or enhance in the form of hefty bank accounts, jewels worth millions, and art collections they had stowed away aboard ships.

As a group they could be separated, said *Fortune*, into three categories: international society types, which included rich American repatriates; royalty; and business tycoons who saw in the United States further entrepreneurial possibilities. The magazine would not hazard a guess as to how the affluent refugees might affect the country, but if nothing else they provided amusing grist for gossip columns. For example, it was said of the Duke of Westminster that he had sent a thousand of his orchid plants to Florida for wartime safety. Similarly, within the year some eighty Rolls-Royces had arrived as refugees and could now be seen tooling along the smarter streets of New York and Long Island.

"Rich Refugees" was mostly whimsical, but "War by Refugee" in the *Saturday Evening Post* the following month was stridently serious. The argument set out by Samuel Lubell—a Washington newspaperman and veteran magazine writer who in the 1950s and 1960s would become widely known as a public opinion analyst—was that the marshaling of refugees from Germany and the occupied countries was yet another tool in the Nazi arsenal of total war. For one thing, the Nazis were disguising Gestapo agents as refugees and taking advantage of relief agencies to scatter them throughout the world as spies, propagandists, and fifth columnists. Equally important, the forced migration of Jews and others was a way of relieving German food shortages while at the same time weakening the United States and other democracies by shifting to them the burden of feeding the newcomers.

The refugee stream, the Nazis also understood, had moneymaking potential. According to Lubell, Germany, operating through the government of Vichy France, proposed to the United States a scheme of shipping, for a per-person charge of $485 paid in New York, Jews of nonmilitary age from Germany or occupied territories to Lisbon, from where they could be sent on to America. Two to five trains a week would leave Aachen for Lisbon, with each train carrying five hundred people, the cars sealed to prevent escapes. The United States Lines would be asked to handle the Lisbon-New York shipping route, with the Nazis guaranteeing 750 passengers every two weeks. "How much money actually was expected to be raised in this human export drive," Lubell wrote, "is a Gestapo secret. The Nazis did let it be known that they were prepared to release as many as 450,000 persons if visas were available, which would have netted them more than $100,000,000, not including the property of the refugees."

The Gestapo pushed ahead with the zany proposal and, Lubell continued, "started the first of its sealed trains rolling into Lisbon without waiting for the completion of arrangements" with the Americans. What happened upon the train's arrival, including how Portugal dealt with its large volume of unexpected guests, was not revealed, though Lubell injected the large qualification that "even if the scheme was blocked, as it almost certainly would be, some trainloads would get through." It only mattered for his dark disclosures that the forceful movement of Jews and others to Lisbon, now or in the future, was evidence of Germany putting into action a strategy in the refugee war "to get rid of those they do not want to feed, squeeze as much as possible from them in the process, and dump them where they will do the most harm." As for the lack of documentation in his clearly specious report, Lubell noted that he had spoken with figures at the State Department and in foreign embassies and had studied more than a thousand reports and letters from abroad. He could not directly quote from anyone or anything, but he assured readers that his every statement had been thoroughly checked against official sources.

★   ★   ★

In late April 1941 William D. Bayles opened "Lisbon: Europe's Bottleneck" in *Life* magazine with a ship arriving at the docks and the passengers gazing down upon the "stranded foreign colony of Europe's last free capital." "Stranded" was only partly accurate since the waiting crowd was made up of American businessmen, filmmakers, Red Cross officials, secretaries of embassies and legations, spies, and "a bevy of Japanese." Joining such figures, all with some reason to be present at shipside, were genuinely marooned Jewish refugees who apparently had come only "to see what kind of lunatic leaves the U.S. for a place as mad as Europe." Well back in the waiting group were poor and patient Portuguese hoping for handouts from the newest batch of visitors.

Important arrivals and the "cream of the refugees," said Bayles, stayed at the Aviz Hotel, a small and luxurious establishment that was once a private residence, where the top suite cost six dollars a day, inexpensive by standards other than Portugal's, where it amounted to a month's wages. Another attraction of the hotel was the absence of Germans, whose "hang-out deluxe" was the Palácio in Estoril. There they mixed with rich Jews, Englishmen, and Americans. The Gestapo agents among them were in plain clothes, but their freshly Alpine-tanned faces easily set them apart. Some gamblers in the Estoril casino humorously imagined the bronzed skin as part of a Nazi intimidation strategy that assumed sun-darkened faces were more fearsome than the pale variety.

The Gestapo, of course, was not to be taken lightly, and Bayles reported that when Biefurn, whom he identified as the Gestapo chief in Portugal, strolled through the casino, he was greeted in German by the croupiers and gamblers who left their tables to shake his hand. When Bayles took up a position near him, Biefurn glared at him before moving away. Everyone assumed Portugal's secret police were in the service of the Gestapo, and one evening Bayles found in his hotel room a Portuguese going through his belongings, then coolly ignoring any need for giving an explanation.

Rich Jews made up half the gamblers in Estoril, and Jews with and without money the bulk of Lisbon's overall refugee population, estimated by Bayles at forty thousand. But in Sintra, the high, forested former summer quarters of Portuguese royalty, he found a group of some six hundred Americans who had stayed in France after World War I, married French women and moved in with their families, had large families of their own, and found work when and where they could. They had largely forgotten English and become essentially French, but because of alien status they failed to qualify for welfare benefits when France entered the war. American officials had evacuated them to Portugal and were maintaining them in Sintra until they could be moved home and to a future viewed without enthusiasm since it meant starting over as refugees in the country of their birth.

Except for Jewish gamblers in Estoril and glum Americans in Sintra, Bayles gave few particulars about Lisbon's refugee population. Photos with his article added useful specificity yet visually glossed over the anxiety felt by many. Refugees were shown sitting with newspapers in a Lisbon café; leaving a hotel on a sailing day; boarding a ship; and crowding the office of

American Export Lines (despite, as the caption noted, the fact that tickets were sold out and bookings had stopped). In all the photos the refugees, well dressed and seemingly well fed, could be mistaken for well heeled, if uniformly somber, tourists.

★   ★   ★

The same month Harvey Klemmer's article appeared in the *National Geographic*, Demaree Bess in the *Saturday Evening Post* reported that Nazi ambition was not the only threat confronting Portugal. An experienced foreign correspondent of the popular weekly, Bess had reached Lisbon at the end of a year-long reporting tour through occupied Europe, and like other newcomers he was struck by the sight of refugees leaving the city, "admirals, aviators and ambassadors" coming in, and the ration-free food markets. But his central observation was conveyed in his article's title, "American Strategy Pains Portugal." "It may startle most Americans," Bess wrote, "to learn that the Portuguese consider us the greatest menace to their continued peace. They think they know what to expect from Germany and from Great Britain, but they frankly admit they don't know what to expect from the United States."

They had, however, some suspicions. Although Portugal had long since ceased to be a world power, it still had extensive and valuable colonial possessions in Africa and the Far East. Of particular wartime importance were its holdings of the Cape Verde islands off the west coast of Africa and the Azores islands in the North Atlantic. In World War I the American navy had operated bases in the Azores by agreement with Portugal, a neutral-turned-ally in the war. More recently Portugal had allowed Pan American Airways to maintain a flying-boat facility in the Azores. Now there was concern that the United States, if it entered the war, would seize the islands under the pretext that the action was necessary before Germany did so and used them for landing fields and ports for marauding submarines.

The apprehension had been sharply heightened on May 27, 1941, when President Franklin Roosevelt, in a fireside chat to the nation about American strategic interests in the European war, had called the Portuguese islands the "outposts of the New World" and said their occupation by Germany "would directly endanger the freedom of the Atlantic and our own physical safety." "Control or occupation by Nazi forces of any of the islands of the Atlantic," he noted in another passage, "would jeopardize the immediate safety of portions of North and South America, and of the island possessions of the United States, and of the ultimate safety of the continental United States itself."

Demaree Bess, in Lisbon at the time of FDR's talk, found that Americans in the city thought the president was merely putting the Nazis on notice. But to the Portuguese the remarks, widely circulated and criticized by Lisbon newspapers and radio, were certain evidence that the United States would move on the islands, which in turn would provoke the Germans to occupy continental Portugal. (A correspondent for the London *Times* suggested that the Portuguese were even troubled that public attention had been drawn to the islands, "which they would like both the belligerents to pretend were part of the moon.") Bess told of a taxi driver taking him along the waterfront and pointing out Portuguese soldiers being loaded on transport ships. "They're sailing to the Azores," said the driver. "When you Americans try to occupy the Azores this time, you will have to fight for them."

So would the Germans. W. E. Lucas, writing in *The Nation* some months after his *PM* reports but before Bess's article appeared, said Hitler surely had his eyes on the Portuguese islands and all else about the country. The Azores and Madeira provided "stepping-stones to the American continent" for launching German sea and air attacks. Within continental Portugal, Lisbon and Porto offered choice ports whose far western location made them strategically critical in the Battle of the Atlantic. Once the Nazi mechanized legions had reached the Pyrenees, Lucas recalled that it had seemed "a matter for wonder then that Hitler did not order his armies to roll into Spain and, fanning out, to occupy Gibraltar and Lisbon. There was nothing at that time to stop them."

And still there was nothing, beyond what Lucas called Hitler's possible calculation that the profit of occupation was not worth the loss that would accompany it. Supplying food to an Iberian peninsula cut off from outside trade by the British blockade would divert Germany's needed homeland requirements. Britain would surely counterattack by seizing the Azores and Madeira. The long coastline of Spain and Portugal would have to be defended against attack. Finally, "in the background looms the shadow of the United States, which is being compelled to push farther afield the frontiers it must defend for its own safety." As Lucas saw it, in early 1941 Hitler's decision about taking Portugal was still pending.

★   ★   ★

So abundant was the news of Lisbon in 1940 and 1941 that it inevitably carried over from newspaper stories and magazine articles into film and fiction. From Hollywood in the summer of 1941 came *One Night in Lisbon*, a light comedy-romance in which the wartime lovers, played by Fred MacMurray and Madeleine Carroll, escape bombed London for a brief interlude of Lisbon's peace and plenty, only to find themselves entangled with a Nazi spy ring. In *Casablanca*, which appeared late the following year, Paul Henreid and Ingrid Bergman merely fly off to Lisbon at the end, yet that in itself—and the film's grave voice-over opening—may have brought the Lisbon route to more international notice than all previous print accounts. A more substantial, if equally oblique, use of wartime Lisbon came in "A Little Door," a short story by the writer and critic Mark Schorer in *The New Yorker* in September 1941. Here everything takes place in the safety and security of America, with Lisbon's frenzied bottleneck of refugees a faraway yet deeply haunting presence.

The time of year in the story is early autumn, the setting a quiet beach in New England, perhaps on Cape Cod. The Abrams family—Harold, Eve, two young children—have come for a picnic lunch; with them is Eve's mother, Mrs. Herman. On the nearly empty beach the air is still, the sunlight mellow, and the ocean quiet as the family glimpse it between two long rocky arms stretching out to the water.

Mrs. Herman, however, is far from quiet. With her gaze fixed at a point where ocean and sky meet, she asks Harold and Eve as the story's opens, "Do you know that we are probably looking directly at Lisbon?" "Lisbon," she answers herself, "a little door toward which half the population of a continent crowds, or yearns to." Eve is impatient with her mother; she tells her not to be so gloomy, especially with the children about. But Mrs. Herman presses on: "Lisbon. Think of it! That one little outlet for the millions who long to pass through. The enormous *aching*."

When Eve maintains she is as aware as her mother of what is taking place across the water ("I feel it as much as you. Everyone does") but refuses to be perpetually burdened by it, Mrs. Herman tries even harder to make her daughter understand:

> It's not a matter of burdening or not burdening ourselves. We are burdened. Form a picture of Europe in your mind. Try to see it. That one open port. The few airplanes and the few ships, the money it costs, and the impossible number of people, and the terrible difficulties. See it as a picture, and you may feel it—all of Europe, and all the roads crowded, and all leading here. In spirit if not in body. All crowding down, or

yearning to. That longing means nothing to you. It's only an idea, all of it, only something you read about. But you're young.

After the children play and the family eat their sandwiches, the weather begins to turn. The wind picks up, there are dark clouds on the horizon, and Harold predicts a storm. The tide, Mrs. Herman notes, has also turned and is now going out, which brings her thoughts back to Portugal and the refugees. "What a strange thing!" she says. "Here the tide rolls out, and I suppose that means that on the other side it is rolling in. That brings us close, doesn't it." She adds that, though she has been abroad many times, she had never been to Lisbon. When Harold remarks that it was never much of a place to go, she returns to the image of Lisbon as the last open door: "But now it's everything. The only door. A little, narrow door, and behind it millions of lives that can't possibly squeeze through it, ache as they may."

With the wind rising, waves hit the rock arms with more force, the sound now like "a distant booming, like remote thunder, or cannon." And to make all the more manifest that the sound evokes the European war, Harold says, "It sounds far away, doesn't it, as though it's from the horizon somewhere, not from that rock at all?" "Yes," Mrs. Herman agrees. In a final scene that paradoxically duplicates the faraway struggle of the refugees to reach Lisbon, the family flees from the beach to the protection of their car before the storm hits. Eve carries one child and drags another behind her, "as if their very lives depended on reaching the car before the rain began."

2

TRAMPING FORWARD

Refugees, refugees, refugees, in various degrees of destitution,
flowed on. Some dropped by the roadside, but the majority
tramped forward. . . . It was a heartbreaking spectacle, and we
drove on in stunned silence.

—Ronald Bodley, *Flight into Portugal*

The sudden change of weather in Mark Schorer's short story might have
been suggested by a powerful hurricane that hit Portugal and Spain in
February 1941. Early reports gave a death toll of nearly two hundred, with
twenty in Lisbon, and injuries numbering in the several hundreds. Later
stories put the number of Portuguese dead at four hundred, with fifteen
hundred injured. Waves up to sixty-feet high had rushed up the Tagus
River, tearing ships and barges loose from their moorings and smashing
them against piers; a British flying boat sank, with three Portuguese guards
aboard lost. At the airport in Sintra ten military planes were destroyed.
Shipwrecks were recorded up and down the coastline; trains were stalled;
trees and electrical lines were down everywhere. The American Red Cross
cabled ten thousand dollars to Lisbon for emergency relief.

Bad as it was, the storm could have been more devastating had it
struck just months earlier during an ambitious national celebration. While
Lisbon's sudden appearance in the limelight as Europe's refugee capital was
an unforeseen consequence of the war, by a surreal coincidence of timing
Portugal, beginning in the summer of 1940, had intended to showcase itself
with a six-month commemoration of two centenaries: eight hundred years
since its founding in 1140 as an independent state, three hundred years
since the restoration of independence in 1640 after sixty years of Spanish
rule. What *Time* magazine labeled an "audacious pageant," at a time when

the country might prefer a low profile, was properly known as the Exposition of the Portuguese World, with Lisbon as its main focus and including programs throughout the nation and the overseas possessions.

Major events were ordered around three historical epochs: the twelfth-century medieval founding of the country; the fifteenth- and sixteenth-century imperial period of exploration and colonization, which saw Portugal at its zenith as a world power; and the seventeenth-century origins of the Braganza era (named for Catherine of Braganza, who in 1662 had become the wife of Charles II of England) and the return of national autonomy. "There is one period of history," observed the London *Times*, "which will not be commemorated, but which will be implicit in everything that is done. It is the Salazar period, now at its height." Clearly the double centenary had the contemporary ideological aim of bolstering the status of António Salazar's authoritarian regime by linking it to a continuum of Portuguese history. The country's propaganda chief, António Ferro, had acknowledged as much when plans for the exposition were unveiled in 1938: "What we will celebrate is not . . . only the Portugal of yesterday but that of today, it is not just the Portugal of D. Afonso Henriques and D. João IV, but the Portugal of [President António] Carmona and Salazar."

A distant and paternal ruler—dubbed a "plainclothes dictator" by *The New Yorker*'s A. J. Liebling in contrast to his uniformed European counterparts—Salazar had begun his rapid rise to power in 1928 when a military government named the University of Coimbra economics professor minister of finance with a mandate to bring financial order to the country. This he did through raising taxes, cutting public spending, banning strikes, and instituting rigid fiscal controls that kept wages and profits low, virtually ended inflation, and created annual budget surpluses.

His ultimate aim was an all-encompassing political order. In 1932 he was appointed president of the Council of Ministers, or prime minister, and a new constitution the following year put in motion his New State, a nationalist dictatorship with some trappings of Benito Mussolini's unitary or corporative regime in Italy. (A signed photograph of Il Duce occupied a place of honor on Salazar's desk until it was replaced by one of Pope Pius XII.) The Portuguese government now had an elected but largely ceremonial president (in keeping with the role of the armed forces in the new order, the president was a senior military figure), a prime minister as effective head of state, and a compliant national assembly. As prime minister, Salazar, while leading the austere personal life of a lifelong bachelor and devout Roman Catholic, would exercise total personal control over the domestic and foreign affairs of Portugal until 1968.

During the double centenary he was lauded in the *Anglo-Portuguese News*—a fortnightly (later a weekly) English-language tabloid miscellany published in Lisbon and mainly given over to the comings and goings of the local British community—for the financial acumen that had brought the country to a position of economic independence. "But financial reform was of no avail," *APN* pointedly added, "if it was not backed up by strict and willing obedience to the orders which were given. Fortunately for Portugal Dr. Salazar, in addition to his financial ability, possessed a moral force of character which won for him the immediate support of all those who had the welfare of the country at heart."

The London *Times* was equally effusive in its praise of the effective ruler. Visitors to the celebration were certain to "appreciate the healthy changes brought about by the present Administration, which, on the philosophical basis of Christianity and the financial basis of solvency and good business, has built up one of the most successful *régimes* of modern times." In an editorial the paper added that "the Portuguese would not be human if they had not grumbled now and then as the firm hand [of Salazar], cruel only to be kind, gave one more twist to the financial screw":

> But they stuck to it, cultivating their garden, going quietly and steadily about their business, working and paying their way, until they have reached a state in which every right-minded man and nation will wish them increased prosperity, and would passionately resent any attempt to disturb their happiness. In the Europe that will follow this war the example set these last twelve years [during which Salazar was in power] by Portugal will be a guiding light.

★   ★   ★

During Salazar's long reign there were many commemorative events to contain domestic grumbling by burnishing Portuguese pride and the authority of the regime, with the 1940 exposition his triumphal effort to date. Long preparation went into it. Artists, architects, composers, and writers were commissioned to create patriotic symbols and produce publications. From village churches and remote monasteries, nearly forgotten Portuguese primitive paintings from the fifteenth and sixteenth centuries were removed to Lisbon for a major exhibition. (Some villagers took the removals as looting and angrily protested. In the northern city of Viseu, church members surrounded a truckload of paintings and kept it hostage for two days.) Academic conferences and sporting events were organized. Official pilgrimages were conducted to historical sites. Large works projects were set in motion, including in the Lisbon area a new international airport at Portela, a new road along the Sun Coast from Lisbon to Estoril to Cascais, and restoration of such landmarks as St. George's Castle and the Romanesque twelfth-century Lisbon Cathedral.

Along the banks of the Tagus in the historic Belém district on the western outskirts of Lisbon, the launching point for Vasco da Gama and other Portuguese explorers, a vast area was cleared for the main exposition site. Erected across from Jerónimos Monastery and east of the Tower of Belém, both structures dating from the early sixteenth century and evoking in their intricate Manueline stonework the country's seafaring past, was the striking riverside Monument to the Discoveries, cast in the form of a massive prow of a caravel lined with figures of explorers and other dignitaries leading, at the head, to Prince Henry the Navigator. (Constructed of temporary material, as were most exposition structures, the monument was redone as a permanent sculpture for an anniversary celebration of Prince Henry in 1960.) A central square was created, with a garden and fountain in the center and Jerónimos Monastery as a backdrop. Flanking the square were the principal pavilions of the exposition, designed in a mildly modernistic style meant to suggest an openness to the future that could be contained within Salazar's vision of a Portugal devoted to traditional values.

Despite the coming of war, and with it a temporary halt of construction in Belém and dashed expectations about world attention directed to the celebration, the double centenary opened as planned on June 2, 1940. A *Te Deum* was sung in the Lisbon Cathedral before an array of clergy, high military officers, city fathers, government officials, the diplomatic corps, Knights of Malta, and the Papal Nuncio to Portugal. The following day German planes bombed the Paris area for the first time, killing more than two hundred people.

Some of the transients passing through Lisbon during the months of celebration left fleeting impressions of it. Lilian Mowrer was struck by the gaiety brought to the city: flags flying; brass bands parading through narrow streets from sundown to dawn; groups of youths in capes carrying banners and singing; fireworks. At the same time she found a "stunning touch of irony in a nightmare world" that Portugal should be "blandly inaugurating a pageant honoring its overseas possessions and recalling the glories of its colonizing days." A hotel porter shrugged off the oddity, telling her that "In France, always war. In Portugal, always fiesta."

The fabled author-aviator Antoine de Saint-Exupéry enjoyed evenings wandering "through the triumphs of this exhibition in perfect taste, where everything was near perfect, including the discreet music, which wafted gently through the garden like the plashing of a fountain." Nonetheless he sensed that in the midst of war Lisbon "smiled a slightly sad smile." It seemed to conceive of its festival fancifully as a shield protecting it from attack:

> "Look, how happy, peaceful, and beautifully illuminated I am," Lisbon said. "Can they choose me as a target when I so carefully refuse to hide? When I am so vulnerable!"

For Saint-Exupéry the answer was obvious: impressive as it might be, the Portuguese exposition afforded no protection against "the monster's voracious appetite." He imagined "the European night inhabited by roving packs of bomber planes pressing down on Lisbon, as if they could have sniffed out this treasure from afar."

Ben Robertson, a correspondent on his way from New York to England to report for the *New York Herald Tribune*, reached Lisbon just as the celebration was about to begin, and as a visiting newsman he received a gold-engraved invitation to the opening ceremony. But the Portuguese censor refused to allow him to cable a story back to the United States, so all he actually witnessed of the festivities was an inaugural torchlight procession glimpsed from the balcony of his hotel. Given the refugees descending upon Lisbon at the same time, he found nothing joyful about the event; it was simply "a ghastly festival." The refugees made him think of trapped rabbits—"and you had the feeling that the hunters and hounds were getting closer and that this eventually would be the field they would use for the kill." The only genuinely carefree people in all of Lisbon, he decided, were American sailors from among the ships massed in the harbor as part of the opening ceremony, since they knew they would soon be crossing the Atlantic for home.

*   *   *

With the closing of the Exposition of the Portuguese World in early December 1940, the London *Times* took stock of the activity that had drawn some three million visitors to various sites and concluded it would propel Portugal into the new year with "determination to fulfill that destiny which the records of the past seem to have laid down for her." From this lofty point, the report might have lowered its sights and pointed out that, the doors of the exposition shut, the question of the moment was whether those to Lisbon would remain open for fleeing refugees. The bleak truth was that Portuguese determination would not be the deciding factor. The fate of the Lisbon route rested with Berlin.

"How easy it would be," wrote Denis de Rougemont about the refugee journeys through France and Spain, "to close off, at any point anywhere, this slender artery through which our old world is being little by little emptied of its elite at the same time as of its parasites." The Nazis, he went on to speculate, were keeping the artery open precisely to rid Europe of its unwanted population of "ex-ministers, ex-directors, ex-Austrians, ex-millionaires, ex-princes" who were, fittingly, leaving Lisbon on American ships bearing names beginning with Ex: *Exeter, Excalibur, Excambion.* By whim or policy, the Third Reich could at any instant pinch shut the thin tube of escape, leaving Europe at the mercy of its new master.

In August 1941 Wes Gallagher of the Associated Press—a veteran wire-service reporter who had covered the German invasion of Norway, would report on the American landings in North Africa, and from London would oversee the AP's coverage of D-Day—filed a brief dispatch that movingly portrayed the refugee lifeline to freedom as a fragile and time-bound hope, nearly as much rumor as reality. His opening sentence read more like a short story than a news story: "Outside the sun beats down in muggy waves, but inside the six stinking railroad cars, fear—like a blanket of dark cobwebs—lies over the lives of 267 passengers." The fear of the train passengers descends from a host of dire possibilities: visas might expire before they can be used; the train might be turned back at the next border crossing; money might not last; the war might overtake their neutral destination before they can reach it.

The train is delivering refugees from Central Europe to Lisbon, from where they will sail to North or South America. The refugees are mostly Jewish, but there are also non-Jewish Czechs, Belgians, and Germans. An American girl is among them, traveling alone now since her fiancé, a young Austrian medical doctor who is a refugee in a neutral country, was forced to leave her at the last border station. Both had tried not to show what they equally knew: he will never get the transit visas needed to take him across countries separating him from Portugal; they will remain apart.

A plump German woman attempts to divert the girl with chocolates and conversation. The woman may, though, be trying to divert herself as well. She has a son in New York, but her husband was refused permission to leave with her. She is trying to reach South America, where she will stay until she can move on to the United States. "It may take years," she tells the girl.

The train stops for hours at remote locations. There are no sleeping cars, and nights pass restlessly in crowded compartments. At border crossings the passengers must produce their passports and other papers. Luggage has to be taken from the train and inspected. Confusion reigns.

A Czech woman is told her visa has not been filled out properly; she must wait while verification is made by telegraph. "It will not take long," an official tells her. "We may hear in a few days." She is on her way to America, and her visa expires in three weeks; already she has waited three years because of American quota regulations. She is led away protesting. None of the other passengers dare come to her aid for fear officials may detain them too.

At the next stop a man, a professor of economics, is approached by two figures in plain clothes. "Come with us," he is told. "A telegram has come. You must stay here awhile." As he is taken from the train the other passengers are careful not to catch his eye. He may not return; they may be considered friends and also removed from the train.

At this stop the luggage search takes longer because there are few inspectors. Trains leave the stop without their passengers, and the refugees are frantic to find other transportation. Police make them stay together, and finally they are put aboard a hot, dusty train made up of passenger and freight cars. Americans in the group are allowed to wait at the station for a faster train.

As the refugee train pulls away, the plump German woman calls out from a window to the American girl on the platform "in a voice meant to be hearty but is cracked with fear." She says: "I'll see you in Lisbon—I hope—soon."

Wes Gallagher's story got fresh life when it was reprinted in 1942 in *Free Men Are Fighting*, a collection of early war reporting (and enduring life in 1995 when it was included in the first volume of the Library of America's *Reporting World War II*). Book publication was appropriate since many firsthand accounts of refugee journeys across Europe found their way into hard covers. Among them, *We Escaped*, published in 1941, collected twelve personal narratives about flights that had eventually reached America. The stories bore no names to protect friends or family still in Europe, with only work or profession as identifying marks; all were written by the refugees themselves or recorded and translated. In each story it was the European journey that mattered, with the final port of exit—Lisbon for five of the refugees, with others leaving, when it was still possible to do so, from Stockholm, Hamburg, and La Havre—briefly mentioned if mentioned at all.

*   *   *

The "Artist from Prague" was in her studio in 1939 when German troops crossed into Czechoslovakia. Earlier, though she had had no political involvement, the Munich Pact of 1938 in which Britain and France acquiesced in Hitler's takeover of the Sudetenland troubled her enough to apply for an American visa. Friends advised her to leave Prague, but, though her prosperous family had already left, she felt strong ties to the city. Finally, a Cook's travel office got her an exit permit for Italy, supposedly for a vacation, and she left with one small suitcase.

From Rome, where she waited for several fruitless months seeking a French visa, she moved to San Remo near the border with France. Here she joined five others in each paying an agent seven hundred lire to smuggle them in a fishing boat along the coast to France. At night they followed a narrow path several hundred meters, their shoes off to mask sounds and sliding on their backs some of the distance to avoid sight; at the sea they were dropped over a high wall to a man in a boat below. When the boat came into French waters it quickly turned to land, the smugglers anxious to return to Italy under cover of darkness.

While getting out of the boat one of the six travelers fell overboard and called out, alerting French police, and everyone was taken into custody. The next morning, after a civilized breakfast of coffee and croissants, they were questioned, photographed, fingerprinted, and driven back to the Italian border. The Italians, however, refused to accept them, so they huddled on a bridge between the two countries while officials squabbled and drivers of passing cars stared at the curious visitors from the French Riviera. When at last an Italian official told them their passports would not be returned until they were transported to the Italy-Germany border, the artist burst into hysterical tears—which saved the day. A woman weeping was more than the Italian could bear, and after much solicitous concern the refugees got their passports back and were driven to San Remo.

The smuggling agent returned their money, and the effort to reach France resumed with another agent. This time money went to a border official, and Italian militia escorted the artist and two men to a border wall with a door in it. On the other side French officers led them to a road and a waiting car. When they reached Nice, there was an argument with the chauffeur about payment. While the artist, able to speak French, was maintaining that the cost of the car was part of the arrangement with the agent, the two men slipped away and she was left alone.

With friends in Nice she settled down to wait for her American visa to come through. In the strange quiet of the phony war after France declared war on Germany, she made a business trip to Paris; then in Nice she got a job teaching drawing to children, some of whom came from refugee families. When Italy joined Germany in the war, many of the refugees fled Nice, fearing an Italian invasion. There were periods of German bombing and rumors of approaching troops, but with the armistice the refugees returned and the city resumed its character.

The artist considered staying in France through the war, but just as food and fuel were beginning to run short she learned that an American visa was waiting for her, and she immediately booked a ticket for a ship leaving from Lisbon. She began making trips back and forth to Marseille in hopes of getting Spanish and Portuguese transit visas, and as time dragged on she was about to cancel her ship reservation when at a party she charmed a French high official and he promised to intervene. In two days she had her transit papers, feeling guilty at being singled out for preference but nonetheless heading without delay for the Spanish border.

Here there were long waiting periods before a train left for Barcelona and the sight throughout Spain of ruined buildings and starving children. Madrid appeared even worse, with men clearing rubble by hand as if they were still in the Middle Ages. In Portugal she found a country "where one could really *eat*," though the bounty of was a brief delight. After just a single day in Lisbon she was on a ship for New York.

★   ★   ★

The "Catholic Writer" was born in Frankfurt, earned a doctorate after serving in World War I, and wrote about cultural matters and politics for a Catholic publication in Frankfurt. With the Nazi rise to power he left Germany for France and found work on a Paris newspaper, interpreting events taking place back in Germany. In France he kept seeing more and more German refugees but believed it important to live as closely as possible within French life and not absorb the exiles' tendency to dream of return. In his work he moved on to the press service of the Austrian legation in Paris, but after the German annexation of Austria he was told to resign. Thereafter he joined a Paris group in an anti-Nazi Austrian information office.

Following France's declaration of war on Germany, he found a position in the French propaganda ministry. The work allowed an exemption from military service demanded of refugees in return for asylum, but it was a disorganized venture whose shortcomings would have been enjoyably comic were it not locked in combat with Germany's efficient propaganda machine. With Nazi forces nearing Paris he was abruptly told to report to an internment camp as part of the general movement of the French government from Paris. He languished for a time in the camp, then, when it was evacuated, he was assigned to a military unit made up mostly of Austrians and sent by train to Nîmes. From there he was posted to the small hill village of Langlade where, given that the Austrians came from a variety of professions and were generally viewed as intellectuals, their French officers had no idea what to do with them.

They were given an imposing name, Compagnie des Travailleurs Intellectuels, and fantastic uniforms of dark blue linen suits, long brown capes, and brown Basque berets. As intellectuals it was assumed they would occupy themselves with books. They were divided into five sections, and every fifth day there was kitchen duty; otherwise there was nothing to do. They ate well, drank well, and were paid a soldier's salary.

The pleasantly unreal interlude ended when retreating French troops came through with stories of how close the Wehrmacht were. With the armistice and demobilization, the Austrians who had come from now-occupied Paris were left to fend for themselves. The writer drew on a connection with a mayor in an unoccupied southern French town and was allowed to make his home there. What followed was another peculiar interlude from war in an ancient and lovely town that easily absorbed the hundreds of refugees who drifted through. Yet despite the contentment the town allowed, the refugees had an ominous feeling that even in unoccupied territory danger was growing.

In the armistice France had infamously agreed to turn over all anti-Nazi refugees wanted by Berlin. Now the Gestapo was requiring that Vichy officials provide exact lists of refugees remaining in France and where they were located. The writer had hoped he could remain in the town through the war, living inconspicuously, yet when he learned of the lists, and later learned that the Gestapo had come looking for him at his Paris home, he knew he had to abandon the country.

He went to Marseille, carrying a letter to the American consul from the mayor of the town where he had been staying. The division of the consulate handling passports and visas had been moved to a mansion outside the town on the Mediterranean coast, the beauty of the setting in vivid contrast to frightened refugees crowding the waiting area. Before he could fully tell his story to a vice consul, he was told a visa was already waiting for him. Some time ago he had written a friend in America about his situation, and the friend had turned over the letter to the American Federation of Labor, with the result that the writer was put on a list of endangered refugees granted emergency visitor visas.

The obstacle that remained was traveling through Spain to Lisbon to claim the visa. Rumors were rife that Spanish officials were cooperating with the Gestapo in stopping wanted figures, but the writer had no trouble crossing the border into Spain, and seven days on a train through the country were uneventful despite the extreme poverty and war damage he saw all about him. Wrecked ships were still in the harbor of Barcelona, and sections of many towns were nothing but rubble. Begging children were everywhere.

When the train reached the Portuguese border he was struck that the officials who boarded it were dressed in civilian clothes rather than the military uniforms of France and Spain, wore white gloves while inspecting his bags, and spoke fluent French. When he reached Lisbon, the city lively and wondrously clean after Marseille, he joined the mass of refugees making the rounds in search of proper papers and overseas transport. While his American visa was waiting for him, arranging ship passage took three months.

★   ★   ★

Just before a chartered Swedish exchange ship carrying diplomats and correspondents was about to leave Lisbon for New York in May 1942, an American who had been interned in Germany had a dramatic change of heart. "I won't go, I won't go," Louis B. Harl cried out as he bolted from the ship and through the customs shed before startled officials could stop him. A journalist with the International News Service, Harl had belatedly ended a long debate with himself about returning to America or rejoining his French wife and five children in occupied Paris, where he had been working before a transfer to Berlin. He had served in the American military during World War I and stayed in France after the war's end.

Faced with a parallel situation of family breakup, Eric Hawkins of the Paris edition of the *New York Herald Tribune* made the opposite decision. A British citizen, Hawkins had joined the daily newspaper in 1915, when it was still under the autocratic hand of its founder James Gordon Bennett, Jr. After inheriting the *New York Herald* from his father, Bennett started a Paris edition in 1887 and hired a mostly British staff. Hawkins rose through the ranks and in 1924 became the paper's managing editor, a position he would hold—the paper now the Paris edition of the merged *New York Herald* and *New York Tribune*—for thirty-six years.

With German troops in the suburbs of Paris in June 1940, the paper put out its final wartime edition, and what remained of the staff scattered. Hawkins and his sixteen-year-old son set off in a car for a country house he owned near

Nérac, some eighty miles inland from Bordeaux, the property bought a few years before with an eye to having a refuge in the event of war. His French wife and daughter were already at the house, and another son would arrive. Reaching it on roads packed with refugees fleeing Paris and troop convoys heading there was a nightmare journey; an artificial fog spread by the French as a screen against bombing added to the misery by covering everything with soot. The sixty miles from Paris to Orléans took sixteen hours.

The day after reaching Nérac, its population of three thousand inflated with refugees, Hawkins went to Bordeaux to survey the situation there. It was equally chaotic: brimming with confused refugees, short of food, thick with tales of the German advance. Accompanying Hawkins was his oldest son, of military age and hoping to escape France for Britain—a feat he managed, being fully bilingual, by talking his way aboard a ship leaving for Britain just hours before the armistice was announced.

The demarcation line between occupied and unoccupied zones put Nérac forty miles inside Vichy France, leaving Hawkins free of German internment but under the rump regime's rule. He had a British passport and wanted to get to London to continue wartime work for his Paris paper's New York parent. Legally, however, getting out of the unoccupied zone required an exit visa, and in turn this required applying for a pass to enter the provincial spa town that was now the capital of Pétain's government. For the time being Hawkins decided to lie low in Nérac, growing potatoes and trying to cultivate the favor of the local police, who were outwardly serving Vichy but, so Hawkins believed, sympathetic to the British.

In the spring of 1941 he went to the American consul in Marseille, an official he had known in Paris, for help in prodding Vichy to issue a pass to the city. One was waiting with the local police when he returned to Nérac. In Vichy, Hawkins found newspaper colleagues who were still working but frustrated by heavy censorship, with one of them annoyed enough to offer Hawkins his own Vichy job so he could leave for Britain. Hawkins was tempted but realized that Germany could at any time decide to occupy France fully, in which case he was certain to be interned.

After fourteen months of trying, Hawkins's exit visa finally came. He dug up sacks of potatoes to help his family get through the winter, then said goodbye to his wife, son, and daughter—believing that as French citizens and in a rural area they were relatively safe—and set out for Cerbère. It was illegal to carry money out of France, but with him he had a dozen ten-pound English banknotes concealed in the pages of a roll of newspapers, and he kept the roll tightly under his arm as, after he was cleared to leave French soil, he hiked up a steep slope and then down into Port Bou in Spain.

In a customs shed an official immediately came up to him, grabbed the roll, tossed it on a bench, and said, "No newspapers allowed in Spain." Hawkins decided the only card he had to play was outrage. He demanded to see the border captain, showed him his press identity cards and a letter from the American consul in Marseille, and insisted the newspapers were an integral part of his profession. Silently the captain went to the bench, picked up the papers, and handed them to Hawkins.

In Lisbon he found a clamoring backlog waiting for air transport to Britain. A friend lucky enough to have a ticket took a message to the London bureau of the *Herald Tribune* saying Hawkins had reached Lisbon but was stranded there. It was autumn and Hawkins found the city, as he later wrote, "gloriously attractive." His enjoyment of Lisbon would stretch on into December, when following the Japanese attack on Pearl Harbor and American entry into the war the British embassy told him a seat on a London flight was at last available.

★   ★   ★

When war broke out in 1939 the Hungarian-born Jewish writer Arthur Koestler was living in Paris with the British sculptor Daphne Hardy and working on *Darkness at Noon*, his soon-to-be-celebrated novel about the brutality of Stalin's Russia. Already a well-traveled life had taken him from Germany to Palestine to Russia to Britain to the Spanish Civil War, where he had worked as a correspondent for a British publication and been imprisoned under order of execution by Franco's Nationalists. After pressure from journalistic groups and the British government, he had been released in a one-for-one prisoner swap.

During the phony war's long stretch of calm, Koestler was taken into French custody as an enemy alien along with Germans, Austrians, and other national groups now considered under the sway of the Reich, and delivered south to Le Vernet, an internment camp at the base of the Pyrenees. Conditions were squalid for the two thousand exiles used as forced laborers; when winter came there were no stoves in Koestler's section of the camp, and few men had blankets. Well-placed friends worked for his release or at least a hearing of his case, but there was no authority that seemed to have charge of the prisoners.

The first break in the dismal situation came in early January 1940 when the Italian consul from Marseille arrived to interview Italian detainees. Those who pledged allegiance to the country's fascist regime were released and sent to Italy; those who refused—the bulk of Italians in the camp—stayed put in Le Vernet. The first person to leave after the few Italians was Koestler. One afternoon he was on a work detail emptying camp latrines; that evening he was on a train to Paris. When an officer told him of his release, Koestler was so overwhelmed he shook the man's hand—an act he would forever regret.

Back in Paris he finished his novel in a furious bout of work, combined with Daphne Hardy in translating it from German to English, and on May 1, 1940, mailed the manuscript to a London publisher, all of which he accomplished while going through a tangled and finally futile bureaucratic effort to gain a new identity card that would give him legal status in France. When it became certain he would be arrested and interned again, he and Hardy joined the flight from Paris, landing first in Limoges. "My memories of those last days of France," Koestler wrote, "are mainly of an acoustic nature":

> the never-ceasing polyphone symphony of motor horns, the roaring and humming of the engines, the thundering of the heavy lorries on the roadway, the asthmatic rattle of old Citroëns, the neighing of horses and the crying of exhausted children, as the chaotic stream flooded through the town on its aimless course. Without interruption, all day and all night, the mechanized divisions of disaster passed by and the people in the streets stared at them; some pityingly, some with hostile contempt, some with anxiously thoughtful eyes, wondering when their turn would come to join the Great Migration to the South.

With the fall of France, Koestler believed there would be total German occupation or a pro-German government under Pétain, and in either case he would soon be in Gestapo hands. He and Hardy had to flee the Continent. They had no visas for the United States, and no money to reach the country in any case. As a British citizen, England was the obvious destination for Hardy, but Koestler had tried and failed to get a British visa, and failed as well to gain permission to volunteer for the British military. Even if he could somehow get across the Channel he believed he would again be interned, a not entirely unhappy fate since he would be in British hands.

Koestler's immediate response was to go underground by walking into a French Foreign Legion recruiting office and, as one Albert Dubert, a former taxi driver from Switzerland, signing on for a five-year tour of duty. When he learned the barracks would fall within occupied territory, he slipped away, rejoined Hardy, and the two managed to hitchhike their way to Bordeaux. At the American consulate they ran into a journalist who had helped in getting Koestler released from Le Vernet, Edgar Mowrer of the *Chicago Daily News*, and the three set off in his Hillman Minx, just purchased from a fleeing British official in Bordeaux, for the Spanish border, believing themselves just a step ahead of German troops.

In Biarritz they were stopped at a military checkpoint. Hardy's and Mowrer's papers passed muster, but Koestler was taken to a jail for questioning. The following day he was moved to a military barracks in Bayonne; meanwhile Hardy and Mowrer had taken the car on to the south. (After Hardy left from St. Jean-de-Luz on a ship to England, Mowrer reached Lisbon after a long holdup on the international bridge between Hendaye and Irun. He rejoined his wife Lilian, and the couple—well-cared-for correspondents rather than harried refugees—switched from a hotel in Lisbon, all the more crowded and noisy with the centenary celebration, to a luxury suite with servants in a British-owned palace near Sintra. Here Mowrer wrote a long newspaper dispatch about the fall of France, and after work he and his wife walked in a grandly landscaped park, went sightseeing in the area, drove into Lisbon for dining, and once went for a swim in Estoril. Mowrer noted the water was chilly.) While he was in the Bayonne barracks, Koestler learned that the German zone in France would include the entire Atlantic coast, and that under terms of the armistice all French troops in occupied territory had to be withdrawn to Vichy France and discharged. His military group, loaded down with equipment and luggage, slogged their way to the east, though not before, in a Bayonne street, Koestler got his first close-up glimpse of the advancing German force: dark green tanks followed by motor bikes with men in black leather and black goggles. In the shuttered, sunbathed street they seemed like a thundering funeral procession.

On the second day of marching with his unit, Koestler went off on his own by joining an older couple driving toward Lourdes. He left them before reaching the town, and for several days he wandered about in the unoccupied zone, still a Legionnaire with an assumed name and now a large walrus mustache altering his looks, before linking up in a tiny village with a detachment of French soldiers waiting to be demobilized. He spent six weeks with the group, sleeping in a barn, feeling more secure than he had in a long time. Although the French troops were free to leave, they continued to wait because of a bonus that came with demobilization and a certificate allowing them to hold jobs. The process was slow because, so it was believed, officers among them wanted to continue drawing their pay.

In early August Koestler and a handful of other enlisted foreigners were sent to the Foreign Legion depot at Fort St. Jean in Marseille for demobilization. His military duties here were light, leaving him free in the evenings to mingle with refugees and relief workers crowded in the city. On September 3 he joined four British soldiers who had been interned in the fort on a tramp steamer bound for Oran in Vichy-controlled French North Africa. Koestler had persuaded the servicemen to take him along as a translator, and had bribed a port official to issue them false Legionaire papers that said they were unfit for duty and were to be discharged in Casablanca.

From Oran the five traveled to Casablanca, where a British intelligence agent provided the soldiers with emergency visas for Britain. Koestler did not qualify for one, but the agent got him aboard a Portuguese fishing boat with the soliders and some fifty others for a seasick-ridden voyage to Lisbon. While the soldiers were at once flown to Britain, Koestler anxiously waited some two months for a British clearance that never came. He took in the delights of Lisbon but with mounting frustration over British inactivity and fear the Portuguese authorities might arrest and deport him, possibly to Franco's Spain. Through cable contact with Daphne Hardy in England, he learned that she and others were laboring behind the scenes on his behalf, but as yet to no avail.

Finally, a stroke of luck came his way. Some months earlier he had applied for a ticket on a British commercial air flight to England, and his name had remained on a list. When a ticket suddenly became available, the British consul-general in Lisbon went against the rules and allowed him to leave Portugal on an emergency permit. Upon arrival in Britain he was arrested for illegal entry and jailed for six weeks, during which *Darkness at Noon* was published. Released from jail just before Christmas 1940, Koestler was now a literary figure of some repute and the holder of a British national registration card—"proof," he would write, "that I had regained my identity, and the right to exist."

★   ★   ★

Rupert Downing's Paris-to-Lisbon escape took place at the same time as Arthur Koestler's and covered some of the same terrain. The book he wrote about the journey appeared in 1941, the year of Koestler's account. But Downing's playful title, *If I Laugh: The Chronicle of My Strange Adventures in the Great Paris Exodus—June 1940*, set his work decidedly apart from Koestler's embittered *Scum of the Earth*. A British playwright and screenwriter, Downing gave full attention to the fear and misery of refugee flight while at the same time recording moments of ease, pleasure, and amusement.

When war came Downing was in Paris, where he had arrived two years before to write a play and was now working on a translating job with a woman named, simply, Dee. For health reasons he had been turned down for military service and as a war correspondent. From the radio he learned that German troops were within twenty miles of Paris—and of a government decree that all civilian men who were not aged or infirm were to leave the city, presumably to avoid ending up as prisoners of war or slave laborers. Nothing was said about where they should go or how.

Downing and Dee set off by bicycle, Dee perched on the handlebars. Soon they were able to buy a second bike, a transaction that seemed miraculous given the demand for transport of any sort, and together rode south through Bordeaux and Biarritz and St. Jean-de-Luz, avoiding main roads that might come under air attack and fearful, before the armistice terms were clarified, that the roads would fall under German control. Among the flow of refugees they also felt an odd sense of community that came from passing and then meeting up again with familiar faces. "And they all seemed," wrote Downing, "as pleased about these chance encounters as we were. At such a time in a stricken country the sight of a face you know (however slightly) can bring a curious glow to the heart."

In the Pyrenees bicycling meant roads twisting up and down and sudden semi-tropical rainstorms. Yet we were "extremely happy in a detached sort of way," Downing recalled. "We talked . . . of this very book (should I have the chance to write it), and discussed possible titles." One bittersweet possibility they tossed about was *Cycling round Europe*. It took two weeks of cycling from Paris before Downing and Dee reached the Spanish frontier. On the French side of the Hendaye-Irun international bridge they found long lines of waiting people and vehicles from Rolls-Royces to taxis to horse-drawn wagons. A barrier on the French side was raised long enough to fill with people and vehicles the gap to the closed barrier on the Spanish side, then closed again until the Spanish barrier was briefly lifted to allow some passage. Here Downing's and Dee's British citizenship came to their aid since British and American consular officials were present at the French barrier and working on behalf of citizens without visas.

One problem still loomed. The Spanish, bowing to German pressure, were not allowing into the country men of military age, with the age limit set at forty, and Downing's papers said he was thirty-eight. The only way around the situation was a doctor's certificate saying he was unfit for military service. Downing had one, but it was in Paris, so he had to seek out a French doctor to examine him, certify he had a weak heart, and hope Spain would accept the French document. Spain did, and after hours on the bridge and several rain showers, Downing and Dee finally were allowed in. Later Downing would learn that British authorities had struck a deal with Spain to get their citizen in and out of the country within forty-eight hours.

Still ahead was rough treatment by Spanish customs officials and a last-minute holdup over the bicycles Downing and Dee still had with them—something about duty or taxes, though they were never certain because everything was announced to them in Spanish. Downing apparently smiled or nodded at the right point, and they were allowed to keep the bikes. A bus transported the British citizens (with another bus for Americans) to San Sebastian, then a train carried them to Lisbon, where they were put up in the Royal British Club, ordinarily male only and still decorated with flags and ferns from the recent visit of the Duke of Kent to the Portuguese exposition. Soon thereafter they were taken to the *Rose of Ireland*, the vessel awaiting more refugees and with no definite date of departure. Once on board no one was allowed to leave, irksome for some but not for Downing.

> For the next four days—some of the sunniest, happiest, laziest days of my life—we lay at the quayside. Lisbon rose in tiers above us on the starboard side; to port the Tagus stretched away blue and twinkling to the far-distant shore on the other side of the river. We slept a lot and ate tremendously.

At last under way for England, the tranquil interlude quickly vanished into seasickness, the specter of German submarines, and the reality of a Heinkel bomber swooping out of a cloud and dropping four bombs, all narrowly missing their target.

★   ★   ★

Otto Strasser was a refugee of a different stripe. An ardent German National Socialist, he had been drummed out of the party in 1930 after disagreement with Hitler, and subsequently started his own political organization, the Black Front, a leftist ex-Nazi group resisting the Führer's continuing ascent to power. Eventually Strasser, a veteran of World War I, began a long period of European exile, which took him to Austria, Czechoslovakia, France, and Switzerland, where he was living when the war began. In November 1939, after hearing a Hitler speech on the radio, he learned that a bomb had exploded shortly after the Führer left the hall—and learned further that he and an unnamed British intelligence officer were behind the assassination attempt.

The following day, after a German ultimatum to surrender him, the Swiss gave Strasser four hours to leave the country. He took an air flight to France, accepting the common belief that the country was safe behind the Maginot Line; when it was speedily proven otherwise, the French government put him in a large concentration camp holding mostly Jews. Through a contact in the French Foreign Office he was released in late May 1940 and, accompanied by Hans, a Dutch friend made while in captivity, took rooms in a small Paris hotel. They were hardly settled before the flight from the city began. By train and auto they made their way to Bordeaux and then Bayonne, where they were able to get tickets on a small freighter making a last sailing to Casablanca.

Amid a wild scene of shouted bribes, bloody fights, and looted luggage as a desperate mob tried to board the ship, it at last set sail—only to turn back to Bayonne when news was radioed of the armistice and a German order that all French ships at sea return to port. Pleas to the freighter's captain to steam for England were ignored. Back in Bayonne the refugee situation was all the more unruly, with the absence still of German troops the only straw of hope. In a taxi acquired with a thick wad of francs, Strasser and Hans quickly made for St. Jean-de-Luz.

At the town's small harbor they found another mob and watched in horror as a German patrol suddenly came into sight and marched in rigid order along a nearby street. Onlookers were stunned to silence, with all chance of escaping France seeming to vanish with the appearance of the troops. Strasser immediately went into hiding while Hans sought to locate transport to take them the short distance to the Spanish border, a seeming impossibility with the Germans now present. Strasser was contemplating suicide rather than ending up in Gestapo hands when Hans appeared with a Belgian chauffeur who, for another wad of cash, drove them not to the border but to Oloron-Sainte-Marie, located just inside unoccupied territory. From here they moved on to a town near Lourdes, putting more distance between themselves and the Wehrmacht.

In Vichy France they felt reasonably safe until Strasser read in a newspaper the complete text of the armistice agreement, with its provision that the French government surrender all refugees wanted by the Reich. He now had to keep an eye out for the French police as well as the Gestapo; at the same time he and Hans concluded that if escaping France by illegal means was nearly hopeless, their only alternative was the complex and equally dangerous way of legality.

Ten days passed before Strasser could get an interview with an official at the Portuguese consulate in Toulouse, who politely explained that an overseas visa was needed before Portugal would consider granting a transit visa. While Strasser stayed in hiding in Toulouse, Hans set out for Vichy, where North and South American countries had consulates. After several days Hans returned, without overseas visas but with the consolation of money provided by friends whom Strasser still had in high places in France.

Strasser was again thinking of suicide when, walking the streets of Toulouse one night, he ran into the official from the Portuguese consulate. After Strasser poured out his story of frustration, though without giving his identity, the official suggested he go to the Netherlands consulate and apply for a visa to the Dutch island of Curaçao. With such a visa in hand, ship passage could be booked by telegraph and both Spanish and Portuguese transit visas issued.

What seemed too easy to be true was not: Strasser was quickly granted a tourist visa for Curaçao, then the Spanish and Portuguese visas. All that remained was the large obstacle of a French exit visa, which Hans solved by making friends with a woman official who after some days saw to it that one was stamped in Strasser's false passport. All went smoothly from here on, with Strasser—while Hans chose to remain in France for family reasons (Strasser had left a wife and children in Switzerland)—moving on to Cerbère for a night before, on August 1, 1940, entering Spain.

In Portugal Strasser located his brother Paul, a Benedictine priest, who had made his own journey of escape across France and found refuge in a monastery in the Portuguese interior. After about a month of living with his brother, two well-dressed men in a large automobile appeared at the monastery and told the abbot that if he turned over Strasser to the German government they would donate a hundred thousand escudos to the monastery along with a car similar to the one they were driving. The abbot at once telephoned the police. The men made no objection since, as they informed the abbot before driving away, they were attached to the German legation in Lisbon and had diplomatic immunity.

Knowing the Gestapo would not stop at trying to suborn the abbot, Strasser left the monastery alone and went into hiding in a remote fishing village in the north of Portugal. BBC broadcasts he could pick up about British endurance under German aerial assault encouraged him to resume his fight against Hitler, which meant leaving the shelter of the Portuguese coast and again living out in the open. An opportunity was handed to him when, at the end of September 1940, a weary and ruffled British figure drove into the village and, speaking to Strasser in French, told him the Gestapo knew where he was and Germany was preparing to seek his extradition. Strasser was wary that the visitor was himself a Gestapo agent; understanding his caution, the visitor suggested Strasser hire a taxi and follow his car at an interval of fifteen minutes to the nearest British consulate, where he would prove his identity. At the consulate in Porto, Strasser learned the British agent had been searching for him for some thirty-six hours, though why England was making a special effort to protect a prominent German was never disclosed.

The British quietly moved Strasser to Lisbon and put him aboard the American liner *Excambion*, which sailed for New York on October 2. At the same time the Portuguese government issued a statement to the effect that it regretted its inability to locate one Dr. Otto Strasser, who was alleged to have entered the country. On October 10 the *Excambion* stopped at Bermuda, and Strasser was taken from the ship on a police launch. The British provided a temporary permit to remain on the island until he could get a visa for a North American country, and there he remained for six months before Canada and Mexico offered him admission. Strasser chose Canada because it was in the war, and once in the country he settled in for the duration and beyond into a secluded life of anti-Hitler writing and lecturing.

★ ★ ★

Like the "Catholic Writer," Franz Schoenberner was among the anti-Nazi German intellectuals who fled the country well before the war. But rather than move to customary peacetime places of exile in Zurich or Paris, he and his wife, Ellie, went south to the French village of Roquebrune-Cap Martin, near Monte Carlo, and in 1933 they began new lives as freelance writers, he with articles for periodicals, she with popular fiction.

It was a Spartan existence. With France now filled with German writers, German-language publications were overwhelmed with manuscripts. Fees dwindled, and even when stories and articles were sold, payment was slow. But the couple believed themselves out of harm's way in France, and especially so in a village where they were known to officials who regularly inspected their identity cards and residence permits.

Then came September 1939. Immediately posters went up announcing that all German and Austrian males between seventeen and fifty were to report without delay to a camp in Antibes, bringing with them blankets and food to last four days. Apparently the exiles were to be screened, and Schoenberner immediately set off, believing he had little to fear since his papers were in order, he had a public record as an anti-Nazi man of letters, and he had lived in France for seven years and volunteered for French military service. If he was too old at forty-five for front-line duty, his knowledge of French and German might be put to use in information or propaganda work.

As it turned out, the camp was for internment rather than screening, and the refugees languished under vague orders of frequently changing commanders and an overall French policy that seemed more concerned with rounding up anti-Nazis than stopping the German army. For Schoenberner, however, internment lasted just six weeks. His editorial work in Germany and his publications caused the literary PEN organization in France to lobby for his release, with the result that one day he was called to the camp office and an officer asked, "Are you this great journalist?" When Schoenberner said yes, he was told he would be released at once. He was a bit of a poet himself, added the officer, and when the two separated they wished each other luck as fellow scribblers.

Freedom was short-lived, as Schoenberner expected it would be. He and his wife prepared themselves, boxing up their belongings for what they believed would be another internment, this one likely lasting through a long struggle with Germany fought along the lines of the slogging trench combat of World War I. It seemed doubtful, at any event, that France could fall as easily as had Poland. When orders finally came, they were for Schoenberner to report to a camp near Aix-en-Provence, while his wife would go to the massive Gurs concentration camp for women and children located just over the Pyrenees from Spain. (A story made the rounds that when the commander of Gurs—set up originally in 1939 to hold Spanish Republicans and men of the International Brigades who had fled into France—was called from Paris and told, "We're sending you ten thousand women to be interned," there was no response from the other end of the line. The commander had fainted.)

There was little or no mistreatment in Schoenberner's camp, yet neglect and indifference made it seem more miserable than the camp in Antibes. Limited faucets and primitive latrines were available for some two thousand Germans and Austrians together with a group of discharged French Foreign Legion soldiers who had the misfortune of having been born in one of the two countries. Everyone slept on piles of straw in what had been an old brickyard. In the congested conditions, ordinary acts of washing, dressing, eating, and cueing up for latrines were so time consuming that everyone felt busy every moment.

The camp held a large number of well-educated and important professionals, among them the rich and acclaimed anti-Nazi literary figure Lion Feuchtwanger. His novel *Success*, inspired by Sinclair Lewis's *Babbitt*, was thought likely to bring him the Nobel Prize for literature. In 1930 it went instead to Lewis, who in his acceptance speech named Feuchtwanger, whom he had once met in Berlin, as among a number of European writers of merit. With news of the fast advance of motorized Nazi divisions through France trickling into Schoenberner's camp, the detainees became frantic. If the Germans reached the camp, in one fell swoop they would have their hands not only on Feuchtwanger but a hundred or so of the most prominent German and Austrian anti-Nazis.

Appeals to the commander to evacuate the camp were met with fuzzy statements that France would see to their safety. With neutral America as the only real hope of the anti-Nazis, cables were sent off (such freedom was possible in the loosely controlled setting, which included a thriving black market run by former Legionnaires and the French guards) to President Roosevelt and the American Red Cross, the only signature on them Lion Feuchtwanger's because of the star-power of his name and the startling fact that he had once met the American president.

Plans were also tossed about for overpowering the small contingent of guards and taking control of the camp, a notion abandoned when one day a company of young and well-equipped French troops came marching in. There was always the possibility of jumping the camp's barbed-wire enclosure and running into nearby woods. But what was to be done then? Always available too was the final escape of suicide with a hidden razor blade. The hope most internees clung to was a rumor that any day the camp would be evacuated and everyone sent by train to an undisclosed destination. The likely direction would be toward the Pyrenees, or possibly through Spain to French labor camps in North Africa. Any destination was preferable to waiting for the arrival of the Wehrmacht.

When the camp was finally abandoned in June 1940 the internees spent five days on a train that kept changing directions—and learned from newspapers picked up along the way of the final fall of France with the acceptance of the armistice. In Nîmes the train stopped, and the men were marched to a new camp in St. Nicolas, which turned out to be a large farm in the middle of a woods. There was no enclosure, and no plans had been made for the new arrivals beyond providing a truckload of army tents. A single farm well with a pump served for everyone.

The absence of guards and barbed wire seemed an open invitation to escape before the Germans came with lists of names that must be turned over by what was now Vichy France. There was, in any case, nothing stopping the internees from walking into Nîmes or simply leaving for their homes in unoccupied territory. On the third day in St. Nicolas a small group of Senegalese troops appeared and strung a single line of barbed wire around the camp. The camp commander dismissed the wire as symbolic and said the new troops were meant only to provide order; the detainees could still move about freely, even go for swims in a stream, and would be released as soon as papers were prepared.

As it happened, Lion Feuchtwanger's departure came about in another fashion. Shortly before the move to St. Nicolas, two cables, addressed solely to him, had come in response to the pleas sent to Roosevelt and the Red Cross. Feuchtwanger had destroyed the cables, which apparently said something about contacting the American consulate in Marseille. Then, after a brief period in St. Nicolas, the writer was seemingly kidnapped by people associated with the consulate and driven to a safe location in Marseille. As Schoenberner interpreted the astonishing development, even before the cables arrived the literary lion's wife and friends were working for him with the consulate—and Feuchtwanger himself, in the all-consuming isolation of his ego, had ignored the fact that the messages were of intense interest to scores of others in the camp.

Feuchtwanger's escape was as dispiriting as it was exhilarating since the remaining internees could hardly expect to be kidnapped one by one by the American consulate. Beyond that, most wanted to put France entirely behind and reach Spain and Portugal, and for this they needed proper documents, with the paper trail beginning with legal release from a concentration camp. So they waited, all the while continuing to plead with authorities for their freedom.

Ellie Schoenberner was suddenly released from Gurs as an essential agricultural worker and went back to Roquebrune-Cap Martin. About the same time Franz Schoenberner learned that Vichy would not release German nationals until a Nazi commission had come to his camp, a delay that might yet take weeks or months. He was now volunteering to work in the camp's office, and one day he initiated a conversation with a captain in charge of inmate records by mentioning that he had been the anti-Nazi editor of the Munich weekly *Simplicissimus*. He added, "I don't know whether this name means anything to you, monsieur—." "But of course, monsieur, I know *Simplicissimus*," replied the captain. "You should have been released long ago." Two hours later Schoenberner was released. He at once took a taxi into Nîmes, a night train to Marseille, and the next day joined his wife at home.

In December 1940 word came that, through the efforts of a German literary friend who had reached New York, an American visa had been recommended for Schoenberner, and he should meet with the consul in Nice. In early January of the new year a precious emergency visitor visa was granted. Later that month Ellie Schoenberner obtained an immigration visa since, with a French father, she came under the American quota for refugees from the country. Still ahead for the Schoenberners were the need for permits to leave France and pass through Spain and Portugal, and then the need of funds for passage to New York.

It took five months of cables, letters, and waiting in lines, all the while wondering if Vichy France would yet turn them over to the Germans, to arrange the required paperwork. Even this effort would not have been enough without work on the couple's behalf and money provided by refugee organizations and individuals in Marseille and New York. On May 25 Franz and Ellie Schoenberner left their village for Marseille to pick up their papers, and four days later they were on a train headed to the Spanish border. When they reached Lisbon the atmosphere of Europe seemed instantly altered. Franz Schoenberner wrote:

> We knew that [Portugal], too, lived under a dictatorship, but, perhaps because Salazar was at least a professor and not a general, the evil of oppression and injustice seemed here less obvious and less ubiquitous. Life on the surface seemed quite civilized and almost normal. You were tempted to accept the omen that this city, which had become the last emergency exit from Europe, had called its most magnificent avenue the Avenue of Liberty.

There was a ten-day wait before their departure on an overburdened Portuguese ship. Finally leaving the haunted house of Europe was a momentous event, and Franz Schoenberner had planned to fix it in his memory with a final look back at the Continent. But onboard tasks delayed him. When at last he came on deck the ship was beyond sight of land; ahead all was ocean and sky. Too excited to sleep, he and his wife spent their first night at sea in deck chairs, celebrating their escape with a bottle of Portuguese brandy, bought with foresight in a seamen's bar on the Lisbon waterfront.

3

WHATEVER WE CAN

What can we do for you? We are ready to do whatever
we can.

—Letter of Varian Fry to Jacques Lipchitz, 1940

Before leaving Marseille for Lisbon, Franz and Ellie Schoenberner paid a
call on Varian Fry to thank him for help he had given them. It was a
fitting response, as it would have been for numerous other exiles, though at
the time few were in the position to know the full extent of Fry's aid effort.
The public manner of the calm, courteous, bespectacled, properly attired
young American gave off no suggestion of his unstinting labor over many
months to get Nazi-hunted refugees from the Vichy-controlled city to
freedom in the United States and elsewhere, using all means at his disposal,
legal or illegal. Nor was it likely the Schoenberners sensed how precarious
Fry's own situation in Marseille was becoming—or suspected that in a short
while he would be forced by Vichy, with the full blessing of American officials, to take the Lisbon route himself.

In early August 1940 Varian Fry had been sent to Marseille by the
Emergency Rescue Committee (ERC), a group formed in New York
in the summer of the year to get figures with backgrounds similar to the
Schoenberners out of Europe. With the German invasion of France, exiles
already in the United States believed the Nazis had lists of former enemies—primarily writers, artists, and intellectuals, many of whom had been
stripped of their German citizenship—and would be searching for them
throughout the country. When later it was learned that in the armistice
the Vichy government had agreed to surrender on demand all Germans
in France or French possessions (with "Germans" also meaning Austrians,

Czechs, Poles, and any other national group the Gestapo wanted to grab), it was clear that evacuation was the best hope of saving them.

With Fry, Paul Hagen (the new name of Karl Frank, an Austrian psychoanalyst who had arrived in the United Sates in the mid-1930s), and others working behind the scenes, a money-raising luncheon was staged in New York's Commodore Hotel on June 25, 1940. Some $3,500 was raised, but Erika Mann, the exiled daughter of Thomas Mann, pointed out in a talk that "money alone is not going to rescue those people. Most of them are trapped without visas, without passports that they dare use. They can't just get on a boat and leave. Somebody has to be there who can *get* them out." With that, the ERC was formed—and need established for an agent operating from a base in Marseille to be its man on the ground to organize and operate the rescue effort.

Frank Kingdon, president of Newark University, was named to chair the committee, and a glittering advisory group was put together that included other university presidents and such well-known journalists and commentators as Elmer Davis, Raymond Gram Swing, and Dorothy Thompson. Exiles of the stature of Jacques Maritain, Jules Romains, and Thomas Mann produced a master list of figures needing rescue. In Washington, First Lady Eleanor Roosevelt sympathized with the work of the committee and lobbied the president, in the face of political resistance and restrictive American quotas on immigration, to authorize special emergency visitor visas for selected exiles.

The ERC's next task was finding the agent to work in France. An American seemed the best choice since U.S. neutrality offered a screen of legality, and when no one else came forward the job fell to the thirty-two-year-old Fry. He was a Harvard graduate with a concentration in classics who had established himself as a foreign affairs journalist by working as an editor for *The Living Age* magazine and later as editor-in-chief of publications on international matters for the Foreign Policy Association. He spoke French and some German and was a political activist and fervent anti-Nazi.

Traveling in Europe in the summer of 1935, Fry had witnessed a vicious mob attack on Jews and Jewish property on Berlin's fashionable Kurfuerstendamm. Although badly shaken by the experience, he put through a call to the Associated Press, and the next day his report of the rioting made the front page of the *New York Times*. That day he also asked for and was granted a meeting with Ernst Franz Sedgwick Hanfstaengl, a fellow Harvard man who had returned to Germany, was an early supporter of Hitler, and was working as the foreign press chief in Joseph Goebbel's Ministry of Propaganda. Fry suspected he had been allowed the meeting because of the

Harvard tie, and Hanfstaengl was indeed in a nostalgic and expansive mood. (Hanfstaengl had another Harvard connection in President Roosevelt, and after falling out of Nazi favor in 1937 and leaving Germany for Britain and then a prisoner-of-war camp in Canada, he ended up in the United States doing special intelligence work for the president under the code name "Dr. Sedgwick.")

When he returned to America, Fry told the *Times* about Hanfstaengl confiding to him that rather than Jews hissing during the showing of a film—the supposed trigger for the 1935 attacks—the disturbance in the theater was the work of brown-shirted Storm Troopers, three days earlier. Fry also reported the Nazi official's observation that there were two views in Germany about solving the Jewish problem, with moderates wishing to segregate them in special areas while radicals favored "bloodshed." The *Times* gave the story prominent play beneath headlines reading "Editor Holds Riots Inspired by Nazis" and "Varian Fry Says Hanfstaengl Admitted Storm Troopers, Not Jews, Hissed Film."

★　　★　　★

Fry's charge from the ERC, set out in a letter, was notably vague. His main task was "to attempt to locate, and to aid with counsel and money as directed, certain individuals whom this Committee will specify, so that they may reach Lisbon or Casablanca and thereby be in a better position to be transported to this continent." His base of operation would be Marseille, teeming with refugees drawn to it as a port city and with a direct rail line to the Spanish frontier, five hours distant. The thin cover for his secret work was an affiliation with the international YMCA, which had a representative in Marseille, and a letter of introduction to the European director of the Red Cross. As for the American consulate in Marseille, it was left to Fry's discretion how much he should share about the nature of his mission.

On August 4, 1940, Fry left on a Clipper flight from New York to Lisbon, carrying with him a list of some two hundred names the ERC wanted rescued, three thousand dollars in cash taped to one leg, and a sleeping bag and air mattress in case he needed to go backpacking in search of his refugees. In his pocket was a small notebook with an amateurish code agreed upon by the ERC for communicating without drawing the attention of Vichy censors: money was "milk," England "Ursula," Germany "Eloise." Thinking his work could be quickly accomplished, Fry also carried a Clipper return ticket that expired within a month.

In Lisbon he was struck by the city's near-African summer heat, its lively commotion and leisurely pace, and the spectacle of rich Europeans pampering themselves while waiting to move on elsewhere. "All very exhausting," he wrote back to his wife, "but none of it boring."

> The hotels are jammed, and business is booming. Everybody from the Archduke Otto down has passed through Lisbon in the past few months. . . . There are all sorts of street cries, gotten off mostly by peasant women who carry their wares in baskets perched precariously on their heads. . . . But it isn't merely the street calls: it is also the bustle of an eastern bazaar—the life is terrific. Yet pleasant. It takes three quarters of an hour to change a travelers check. And yet one doesn't mind. I don't know why. One just doesn't. . . .

While settling for a week in the Hotel Métropole and enjoying what seemed almost like a vacation in a place far removed from war, Fry got a piece of information about the whereabouts of one of the prominent names on his rescue list. A sister of Franz Werfel told him the writer and his wife were already lodged in a hotel in Marseille.

The city when Fry reached it presented stark contrasts with Lisbon. On the surface it was another hot and bustling port while underneath was an ancient trading center—grimy, hard-used, burdened with a history of crime and corruption, and now riding the wave of a booming black-market economy in visas, passports, food, and nearly all else. Yet like Lisbon, Marseille gave Fry little sense of life in wartime, let alone life in fallen France. He wrote his wife: "There is no disorder, there are no children starving in the streets, and there are very few signs of war of any kind. The people of Marseille seem to have resigned themselves to defeat, and even to take it rather lightly—as they take everything." In short order he would become aware of several thousands of refugees who spent their nights in crowded hotels and boardinghouses, their days in the waiting rooms of consulates—and would realize that despite being under Vichy authority, Nazi officials came and went in the city as they pleased.

His first evening in Marseille Fry met with Franz Werfel and his wife Alma, who were booked into the Hôtel du Louvre as Mr. and Mrs. Gustav Mahler, a disguise that if anything drew more attention to them. Anna Werfel had been married to the famed composer, as she had been to the famed architect Walter Gropius. "I only marry geniuses," she is said to have remarked. Her present genius, Franz Werfel, was now the first figure on his list Fry had found, and he listened as husband and wife said they had visas for America, had picked them up at the consulate, but had no idea what to do next. "You must save us, Mr. Fry," they cried. "Oh, *ja*, you must save us!" Fry was in Marseille to do precisely that, but—as he later wrote—"the truth was that I was at a complete loss about how to begin, and where. My job was to save certain refugees. But how was I to do it? How was I to get in touch with them? What could I do for them when I found them?"

Other important writers on his list had also reached Marseille. Heinrich Mann was living in the Hôtel Normandie. The poet Walter Mehring was tucked away in a suburb of the city. Lion Feuchtwanger was in hiding at a villa occupied by Hiram (Harry) Bingham, the American vice consul in Marseille, who had sent his pregnant wife and four children back to America upon the German invasion of France. Bingham, whose father was a United States senator, would prove helpful to Fry in many ways while his boss, Consul Hugh Fullerton, remained stiffly opposed to an American citizen undertaking undercover work in Vichy France at a time when government policy called for friendly relations with the Pétain regime.

Feuchtwanger's removal from the concentration camp at St. Nicolas had come about at the hands of Harry Bingham's assistant in the consulate, the improbably named Myles Standish. He had visited the writer and his wife when they were living in Sanary in the south of France before the war; now, learning Feuchtwanger was held in the camp, Standish made plans to free him. In Bingham's undiplomatic-looking red Chevrolet, he drove to the lightly policed facility with the wife of a doctor from Nîmes who regularly brought food and medicine to the camp and consequently was known to the guards. Called "Madame L" in an account Feuchtwanger later wrote of his rescue, she carried a message to him written by his wife that said in French, "Do what you're told. Don't waste time wondering, it's all absolutely sound and serious."

At the camp Standish and the doctor's wife waited until late afternoon before they located Feuchtwanger on his way back from a walk to a nearby town for a meal with other inmates. As he was about to leave the road for a path to the camp, Madame L came up to him, handed him the note, and said, "I've been waiting for you. I have news for you from your wife. Read it. Do read it straightaway." Feuchtwanger read the note, read it again, then noticed the red car pulled up by the side of the road. A youngish man he recognized, dressed in a white suit and wearing string gloves, emerged and said in English, "Please don't ask questions. But get in. Don't hesitate—I'll tell you everything as we go along."

Feuchtwanger played his part and, along with Madame L, entered the car, where he found waiting for him a woman's coat with an English badge on it, a shawl for his head, and dark glasses. When the car was stopped on the way back to Marseille, the driver identified himself as an American from the consulate and the two passengers as his wife and mother-in-law.

★   ★   ★

Werfels, Mann, Mehring, Feuchtwanger—all were important figures with recognizable faces, and as such they lived in daily dread of being spotted by the police or by fellow exiles who might call out their names in public. All had longed to reach Marseille because of its large, diverse, and generally accepting population along with a port that offered hope of sailing to freedom on a ship. But now they were blocked in the city, uncertain about where to go next, terrified of moving at all. Fry got his first ideas on how to proceed with these and lesser-known exiles from Frank Bohn, the European representative of a coalition of American labor groups. After the fall of France the coalition had persuaded the State Department to give emergency visitor visas to a list of European labor leaders, union officials, and democratic politicians in danger of arrest by the Nazis, and Bohn had been sent to France to get them out. He had arrived in Marseille only shortly before Fry but had already developed considerable knowledge about the local refugee situation.

Among other things, Bohn was a font of information about the maze of documents needed to travel legally in France and beyond. Since visas had time limits and were constantly expiring, possessing a full set of up-to-date documents was difficult at best. And there were some refugees, largely German and Austrian Jews, who were stateless and carried only "affidavits in lieu of passports" that might or might not be acceptable. But Bohn was hopeful about present conditions, believing a window of opportunity still existed before the Gestapo and French authorities in Vichy were fully organized and tightened the noose on refugees they wanted.

Fry found Bohn's unguarded way of talking about his work troubling, and he was skeptical about a particular plan to move some of his refugees from Marseille illegally by boat. But he decided to scrap his earlier thought of traveling around southern France and hunting for his refugees and to operate in Bohn's open manner by taking a room in the same hotel, the Splendide, writing to all the refugees for whom he had addresses about his arrival in Marseille, and waiting for them to come to him. He also made the rounds of the many relief agencies operating in Marseille to see what support they might give him. Donald Lowrie of the International YMCA, an experienced relief worker, would become a valued resource.

Within a week of his arrival Fry was running what appeared to be a thriving business from unlikely quarters. Waiting refugees lined a corridor outside his hotel room and trailed down a stairway. From the numbers it was clear the refugee problem was far greater than New York knew, and clear as well that lists provided him favored already successful cultural figures as against those soon to be. A young German writer named Hannah Arendt was among the latter, as was Arthur Koestler. Nonetheless the lists were meant to be followed. Fry could only appeal to New York to add new names, then begin the drawn-out process of appealing for one of the emergency visas.

★   ★   ★

To refugees who climbed to the fourth floor of the Hôtel Splendide, the presence in Marseille of the concerned American with a mission to save them and the money to do so seemed a scarcely believable gift. Hans Sahl, a German writer on the ERC list, recalled (in the form of an autobiographical novel) the strong emotion of their first meeting in Fry's room.

> Imagine the situation: the borders closed; you're caught in a trap, might be arrested again at any moment; life is as good as over—and suddenly a young American in shirt sleeves is stuffing your pocket full of money, putting his arm around your shoulders and whispering in a poor imitation of a conspirator's manner: "Oh, there are ways to get you out of here," while damn it all, the tears were streaming down my face, actual tears, big, round, and wet; and that pleasant fellow, a Harvard man incidentally, takes a silk handkerchief from his jacket and says: "Here, have this. Sorry it isn't cleaner."

Hertha Pauli's first meeting with Fry, on the other hand, was brief and businesslike. From other exiles huddled in Marseille the young Austrian writer had heard of the American rescuer who had come to town, and from a former colleague, a journalist from Vienna, she learned he was staying at the Splendide. "I've been turned away already; I'm not on his list," the colleague said. "But perhaps you are, and he'll see you."

In the hotel room she found a young man sitting at a table and examining a sheet of paper. When she told him her name he raised his head and looked at her through his glasses. "Well, Miss Pauli," he said in an expressionless voice, "I've got you on my list." He put a few questions to her—switching to French when he realized her English was poor—as if she were having a job interview. He then asked about other names on his list, and one of them, the German poet Walter Mehring, she knew was hiding in nearby Bar Mistral. "Bring Mehring with you tomorrow," Fry said to her. "Au revoir."

Fry soon took on two assistants to help in his work: Albert Hirschman, a German who was using the name Albert Hermant but was called "Beamish" by Fry because of his broad smile, and Franz von Hildebrand, an Austrian Catholic whom he called "Franzi." (The nicknames helped as well to disguise real names that might be overheard in conversations.) Together the three developed a work routine. At eight in the morning refugees were ushered into the hotel room one at a time. Fry talked with them first to see if they were "his" cases; if so, they were turned over to Beamish or Franzi for interviews and their information recorded on file cards. Work went on well into the night.

With the refugees gone, the cards were reviewed and action decided upon. Always three main questions needed answers: who, and on what grounds, should be added to the list? What papers had to be procured for the escapees? How and when would movement to the Spanish border take place? Since there was fear of a police microphone placed in the room or someone listening in a connecting room, major decisions were made in the toilet with the water taps turned on. The last job of the three men each evening was to write out a daily cable to New York with the names and references of refugees judged right for visas.

In time the refugees streaming through the hotel caused management to complain, and the police appeared. The only surprise was that, with German and Italian officers living in the hotel and circulating in and out themselves, they had not come sooner. Fry said under questioning that he was doing nothing more than studying the refugees' needs and giving them advice. The explanation was accepted, but it was evident that to carry on he needed a more formal operation with a name, a real office, and additional assistants. His work, he told his wife in a letter, had become "a crushing job. I have never worked so hard in my life, or such long hours. Strangely, though there are a dozen harrowing scenes every day, I love the work. The pleasure of being able to help even a few people more than makes up for the pain of having to turn others down."

The pain of rejecting refugees only increased. Despite sharing his work with others, ultimate decisions were Fry's alone, and he agonized over a litany of vexing concerns. How could refugee claims be genuinely verified? What did being an intellectual really mean? Were scientists intellectuals? Were journalists? Could nothing be done for refugees who were clearly anti-Nazi and in danger but fit none of his categories for saving? Fry continually cabled New York with names to add to his list, yet finally there were always those he had to turn away.

Despite the guilt that weighed on him, Fry was able to unwind. During nightly conferences with fellow workers in his hotel room he would remove his Brooks Brothers clothing down to Black Watch or Royal Stewart tartan boxer shorts while all others stayed fully dressed, join in generous consumption of French wine, and hold up his end of often bawdy conversations. And he found time to leave his duties behind for bicycling trips through Provence to explore churches and old ruins.

★   ★   ★

In early September 1940 Fry set up shop as the innocently named Centre Américain de Secours (CAS), the American Relief Center, in an office on a side street near the Marseille harbor. There were three rooms, two for interviews, and the other for Fry's office. He had taken on a secretary and had new staff members with varying backgrounds and language abilities. One of them, Miriam Davenport, had another useful skill beyond speaking German and French. An American, she had gone to Paris for art study after finishing Smith College, and with the war she joined the refugee escape to the south; in Marseille she began working for Fry for what she thought a grand salary under the conditions of about twenty-seven dollars a month. When refugees came to the CAS calling themselves artists though no one had heard of them, Davenport sent them to the harbor to make a sketch. When they returned with their work she made a quick judgment of their ability. With poets carrying folders of work, her judgment was made on the spot.

The new quarters were meant to bolster the cover that Fry was running just another relief agency, his specializing in immigration to America, and giving financial help when and where it was needed. In fact the CAS was a rescue operation and was soon up to its neck in a range of illegal activities: dealing with a Marseille crime figure in exchanging dollars for francs; forging a variety of documents from the nimble hand of a Viennese political cartoonist then calling himself Bill Freier; and smuggling refugees in immediate danger and without exit visas across the French border and into Spain. Leon Ball, who had been with the American Volunteer Ambulance Corps before the armistice and knew France well, was one of a small band making regular clandestine trips with two or three refugees to the border, seeing them across into Spain, then returning to Marseille for another trip. Cryptic cables would be sent back when a refugee finally reached Lisbon.

When Frank Bohn's cherished scheme for a boat from Marseille fell through, Fry became directly involved in the smuggling operation. He had intended to put three major figures from his lists, all lacking French exit visas, on the boat: Heinrich Mann, Franz Werfel, Lion Feuchtwanger. The last told Fry that, the boat no longer an option, he would attempt a border crossing on foot only if Fry went with him. Fry agreed and invited Werfel, Mann, and their wives to join them.

Fry had his own reasons for going to Spain and then on to Portugal. Five of his clients, as he called them, had been arrested in Spain; he wanted to learn why and, if possible, get them out of jail. In Lisbon he wanted freedom to send a frank report to the ERC in New York, which included bringing up the matter of his possible replacement.

Learning at the last moment that Spain would not allow into the country refugees without national identities, Feuchtwanger—in lieu of a passport he had only an affidavit provided by the U.S. consulate under a pen name used in some of his early writings, James Wetcheek (the surname of an English translator of Feuchtwanger)—and his wife were left behind in Marseille. The traveling party, which along with the Manns and Werfels included Golo Mann, Thomas Mann's son, and the smuggling expert Leon Ball, took a train to Cerbère on the odd chance the refugees might somehow be allowed across the French border without an exit visa. When this failed to happen, Fry, who did have the pass, went across with the luggage—twelve suitcases belonged to the Werfels—while Ball led the others across the steep overland route.

Ball shook hands and left them when they were in sight of a Spanish entry post. Except for Golo Mann, all the traveling party had passports; he had an affidavit in lieu of passport that said he was going to visit his father, who at the time was teaching at Princeton University. A sentry gave the affidavit close inspection and said, "I am honored to make the acquaintance of the son of so great a man," then shook hands with Golo and called for a car to bring the entire party to a station in town, where they were reunited eventually with Fry.

In Madrid, trying to get information about his clients jailed in Spain, Fry learned at the British embassy that Germany had Panzer divisions massed on the Spanish border, though it was unclear whether they intended to enter Spain or move east into unoccupied France. In Lisbon he met with Charles R. Joy, a Unitarian minister and European head of the Unitarian Service Committee, which was based in the city but had expanded its work into France with an office in Marseille. Joy's Lisbon operation in the Hotel Métropole on busy Rossio Square was an important base point for Fry's clients who reached the city, and here he had a happy reunion with Franzi, who was now working with Joy. From Joy and Franzi he learned that the Werfels were settled in a plush hotel in Estoril while the Manns were more modestly housed in Lisbon.

The city seemed changed since Fry had passed through on his way to Marseille just over a month before. On the newsstands there seemed fewer American and British publications and more from Germany; and there were more Germans in the city trying to pass as tourists. Lisbon was also darkened for him by news that the Gestapo was lifting refugees off the streets and moving them back to Spain or Germany. To date a half-dozen or so anti-Nazis had disappeared in this way, none of them so far Fry's clients, but the possibility remained that one could be kidnapped and as a result the whole underground rescue operation exposed. Fry met with clients who had made it to Lisbon and learned that their experiences in getting through Spain were so varied it was hard to come to any general conclusions; plainly, much depended on sheer luck. Despite the five arrested in Spain, the best route from France still seemed overland through Spain to Lisbon. The many schemes floated for sea transport from Marseille had all come to nothing, and when he returned to the city Fry was all the more determined to tell his refugees to take the Lisbon route before it was too late.

Before leaving Lisbon he had bought a couple dozen bars of soap, a desperate need back at the CAS office. The committee's invaluable secretary, Lena Fischmann, had buried notes throughout his luggage, using the several languages she commanded, as reminders to bring as much as he could.

★   ★   ★

After weeks of waiting in Lisbon, the Manns and Werfels finally departed for New York on the Greek ship *Nea Hellas*. The leave-taking, as Heinrich Mann recorded it, was tinged with a sense of loss: "The view towards Lisbon presented the harbour—the last image as Europe faded. It seemed indescribably beautiful. A lost lover is not more beautiful. Everything life had given us had come from this continent. . . . It was a parting of exceeding sadness." Lion Feuchtwanger and his wife, as Fry learned when he returned to Marseille, also had been led across the frontier by Ball (with Feuchtwanger bearing several packs of American cigarettes to persuade Spanish officials to look the other way if his affidavit were questioned) and were safely in Lisbon and waiting for ship transport.

Later came the appalling news that when Feuchtwanger reached New York (while his wife was still stuck in Lisbon) he told reporters gathered at the dock both about his escape from a French concentration camp and how he had been taken over the Pyrenees into Spain. "The author spoke repeatedly," said the *New York Times*, "of unidentified American friends who seemed to turn up miraculously in various parts of France to aid him at crucial moments in his flight." He refused to name the friends or the French city in which he had hidden after he was freed from the camp, but he did not shy away from revealing details of his crossing into Spain.

> After hiding in this unnamed southern city [the newspaper account went on], he received a false passport already provided with Spanish and Portuguese visas, and again he started out by train for the Spanish border. The way had been well prepared, and although he was questioned and his papers examined several times he passed through successfully. Mrs. Feuchtwanger had joined him, and together they were guided, again by friends, to a smuggler's pass over the Pyrenees, and they climbed together for four hours, entering Spain. It then took them a week to get to Lisbon, where Mr. Feuchtwanger identified himself to an American consul.

Fry's repeated denials to French and American officials of CAS involvement in illegal operations was deeply compromised by Feuchtwanger's reckless talk, as a follow-up round of press stories made all the more clear. "Refugee Tales Wreck Underground Railway," read a headline in the *New York Post*. *Time* magazine reported that "charmed were newshawks by [Feuchtwanger's] colorful details, lack of the reticence usual in such cases. Far from charmed was the Emergency Rescue Committee. They thought Author Feuchtwanger might as well be talking to the Gestapo. They wondered why he talked at all, believed that, whatever his motives, he had gravely jeopardized the Committee's undercover rescue work in France."

While the notoriety surrounding Feuchtwanger's American arrival caused Fry ongoing headaches, the writer's movement from Marseille to Lisbon to New York was a major CAS success story. Walter Benjamin's similar attempt was a tragic failure. The eminent German intellectual, age forty-eight but in poor health and looking much older, took the mountain route into Spain while carrying with him his latest manuscript in a heavy briefcase. He had been advised to leave the briefcase behind or have it carried from France by someone with an exit visa, but he refused to let it out of his sight. Fry's instructions to Benjamin were that if he were turned back for any reason after crossing the Spanish border, he should go back to France and keep trying; eventually luck would be on his side. Instead Benjamin took his own life with morphine pills in a hotel in Port-Bou, where Spanish police, given his exhausted condition after the border cross-ing, had allowed him to rest for a night before returning to France. (While in Marseille before attempting his escape, Benjamin had met with Arthur Koestler in a bar near the harbor and told him that, in event of failure, he was carrying morphine pills. Since he had more than he needed, he offered Koestler half his supply, and Koestler accepted with gratitude.) In a letter to New York, Fry made only brief mention of Benjamin's death, adding in a note that it was the third suicide of a figure on his rescue list.

★   ★   ★

Lisa Fittko had just recently discovered the route Walter Benjamin had taken over the Pyrenees. She and her husband Hans had been on the run across Europe since 1933; now in hiding in Marseille, they were finally in a position to leave France. They had Czech passports, transit visas for Spain and Portugal, and overseas visas for China; all they lacked were exit visas for France, which meant they would have to cross the mountains.

While Hans remained in Marseille, Lisa had gone to Port-Vendres on the Mediterranean coast in unoccupied France near the Spanish border to scout out a path to replace the one from Cerbère that had become too dan-gerous. At the harbor she had spoken with dockworkers and was advised to contact the socialist mayor of the nearby fishing town of Banyuls-sur-Mer, who was believed to have sympathy for the refugees. He had gone to great lengths, including drawing a map from memory, to instruct her about a trail at higher elevation that had been used in the Spanish Civil War to evacu-ate Republican troops. Lisa had taken the route to guide Walter Benjamin, together with a woman and her son, leaving them when they were inside Spain and retracing the route alone. When she returned to Marseille she learned from Hans that two Americans wanted to speak with them.

The small bistro on a narrow side street near the harbor struck Lisa as exactly the wrong place for the meeting. The neatly dressed refugee agents, Varian Fry and Frank Bohn, were conspicuously out of place. Al-bert Hirschman, a refugee who worked closely with Fry, had come with them, and that much was reassuring. The Fittkos knew that Hirschman was a fellow anti-Nazi German and aware of the underground work of getting Gestapo-hunted refugees into Spain.

Still, Lisa was concerned since she and Hans were close to making their own flight to freedom and she wanted nothing to endanger that. Only when Fry started talking did she begin to relax. Hans had suspected the Americans wanted information about the new route she had discovered, and that turned out to be the case. She was happy to supply the details;

she and Hans had intended that others use the route after they did. It soon became apparent, however, that Fry and Bohn had something more in mind. With hundreds of endangered figures needing to escape, the agents believed the crossing should be organized in the sense of having definite starting and ending points, guides taking the refugees along the route, and someone permanently in place and in charge.

Fry asked, "Would you, for a few months—?" He promised that if Lisa and Hans took on what he was calling the "border project," he would get them out of France when the work was finished.

Hans relented to the extent of saying, "Oh, maybe for a short time we can break someone in there." Lisa agreed but thought it best that a Frenchman take on the job. And she had reservations about the ability of the Americans to keep their promise of future help.

At this point Hirschman joined in the conversation, speaking in German and telling Lisa and Hans that the Americans could be trusted and had money and connections. Hearing the mention of money, Fry misunderstood and asked how much the Fittkos wanted. Hans erupted in irritation. "Do you know," he told Fry, "that assisting men of military age in illegal border crossings now rates the death penalty? And you offer us money. We would have to be insane indeed. Do you actually understand what an anti-Fascist is? Do you understand the word . . . convictions?"

Fry apologized for the confusion, explaining that he only meant money would be needed for living expenses and emergencies. Once the new route was organized, he and Bohn would provide the necessary funds.

Lisa and Hans said they needed time to consider the project. They knew putting their own plans on hold was unwise, as was trusting two men they had just met. They also knew they could not shrug off the opportunity to set up a border-crossing base by telling themselves, "Let others do it."

From a house in Banyuls-sur-Mer using forged French identity cards and posing as French refugees who could not return home (which qualified them for a small allowance from the Vichy government), Hans and Lisa Fittko operated as refugee guides on the new route over the Pyrenees from mid-October 1940 to early April 1941, taking as many as three trips a week with Fry's and Bohn's refugees as well as British soldiers and airmen who had been captured in France and were interned in Fort St. Jean in Marseille. Officially prisoners of war, the British were allowed to roam about town during the day. Officers had to report only for Monday roll call; with food rations issued at the time, many sold their allotment on the black market and lived in town the rest of the week on the earnings. Since the fort held more than three hundred POWs, it was relatively easy for

Fry—drawing on funds supplied by the British embassy in Madrid (about which more in a later chapter)—to move two or three at a time to Banyuls. Once across the border they reported to Spanish authorities as prisoners of war and waited for British officials from Barcelona to pick them up and move them to Gibraltar.

The Fittkos identified the refugees who came to them, ordinarily no more than three at a time, with a simple checking method. A go-between from Marseille would bring them a torn piece of colored paper with a number on it, and a refugee when he appeared would give them the other half of the torn sheet with a matching number. Among those led across the frontier was Hirschman, forced to make a last-minute dash from Marseille when police came looking for him.

The end for the border project came when Vichy ordered all frontier areas cleared of foreigners, and the Fittkos left Banyuls. They had succeeded in getting more than a hundred people across the border. Back in the Marseille area, they were supported with funds from the CAS before new overseas visas to Cuba were obtained for them and they began their own exit from France to Lisbon. "It had been exactly one year," Lisa recorded, "since the [Fry] committee had given us its assurance that it would help us in our own flight when the time came. We had always considered this promise to be a dim glimmer of hope; the more time that passed, the nearer it got to cutoff time, the dimmer it seemed to be." Now, the time come, Fry was as good as his word.

★   ★   ★

In the wake of the Lion Feuchtwanger affair and Walter Benjamin's suicide, Fry learned that the Vichy government had complained about his work to the U.S. State Department, which in turn had done nothing to defend him. The chilly advice of the American consulate in Marseille was that Fry should leave France before he was arrested or expelled. The ERC in New York, yielding to pressure from the State Department, said he should come home—which he agreed to do, with the delaying caveat that he would leave the moment his replacement arrived in Marseille.

A more immediate concern for Fry was news that Gestapo agents were now on the frontier and that Spain had closed the border. In fact the border would open and close erratically, but the escape route through the country could not be relied on as before. At the same time Portugal tightened its transit visa requirements by having all requests handled in Lisbon and acting only with documentary proof of an overseas visa and a paid ticket for ship or plane transport to the destination. The Portuguese action was understandable; Fry knew, as he wrote, that "their country was already jammed to the gunwales with stranded refugees." But when shortly afterward the Spanish followed suit with visa restrictions, he was deeply troubled. His refugees, with no wish to stay in Spain, had always moved through the country as quickly as possible; the only explanation seemed to be that the Gestapo was intent on keeping refugees bottled up in France. Fry had also learned that the Kundt Commission—a group of Gestapo agents and German officials, under the leadership of a Dr. Kundt, whom Fry had heard about but had not been certain existed—was combing French concentration camps for names of those to force back to Germany under the armistice terms.

The new developments meant reorganizing the CAS's work. If refugees were to be held in France, the main effort had to shift from arranging their escapes to keeping them out of concentration camps and providing for their needs while in hiding. When Frank Bohn took the repeated advice of the American consulate that he and Fry should get out of France, Fry added Bohn's list of labor and socialist leaders to his own and began turning the center into an actual relief agency. New staff members were added, most of them French and with professional aid experience. One of them, Danny Bénédite, became Fry's chief associate and close friend. And since refugees kept coming and many had no money, the center began handing out weekly living allowances from ERC funds. To those held in camps it sent regular food parcels.

The dramatic shift in work was accompanied by one in living arrangements. The first time he saw the Villa Air-Bel, as Fry recalled,

> it was closed as tight as a fortress, the walks and gardens were overrun with weeds, and the hedges hadn't been trimmed for years. But the view across the valley to the Mediterranean was enchanting and I was impressed by the terrace with its enormous plane trees and the double flight of steps which led down, right and left, to a formal garden and a fish pond.

The three-story, eighteen-room tumbledown château was located on eighty-five acres about a half-hour drive from Marseille. The distance was part of its appeal; Fry wanted a place where he was free of around-the-clock availability to the refugees, and free of confinement in the Splendide. Leasing the Villa Air-Bel also made financial sense. The monthly rent was little more than his hotel, and the many bedrooms could be filled with staff members, including Danny Bénédite and his wife Theo, Miriam Davenport, and Davenport's friend Mary Jayne Gold.

Blonde, beautiful, and an heiress from the Midwest, Gold seemed to have stepped from the pages of an F. Scott Fitzgerald story. She had been educated in Europe, then stayed on and from Paris led the life, by her own account, of an expatriate playgirl, which included owning her own airplane and flying off for Swiss skiing and Riviera sun. When war came she had donated the plane to the French air force, joined the refugee exodus from Paris, and met Miriam Davenport in Toulouse, from where the pair gravitated to Marseille and Fry's staff at the CES. The women, along with Danny Bénédite's wife, had found Villa Air-Bel, and Danny, as a French citizen, had signed the lease while the "made-to-order charmer"—as Fry thought of her—Mary Jayne Gold paid the rent.

Two of Fry's clients, the Russian novelist Victor Serge and the French poet and leading light of the surrealist movement André Breton, also took rooms in the villa. And there were visitors: the German surrealist artist Max Ernst; the American expatriate writer Kay Boyle; and the estranged wife of Antoine de Saint-Exupéry, who appeared one night and stayed on for weeks. When Mary Jayne Gold left for Lisbon (carrying with her smuggled information in condoms inserted into squeezed-out toothpaste and face cream tubes), her room was taken by the heiress and collector of modern art Peggy Guggenheim. Not certain at first about the nature of Fry's work, Guggenheim went to the American consul in Marseilles for advice—and was told to steer clear of it. She paid no attention, and Fry had with her, as he had had with Gold, a generous donor to his operation.

Victor Serge nicknamed the château Espèrvisa, Hopevisa, since many staying or passing through were waiting for visas to be issued, or purchased for a price. ("A fine trade this," Serge remarked, "selling lifebelts on a shipwrecked continent!") There was no escaping the long hours and tense work going on in Marseille, but Villa Air-Bel provided periods of needed release and communal gaiety in Fry's life. Others found time to get in some literary work, Victor Serge turning out pages of a novel and André Breton writing poetry in the château's greenhouse. The house had no central heating, food was in short supply, but wine was always plentiful. A cook and a maid were on hand, and a refugee Spanish barber came every morning to shave the men. When warm weather arrived a vegetable garden was started, and workers removed muck from an irrigation basin and turned it into a swimming pool. On Sunday afternoon surrealists flocked to the house to auction their pictures on the terrace, and afterward stayed for tea or cognac.

★　　★　　★

Toward the end of January 1941, a sudden and unexplained shift in Vichy policy allowed many refugees to get exit visas from France. Fry assumed it meant the Gestapo was finished grabbing those it wanted from the country. Whatever the reason, his center became a travel bureau as well as relief operation and functioned legally in moving refugees on their way to Lisbon. While there was still the endless need of cajoling authorities for transit visas for Spain and Portugal as well as overseas visas, important figures—historians, literary critics, poets and novelists, physicists and mathematicians, film and theater producers—passed through Fry's hands in this period. Two especially notable artists were also among them, Jacques Lipchitz and Marc Chagall.

When Fry had first contacted him, Chagall was working in his studio in Gordes and, as a naturalized French citizen, saw no reason to leave the country. With the proclamation of anti-Jewish laws he changed his mind, and in Marseille Harry Bingham provided Chagall and his wife with American visas. While they waited in a hotel before journeying to Lisbon, police swept through and arrested everyone they took to be Jewish. When Fry learned of the action he phoned a police official and informed him that Chagall was one of the world's great artists. The official was unimpressed, so Fry added that unless Chagall was released in a half-hour he would call the *New York Times* correspondent in Vichy, Gaston Archambault, with the news of the artist's arrest. Chagall was quickly released.

For Marc and Bella Chagall, refugee flight was anything but difficult. Fry provided train tickets that took them across the Spanish border and on to Portugal. They reached Lisbon on May 11, 1941, and while waiting for a crate of Chagall's paintings that had been left behind and were coming by train—Chagall's daughter and her husband eventually brought them to Lisbon and then to New York—the artist dropped a note to one of his wealthy patrons, Solomon R. Guggenheim, letting him know he would soon be in America. When the ship bearing the Chagalls reached New York in late June, Pierre Matisse, a New York art dealer and son of Henri Matisse, met them at the dock. Guggenheim subsequently treated the couple to an introductory boat tour around Manhattan.

Jacques Lipchitz knew he was in danger as a Jew but still was reluctant to leave France. He spoke no English, and starting his career over in America was a daunting prospect. Fry kept writing to him at his studio in Toulouse—"What can we do for you? We are ready to do whatever we can"—and arranged to have the sculptor and his wife pick up visas at the Marseille consulate. But even with the visas in hand Lipchitz was unwilling to move until friends convinced him the Nazis would soon occupy all of France, leaving him trapped. Fry gave the couple money and train tickets to

Barcelona and Lisbon, where they waited for weeks while living on a room allowance and eating meals at a Jewish relief center. Lipchitz later said of Fry, "In some ways I owe him my life. . . . I did not want to go away from France. It was his severe and clairvoyant letters which helped me finally to do so. . . . And of what help he was once I decided to go to America!"

Other celebrated names on Fry's list to be saved refused to leave for any reason. When he tracked down André Gide in his mountain hideaway beyond Cannes, the author said the Germans were trying hard to entice him into collaboration; he would not agree, but neither would he abandon France. Henri Matisse turned down help as well despite Fry's argument that even if the Germans left him alone in his studio at Niceff, he might starve to death. Both Gide and Matisse were willing, though, to have their names used to bolster the CES's image as a proper relief agency by becoming members of its Committee of Patrons.

Along with the easing of exit visas, another new development was the possibility of bypassing Spain and Portugal and sending refugees by ship directly from Marseille to Martinique, the French colonial possession in the Caribbean, on a meandering course through the Mediterranean and down the African coast. Although the French colonies were under Vichy control, Martinique was a long reach for the Gestapo in pulling a refugee back to Europe; and from the island there was passage to Cuba, Florida, and South America. When Fry learned that space was available on a converted French cargo vessel called the *Winnipeg*, he immediately began buying passenger tickets for those of his clients with exit visas. The route was slow to develop, with nine refugees leaving in mid-February, then forty more by the end of March. By May there were regular sailings every four or five days on Vichy ships with navicerts, or shipping passports, allowing passage through the British blockade.

Compared to days of sending groups of two or three to the Fittkos in Banyuls, the opening of the Martinique route was the busiest and most fruitful period of Fry's operation in Marseille. The CAS staff grew to more than twenty to handle the new workload of getting clients prepared with paperwork and money while also attending to last-minute panic attacks about the long and tedious journey. Among those taking the new sea route was Walter Mehring, who promptly cast his journey—aboard the *Wyoming*, as surprisingly named as the *Winnipeg*—in verse in "Love Song a la Martinique":

> In uneventful faring over sea, with battle freight
> And negro soldier lads, the staunch "Wyoming" bore
> Us through the oceanic muck. . . .

Victor Serge and André Breton got out with three hundred other refugees on the *Capitaine Paul Lemerle*, and after reaching Martinique went on to the Dominican Republic, Cuba, and at last Mexico. But not all of Fry's clients could get French exit permits, and there was still a list of forbidden names. So for those without the permits but able to get Spanish and Portuguese transit visas and overseas visas, the Pyrenees crossing routes to Lisbon were again in operation. Some others were smuggled through Spain to North Africa, then taken by fishing boats to Lisbon.

When Britain suddenly seized one of the Martinique-bound ships and sailed her to Trinidad as a prize of war, Vichy canceled future sailings and ordered two vessels already at sea to land at Casablanca, with all passengers interned. It took Fry's committee long labor to get them released and sent on through Spain to Lisbon. In at least one instance, another relief group, the Hebrew Immigrant Aid Society (HIAS), also came to the rescue of the stranded refugees.

Richard Berczeller, an Austrian Jew and a medical doctor, had reached Marseille with his wife and son only to learn that American visas would be available to them if they could produce tickets for a ship leaving France. When he contacted Fry's committee, Berczeller was informed about ships going to Martinique and told to keep in touch. The family was granted exit permits but waited some four weeks before learning of available space on the *Wyoming*.

Once at sea they began to feel safe, especially as the freighter made its sluggish passage through the Straits of Gibraltar and put up at the port of Casablanca. But there the vessel sat in boiling heat and with meager food supplies supplemented by stringing baskets from the deck for merchants below to sell them bread and fruit. On the fifth day of waiting, the passengers were told the ship would not leave Casablanca, and under orders from Vichy they could choose to return to France or go to an internment camp. Everyone aboard selected the camp, and guarded trucks took them to an old Foreign Legion base sixty miles from the city.

Some six hundred people were wedged in barracks with primitive sanitation; soon another three hundred ship passengers were added to the number, increasing the rampant sickness in the unceasing heat. Abruptly one morning the camp commandant informed Berczeller, with no explanation, that he and his family had tickets on a ship to America. An aged bus took them to Casablanca, where they learned that HIAS had chartered a liner in Lisbon, the *Nyassa*, which was about to weigh anchor on a voyage that would eventually get them to New York.

★   ★   ★

About the same time the Martinique route closed down, Harry Bingham was assigned to Lisbon as vice consul (and shortly thereafter moved
again, this time to Buenos Aires for the duration of the war), leaving Fry
without a source of information or support at the American consulate
in Marseille and the ministry in Vichy. It also became apparent that the
police were taking more interest in the CAS's work. Danny Bénédite
was arrested on the serious charge of trading gold bullion on the black
market, though he was finally let off. Fry's telephone was tapped, and one
day detectives searched the committee's office for false documents and
the means of turning them out—finding nothing since the staff was careful enough to keep both elsewhere. Two days later police searched the
Villa Bel-Air for a nonexistent radio transmitter. Shortly thereafter they
were back at the CAS office and then the villa, ransacking both places for
money Fry had recently been given by a Frenchwoman leaving for New
York, again finding nothing.

Danny Bénédite believed the searches were part of a calculated campaign to scare Fry out of France, since as an American citizen Vichy was
unable to dispel him without proof of illegal actions. Fry was determined
not to be frightened away, but he knew the inescapable weak link in his
continuing work was lack of support from the American authorities in
France, and behind them the State Department in Washington. In January
he had gone to the Marseille consulate to have his passport renewed and
was told updating would be only for immediate return to the United States,
with the passport held by the consulate until he was ready to leave. In May
he tried again and learned the same thing.

Then on July 10 a motorcyclist brought to the committee office a
summons for Fry to appear the following morning before the district chief
of police. The American consul had warned him that the Gestapo was
pressuring the French to arrest him, and the police official told him directly
that unless he left France he would be confined in a small town outside
Marseille, where he could do no harm. Fry appealed for time by saying he
needed to prepare his committee to continue work after he left; he would
need at least until August 15, and the official agreed. "Tell me, frankly, why
are you so much opposed to me?" Fry asked before he left. "Because you
have protected Jews and anti-Nazis," the official replied.

A day or so later the American consul returned Fry's passport for
travel within the next thirty days, with a French exit visa and Spanish and
Portuguese transit visas already stamped within. For Fry's work in Marseille
it was the beginning of the end. Danny Bénédite still thought the French
police were bluffing about the arrest, and Fry took a vacation on the French

Riviera and in Monaco that included meeting again with Matisse and Gide. By the time he returned to Marseille his passport and visas had expired.

On his desk was a cable from the ERC in New York informing him his successor had been named and was preparing to leave for France (though in fact none ever arrived). Two weeks or so went by before the police returned and told him he was being expelled from the country as an undesirable alien. He was given a little time to clear out his belongings from the office and the villa before he was taken to a train by a police inspector, who would be with him the rest of the journey. Staff members gathered at the Marseille station to say goodbye, and Danny Bénédite arrived back from a hurried trip to Vichy to say that nothing could be done about the expulsion. It had been ordered by the Ministry of the Interior and approved by the American legation.

There was delay at the border at Cerbère while the American consulate in Marseille renewed Fry's passport and got the new visas on it. When all the paperwork was in order, CAS workers gathered at the Cerbère rail station for another farewell. The police inspector accompanied Fry across the border to Port-Bou, and he helped open his bags for inspection and then repack them. When it was time to take the train to Barcelona, he shook Fry's hand and said, "I hope you will not think ill of France." "Of France, never," Fry said. "Of certain Frenchmen, yes." The policeman indicated he understood.

In Lisbon, Fry put his name on the waiting list for a Clipper to New York, met with Charles Joy in the Unitarian Service Committee's office, and took advantage of the city's carnival of abundance. He felt "like a child taken for the first time to the circus, goggle-eyed," he wrote in a letter. All about him were

> camera shops *filled* with cameras. . . . Typewriters—*new* typewriters—for sale at perfectly ordinary prices. Tailors' shops displaying *English* cloth in their windows. The latest books from England and the United States. *Yesterday's* Times, Daily Mail, and Daily Telegraph. . . . Time and Harper's Magazine, the Saturday Evening Post and the New Yorker, all for sale as if it were perfectly natural to be so. A grocer's window boasting boxes and boxes of MacVitie and Price's Petits Buerres, Clotted creams—and Scotch Shortbread. Haig and Haig, Johnny Walker, and Dewar's White Label. Shops where you just walk in and buy any number of packages of Player's Navy Cut, Goldflake, or Lucky Strike cigarettes, for less than 25c a package.

What he needed most of all was Lisbon's plentiful food. He was seriously malnourished, and a vitamin shortage was causing memory loss. Nonetheless he spent his six weeks of waiting in Lisbon working for the refugee cause with Charles Joy and meeting with exiles waiting for transport.

★   ★   ★

Before departing Lisbon on November 1, 1941, Fry wrote in an emotional letter to Danny Bénédite that he had no wish to put Europe behind: "I *prefer* the blackout, and would gladly trade even an occasional bombardment for what lies in wait for me in America. But I have to go home . . . to the hard geometry of New York." What awaited him in that hard geometry was a drawn-out and never wholly successful struggle to find a new role. For a time he continued his involvement with the ERC. Miriam Davenport and Hans Sahl from his Marseille committee were now working in the New York office, yet Fry found the group lacking the passion for exiles he had known at the CAS. His attacks on the State Department's foot-dragging attitude toward refugees also had done nothing to endear him to the ERC leadership. When his Clipper flight landed in New York he had complained to reporters about the red tape "in which the American State Department enshrouds refugee procedures." "The State Department," he went on, "is pursuing a very stupid policy."

By letter and cable Fry kept in close contact with Danny Bénédite and others in France. American entry into the war sharply increased activity at the CAS, the Marseille consulate now issuing visas to refugees whose applications had long been delayed. Over the next few months a great number were able to leave France, including such luminaries as the artists Marcel Duchamp and Jean Arp and the harpsichordist Wanda Landowska. Fry also learned that Lisa and Hans Fittko had reached Lisbon and then taken a ship to Cuba. And he heard that an anti-Nazi journalist and editor named Berthold Jacob had reached Lisbon on a false passport, then had been kidnapped off a street after leaving the Unitarian office at the Hotel Métropole and taken to a concentration camp in Spain or Germany.

The news about Jacob was distressing but not surprising. On his arrival in New York Fry had warned, as the press reported, of a "secret kidnapping organization" operated by the Gestapo in Portugal that was abducting anti-Nazis from the country. They posed as police and brazenly snatched their victims off streets and rushed them into fast cars. The Portuguese police were trying to preserve the country's neutrality by stopping the Gestapo, but so far they had been unsuccessful, with the result that "at least a dozen valuable refugees have disappeared from Portugal in the past two months."

On June 2, 1942, French police confiscated the files and typewriters of the CAS, closed the office, and arrested the staff together with some refugees who had the misfortune to arrive that day. After hours of questioning the staff was released, but the office remained permanently sealed. Bénédite and other staff members carried on the center's work elsewhere until, with the Allied landings in North Africa, German troops poured across the demarcation line to take control of the Mediterranean coast and occupy Marseille. Two years of silence passed before Fry learned that Bénédite had eluded capture but remained in France and joined the underground work of the French resistance.

$\star$ $\star$ $\star$

Eventually Fry was pushed out of the ERC by its head, Frank Kingdon. "Dr. Kingdon does not like me," Fry informed Danny Bénédite, "and will not hear of me having anything to do with the committee. That's that." He moved on to usually short-lived editorial positions with various magazines, including a stint with the *The New Republic*, and began work on a memoir of his Marseille period. Published in 1945, *Surrender on Demand* closed with a capsule account of what some of his former clients had done after reaching the United States. "Not all, perhaps, have justified the efforts we made for them," Fry added. "Some have died, and, in a very real sense, some have been crippled for life by what they have been through. But, as Beamish said, we had to bring them *all* back. At least we had to try."

4

THE LAST LAP

Lisbon became the new and magic goal of the growing thousands of refugees. There, if they were lucky, they would be
able to begin the last lap in their long escape.

—Lilian Mowrer, *The New Yorker,* July 20, 1940

Despite having lost support of both the State Department and the Emergency Rescue Committee by the time he left Lisbon, Varian Fry retained
enough status—and had sufficient money, thanks to funds cabled by the
ERC—to return to New York aboard a Pan American Airways Clipper.
This set him well apart from the great mass of transients coming and going
through the city, given that limited space on flights ordinarily went to the
prominent and the influential. As a top-tier foreign correspondent, William
L. Shirer qualified as well, but when weather conditions intervened—the
constant bugbear of air travel, especially on flying boats—the familiar CBS
radio voice from Berlin abandoned plans to take a Clipper and went home
by ship a few months after Fry left by air.

In the autumn of 1940 Shirer concluded that censorship was making
his reporting from within Germany impossibly difficult. He had to leave,
and he knew the route to take. "The only way you can get to America
now from Europe," he wrote in his diary, "is through Switzerland, unoccupied France, Spain, and Portugal to Lisbon, the one remaining port on
the Continent from which you can get a boat or a plane to New York."
It was early December, his wife and young daughter already in the United
States, before Shirer himself departed.

From Berlin he flew on Lufthansa to Barcelona, Madrid, and finally
Lisbon, where airport officials briefly held him since he lacked a booked

ticket for further travel to New York. "Lisbon and light and freedom and sanity at last!" he exulted when he was released. He found a room in Estoril, as did his CBS boss Edward R. Murrow, who came in from London for a brief reunion. After learning that bad weather was holding up Atlantic flights, Shirer tried the shipping office of American Export Lines, finding it

> jammed with a mob of refugees—jittery, desperate, tragic victims of Hitler's fury—begging for a place—any place—on the next ship. But as one of the company officials explained to me, there are three thousand of them in Lisbon and the boats only carry one hundred and fifty passengers and there is only one boat a week. He promised me a place on the *Excambion*, sailing next Friday the 13th, though it may only be a mattress in the writing room.

The date was ominous, but Shirer was anxious to move on. Aboard ship he joined a group of other American correspondents gathered in Lisbon— among them, James Reston of the *New York Times* and Whitelaw Reid of the *New York Herald Tribune*—and as it slid down the Tagus to the ocean he was entranced by a full moon above and "all the million lights of Lisbon and more across the broad river on the hills." Like others, though, who marveled at the wartime show of light, he questioned how long it could continue.

> Beyond Lisbon over almost all of Europe the lights were out. This little fringe on the southwest corner of the Continent kept them burning. Civilization, such as it was, had not yet been stamped out here by a Nazi boot. But next week? Next month? The month after? Would not Hitler's hordes take this too and extinguish the last lights?

★   ★   ★

What William L. Shirer had noted about Lisbon's unique position as the last Continental port with regular passenger transport to New York had come about only recently. Before the war political and other exiles could leave on scheduled liners sailing from several European ports; with the fighting, departure points rapidly shut down. In April 1940, with German troops in Scandinavia, Baltic Sea routes were closed. In June, Italy entered the war and closed its ports. After Italy attacked France, the western Mediterranean was among the combat areas blocked to all American-flag shipping because of the Neutrality Act of 1939, leaving only the ports of Ireland, Portugal, and the Atlantic coast of Spain available to American vessels.

By June 1940 passenger shipping from Western Europe had effectively narrowed to Lisbon and British ports, with transport from England in short supply due to German U-boat activity and too few protective convoy ships. Some refugees were still able to escape from French and Spanish fishing ports; some crossed the Mediterranean in small boats and got out from Casablanca; and, as mentioned before, some sailed from Marseille to the French island of Martinique. But from mid-1940 forward there was little choice for scheduled ship transport other than Lisbon.

Promptly after the ban on shipping in Mediterranean waters, American Export Lines moved its European headquarters from Genoa to Lisbon and announced it would have one sailing a week between New York and Lisbon using its four *Ex*-named vessels, each a small liner with an expanded capacity of about 185 passengers. "Portugal is neutral," said the firm's passenger traffic manager, "and the port is the terminus of extensive rail and air connections to France, England, Spain and many parts of Europe. We will thus employ our four passenger ships on a route that has a lot of promise."

Far more than merely promising, the Lisbon-New York run became golden for the shipping firm—literally so when Portugal used the liners to transport gold reserves to the United States for safekeeping for the duration of the war. News stories of ship arrivals in New York often disclosed the value of a shipment—for example, when the *Excambion* docked in August 1940 a report said it carried "$2,500,000 in gold, consigned by the Portuguese Government to the Federal Reserve Bank." In October the *Excalibur* brought a gold shipment worth $3 million. Gold transfers aside, the Lisbon end of the route was a business bonanza for the shipping firm, with refugees besieging its office in numbers that swamped the capacity of its vessels and those of other national passenger lines.

When tickets were acquired they were usually for overloaded ships on which passengers complained of *Queen Mary* rates for makeshift quarters, unsanitary conditions, and poor food. When the Portuguese liner *Myassa* arrived in New York in December 1940 it was considered at full capacity with 451 passengers; on a later voyage from Lisbon in April 1941 it carried 816, the added numbers stuffed in dormitories set up in compartments usually carrying cargo. On the *Mouzinho* bringing Franz and Ellie Schoenberner to New York, the vessel filled with more than 800 passengers, men and women occupied separate dormitories in the hold, with long rows of double-decker beds and just enough aisle room to squeeze through. The sleeping space allowed for a single suitcase, with other luggage stored elsewhere in the hold—and with luck left undisturbed. Rates on ships like the *Myassa* and the *Mouzinho* typically ranged from $480 in first class to $160 for third class in the cargo holds. On the Spanish vessel *Villa de Madrid*, first-class passage soared to $1,200, and rough bunks set up between decks went for $450. Tacked on to stated prices could be payments demanded by speculators or by shipping-line agents for tickets reserved by refugees who were unable to reach Lisbon by their sailing dates, leaving empty spaces aboard ships that could be put up for sale.

An infamous case of refugee overcrowding and overcharging came to light in September 1941 when the small Spanish ship *Navemar*, converted from a freighter with quarters ordinarily for fifteen passengers, docked in Brooklyn on a voyage that had begun in Seville and gone on to Lisbon before setting sail for the United States with more than a thousand people aboard. Of that number, eleven had left the ship in Bermuda, 330 in Havana, and six passengers died, with four of them buried at sea. Health officials who inspected the ship on its American arrival expressed surprise that more had not perished, given what those aboard called "floating concentration camp" conditions. Some of the refugees later filed a lawsuit to collect damages for inadequate accommodations, food, and medical services and to recover passenger fares said to have been from $375 to $604. In turn, the Spanish owners of the *Navemar* brought suit against a figure identified as A. S. Montiero of Lisbon, claiming he was the vessel's agent when the refugees purchased passage in Marseille and set out for Seville. (On its return to Europe in January 1942, the *Navemar* was sunk by an Axis submarine off the Portuguese coast. Rather than passengers in its hold, the freighter carried wheat destined for Switzerland.)

★   ★   ★

At the same time passenger shipping from Lisbon was booming, news reports coming from the city disclosed another grim side of the transportation business—stories of fake passports and visas for South American countries going to the highest bidders at auctions run by consuls of small nations. A Japanese liner that had recently docked in Panama was filled with Jewish refugees who each paid $2,400 for visas that proved to be useless. Other reports told of refugee ships prevented from docking anywhere and left wandering the seas, usually the Caribbean or the Mediterranean, while various countries squabbled about proper visas and immigration quotas.

For their part, ship operators voiced complaints of a business sort. A half-year after finding promise in its Lisbon-New York run, American Export Lines' traffic manager moaned in the press that the route had become "little more than a constant headache":

> We have had to raise our rates to continue operation; we have had to put in extra sleeping quarters for anxious refugees who plead with us

in Lisbon to provide any kind of space available. Then when they get safely here some of them write in to complain about accommodations, service and the fares.

An unforeseen problem in handling refugees coming to the United States was that those found with unacceptable visas were held on Ellis Island, and the shipping line had to pay for their keep. One group of twenty-two refugees, said the traffic manager, had spent fifty-five days on the island while waiting for their paperwork to be cleared up. "We paid 44 cents a meal each day for those refugees on the island, and 50 cents a day each for their rooms," he added. "And if one of our 'guests' require hospital treatment it costs us $2.75 a day." And there were always cases in which the paperwork could never be straightened out.

> One man who came from Lisbon with a fraudulent Honduran passport, for which he paid 25,000 francs in France, was rejected here, and we had to keep him on Ellis Island. The government threatens to fine us $1,000 for bringing him here. And we have to take him back, with the definite prospect of entertaining him indefinitely when the Portuguese Government declines to permit him to land in Lisbon. The tug that we must hire to transport him from Ellis Island to the ship costs around $18 an hour.

Yet another grumble from the shipping firm was that on the Lisbon end of the route a Portuguese law prohibited the use of trained American staff to handle the rush of business. With the exception of executives, all workers had to be Portuguese citizens. A further irritant was the belief, said to be common among refugees, that ticket allotments depended on bribes. Lisbon newspapers, it was pointed out, carried notices offering up to two hundred dollars to anyone who could influence steamship officials to arrange early passage.

In March 1941, less that a year after saying it would employ four ships on the New York-Lisbon run, American Export Lines suspended advance bookings between the cities until further notice. The reason, as explained by a shipping official, was that increased demand in Lisbon had created a backlog of ticket seekers estimated to be in excess of ten thousand. With its present number of ships, the company could not expect to fulfill the need until the last of June at the earliest. Press stories added that a request by refugee organizations and the President's Advisory Committee (a group formed to counsel President Roosevelt on refugee matters) to use on the route the United States Lines' *Washington*, a large ship normally carrying

eleven-hundred passengers, had been denied by the U.S. Maritime Commission due, among other reasons, to the danger of a ship so large in or
near war zones. With tickets sales temporarily ended at American Export
Lines, the only ships still offering passage between Lisbon and New York
were small and irregularly scheduled Portuguese vessels that were equally
booked solid for weeks ahead.

★   ★   ★

On December 10, 1941, three days after Pearl Harbor, American Export
Lines canceled a steamer set to leave New York for Lisbon and announced
all future sailings were ended. The company also ordered its Lisbon staff to
return home by any means possible. The United States' legation in Portugal
had already advised American businesses in the country to send employees
home on the *Excambion*, the last sailing of an American ship from Lisbon.
While passengers boarded, workmen were hastily painting out the Stars and
Stripes on the sides—and rumors were rife that, with U-boats lurking just
beyond the Tagus estuary, she was doomed nonetheless. (The *Excambion*
made the journey unscathed. She was turned over to the U.S. Navy as a
troop transport, renamed the *John Penn*, and eventually sunk by a Japanese
torpedo plane off Guadalcanal.) For the duration of the war, Portuguese,
Spanish, and a few other national liners continued making the Atlantic
crossing, this despite the danger of coming under German attack, either by
accident or intention. A chilling case in point was the *Zamzam*, sunk in the
South Atlantic by a German surface raider on April 17, 1941.

The aged vessel, sailing under the flag of neutral Egypt, had left New
York for Alexandria, and after taking on cargo and passengers in Baltimore
and refueling in Brazil, was on its way to South Africa when the attack
came. In the first news stories in what became an extended saga of coverage, it was feared that more than 300 people—129 crew members, including the British captain and chief engineer, and 202 passengers, among them
a large number of mostly American missionaries on their way to Africa—
were lost at sea. Then it was learned that after the ship came under fire it
had managed to indicate it was unarmed and neutral, with the result that all
aboard were removed to the raider before the liner was sunk.

The wounded were treated on the German vessel, and a small group
of the survivors met with the captain. After shaking hands with them, he
both apologized for the sinking and justified it on grounds the *Zamzam*
had been running without lights, keeping radio silence, and was under the
direction of the British Admiralty (a coded British radio message warn-

ing of the German ship's presence had been found during a search of the captain's quarters). "I am sorry this had to happen," the captain told the group. "I can only tell you that we shall do everything in our power to put you safely ashore but you must remember that this is war and in traveling on the ocean you have assumed many risks." The following day the *Zamzam*'s survivors were transferred to the *Dresden*, a supply ship carrying cargo to Germany and oil for the raider. The raider then vanished, and for thirty-five days the *Dresden* was at sea before reaching St. Jean-de-Luz in occupied France.

Here the survivors were separated. British, Canadian, Egyptian, and some other national groups, women and children included, were sent to Bordeaux for internment. Americans—including the missionaries bound for Africa, though not twenty-four adventurous ambulance drivers who had enlisted in the British-American Ambulance Corps with plans to join Free French forces in North Africa (their ambulances had been aboard the *Zamzam* as cargo)—went to hotels in Biarritz. With the United States still out of the war, the Americans were treated with special care. News reports said they were free to circulate where they pleased in the occupied city, and while the weather was thought too chilly for bathing, some had "attended a cocktail party or two."

From the Spanish border the Americans made the two-day train ride to Portugal, where at a border town they found a welcoming celebration with the entire population turning out to watch the survivors eat a Red Cross meal on tables set up on the station platform. A string of press accounts about the American survivors came to a close when they reached Lisbon and were moved to Sintra to await transport out of the country. The missionaries said they still hoped to get to Africa; the ambulance drivers, after being briefly held by the Germans, trickled into Lisbon and talked of returning to America or reaching Britain. (One of the drivers, wounded in the attack on the *Zamzam*, had remained on the German raider after treatment. When America entered the war he was interned by the Germans and eventually released in a prisoner-of-war swap.)

Among the *Zamzam*'s survivors was a *Life* magazine photographer, David Scherman, and an editor of *Fortune* magazine, Charles J. V. Murphy. Both got places on a Clipper flight and, along with one of the ambulance drivers, were the first to get back to New York. Scherman had snapped photos of the sinking of the ship and of the following journey to the French port. In Biarritz, German officials allowed him to develop the pictures, then—according to reports at the time—confiscated them. But not all were lost, and on June 23, 1941, seventeen of the photos (including one of the

German raider closing in on the *Zamzam* after the shelling) appeared in a *Life* exclusive together with Murphy's dramatic account of the long ordeal.

★   ★   ★

For most of those trying to leave or reach Lisbon, travel by air was rarely an alternative. Although there was scheduled plane service to and from the United States and Britain, and within Europe to and from Spain, Germany, and (early in the war) Italy and North Africa, tickets were expensive and hard to come by, with preference given to the citizens of countries with national airlines and, as noted above, figures with high-level connections. Those fitting neither category found themselves—as they gloomily characterized their plight among one another—members of a lost tribe of forgotten spirits who spent their days haunting the beaches, the casino, and, in dim hope of a canceled passage, the airline offices.

Seats on land-based planes flying to and from Lisbon were highly prized, but the real cachet attached to wartime air journeys belonged to Pan American's mammoth blue-and-white Clipper flying boats winging their way between Lisbon and New York. After prolonged negotiations, Pan American in 1937 had reached a twenty-five-year agreement with Portugal for landing rights at Horta in the Azores and at Lisbon, a choice deal that excluded other carriers for a fifteen-year period unless the U.S. government nominated another airline. Late the next year Pan American took delivery of the first of what would become a fleet of twelve Boeing B-314 Clippers, four-engine whale-shaped seaplanes capable of crossing the Atlantic on two routes: a northern course via Newfoundland to Foynes in Ireland and Southampton in England; a southern course to Hamilton in Bermuda, Horta, Lisbon, and finally Marseille. When the war made the northern way too dangerous, Pan American narrowed its transatlantic flights to the southerly course, and Lisbon rather than Marseille became the terminus.

On eastbound flights, Clippers—named for the high-peaked sailing ships that had given way to steam-powered vessels—left from Port Washington on Long Island Sound (later from the La Guardia Marine Air Terminal) or from Baltimore. If all went well, the journey ended some twenty-four hours later at a seaplane docking facility constructed at Cabo Ruivo on the Tagus River, the watery landing path illuminated with flares. Westbound flights took longer due to headwinds, and far longer when weather conditions in the Azores sent them along the west coast of Africa to South America to New York. Since Clippers also carried large volumes of mail—a highly lucrative part of Pan American's business, which only increased as ship transport dwindled—space available for passengers varied considerably. At times the volume of mail was such that no passengers were carried.

A flight to Lisbon to open the Tagus landing port was made by the *Yankee Clipper* at the end of March 1939 in twenty-four hours and thirty-nine minutes. The American minister, consul, and a gathering from Lisbon's small American colony were on hand to greet the arrival. Speaking from Lisbon on an NBC radio hookup, the plane's captain said he had encountered some light storms but otherwise pronounced the flight uneventful. On May 20, 1939, the twelfth anniversary of Charles Lindbergh's solo flight to Paris, the *Yankee Clipper* left Port Washington for Lisbon and Marseille on the first commercial round-trip flight across the Atlantic. Before heading out over the ocean, the plane, with some eighteen hundred pounds of mail aboard and no passengers, circled the grounds of the New York World's Fair while the captain spoke on a two-way radio phone to dignitaries on the ground, the conversation relayed to the crowd through loudspeakers hung from trees. In mid-June the *Atlantic Clipper* carried a delegation of newspaper and radio correspondents to Lisbon on a survey flight—the total of thirty people on board the largest number ever to cross the Atlantic in an airplane.

The first Pan American transatlantic flight with paying customers left Port Washington on June 28, 1939—a momentous occasion, declared the *New York Times*, marking "man's aerial conquest of the last, and commercially most important of the earth's oceans. It is now possible for the traveler to circle the globe on scheduled airplanes." Port Washington declared a partial holiday to allow residents to be on hand, and the high school band played as police escorted coaches taking passengers along the decorated main street to a long dock leading to a float where the *Dixie Clipper* was moored. The plane that day would carry a crew of eleven and twenty-two passengers—a mixture of corporate officials, the wife of Juan Trippe, Pan American's president, and self-styled world travelers who for years had held standing reservations for the first transatlantic crossing by air. The announced fare was $375 one way, $675 round trip.

Passengers entered an enormous aircraft, with wings so thick that companionways allowed the engines to be serviced in flight. There were two carpeted decks, an upper solely for the crew, a lower separated into spacious passenger compartments, which included a dining room, a lounge, and a self-contained compartment in the rear variously known as a honeymoon or bridal suite. Separate dressing rooms for men and women each had a toilet and hot and cold running water.

As soon as the flying boat was airborne—in normal conditions the run across the water took about thirty seconds—a steward passed out a printed passenger list, letting everyone know who else was on the flight. Then a passenger produced a bottle (since no liquor was served, a safety precaution Pan American soon abandoned), and cocktails were mixed. Stewards served dinner on white-clothed tables, and afterward the captain came down and had a cigarette with the travelers. Berths were then made up into beds resembling those of Pullman railway cars.

It was morning when the plane landed at Horta, fifteen and a half hours after takeoff. While it was refueled, passengers were taken in open cars about the island, lush with flowers and dotted with white-sailed windmills. The stop took ninety minutes; seven hours later the plane landed on the river in Lisbon. After passengers went through customs they were driven to the Aviz Hotel for the night. The following morning they were off again, with breakfast aboard the plane, for Marseille, taking a roundabout course since Spain did not allow passage through its airspace. From Marseille passengers could make further connections by air or rail to Paris. The next day the *Dixie Clipper*, with twelve travelers now aboard, left Marseille on the return journey to Lisbon and New York.

The overriding appeal of the Clippers was plainly speed: eastbound, a day's journey now separated America and Europe. Close behind was the moderate luxury the planes provided, with flights typically likened to being in a country club lounge or on a yachting party in the sky. The inescapable downside was foul sea and sky weather conditions. Winter in New York and Baltimore could divert takeoffs and landings south to Norfolk or Miami. Horta was especially hostage to weather since the port offered virtually no shelter; heavy seas, especially in winter, meant long layovers in the town of seven thousand while waiting for calm water, or delays at Bermuda or Lisbon while meteorologists kept abreast of Horta's wave heights. As for air conditions, at Horta and other Pan American sites small balloons were inflated and released to gauge the ceiling during rain and fog, the findings correlated with reports from the company's scattered radio stations.

Flights bypassing Horta because of weather meant adding some four thousand miles and five days to the journey, as the American diplomat George F. Kennan painfully learned when on government business in 1943 he made a Clipper flight from Lisbon to New York. The route took him to Portuguese Guinea in Africa, across the South Atlantic to Brazil, and north through the Caribbean to New York, with frequent refueling stops along the way. The plane's crew changed three times. The ordeal, Kennan later wrote, left him feeling as one might after "some sort of five-day debauch: unnerved, overtired, jittery, not myself."

The American foreign correspondent Henry J. Taylor also made the extended Clipper journey from Lisbon, though at the time he did so, immediately after Hitler declared war on the United States in December 1941, the presumed safety of the far southern route eased whatever annoyance he felt. Taylor had come from London and was staying at the Pálacio in Estoril when news came over Vichy radio that the Japanese had bombed Pearl Harbor. Immediately, high-ranking American military figures and important British civilians began arriving from London for Clipper flights to America.

On December 11 a Clipper arrived from New York, and that afternoon Taylor, settled with the American minister Bert Fish in chairs in his bedroom, listened to a radio address by Hitler in Berlin. The talk began at one o'clock Lisbon time, and Taylor and Fish waged a dollar on when the Führer would actually declare war on the United States. He did so at 2:26, with Fish the winner. Late that night Taylor went out on the Clipper's return flight to New York. Due to the new and uncertain war situation, the plane was going the long way via Africa and South America. To reduce weight for fuel and passengers, berths were taken out, mail was left piled on the pier, and seven pounds of luggage was allotted to each passenger. Clothes and shoes above the limit were given to Portuguese dock workers.

Stops in Bermuda could hold up Clippers for a reason other than weather: British censorship of American mail to and from continental Europe. In early January 1940 a spat developed when the *American Clipper* was delayed for a day while its mail, some three hundred sacks, was removed, opened, and read. Britain had previously censored mail for Europe carried aboard American Export Lines ships stopping at Bermuda, but this was the first time it had done so with airmail. (Sending mail by sea was a risky venture. In the first year and a half of the war seven ships carrying mail from America were sunk in the Atlantic.) The State Department protested, and there was angry talk in the Senate (the British action was "a hell of a note," said Harry S Truman of Missouri), yet at issue was not the right of a belligerent to censor mail passing through one of its ports but the manner in which it was done. According to first reports, the Clipper's captain refused to allow censors to enter the plane, so mail had been removed at bayonet point by British marines—a report the British ambassador to Washington labeled "complete eyewash." Britain went on exercising censorship at Bermuda. Some six months after the purported bayonet incident a hundred people were added to the Hamilton censorship staff because, as the British explained, of an increased number of mail-laden American ships stopping in Bermuda—and Pan American partially skirted the matter by canceling some stops at Bermuda on its eastbound flights to Lisbon, weather permitting. In his 1941 *National Geographic* article about Lisbon, Harvey Klemmer reported that the last time he passed through Hamilton the British had nine hundred censors on duty.

★   ★   ★

The wartime monopoly of Clipper flights carrying passengers and mail between New York and Lisbon brought Pan American record profits. At the same time the war marked the beginning of the end for commercial Clipper service everywhere in the world. After Pearl Harbor, American aircraft production went to military needs, and no new Clippers were built. The war also accelerated developments in landplane technology and the construction of ground facilities. At the war's end the remaining Boeing Clippers—eleven of the original twelve—were unceremoniously sold and scrapped. Yet however short-lived the era of the great flying boats, while they flew their hold on the imagination was strong.

A lengthy *New York Times* report on the second anniversary of Clipper passenger service to Europe opened by reproducing the detailed loudspeaker announcement to passengers before boarding a flight—even that, apparently, had a certain distinction about it. The announcement began: "In a few minutes, ladies and gentlemen, you will hear a bell ring. A short interval later you will hear two bells sounding. The first will be the signal for the crew of the *Yankee Clipper* to board their airliner. The second will be the boarding signal for passengers." And ended: "The *Yankee Clipper* is now departing for Bermuda, the Azores and Lisbon. All aboard, please."

The *Times* report gave information about the plane's food and drink, both now fashioned around wartime rationing. Westbound flights featured veal or chicken since they were easiest to buy in Lisbon, while eastbound planes from Bermuda offered lamb chops or chicken since the British colony had little beef. Between New York and Bermuda there was a wide choice of bar drinks, but between Bermuda and Lisbon—for reasons unexplained—they tapered off to Scotch whiskey and brandy. Ice cream, on the other hand, was packed in dry ice in New York and available on Clippers leaving the port for a full forty-eight hours thereafter.

The newspaper account even went into luggage matters, though there seemed minimal charm here. Fifty-five pounds was the limit—but, it was explained, that amount "translated into terms of wardrobe" allowed "five suits and accessories or four street dresses, three evening gowns and all that goes with them." For highly important figures the luggage allotment could be expanded, at a charge. After passenger luggage was weighed it was inspected for contraband; if a camera was found it was placed in a container for the duration of a flight. Passengers were finally weighed themselves, with the number (nothing was said about a weight limit) recorded behind a counter—"a concession to sensitive women."

★   ★   ★

The allure of the flying boats even reached Broadway in Elmer Rice's anti-Nazi play *Flight to the West*, where—as detailed staging directions noted—all action takes place on two successive days aboard a Clipper flying from Lisbon to New York in July 1940. The set for the production, which opened in New York's Guild Theatre on December 30, 1940, with Rice also the director, was a Clipper's midsection: a smoking lounge, a compartment on either side, and parts of two other compartments at the ends. A hinged door in the center of the set opened out, when the plane was supposedly in port, to show broad pontoons that served as a gangplank. The overall design was intended to give the audience the feeling that everything of the Clipper's interior was entirely functional yet of high quality, suggesting—said the stage directions—"the living quarters of a small, but very modern yacht, rather than the inside of an airplane."

As the curtain rises, the Clipper is about to leave port on the Tagus. The door is open, presenting a distant view of the far outskirts of Lisbon, and two Portuguese mechanics are at work on the pontoons. Near the door one of Pan American's flight officers barks instructions to them in Portuguese while two uniformed stewards carry luggage to the sleeping compartments. Soon the passengers file into the lounge, greeted by the junior officer; when all are aboard there is the increased sound of the engines, then a moving landscape appears through the three windows until sprayed water obscures the view. With the plane in the air, the passengers are told they can freely move about; they are to ask for anything they want—cigarettes, coffee, cocktails—and berths will be made up for naps. They will be in the Azores in late afternoon, in New York the following morning.

The passengers talk among themselves, play cards, drink, retire to the berths—and plots emerge. The main one is a melodrama that results in a pistol shot, intended for a German diplomat who is actually a spy handler, striking a young Jewish man when he attempts to intervene. They heavy irony is that a Jew saves a German's life. By the time the plane descends to

Long Island, accompanied by the added noise of the engines, all has been sorted out: the wounded man will be rushed to a hospital; the German will be handed over to authorities; and an American author, Rice's spokesman throughout the play, announces an overarching theme of renewal. With the Jewish man's act, he proclaims, "my faith and my sense of values have been restored."

The play's setting aboard a Clipper was drawn from the well-traveled Rice's own experience. Just before the war broke out he had flown from London to Marseille to begin a transatlantic flight, a long-standing ambition. The Clipper to New York, carrying just eight passengers, stopped at Horta for refueling, and at first Rice regretted such a brief stay on the green island. When it was learned the plane had been damaged by a wave and the flight would not continue, he was faced with a long wait until a plane from New York stopped at Horta and the stranded passengers were delivered back eastward. In Lisbon they spent several comfortable days as guests of Pan American. When they were finally flown back to Horta, they transferred to their original New York–bound Clipper and flew into the setting sun while treated to a champagne dinner followed by cigars and brandy in the lounge.

★   ★   ★

Eric Sevareid, another Clipper veteran, was intrigued enough by the dramatic possibilities of the flights that he wrote a fifteen-page plot sketch for a Hollywood film to be called *Lisbon Clipper*. An executive at Warner Brothers had provided the title and urged Sevareid to produce a story. What he came up with was a thriller-romance involving an American vice consul in Lisbon and a glamorous Czech actress pursued by both the Gestapo and a young Czech refugee, who loves her yet is attracted to the Nazi cause.

In the end the refugee betrays the Germans, foils their efforts to capture the actress, and she and the vice consul flee to safety on a Clipper to New York. Whether Sevareid actually submitted his sketch is unknown. At any event, when *Casablanca* appeared in late 1942 he might have detected a distant resemblance to his plot for *Lisbon Clipper*, despite the large difference that the film's last-minute escape is *to* Lisbon and not aboard a Clipper.

★   ★   ★

On February 22, 1943, tragedy jolted the romance of the Clippers. After nearly four years of operations and some 240 transatlantic crossings, the *Yankee Clipper* crashed and sank while landing in Lisbon, with twenty-four lives lost among the thirty-nine passengers and crew. During a shallow bank on the approach a wing tip had caught in the Tagus, and the plane cartwheeled into the water—a matter, as later determined, of pilot error. Among the survivors swimming to shore or rescued by boats was Lorraine Rognan, who performed with her husband in the comedy dance team of Lorraine and Roy Rognan and was traveling in a group of seven entertainers to put on shows for American troops in England and North Africa. Later she gave reporters an horrific account of escaping from the swiftly sinking plane while her husband vanished.

> The confusion was terrific. My husband yelled to me to "hold this briefcase while I remove my trousers to swim better and take you." The water was coming up and I desperately kicked at a window to free him. But he was knocked down as the Clipper began sinking. He cried my name and waved. I cried back his name and saw him go down. The water pushed me out and in less than two minutes I found myself floating on the surface and I was pulled into a boat.

Another survivor from the entertainment group, the popular radio singer Jane Froman, was thrown from the plane into icy water. Unable to swim because of a badly damaged arm and leg, she clung to debris from the wreckage along with an officer of the crew, John C. Burn, until a rescue boat arrived. Both were taken to a small emergency hospital in Lisbon, and for a time it looked as if Froman's injured leg might have to come off. After long surgery to repair the leg and other serious injuries, she was moved to a convalescent home in a Lisbon suburb. Burn, recovering from a broken back and fractured skull, was transferred to the same facility, and as time went on his relationship with Froman, begun in the Tagus, deepened.

A month after the crash Froman's husband reached Lisbon on a Clipper and, determining she needed more medical treatment, brought her home on a Portuguese ship, an agonizing two-week journey with Froman in a body cast and strapped to a board. Following more surgeries and bone grafts, she was able to return to performing—even, with the war just ended, flying to Europe to sing before servicemen. After her divorce from her husband in 1948, she and John Burn, now a Pan American pilot, were married. Froman went down the aisle on crutches.

Among those killed in the crash were two correspondents, Frank J. Cuhel of the Mutual Broadcasting System and Ben Robertson of the *New York Herald Tribune*. Robertson's death drew wide notice. During the Battle of Britain he had covered London for the newspaper *PM* in the company of Eric Sevareid, Edward R. Murrow, and other newsmen whom the blitz made household names. His critically praised book about the experience, *I Saw England*, had ended with Robertson flying from England to Portugal, where he had booked ship passage aboard the *Exeter* for America.

> Here in Lisbon [he wrote in the book's closing paragraph] we had lights and butter and sugar. And in Lisbon we realized how little such things meant to us. In Lisbon we turned our thoughts back to a country that was fighting in darkness—to a great generation of British people who . . . had learned through suffering. They had learned, and I too had learned, by being with them through those months. In the depth of the English blackout I had seen the stars.

★   ★   ★

In his fatal flight aboard the *Yankee Clipper* to Lisbon, Ben Robertson was on the first leg of a return to England to take up a new position with the *Herald Tribune*. For correspondents and others for whom England was the final destination, the next stage, following a hotel stay of long or short duration in Lisbon, was ordinarily a flight on a British Overseas Airways Corporation land-based plane or a flying boat taking off from Pan American's site at Cabo Ruivo. One who went by flying boat was Sheilah Graham, the Hollywood columnist and late love of F. Scott Fitzgerald. In early 1941, shortly after his death, she set off for her native England as a correspondent for the North American Newspaper Alliance and a first assignment of interviewing George Bernard Shaw. After reaching Lisbon on a Clipper, she spent only a single night in a hotel before boarding in predawn darkness a BOAC Empire flying boat, which had been stealthily loaded with exhausted and wounded British troops from the fighting in North Africa. The windows of the plane on the flight to Southampton were covered with black cloth and passengers were told to keep complete silence. "For the first time," Graham wrote of the experience, "I realized that there was a war on."

The more typical air journey from Lisbon to Britain was aboard BOAC's commercial service operating from Sintra, and later from the new airfield at Portela, located farther up the Tagus from Lisbon. Landings in England were normally in the west of the country at Whitchurch airfield outside Bristol. When Henry J. Taylor took the route in late 1941, he left his hotel in Estoril in morning darkness, carrying with him a package of a thousand boxes of matches and his overcoat pockets stuffed with lumps of sugar, both gifts for friends in England. On the twisting road to the airport—the sign for it seeming strangely out of place in the ancient hills—he could see the fairyland castles of Sintra in dim silhouettes. The camouflaged civilian plane was ready on the field, the Dutch crew—pilot, co-pilot, engineer, and radio operator—waiting in the office. The aircraft was one of the four American-made Douglas DC-3s that KLM pilots had flown to Britain before German occupation of the Netherlands and were now in use by BOAC. Inside the cabins small signs proclaimed "KLM—Still Flying." (Some of the Dutch aircraft remained in German hands and were flown by Lufthansa.) Usually the planes had fourteen seats for passengers, with the actual number aboard determined by the amount of mail carried.

At dawn Taylor's flight lifted off on a circuitous course over the Bay of Biscay to avoid enemy aircraft. After refueling in Porto, it swung out to the ocean, and the co-pilot came back and led Taylor to the cockpit. He wanted him to see through binoculars a pair of German U-boats running on the surface. When the submarines began to submerge, the plane swiftly sought the cover of clouds. It was possible, the co-pilot pointed out, that the submarines below had Luftwaffe escorts above.

5

GAIETY, PLENTY, AND BRILLIANT LIGHTS

We never realized how miserable we had been in warring
Italy, before as well as during internment, until we arrived in
Lisbon, where the gaiety, plenty and brilliant lights made the
somberness of blacked-out, half-starved Europe we had left
seem all the more dismal by comparison.

—Reynolds and Eleanor Packard, *Balcony Empire*

A ir transport back to England was hardly an option for several thousand
troops of the British Expeditionary Force left stranded behind German
lines after the mass evacuation from Dunkirk in May and June 1940. Along
with downed Royal Air Force flyers, their best chance of escape was to
try, following the armistice in late June, to make their way south through
unoccupied France to Spain and Portugal. Those picked up along the way
by Vichy authorities were interned as prisoners of war in such places as
Marseille's Fort St. Jean, where their confinement was light. Yet they were
still considered fighting men and expected to plot returns to duty.

In July 1940 Donald Darling, a young military officer of M19, a British unit with a mission of helping get escapees and evaders back to England,
was sent to Lisbon to organize overland escape lines running from Marseille
to Barcelona and finally to either Gibraltar or Lisbon. (A parallel American
group, MIS-X, worked closely with the British after American entry into
the war.) Darling was a good fit for the job since he had lived in France and
Spain, spoke both languages, and had knowledge of the mountain terrain
of the Pyrenees. After meetings with the British ambassador in Lisbon, he
moved on to Madrid to examine the situation there, and found Ambassador
Samuel Hoare opposed to clandestine British operations inside Spain on
grounds that they put Anglo-Spanish relations at risk.

Darling returned to Lisbon and, under cover in the British embassy as the repatriation officer, set up his escape operation. With easy access to people coming and going between Lisbon and Marseille, he soon was in contact and passing money to the highest-ranking officer of troops held in Fort St. Jean. Darling also learned of Varian Fry's rescue effort in Marseille, one that now included getting British soldiers and airmen as well as important exiles out of France. In effect, Fry had become a British secret agent, recruited for the work—as Darling might have been startled to learn—by Samuel Hoare.

In the autumn of 1940, after accompanying Heinrich Mann and Franz Werfel and their wives and Golo Mann on their journey from Marseille to Lisbon, Fry had returned through Madrid and made a call at the British embassy. Here the ambassador struck a deal with the neutral American whose undercover work presumably posed less of a threat to his relations with Franco: he would give Fry ten thousand dollars for use in moving captured or hidden British troops in France over his mountain routes into Spain, from where the British would provide Spanish fishing boats to carry them to Gibraltar. The British also agreed to transport to Gibraltar a group of Italian and Spanish refugees Fry was helping, though with the condition that troops and refugees move on separate vessels.

Hoare offered Fry the money in British pounds, but there was risk in bringing such a sum across the border. Fry asked to have it wired to New York, from where it could be drawn on from Marseille. Besides, acting as a British agent was dangerous enough without worrying about carrying around a large amount of money. Fry was not only expanding his assignment for the Emergency Rescue Committee but, of more concern, threatening his entire Marseille operation if the covert work for the British came to light. Nonetheless, as soon as he was back in Marseille he got in touch with the British internees in Fort St. Jean through a young British officer, Captain Frederic Fitch. Fry told him about the border escape routes he used and passed along some of Hoare's money. Fitch thought the overland way a better bet than waiting around for ships, and fugitive British troops were soon on their way from Marseille to the Pyrenees route operated by Lisa and Hans Fittko from Banyuls. Once across the French border the men were instructed to surrender to the Spanish authorities as POWs under the Geneva Conventions, then wait for a British consular official from Barcelona to pick them up and dispatch them to Gibraltar.

For the Fittkos, working with the troops was a pleasure since they were young, strong, cheerful, and did exactly what they were told without asking questions. They were mostly tall and pale, however, and stood out from the local population, causing the Fittkos to resort to what they called the "Britannia-Special" method in guiding them out of the village to the mountain trail. They got the troops on the move between three and four in the morning, when it was unlikely that French border police had yet stirred for duty.

By early February 1941 the money the British had given Fry, now mostly spent, had by his account "gotten out about 125 officers and men, including at least one secret agent and a handful of veteran pilots." Another fifty thousand dollars, he calculated, "would have been enough to take care of the remaining 300 members of the B.E.F. [British Expeditionary Force] in Southern France and the next 200 R.A.F. men to come down from the occupied zone." When his secretary Lena Fischmann decided to take the Lisbon route herself, she carried a message to Ambassador Hoare in Madrid requesting the additional funds. Fry heard nothing back.

Eventually he learned from Donald Darling—the message delivered by Charles Joy, who had come from Lisbon to Marseille on Unitarian relief work—not to send any more British troops overland into Spain. Fry understood this to mean the Spanish were no longer cooperating in releasing the men to British officials. In the future, said Darling, he was to send escapees directly to Gibraltar by sea. Fry had virtually given up hope of finding boats in Marseille, and when Leon Ball located a seaworthy fishing trawler with sails and a backup motor capable of carrying seventy-five to Gibraltar, it seemed too good to be true. The price was steep, about $4,500, but Fry decided it was worth a try. But he would hand over all the money only when the passengers were actually at sea.

The plan was to bring the trawler from where it was anchored to the harbor; the passengers—sixty British troops and fifteen refugees, including some Italians—would gather with food and water to last four days in a location near the lighthouse, where the trawler would pick them up and head directly out to sea. When Fry informed Captain Fitch about his agreement with Hoare not to mix troops with refugees, Fitch said the chance for large-scale escape was too rare to worry about such niceties.

As a precaution, Fry left Marseille on the night of the escape so, if it went wrong, he could deny involvement. When he returned he learned how it went wrong. The passengers had waited until two o'clock in the morning before returning to town in small groups to avoid attracting police attention; meanwhile there had been negotiations in Snappy's Bar, a favorite hangout of officers held in Fort St. Jean, involving the trawler captain, Captain Fitch, and Leon Ball. The trawler captain maintained he could get the boat from the owner only when all the money due was paid up front.

Fitch resisted but finally was persuaded to hand it over. The trawler captain left with the money, never to return.

For Fitch, though, the affair was far from over. The British POWs kidnapped two or three men said to be members of the trawler captain's gang, took them to Fort St. Jean as hostages, and roughed them up to find out the whereabouts of the captain and the money. In time the police came and removed the hostages. Since Fitch and the troops were already prisoners, they were not arrested, but a trial of the hostages ensued during which Fitch in testimony claimed that the money given the trawler captain had come from a collection taken up among men interned in the fort. The court accepted his word, and the hostages were given short sentences for being parties to fraud. The trawler captain and the money remained at large.

★   ★   ★

In January 1942 Donald Darling switched his escape operation from Lisbon to Gibraltar, the Rock being the only piece of Europe still in British hands. Here he ran a one-man MI9 center both welcoming newly arrived escapees and evaders from occupied territory and quizzing them about details of their movements. It took time to confirm identities, then time to line up ship transport or, for special cases, air flights to England.

In the same period the American embassy in Madrid was engaged in its own work of gathering information from downed American airmen reaching Spain and refugees crossing from France. Pumping informants, as Ambassador Carlton Hayes termed it, was a top priority of the Allies, the work in Madrid carried out by the embassy's military attaché officers. Later in the war, with the Allies on the march across France, Hayes would tell President Roosevelt (in the hope that neutral Spain and Portugal would not be pressed too hard to end all trade arrangements with Germany) that "65 percent of Allied intelligence—and 90 percent of American—concerning German military dispositions in France are derived from our intelligence services in Spain while the Spanish looked away."

Hayes also informed Roosevelt that Spain had allowed large numbers of American flyers to leave the country and return to combat. The first American airmen to find themselves in Spanish territory came with the Allies' Operation Torch landings in North Africa. In November 1942 three transport planes carrying paratroopers from England mistakenly landed in the Spanish rather than French zone of Morocco. Spain moved the planes, pilots, and troops to Madrid, but rather than keeping the men interned, the usual practice in neutral countries, they were put in the custody of the embassy's military attachés and housed in hotels.

When Hayes began working with the Spanish foreign office for their release, he ran into a precedent established by the British. In the early part of the war more German and Italian planes on bombing runs over Gibraltar had been forced down in Spain than British planes, and consequently more Axis men were interned in the country. Britain had worked out an informal deal with Spain for the release of crew members: one Axis flyer for one British flyer. With the North African invasion and more Allied planes in the air, Hayes thought the arrangement needed change and launched a dubious argument that airmen forced to land were like shipwrecked mariners rather than fighting men, and should be helped in leaving the country. After some pondering, the Spanish foreign ministry agreed, and in February 1943 the paratroopers were moved through Gibraltar to their command in North Africa.

Spain continued the procedure as the war went on and increasing numbers of Allied flyers made forced landings in the country or were pulled from the sea by fishermen. Many now had also been downed in occupied Europe and made their way along the escape lines to Spain. Hayes estimated that between the North African landings in 1942 and the Normandy invasion in 1944 some eleven hundred American airmen found safety in Spain. None were refused entry, none interned. After declaring their citizenship they were turned over to American consuls, then to the embassy's military attachés who were responsible for their care and movement to Gibraltar. The wounded and those in ill health because of the escape journey were cared for in Spanish hospitals and Madrid's British-American Hospital. For the able-bodied, the release system got them out of Spain and to Gibraltar, on average, in about two weeks.

★   ★   ★

Among American flyers who escaped on the France-Spain-Gibraltar route was twenty-one-year-old Lieutenant Chuck Yeager (later an air force general and one of the intrepid fighter jocks of Tom Wolfe's *The Right Stuff*). On his eighth combat mission Yeager had gotten out of a burning P-51 and parachuted to the ground in occupied France, about fifty miles east of Bordeaux. He sprinkled sulfa powder from his survival kit on a leg wound, bandaged it, and studied a silk map of Europe sewn into his flying suit for the escape lines across the Pyrenees to Spain. Getting to the mountains meant eluding German troops, finding friendly locals, and getting help from the French underground. Yeager gripped the .45 automatic pistol that pilots carried and decided to stay hidden until dark, using his parachute for cover against the wet and cold.

In the morning he saw a woodcutter with an axe and rushed him from behind. The man dropped the axe and stared with fright at the pistol. He spoke no English yet seemed to understand when Yeager said he was an American and needed help, and seemed to reply that he would get someone who could speak English. Yeager waited in a nearby stand of trees, wondering if he could trust the woodcutter not to come back with a squad of Germans. When the woodcutter returned he had with him an old man who called out softly, "American, a friend is here. Come out."

Yeager was taken to a barn behind a stone farmhouse and put in a small tool room in a hayloft. When the door was shut, hay was pitched outside to cover it. Eventually he heard German voices climbing the ladder to the hayloft and imagined them searching the hay. He never heard them leave, and several hours passed before he made out the sound of hay being moved. He had the .45 ready when he heard the old man say outside the door, "It's me. You're okay. They've gone."

From the barn he was taken to the farmhouse where a middle-aged woman quizzed him in perfect English about his background and his West Virginia accent. Satisfied with his answers, she told him, "We must be very careful. The Nazis are using English-speaking infiltrators to pose as downed American fliers." He would be helped, she added, but he must do precisely what he was told. He was taken to the kitchen and given a meal before being returned to the room in the hayloft. Late in the night the village doctor came to the farm to attend to his wound, after which he made a brief speech in French, not a word of which Yeager understood.

About a week later the doctor returned, had Yeager put on the clothes of a French woodcutter, gave him forged identity papers, and the two set off together on bicycles. For two days they traveled at night on country roads and stayed during daylight in farmhouses. At Nerac the doctor turned Yeager over to a farmer, where for the next weeks he was kept in a shed and allowed into the house only to share the family meals. "We *loove* Americains," the farmwife would tell him, a line of English that Yeager imagined was learned just for him.

One dark night Yeager and the farmer left on foot, and after a two-day upland walk in deep pine forests he was turned over to a heavily armed band of French resistance fighters who lived in the mountainous region and conducted nighttime sabotage raids. The farmer told Yeager he would stay and work with the band until snow thawed in the high Pyrenees, when he would be led over to Spain.

The commander of the group of twenty-six was a lawyer who spoke English. Few of the other fighters did. They were men who knew the deep woods intimately and stayed constantly on the move, shifting camps twice a day, staying nowhere more than a few hours. If caught they would be turned over to the Gestapo, tortured for information, and shot. As long as he was with them and dressed like a Frenchmen, Yeager believed his fate would be the same since the Geneva Conventions on treatment of POWs would no longer apply to him. Yet he needed the band. He could not cross the mountains alone.

At first he was excluded from nighttime operations, staying behind with a cook and others guarding the camp. Finally the commander invited him to take part in a supply drop. The men lighted flares to illuminate a field, and when a British Lancaster bomber made a low pass a signal was sent with a flashlight. The plane then made another pass at a higher altitude and dropped a fifteen-hundred pound canister on two parachutes. The men rushed to the drop and hoisted the canister onto a cart pulled by two oxen. The entire operation took fewer than five minutes.

In a barn under lantern light the canister was opened; inside were weapons, ammunition, counterfeit franc notes, bread and meat ration stamps, plastique explosives, and fuses and timing devices. Yeager told the commander he knew how to use the explosives. Back in camp after the weapons had been buried in caches around the countryside, he showed how to set the timing on the fuse devices and how to cut up cords of plastique and attach fuses. Impressed, the band put him in charge of the work, their terrorist bomb maker.

Despite the danger involved, resistance fighters slipped into villages to make purchases, using their counterfeit rations stamps and money. One day Yeager was told to accompany two men to town. "Don't worry," the commander said. "Just stay with the men." After a short walk they reached a van on a logging road; when the back door opened a young man motioned Yeager inside. Nothing was said, but Yeager understood the time had come: the van was headed south into the Pyrenees. They drove for hours before the van stopped in the backstreet of a village, and Yeager was taken to another truck with its engine idling.

Three other escaping airmen were in the truck together with a Frenchmen who spoke English and explained they were outside Lourdes and heading into the foothills. He gave hand-drawn maps to each of the flyers showing the paths they were to take over the mountains. He told them they could go as a team or in pairs, and it would take them four or five days, depending on the weather. The crossing would be hard and dangerous; they might meet German patrols, smugglers, refugees, other escaping military men. The way mapped out for them was to the south because Spaniards in the north were said to turn in American pilots to the Gestapo for a reward.

It was after midnight when the truck stopped. The flyers were given filled knapsacks and told they were at the starting point. A hundred yards ahead was a shed where they could spend the night, but they were not to talk or start fires. At first light they should begin the climb.

In morning rain they set off. By noon Yeager and another flyer, a navigator on a B-24 downed in France, had reached the timberline. The other two flyers were far behind. Yeager and the navigator stopped to eat bread, cheese, and chocolate from their knapsacks; when the others still had not reached them, they moved on. They were at six or seven thousand feet and in freezing wind and wet snow, the ridges they crossed slick with ice. As they climbed higher the air thinned, and they stopped every ten or fifteen minutes, nearly exhausted and leaving Yeager wondering how many escapees actually made it over the Pyrenees. They had been given four pairs of socks and wore two pairs at a time, but their boots leaked and they worried about frostbite.

Late into their fourth day the two men were ready to give up. They thought they were near the Spanish border, but clouds limited visibility to fifty feet. They nearly bumped into a lumberman's cabin, and with pistols drawn went in and found it empty. The navigator took off his boots, hung his wet socks on a bush outside, and both men fell asleep inside the cabin. When a passing German patrol noticed the socks and opened fire through the cabin door, both men went through a rear window and spun down a long log slide into a creek deep with water.

Yeager's partner had been hit in the knee by the German fire, and when the two got across the creek Yeager saw that only a tendon attached his upper and lower leg. With a penknife Yeager cut the tendon and used the silk remains of his parachute in his knapsack to wrap and tie the stump of the leg. The navigator was unconscious but breathing; they were now fairly well hidden from the Germans above. Yeager decided to stay where they were until dark, then somehow try to drag the navigator up the glazed mountainside and continue on to Spain.

He did just that, a staggering feat of will and endurance. At the summit of the mountain, at sunrise, he saw in the distance a road he believed was in

Spain. He slid his partner back down the mountain, and when they reached the road, the man only faintly breathing, left him beside it in the hope a passing motorist would see him. (A police vehicle, Yeager later learned, passed within an hour. The flyer was taken to a hospital where most of his stump was removed. Six weeks later he was sent home.) Yeager continued south on the road for some twenty miles, and when he found a village turned himself in to the local police. He was put in a filthy jail cell but not searched, which allowed him to use a small saw from the survival kit still with him to cut through brass bars and locate a small rooming house a few blocks from the police station. The police ignored his escape, and after dinner and a hot bath he fell into a long sleep. Two days later an American consul knocked on his door.

When Yeager left Spain for Britain, the first evader in his squadron to make it back, he was twenty pounds heavier and deeply tanned. The American consul had settled him in a resort hotel in Alma de Aragon, where for six weeks he ate and took the sun while his release and that of other evaders was worked out in a deal for shipments of oil to Spain.

★   ★   ★

With the Allied landings in North Africa, a tide of Frenchmen swept over the Pyrenees into Spain in hopes of joining the forces matched against Germany and Italy. Within three months of the landings, Ambassador Hayes in Madrid put the number of Frenchmen already in Spain at ten thousand. Germany pressured Spain to ship them back to France or intern them; Britain and America wanted them accepted humanely as refugees, then moved on to North Africa. The latter request put Spain in the dicey position of allowing on its soil what could be construed by the Third Reich as recruitment of military men for the Allied cause.

After lengthy discussion Spain took the chance, and the government informed Hayes that the refugees could be evacuated on French ships from the port of Cadiz. Then, just before the first group of some fourteen hundred held in northern Spain was set to move by rail to the southern port, the government decided that Cadiz could not be used, nor could any Spanish port. The reason was the flexing of Nazi muscle: Spain had been told that any refugee ships leaving her ports would be sunk. As an alternative, Spain suggested the use of Portuguese ports, either Lisbon or Setúbal, and Hayes flew to Lisbon to begin talks with American minister Bert Fish and Portuguese authorities. Salazar, who had the final word, delayed his decision yet finally consented to the French leaving from Portugal if the United States made a formal request, and made it in a form he found acceptable. Setúbal, a large port just south of Lisbon, was agreed upon as the embarkation point.

At the end of April 1943, after complicated arrangements for exit and transit visas, trains, food supplies, and British ships, 850 French military men sailed at midnight from Setúbal for Tunisia. Through that spring and summer other groups followed, with finally 16,000 of what Hayes called fighting Frenchmen were moved to North Africa and integrated with Allied forces.

★   ★   ★

In January 1943 Minister Fish in Lisbon sent a telegram to the State Department outlining Portugal's manner of handling Allied airmen and planes downed on its territory. Both were immediately interned, with the planes never released (before the North African invasion, Fish noted, none were in a condition worth retrieving), and crews were held in custody until—as the minister prudently put it—authorities were able to "convince themselves that due respect had been shown to the principle of Portuguese sovereignty," then quietly moved to Allied control. With the Portuguese endlessly cautious about neutrality issues, the release process was always delicate—and best conducted, Fish added, outside the attention of the American press and radio. (Fish may have feared Portugal's reaction to reports such as one that appeared in the *Saturday Evening Post* in 1943: the Portuguese police, said the article, had the habit of looking the other way with downed American flyers since, in their practical way, they "do not relish feeding and housing interned pilots for the duration.")

What Fish sketched out for Washington was the rule with downed flyers. Lieutenant Jack Ilfrey was the exception. Two months before the minister's telegram to Washington, the young American fighter pilot had bypassed diplomatic delicacy by releasing himself from Portuguese custody.

At first light on November 9, 1942, Ilfrey had left a base at Land's End in England as part of a large nonstop flight of twin-engine, twin-tailed P-38 Lightnings on their way to Oran in North Africa for combat in Operation Torch. (After Antoine de Saint-Exupéry, age forty-three, flew Lightnings in North Africa in 1943—he was attached to an aerial photo group commanded by the president's son, Colonel Elliott Roosevelt—he wrote: "It's a fine machine. I wish I'd been given that present in my twenties." He was flying a Lightning over France in 1944 when he and the plane were mysteriously lost.) A B-26 bomber led the way on a flight plan across the Bay of Biscay, down the Spanish and Portuguese coasts to the Straits of Gibraltar, and along the African coast to French Morocco and Oran. The distance was fifteen hundred miles, and the fighter planes were outfitted with external fuel tanks that could be dropped when emptied. Still, they would be squeezing out every drop of fuel to make the flight. If they ran short, the pilots were instructed that Gibraltar was the first place for an emergency stop.

Ilfrey, flying in a group of eight fighters, was over the Bay of Biscay when one of his plane's external tanks accidentally fell off, taking with it 150 gallons of fuel. Another pilot flew close and held up a printed sign: ONE BELLY TANK. The pilots had been told to keep radio silence, and Ilfrey nodded that he understood about the lost tank. The decision he now faced was whether to return to England or see if his fuel would hold out to Gibraltar. He wanted to remain with his squadron and not miss out on combat in North Africa, so he chose Gibraltar.

Over the Bay of Biscay the bomber and the fighters had to alter course to avoid thunderheads, and Ilfrey realized he was using up too much fuel. He veered off from his group and headed for what he hoped was land. When he saw it, he checked his maps and plotted his position as about at Portugal's northern boundary with Spain. He turned south and flew down the coastline to the mouth of the Tagus River. His maps indicated Lisbon was twenty to thirty miles upriver. He had been given little briefing about forced landings in enemy or neutral countries beyond a pilot's duty to destroy his plane and equipment. But briefings or not, his fuel was so short he had no choice but to come down. When he saw a big airport with inviting runways just outside Lisbon, he circled once and landed.

Immediately six men on horseback, armed with pistols and sabers and outfitted in plumed hats and colorful trousers, charged toward him. They gestured frantically that he was to taxi toward an administration building, and while Ilfrey did so he tore up his maps and papers and tossed the pieces out the cockpit.

When he shut down his engines in front of the building, people rushed the plane from every direction while the horsemen surrounded it. With a man who spoke English, Ilfrey was led toward the administration building, along the way noticing on the airport apron American-made Douglas DC-3s with German markings. The pilots of the airliners were inside the building and remained present and silent while Ilfrey was given cake and coffee, told the American legation had been notified of his presence, and then questioned at length by a Portuguese official. Ilfrey refused all answers. The crowd about him seemed decidedly pro-German, and he assumed anything he said about his plane or his mission would be handed over to the Nazis.

Another official told him that Portuguese policy was to intern all foreign pilots and planes. Ilfrey was then introduced to a Portuguese pilot, who explained that the country's air force was made up mostly of interned British, German, and French planes; the P-38 would be its first American fighter, and he would fly it to a military base. Ilfrey and the pilot walked together out to the P-38, and while it was being refueled the pilot asked questions about the cockpit mechanism. Ilfrey, seated in the cockpit, saw that his parachute and Mae West were gone along with his billfold and overnight bag. With the Portuguese pilot sitting on the wing, Ilfrey showed him how the plane was operated, all the while feeling guilty that he had not followed orders to destroy it. Beyond the plane, the horsemen were still present together with a large crowd of onlookers. No one from the American legation had yet appeared.

A familiar sound in the air caught Ilfrey's attention, and when he looked up he saw another P-38 on one engine coming in for a forced landing. As the horsemen dashed off toward it, Ilfrey seized the moment. He fired his plane's two engines, creating a gust of wind that, the plane holding still, blew the Portuguese pilot from the wing and sent the crowd beyond chasing their hats. Ilfrey shut the canopy, gave the plane full power, and shot straight ahead, ignoring the runway and all else until he was in the air. Looking back, he caught the identification mark of the P-38 on the runway. It was Jim Harman's, a pilot in his squadron.

Once he had altitude, Ilfrey realized he did not know if enough fuel had been put into the plane to get him to Gibraltar—and also realized he was without parachute or helmet. But the weather was good, the Portuguese villages below were picturesque, and he reached the Rock without incident. Only when he was on the ground and warmly greeted by other members of his squadron who had also failed to reach Oran did it sink in that he had escaped one situation for another.

An American colonel gave Ilfrey a vigorous dressing down for not destroying his plane in Lisbon and threatened to send both pilot and plane back for internment in Portugal. Then he changed course and told Ilfrey not to worry. Ilfrey later heard through rumor that the colonel had cabled Washington that orders to send the offending pilot back to Lisbon had unfortunately come too late, and he had already rejoined his squadron in North Africa. From the published diaries of Captain Harry C. Butcher, General Eisenhower's wartime aide, Ilfrey would also learn that a diplomatic flap over his escape had reached all the way to the supreme commander, who had at least been willing to consider sending him back to

Lisbon since the Portuguese, in a recent incident, had rescued and returned a group of American servicemen. Butcher wrote about Ilfrey:

> One of our American pilots flying a P-38 from U.K. to Gib landed at Lisbon for gas, having lost one spare belly tank, was told he was thereby interned. Told the airdrome official he wanted to clear his supercharger, or something, got back in plane, started motor, and dashed away, leaving his jacket with identification papers. Fearful of a diplomatic upset for thus flaunting Portugal, which has been friendly, and of indicating a "mightier than thou" attitude, Ike had [General Albert] Gruenther radio our Ambassador at Lisbon the story and to be prepared to answer questions frankly. Consideration would be given to return the lad and plane for internment. Recently an American paratroop plane came down at sea off Portugal, the crew was rescued, taken ashore in Portugal, and allowed to depart as "experienced seamen."

As for Jim Harman, he rejoined the flying group in North Africa some four months after Ilfrey. Engine trouble had forced him down in Lisbon, and the Portuguese had immediately clamped him in jail for a few days, then moved him to an internment camp. Toward the end of his third month in the camp the American legation had provided him with civilian clothes and moved him out of Portugal on a foreign liner. Unsurprisingly, Harman held Jack Ilfrey personally responsible for his Portuguese sojourn.

★   ★   ★

A series of forced landings inside Portugal had provided the backdrop for Minister Fish's communication with the State Department about Portugal's treatment of downed men and aircraft. When at the end of 1942 two fighter planes had come down in Lisbon, the pilots had tried and failed to destroy them. At the same time a twin-engine bomber was damaged in a landing in northern Portugal near Porto. The pilot of the bomber made no resistance and turned over his papers to authorities. Some two weeks later eleven P-39 Airacobra fighter planes, blown off course by storms and short on fuel, landed in Lisbon, after which one of the pilots tried unsuccessfully to destroy his plane by flinging a grenade at it. A front-page story in the *New York Times* reported that Portuguese pilots flew the Airacobras to a military base near Sintra while the American pilots were interned in a fortress in Elvas, some one hundred miles east of Lisbon near the Spanish frontier.

The press account added that the eleven fighters had been escorting two four-engine American bombers passing over Portuguese territory, but a follow-up story the next day said reports from Lisbon indicated the fighters were part of a much larger formation on the way from England to Gibraltar to bolster Allied air strength in North Africa. A third story, by the *Times'* military expert, Hanson W. Baldwin, supplied more detail. The P-39s were being "flight-ferried" to Gibraltar, and rather than escorting the bombers, the fighters, flying at reduced speed, were guided by the navigational capability of the larger planes on a flight across the Bay of Biscay and over or around the Iberian peninsula.

With the Airacobras held in Portugal, all in good condition, the State Department suggested that Fish argue for their release on grounds they should be treated like belligerent warships and permitted to depart within forty-eight hours. Mounting such an effort, Fish responded, was unwise. It was British practice not to seek release of planes; moreover, the planes had been on military missions and armed, and if allowed to leave Portugal—so Portuguese authorities would likely reason—all the belligerent powers "would soon take much greater liberty with operations in the neighborhood of Portugal confident that if they had fueling difficulties they could always fall back on Portuguese airports to save themselves." Fish added: "It would not appear to me to be to our advantage to have the German long-range bombers which occasionally operate off the Portuguese coast placed in a position where they could regularly risk running short of fuel and count on the Portuguese to help them get home."

The fate of the planes was resolved not by release but purchase. Fish was told that the Joint Chiefs of Staff in Washington were recommending a policy of selling Portugal aircraft of "non-confidential character" forced down in the country. Pilots consequently would be instructed not to attempt destruction of such planes. When the State Department contacted the British about adopting a similar policy, it learned that one was already in place. Fish replied to news of the Joint Chiefs' policy by reminding the State Department that three months earlier he had reported Portugal's offer to buy the planes presently interned and had heard nothing back from Washington.

In subsequent telegrams Fish was ordered to pursue the sale, with the War Department placing a price tag on P-38s and P-39s, without spare parts or munitions, of twenty thousand dollars each. Fish expected the Portuguese Ministry of War to accept the terms (it did, with the transferred planes put in service by the country's military) and concluded in a message to the State Department that "this appears to be the most satisfactory solution practicable inasmuch as [the] Portuguese obviously will not consider any action *in re* these planes which might be possibly interpreted as a violation of neutrality." The sale, he added, might also bring about the early release of eighteen American pilots presently held in Portugal.

★   ★   ★

Among the advantages to the warring powers of having Portugal outside the war was that Lisbon's open port offered a mutually acceptable meeting ground for formal exchange programs, with arrivals and departures carefully timed to maintain the country's balancing act of equal treatment. For the United States, exchange deals began soon after Pearl Harbor and the declarations of war by Germany and Italy. In Rome at the time, Reynolds and Eleanor Packard gloomily recalled an old wartime joke: "What is the difference between a diplomat and a foreign correspondent? The diplomat is sure to get home." The Rome bureau chief of the United Press for the preceding three years, Reynolds Packard realized that he and his wife Eleanor, also an accredited correspondent, might well be interned for the length of the fighting. On the other hand, with important contacts in and out of Italy, they both knew their chances of getting away were better than most aliens who suddenly found themselves on enemy soil.

Shortly after going to the American embassy to have their passports renewed, the Packards were taken into police custody, with Eleanor allowed to return to the couple's apartment under watch of a detective while Reynolds was put in Regina Coeli prison with other male correspondents. The following day he was released and placed with five other correspondents in a bleak boardinghouse. After a time it was learned that all American correspondents would be moved to Siena while the American and Italian governments haggled over a list of names for exchange between the two countries—and haggled too over dividing up apartments, cars, furniture, radios, and other goods that would be left behind.

In late December the correspondents were taken by police escort to Siena, where they put themselves up in the Excelsior Hotel, nearly empty except for a few other detained guests. The newsmen, seven in all, split the cost of another room to convert to a common area despite the fact, as the Packards noted, "from then on, it was a plot out of a Dostoevski novel." In Rome they had all been cutthroat competitors; now they had to live together in a tight society with no end in sight. They were allowed nearly full freedom to do as they wished in Siena but strictly forbidden any contact with the local population.

Soon grown to nine, the group—along with the Packards it included Herbert L. Matthews and Harold Denny of the *New York Times*, Mrs. Paul

Getty of the *New York Herald Tribune*, David Colin of NBC, and Dick Massock of the Associated Press—ran through a string of hobbies: bridge; visiting churches, galleries, and antique shops; bicycling (the police made no objection to long excursions); drawing with charcoal and crayons, using themselves as models; ping pong and tennis; beard-growing competitions; and bird-raising contests based on the number of hatched eggs. Everywhere they went in Siena they were given, surreptitiously, preferred treatment by the locals: cinema tickets were often free; grocery stores allowed them more food than rationing permitted; anonymous presents of champagne came from Italian businessmen passing through town. One of the correspondents kept a rented radio in his room, monitored BBC broadcasts, and kept the others informed of war news with written summaries.

Reynolds Packard was playing billiards in a Siena café when he learned the Americans were to report to the local police chief. When told they were moving to Rome, one of the correspondents let out a loud cheer. "I'm as relieved to get rid of you as you are to go," the chief responded with a smile. The Excelsior Hotel presented the internees with bottles of champagne as a parting gift.

The correspondents were escorted to Rome by detectives and installed in the Grand Hotel, where they spent eight days, eating in the best restaurants and enjoying relative freedom. On May 13, 1942, they left Rome on the last of four trains departing at different intervals for the French-Spanish border and carrying diplomats and American citizens who had been detained in the country, the number equal to that of Italians allowed out of America. In unoccupied France the train took on Vichy detectives, and from the windows the correspondents got glimpses of the Riviera: hotels shut up, tennis courts and golf courses overgrown with weeds, people walking or bicycling and carrying knapsacks to pick up any fruit or wood they might find off the roads. When the train arrived at Cerbère on the Spanish border, the passengers boarded another exchange train for Barcelona, Madrid, and eventually Lisbon.

Late at night the train reached the Portuguese border, but it was not allowed to cross until the chartered Swedish liner *Drottningholm*, bringing Italian and German diplomats from America, had docked in Lisbon. When at last the train entered Portugal, the correspondents rushed to a frontier café for the first genuine coffee they had drunk in months. But only in the Lisbon railway station did they finally have a sense of complete freedom, though there remained an ocean to cross. British and Yugoslav correspondents they had known in the past came to shake their hands while Italian detectives, who had been with them the entire journey, said polite goodbyes and hurried to shops to buy goods no longer available at home.

Like other new arrivals in Lisbon, Reynolds and Eleanor Packard were dazzled by the bright lights and abundant food. "To eat what one wanted," they wrote, "to dance, to walk on brightly lighted streets at night, to drink real coffee, to smoke American cigarettes—all trivial things in themselves, but in their sum total they went a long way toward representing the differences between comfort and hardship. The Portuguese complained of a shortage of gasoline, but there were many taxis, and we thought that if the Portuguese had nothing more than that to worry about they were indeed lucky." For their first days in the city the Packards and other correspondents also were allowed to write and transmit what the Packards called "really good broadsides at the Axis." Then, after Rome and Berlin protested, the Portuguese censors clamped down.

The overcrowded *Drottningholm*—painted white, brightly lit, DIPLOMAT in bold lettering on each side—weighed anchor on May 22 and arrived in New York near the end of the month. The official passenger list issued by the State Department included 25 correspondents and their families from Italy and Central Europe along with a 154 American diplomatic officials and families and a few private citizens. Among the diplomats was Admiral William D. Leahy, who had resigned as ambassador to Vichy France after he was appointed President Roosevelt's chief of staff. His wife had died shortly before, and her body was being returned home.

Also with the diplomats was the American minister to Hungary, Herbert C. Pell, a wealthy aristocrat who had begun his foreign service career in 1937 when his friend President Roosevelt appointed him to head the ministry in Lisbon. (The U.S. diplomatic presence in Portugal was elevated to embassy status only in 1944.) Pell soon found himself in what he called "the dullest and least important post in Europe." About his only task was to send a required weekly report to Washington: "Every Friday I would write a letter to the Secretary of State: 'Sir, I have the honor to enclose a copy of the official journal. I am, respectfully.' There was nothing more to do until the next Friday when the same letter had to be signed again." With time on his hands, Pell spent most of it on leisurely drives about Portugal. Then came the war, and with it his reassignment in early 1941 from Portugal to Hungary. (When the exchange ship arrived in New York, reporters noted that Pell's mass of luggage included eighty-five cases of French, Spanish, and Portuguese wine. He was never one to travel lightly or inconspicuously. When he left Lisbon for his new post in Budapest, he journeyed across wartime Europe in a three-vehicle motorcade—an American station wagon loaded with belongings, a limousine in which Pell and a secretary rode, and a truck carrying gasoline and spare parts, each vehicle with its own chauffeur.)

★   ★   ★

Still another diplomat in the *Drottningholm* group was the former first secretary of the American embassy in Berlin, George Kennan. With the German declaration of war on the United States, Kennan and other Berlin personnel and their families together with American officials and journalists from throughout Europe had been swiftly interned under Gestapo supervision in a hotel in Bad Nauheim, a small spa town near Frankfurt. For five months Kennan was both in charge of what he termed "this motley group of hungry, cold, and worried prisoners" and the intermediary with their captors. Complaint among the internees was constant, with grousing about food topping the list. The daily fare was German civilian rations, not as ample as prisoners of war were entitled to; nor were the internees allowed Red Cross parcels that normally went to prisoners. When the 130 captives finally left Frankfort for Lisbon and the exchange ship, all were emaciated.

The trip was made aboard two special trains. Crossing Spain at night it was necessary to lock the doors to keep the prisoners, especially the journalists among them, from getting off at rail stations in a hunt for liquor and possibly being left behind. Kennan had charge of one of the trains, and when it reached a Portuguese border town ("our first breath of peace and normalcy," he recalled) a member of Lisbon's American legation was waiting. Kennan went out for a meeting, leaving the train locked behind him, and afterward asked if breakfast was possible at the station. It was.

> Thereupon I [Kennan wrote], who had been for five months on the receiving end of the food complaints, took final revenge upon my fellow internees by repairing to the station buffet and eating a breakfast of several eggs, leaving the rest of them to nurse their empty bellies over the remaining six or seven hours of rail journey before making themselves sick, as all of us did, on the rich fare of Lisbon.

★   ★   ★

One of the war's late exchanges in Lisbon took place in early March 1944 when a group of some 600—mostly American diplomats, correspondents, relief workers, and wounded POWs—left on the chartered Swedish liner *Gripsholm* for New York. The ship had just brought more than twelve hundred French and German internees to Lisbon. Among the French-German collection were former Vichy diplomats, 130 German troops who had been wounded or were considered mental cases, and a large number of women and children. Most of the 150 American civilians on the outgoing ship had been seized from Vichy France after its occupation by German troops and held for barter for more than a year in the resort town of Baden-Baden.

The wounded Americans in the exchange party had come by rail to Lisbon, and the Portuguese Red Cross had cared for them in an emergency hospital before sending them in ambulances to the ship. One of the men, Lieutenant Robert Janson, had bailed out of a burning B-17 bomber over Germany and, his back broken, had spent seven months in German hospitals before ending up in a camp for captured airmen, Stalag Luft III in Poland. (A month after Janson was brought to Lisbon, the camp was the site of a mass tunnel escape that became the subject of *The Great Escape*, a 1950 book by an Australian writer and camp prisoner, Paul Brickhill, and in 1963 a popular film of the same name.) In a log he kept, Janson wrote of the train journey in unheated cars through Germany and France to Hendaye, where the occupants were housed in a German camp and served dinner by Spanish women. They could now glimpse Irun in Spain and on Sunday hear chimes from a church. From Sunday to Thursday they waited in the camp; then, at 3:30 in the morning, they were roused from sleep and led in heavy snow to a train station, where one car was waiting for them, again without heat. At the station a trainload of diplomats came in, most of them from Latin America, and half were placed on the same train as the POWs.

It was a happy moment when the train crossed the border with, as Janson wrote in reference to his prison captors, "no goons on board" and the diplomats in good humor after their own long internment. At the first stop in Spain a doctor and nurses dressed the wounds of some of the men and attended the sick. An American colonel appeared and gave out information about what to expect in Lisbon and on the exchange ship. For the first time Janson began feeling he was on his way to home.

In Lisbon's crowded railway station Red Cross workers quickly moved the wounded prisoners to a room with a large table arranged with flowers, oranges, and sandwiches, then transported them to a hospital. "Nice clean bed," Janson said of the ward, "new linens. Flowers. Treated us fine." After a good sleep in a comfortable bed, he "took a very thankful shower. Also 3 barbers spruced us up. Received Pajamas—Robe. Sunday went to Mass in a very pretty Church. Felt swell." The ward had American magazines, and a movie was shown—Leslie Howard in *Pimpernel Smith*. Another evening the movie was Bob Hope in *Road to Morocco*.

Janson and other prisoners were also invited to meals at the Lisbon homes of American diplomats. After one, taxis called for them shortly before midnight—still early by Portuguese custom—and they were taken on a sightseeing tour. "The center of the town is very modernistic," Janson noted. "Great sight to see theater crowd. The sight of all this gave us quite a tingling sensation." On another evening the movies were replaced by "swell entertainment" provided by a "fine smiling bunch of kids" from northern Portugal.

★   ★   ★

At the same time Lisbon provided a gateway home for exchanged figures, it gave the belligerents a connecting point for exchanging information. But while the transfer of people was conducted openly—the progress of exchange ships sailing between Lisbon and New York drew wide press attention, and when they docked prominent returnees were interviewed and photographed—Allied-Axis communication took place in the shadow world of wartime. This was all the more so when contact involved conditions for possibly ending the war.

In August 1943, Italy—with Mussolini now deposed and Marshal Pietro Badoglio the new head of government—reached out to the Allies for surrender terms while yet officially linked with Germany. After an initial contact in Lisbon between the British ambassador and the new counselor of the Italian legation, Allied authorities instructed General Eisenhower to send two officers from his headquarters in Algiers to Lisbon for a clandestine meeting with an Italian emissary.

General Walter Bedell Smith, Eisenhower's American chief of staff, and Brigadier Kenneth W. D. Strong, the British head of his intelligence staff, flew from Tangiers to Gibraltar, after which—with forged papers, dressed in plain clothes, and traveling in a civilian plane—they went on to Lisbon, where George Kennan, now attached to the American legation, drove them about in an aged Buick. The ultra-secret "atmosphere of amateur theatricals"—in the phrase of Harold Macmillan (at the time, the future British prime minister was his country's political representative at Allied headquarters)—that characterized the powwow of the enemies, was adopted to avoid detection by Lisbon's international press corps and the German secret service. From Italy came General Giuseppe Castellano, also disguised as a civilian, carrying a false passport, and ostensibly a member of an Italian delegation accompanying a group of Chilean diplomats being exchanged in Lisbon for Italian officials who had left Chile when the country ended relations with Italy. At a stopover in Madrid, the officer had told the British ambassador that if the Germans learned of his mission he would be killed the moment he returned to Italy.

An all-night meeting in the Lisbon residence of the British ambassador revealed that the two sides were miles apart. The Italian emissary understood his mission as arranging to abandon Germany and then joining Britain and the United States in the war; the two Allied representatives made clear that Italy's only choice was between complete capitulation and total war. "We are not in a position to make terms," Castellano acknowledged after Smith read aloud a proposed military armistice. Before leaving for home in the early hours—carrying with him a special radio transmitter, previously installed in the British embassy, which would allow the Italian general staff in Rome to secretly contact Allied headquarters—Castellano drew up a map that set out the location of some 400,000 German troops in Italy.

What followed was a melodrama of several acts, as Harold Macmillan described it, that included Rome sending another and unexpected emissary to meet with Smith and Strong. With Castellano stalled while waiting for the exchange between Italy and Chile to take place, General Giacomo Zanussi appeared in Lisbon—accompanied, apparently as a gesture of good faith, by a high-level British prisoner of war, General Adrian Carton de Wiart—with instructions from his government to move on to London as soon as possible. But the British ambassador, thinking the second Italian general would only muddy negotiations under way with Castellano, instead hid him for the time being in a Lisbon flat. Eventually Zanussi flew to Algiers with Smith and Strong, then moved to Sicily, where on September 3, in an olive grove near Syracuse, General Castellano finally signed for the Italian government an armistice of so-called short terms dealing only with military matters as against the long terms of an unconditional surrender. On September 8, less than a month since the first peace overtures in Lisbon, Eisenhower announced over Radio Algiers Italy's full capitulation. The following day Allied troops of Operation Avalanche landed on the Italian mainland at Salerno. On October 13, with German forces occupying central and northern parts of the country, the new Italian government declared war on its former ally.

Earlier an incident that had taken place during General Zanussi's strange mission to Portugal was brought to conclusion. Perhaps thinking them useful in surrender negotiations, the officer had deposited at Lisbon's Italian legation two packets of valuable information about German forces in Italy. The Italian minister, realizing the danger involved, was eager to get the packets off his hands, and coded messages flew back and forth to the Allies before Harold Macmillan sent his press attaché to Lisbon to retrieve them. In the guise of a Spaniard, he arrived at the legation and, as Macmillan wrote, "obtained the two packages from the trembling hands of Signor Prunas" and carried them safely to Allied headquarters.

★   ★   ★

After Badoglio replaced Mussolini, Hitler, worried about the Italians seeking a separate peace, had sent Admiral Wilhelm Canaris, head of Germany's military intelligence, the Abwehr, to Italy to survey the situation. In a secret meeting in Venice, Canaris consented to a request of General Cesare Amé, head of Italy's military intelligence, to join in masking Italy's planned departure from the war. In a conference attended by intelligence members of both Axis nations, Amé vigorously affirmed Badoglio's commitment to the war as a Nazi ally. Canaris went along with the deception in a report on the conference written after he returned to Germany, though he took the precaution of having an underling attach his name to it. Hitler, though not fully convinced of Badoglio's loyalty, made no effort to remove him from power. Thus Italy's surrender to the Allies was an unwelcome surprise.

The Abwehr chief's duplicitous role in the scheme is understandable in light of his long involvement in a German anti-Nazi opposition group with roots going back to the 1930s. As it was later dubbed by the Gestapo, the Schwarze Kapelle—the Black Orchestra—numbered among its members aristocrats, diplomats, businessmen, and such leading military figures as Field Marshal Erwin Rommel as well as Canaris. The conspirators' aim, as it ultimately developed, was a coup d'état in which Hitler would be assassinated, top Nazi leaders arrested, and a military government installed in Berlin that would sue for peace. To gain support from the Western Allies and favorable surrender terms, the Schwarze Kapelle betrayed important details of German military planning and capability through contact with the Allies in the neutral settings of Bern, Stockholm, and, in 1943, Lisbon.

In July and August one of the plotters, Otto John, a lawyer with Lufthansa airlines who also carried out intelligence missions for the Abwehr, was sent to both Madrid and Lisbon to see if communication links could be established to Washington and London. Over dinner in Madrid with William Hohenthal, an Office of Strategic Services (OSS) agent under cover as a military attaché at the American embassy, John confided that an attempt would soon be made to change the régime in Berlin. What was needed for the effort was some indication from the Allied high command that German field marshals would receive the same lenient treatment given Marshal Badoglio when Italy left the war. The evening ended with Hohenthal agreeing to stay in contact and giving John a secret telephone number to the embassy.

John's Lufthansa position made travel about the Iberian peninsula easy and above suspicion, and earlier he had met in Lisbon with Graham Maingot, an agent of Britain's MI6, the country's Secret Intelligence Service operating overseas. The two had left the city by car and walked country lanes to avoid observation, the British operative convinced of John's authenticity but explaining to him why others might be wary:

> I see no reason why I should not believe you. . . . But there are people here in Portugal claiming to belong to the German opposition who would like to mislead us. Before the war German opposition emissaries came to London and told us that they were in touch with German generals who wished to overthrow Hitler. But what happened? Nothing. The German generals are fighting for Hitler and they're not doing it badly either.

It was necessary, added Maingot, for the German resistance to "prove itself by doing something if it wishes to get a hearing in Lisbon."

In February 1944, the planned coup near at hand, John returned to Madrid and Lisbon to try to establish some link with the Allied military leadership. In Madrid, William Hohenthal said he would look into the possibility of a connection with Eisenhower; in Lisbon, however, John hit a stonewall. Another officer of MI6's Lisbon station, Rita Winsor, met John in a car parked on a dark side street and, as they drove through the city, told him that instructions from London were that all contact with the German opposition should cease. The war would be decided only on the battlefield. After delivering this disheartening news, Winsor invited John to her home for a farewell drink. He would return to Lisbon under quite different circumstances, but for the time being his work as an emissary of the anti-Nazi resistance was over.

However, in the German minister in Portugal, Baron Oswald von Hoyningen-Huene, the Schwarze Kapelle had long had a highly placed member in Lisbon. In the summer of 1943 Hoyningen-Huene was the link in an invitation from Admiral Canaris to the head of MI6, Stewart Menzies, to meet on neutral ground, possibly in Portugal, to discuss an alliance between the German conspirators and British intelligence. Menzies was prepared to chance the danger involved, but Foreign Secretary Anthony

Eden was not. He vetoed both the meeting and a response to the invitation on grounds it would stoke the fear of the Russians, if they learned of it, that Britain would seek a separate peace with Germany.

As perhaps part of an attempt by Canaris to sway Menzies's agreement to a meeting, in that summer of 1943 an Abwehr officer turned over to the MI6 station in Lisbon a detailed dossier about Hitler's secret V1 and V2 rocket program under way at Peenemünde, on an island in the Baltic Sea. Germans later considered the material, which came to be known as the Lisbon Report, as the most devastating betrayal of the Third Reich during the war. The report confirmed other information about the rocket program available to the British and Americans through intercepts of German wireless communications, and on August 17 and 18, 1943, the RAF staged a massive assault on Peenemünde.

With the Allies committed to unconditional surrender, the Schwarze Kapelle's attempts to trade information for aid and concessions had no chance of success. Likewise, the plotters' efforts to remove Hitler produced a series of failures. When a fourth assassination attempt on July 20, 1944, went awry—a bomb placed beneath the Führer's desk exploded but only wounded him—most of the conspirators, among them Canaris, were rounded up and executed. Rommel was allowed the questionable honor of taking his own life.

A final German attempt in Lisbon to reach the Western Allies, this initiated by some members of the military high command following the Normandy landings, took place in or about August 1944. Heinz Carl Weber, identified as the figure in charge of German mineral purchasing in Portugal, contacted the American and British embassies in Lisbon through, presumably, Hoyningen-Huene or key subordinates. According to a document prepared by the American OSS and circulated to the president, the secretary of state, and others in Washington, Weber said that German general headquarters had asked him to determine the response of the United States to the surrender of German forces to the Western Allies, "provided the latter act at once to occupy the Reich and keep out the Soviet." The OSS added that "the report may merit attention in view of the channels employed and the apparent sincerity of the source." There is no evidence, however, that Weber received a reply; if he did, it would only have restated the Allied position of surrender without conditions. The war, in any case, went on for another nine months.

★   ★   ★

Otto John, who had returned to Berlin in anticipation of Hitler's assassination, escaped Gestapo retribution by fleeing to Madrid on a Lufthansa flight. "A dagger's the right way to murder a man like Hitler," a Spanish friend bitterly admonished him. "If one of you had the courage to do that, the coup would have succeeded. What you did was wrong and too late." He also told John that he could not stay in Madrid; the Spanish police would surely hand him over to the Gestapo. John considered going to the American embassy, meeting again with William Hohenthal, and asking for asylum. Instead he chose, with the help of British friends, to try to reach Lisbon and then London, where he hoped, through the medium of BBC broadcasts, to provide a full account of the German resistance.

After a series of moves in Madrid to avoid detection, John was driven by a man from the British embassy to the Spanish port of Vigo, from where he was transported to a village on the frontier with Portugal. Before dawn the following day he was taken by rowboat across the Minho River to waiting Portuguese, who provided him with breakfast. When a large car marked with a Union Jack appeared, John proved his identity to the Portuguese driver with a method agreed upon in Madrid—a matchbox with a hundred-peseta note inside—and was promptly taken to Lisbon. At the British embassy, his identity again demonstrated with the matchbox, he was told he would be lodged in a small inn outside Lisbon until he was sent on to London.

A Portuguese agent working with the embassy led him to the inn, where a meal was provided. But John's room turned out to be a corner of a barn filled with straw and corn. He was next taken to the agent's home near Lisbon, where his movements were confined to an inner courtyard. Days passed, and though the agent preached patience, John began thinking the British had little interest in getting him to London.

One evening two members of the Portuguese secret police burst into the home and demanded John's identity card. After claiming he was an RAF officer who had been shot down over Germany and was on his way to Britain, he was taken to a prison on the edge of Lisbon—the medieval fortress of Aljube, he later learned—while his story was checked. The worst that could befall him, John assumed, was internment in Portugal, in every sense a better fate than that of his fellow conspirators in Germany.

During questioning in Aljube he held to his RAF story. But when the Portuguese interrogator produced a suitcase that had been forwarded from Madrid without John's knowledge and found in the Portuguese agent's home, the game was up: in the suitcase was a dinner jacket with the label of a German tailor. John admitted his true identity but said he was in Madrid at the time of the attempt on Hitler's life and had fled to Lisbon to escape the reach of the Gestapo. He asked for political asylum in Portugal.

The interrogator had him write down what he had said, and left him alone to do so. At the same time John wrote a letter to Salazar, hoping to gain his support for asylum. From the interrogator he learned that the police had stumbled on him when they came to the agent's home to arrest him for supposed Communist connections. John was returned to his dismal prison cell and days passed while, seemingly, his asylum request was under consideration. He would eventually discover that, after Portugal had refused a German request for extradition, the Gestapo intended to abduct him in Portugal and bring him, dead or alive, to Germany. When the British embassy got wind of the Gestapo's plans, it had contacted the Portuguese minister of the interior on John's behalf, who in turn said Portugal could not guarantee his long-term security and he should be moved to England. Rita Winsor, John's earlier MI6 contact in Lisbon, remembered him and prodded embassy officials to take action on his behalf.

One day, without preliminaries, John was taken from the prison to the embassy, given a British emergency passport, and put up for a night with a British couple. The next day, accompanied by a friend of Rita Winsor's, he was placed on a plane to Gibraltar—but when the plane could not land due to weather it returned to Lisbon. The next night Rita Winsor herself took him to a flying boat on the Tagus for a flight to England. After brief internment, the British set Otto John to work advising on BBC broadcasts directed to German troops and interviewing prisoners of war.

6

LIVING THERE

I know of no capital city that is pleasanter for an exile to live
in than Lisbon.

—Hugh Muir, *European Junction*

For Denis de Rougemont, the Swiss-born writer, the Lisbon route from war
ultimately led to one destination, as he made emphatically clear in a journal
entry on September 10, 1940: "White and blue in the light of the immense
Atlantic freedom with all its flags snapping and its streets leading to the sky,
the city of seven hills denies the war, forgets Europe. Tomorrow we embark
for America." And the next day he indeed boarded the *Exeter* for New York,
leaving Lisbon and Europe behind. Still, there were always exceptions in the
determined rush to move on, whether to America or elsewhere. Some refugees who reached Lisbon purposely prolonged their stay there, even decided
it was an agreeable place to sit out some or all of the war. And throughout the
period there were those for whom the city was a goal rather than a stopping
off place, and they settled into long stretches of residence.

Even for exiles bent solely on getting away, delays in doing so could
stretch so long that they seemed to be living in Lisbon. The American
novelist and poet Frederic Prokosch reported that after going through a
furious phase of trying to leave—"straggling in and out of the Consulates,
gathering for gossip, begging for introductions, ferreting for loans, gambling, bribing, bickering, pawning; waiting and waiting"—many refugees
gave up and made homes of a sort in the city and took up familiar national
routines. "Their complaints," he went on "grew stylized; people stopped
listening. A strange kind of peacefulness swept over them. The drab, gentle
lethargy of Lisbon gathered them in."

121

Lisbon became Munich, Manchester, Marseilles. Small replicas of a dead Europe were erected all over the city, tenderly, rather shabbily. French and Belgians flocked to the boulevard cafés; Germans to the shady beauty spots; English to the tennis-courts; Jews and South Americans to the fashionable tea-shops; Dutch and Norwegians and Jugoslavs to the cliff-lined beaches. Everyone managed, after a while, to be contented; or almost everyone. There was plenty of coffee, butter, beef. Warsaw, Rotterdam, Belgrade were never mentioned.

Prokosch himself settled in. At the time he reached Lisbon on the early wave of fleeing refugees he was an ascendant literary star, having published collections of poetry and novels—his first novel, *The Asiatics*, was a major success—and in 1937 been awarded a prestigious Guggenheim fellowship. With the award he put aside plans for an academic career, following a master's degree from King's College, Cambridge, and a doctorate from Yale, in favor of imaginative writing and a wandering life spent mostly in Europe. He was in France and subsisting on a publisher's advance when the war began. Immediately he drove a Ford convertible to Bordeaux and booked passage on a steamship, then discovered he was not yet ready to abandon Europe, and so drove south to Spain.

After a week in Madrid and Seville he went on to Lisbon. In the Pálacio in Estoril he found a dollar-a-day maid's room in which he felt, as he later wrote, "safe and inaccessible. The war was thrillingly near yet intriguingly remote. The refugees swept down from Brussels and Oslo and Amsterdam and the beach rang with the accents of Dutch, Norwegian, Flemish." His intent to stay two weeks in Portugal stretched to two years.

Prokosch spent his mornings working on a new novel about Europe in the time just before the war, his afternoons at the beach with a polyglot group of new friends. They lunched together on cheese from Algarve, sausages from Minho, and joked about the Nazi leaders while also making fifty-escudo bets among themselves about when the Wehrmacht would take Moscow. One night at a large beach at Guincho (located some four miles beyond Cascais, near the westernmost edge of Europe), with breakers crashing in beneath steep cliffs, he and his new friends went swimming nude—and he rescued one of them from the surging water by grabbing her hair and dragging her to the beach. Praised for his brave act, he passed it off as simply reaction to fear, though possibly it also had something to do with his level of physical conditioning. Prokosch was a skilled tennis and squash player who had played in many tournaments and in 1939 had won the French national championship in squash.

While he worked on his novel the war suddenly came close in Prokosch's awareness of "ambiguous and slippery personalities" staying with him at the Pálacio. Some of his evenings he spent in the hotel's lounge going over notes for his book, causing an Italian guest to caution him, "Shouldn't you be a bit more circumspect? People are beginning to be suspicious!" Another figure, suddenly appearing before Prokosch during a nighttime walk on the beach, warned him about a drink he had recently had with a Prussian aristocrat named Baron von Rheinbaben.

> One of the big shots in the Gestapo but please don't tell him that I told you so! But be careful with the Baron. He sends his cables straight to Hitler and nothing would please him more than to establish a rapport with America—a friendly little dialogue with a famous poet or novelist. And besides, you are being watched, my boy. Not only by *me*, who am innocuous, but by an odalisque draped in pearls and by a lady who is wearing sunglasses. So do be careful from now on! What a delicious place, Portugal!

With the novel finished after many months of work (reports in the press in June 1941 said that Harper and Brothers had received from the Pálacio Hotel in Estoril the manuscript of a new Prokosch novel called *The Skies of Europe*), Prokosch took a lesiurely driving tour north to the fishing village of Nazaré, the cities of Coimbra and Porto, and into the mountains of Minho, which struck him as the loveliest he had ever seen. Back in Estoril, his friends now departing for places in South America, he decided the time had come for him to leave as well. He booked passage to New York on the Portuguese vessel *Serpa Pinto* and, as he wrote,

> I waved goodbye to my lovely Portugal on a gray October morning and the ship slid from the Tagus into the gray, sullen, seas. Every night the deck was illuminated by brilliant lights spelling PORTUGAL and at dawn a flock of gulls swooped over the ship with screams of warning.

A chance of returning to Lisbon came when the playwright Robert Sherwood, head of the Overseas Branch of the U.S. Office of War Information, suggested Prokosch might be a good fit for propaganda work in a neutral country. "You know the Portuguese mentality," Sherwood told him. "You might be useful to us in Lisbon." Prokosch preferred a new neutral location and mentioned Stockholm, and there he went in 1943 on what Sherwood called "a cultural exploration." Prokosch characterized it as "my erratic little career in espionage."

Prokosch's only return to Portugal was imaginatively in the brief 1943 novel *The Conspirators*, a story of betrayal and retribution set in wartime Lisbon. In an opening scene, Vincent Van der Lyn, a Dutch refugee caught up in undisclosed anti-Nazi activity, escapes from prison and sets about finding who has named him to Portuguese authorities. From Quintanilla, a mysterious veteran of the Spanish Civil War, he learns that the villain, wearing a white dinner jacket with a red carnation, will appear that very night at the second roulette table of the Estoril casino. If he misses him there, the man will spend the night at a small inn at Guincho before departing the following day for Madrid. When he leaves Quintanilla's quarters, Vincent takes with him a silver letter opener, which of course he is destined to employ as a weapon.

Intertwined with Vincent's story is that of Irina Petrova, his Russian mistress but also the lover of the man he seeks, Hugo von Mohr, supposedly an anti-fascist Anglophile but in reality a Nazi agent. Over the course of the compressed story's single evening, Irina comes to realize that von Mohr is as coldly betraying her as he has Vincent.

Both Irina and Vincent in their movements through Lisbon become Prokosch's vehicles for evoking the overflowing city of the refugees, including those for whom it becomes the sad end of their journeys. For instance, Irina, passing cafés on the Rua Augusta, glimpses many familiar exiles but knows "each day there would be new ones."

> Each day some of the old ones vanished. Most of them took the Clipper or the *Excalibur* for New York; a few sailed to Rio on the *Siqueira Campos*; others left, one by one, for Capetown or Brazzaville or Batavia; a few settled in small hotels or cottages along the shore "for the duration." And a few of them quietly disappeared. The distinguished Dutch explorer, for example, had been found in his bedroom with a bullet in his right temple; the Austrian baroness had been jailed for stealing a sapphire bracelet in the Casino; the stammering Norwegian school teacher had fallen a victim to typhoid; the Latvian journalist had thrown himself into the Tagus; the Hungarian ballet dancer had suddenly gone blind with syphilis. They were gone, all gone. And others were going day by day.

In the novel's final scene Vincent pries open the window of the room in the inn at Guincho and kills von Mohr with the letter knife. (On the terrace outside the Estoril casino, as von Mohr left after winning at roulette, they had passed each other, Vincent pausing and staring, the other ignoring him.) He then calmly awaits the police, knowing he will return to prison but feeling strengthened by his deed. Mild and self-questioning to this point, Prokosch has Vincent now think: "I am at last a participant in the world. A part of history." And add: "By a single brutal act I have cut myself from the life of men; yet in this very act, I have united myself to humanity."

More substantial than the characters or the plot of the novel is Lisbon itself, sketched by Prokosch in moody detail. Seemingly he intends to illustrate how the "most old-fashioned capital in Europe" was transformed into a "frenzied bazaar" by the great rush of refugees, its once sleepy atmosphere now thick with conspiratorial feeling and moral uncertainty yet, in some ambiguous fashion, also charged with fresh energy. He has Irina, whom the police bring to Guincho to see both killer and victim, believe in the story's closing lines that "from the very core of disaster and loss she was drawing a new vitality, and a boundless strength; she was in the act of creating, at this very moment, a new way of living."

In 1944 Hollywood turned *The Conspirators* into a film of that name, with Vincent recast as a gallant Dutch freedom fighter and the murky foreboding of the novel blown into a full-scale spy melodrama. Prokosch had no role in the adaptation, which was the sole pleasure he took from a screening he saw. The film seemed to him to go out of its way to avoid such construction staples as suspense, characterization, or verisimilitude in portraying the Lisbon setting. "After all," Prokosch wrote, "I had lived in Lisbon; I hadn't imagined that the quality of that city could be so widely misrepresented, could be turned into such excruciating silliness. I kept smiling when I thought of the bewilderment the Portuguese will feel when that film finally reaches them. (If it ever does.)" The only things he was willing to accept as a bit right were a couple of costumes of Hedy Lamarr, who shared lead roles with Paul Henreid, and shots of a fine Rolls-Royce.

★   ★   ★

Hugh Muir's writing in Lisbon was newspaper writing. He had worked in Paris on an American paper, the Paris *Herald*, in the World War I period, then moved back to his native England as a correspondent and eventually editor of London's *Sunday Express*. When World War II began Muir was again in Paris as editor the *Continental Daily Mail*, the local edition of the London *Daily Mail*. With German forces advancing on the city, he fled in his car and in July 1940 came to Lisbon, where for the next eighteen months he was resident correspondent of the *Daily Mail*'s London edition. (A planned *Continental Daily Mail* edition in Lisbon, with Muir presumably in charge, never materialized.)

Muir assumed that because Lisbon was the escape point for refugees leaving Europe and a crossroads for diplomats and high-profile wartime officials shuffling in and out, the city would be a journalist's paradise. The day-to-day actuality, he soon learned, fell far short: the place was rife with rumor and propaganda clothed as news. "With dull regularity," he observed, "we heard that German troops were about to march into the Peninsula, that revolt had broken out in Spain, that France had surrendered her fleet, and that the Americans were going to occupy the Azores." If any such things really happened, Lisbon-based correspondents were often the last to know, with the result that most Allied newspapers and wire services relied on Portuguese stringers rather than staff writers for coverage of what firm news there was. An American correspondent for *Collier's* magazine, Alice-Leone Moats, considered herself fortunate to be passing through Lisbon rather than working there since the unceasing rumor mill made it impossible to separate fact and fiction. "Five times a day," she wrote, echoing Muir, "I would hear a different version of some wild report that was going the rounds. Each one was believed implicitly and repeated with embroidery."

Beyond rumor and propaganda newsmen faced structural difficulties: refugees were reluctant to tell their stories because of fear for friends and relatives still in occupied territory; visiting diplomats and officials were tight-lipped; and Portuguese censors were courteous but rigorous. Local correspondents frequently read better versions of their best stories when informants got to America and gave interviews free of Portuguese blue pencils.

Work aside, and the swelling population of refugees also aside, Muir found Lisbon a delightful place to live. Its neighborhoods had a small-town intimacy about them, and the animated life of streets and cafés was a day-and-night magnet drawing nearly everyone outside or hanging from windows or leaning in doorways. Despite shabby districts and obvious poverty, the city was clean, its inhabitants relaxed and friendly, and there was a general air of modest commercial prosperity. Although the government was authoritarian, the law-abiding felt free to do as they pleased.

For Muir's countrymen the city had added charms. Sun and warmth were high on the list, but also in many ways Lisbon felt like home. There were British schools and churches, a British hospital and cemetery; there was English marmalade, Worcestershire sauce, English newspapers and tea-rooms and bars. Names of many familiar English businesses were on store-fronts. There was the Royal British Club for gin and bridge. And there was nearby Estoril or Cascais to replace homesickness, if one were not overly stricken, for the wonders of Brighton or Blackpool.

Lisbon and its seaside communities were so compelling, and wartime conditions back home so cheerless, that some British citizens resisted repatriation. If they were refugees and had gone through their funds in reaching Lisbon—and due to British regulations were unable to export funds from home accounts or friends—they could draw ten pounds a month from the British consulate after signing an agreement to repay the debt. The amount, supplemented for medical fees, was adequate for life in a cheap hotel or boardinghouse. But with British refugees constantly arriving and the local community thus expanding, the financial drain on the consulate brought forth an order that anyone refusing to accept transport home when available would forfeit the monthly allowance. A loophole, though, made an exception for those producing a medical certificate indicating they were too ill to travel. When some laggards found agreeable medical men to so certify them, the order was altered: only a medical certificate issued by the consulate's doctor would do.

A number of British seamen stayed on in Lisbon for another reason. They were survivors of merchant ships sunk by U-boats or German planes and had been rescued by Portuguese vessels or managed to paddle lifeboats or rafts to the Azores or Cape Verde islands. Now under the care of the embassy, the Mercantile Marine Office in Lisbon, and the British Seamen's Institute, they were happily taking in Lisbon's sun and food while regaining their health before again shipping off to sea. They lingered in the English bars in Cais de Sodré Square, easily recognizable in their new clothes but sternly forbidden to speak of their ships or convoys.

When Hugh Muir gained permission to talk with the chief officer of one torpedoed freighter, he was told a story of being hit about 150 miles off the Azores and climbing in a lifeboat, one of the few to get free of the burning ship. From the lifeboat the officer got into a dinghy with six others, then transferred to another lifeboat with 40 men and spent nine days at sea before a fishing boat spotted them and they were towed to a village on one of the islands. Injured and splotched with fuel oil, the officer was carried ashore on a stretcher. When he was able to get to his feet, two Portuguese soldiers helped him stagger up the village street and pass before, to his considerable embarrassment, a lineup of weeping local women.

After eighteen months of working in Lisbon, Muir returned to England for good. Through a friend in the British embassy he got priority booking on a flying boat. It was winter in Portugal, but the morning his plane left from Cabo Ruivo—with fourteen passengers aboard in bucket seats in an otherwise bare interior—the weather was fine and the flight was made without incident. London when he arrived was in blackout and it was raining, but, as Muir wrote of the moment, "it was London, and thoughts of Lisbon's sunshine and a land of no war could not spoil my satisfaction at being home."

★   ★   ★

Among Hugh Muir's countrymen drawing on consular funds was the author Norman Douglas. Now in his seventies and long a resident of Europe, he was believed missing when the war began but turned up in Lisbon, as the *New York Times* disclosed with a story in March 15, 1941, headlined "Norman Douglas Safe in Lisbon." He had left Antibes in the south of France and reached Lisbon by rail in February, and after a few days in the city moved to the far north of Portugal to stay in the large and elegant home of a British acquaintance. "I shall stay till I am kicked out," he wrote in a letter, "or failing that, till the war ends, or failing that, and supposing the war to last longer than I do—then, presumably, for ever. . . . I do nothing but eat and sleep which fills up the 24 hours nicely." Unable to carry money with him out of France, he was living on his host's hospitality and the British handout.

Douglas may have been trying to fix his legal status in Portugal for the duration, or possibly he had been turned out by his host (who eventually left for the United States), when he went down to Lisbon in May. After a couple weeks there, Neil Hogg, the second secretary of the British embassy, put him up in a spare room in his Lisbon flat. With his Portuguese visa renewed, and the British raising his monthly payment to twenty pounds due to age and certification by the British Hospital that he was not up to further travel, he was prepared for another long wait in Portugal. Before leaving France he had booked an air flight from Lisbon to England as a requirement for getting Spanish and Portuguese transit visas, but he now wrote his close friend Nancy Cunard in London (who had published some of his work at her Hours Press in Paris) that his prospects of getting out were poor: ". . . there are 80 people ahead of me, and some 700 others, waiting their chance to go to England, and many of them much more important than myself. A pretty tangle!"

Douglas seems not to have tried overly hard to improve his chances of leaving. He was of two minds about returning to a country he had not seen in a quarter century, and he dreaded having to deal with English food, weather, and social attitudes. He wrote Nancy Cunard, "If the police renew my passport, and if Neil Hogg does not get recalled, I shan't move from here. The idea of England makes me rather creepy." Later, with Douglas back in England, Cunard prodded him in written notes to recall his experience in France and Portugal.

And Lisbon [she asked him]—you were there for many months. Did you find the Portuguese in general—or which classes in particular—as friendly to the British as tradition states them to be? Do you think it is a hotbed of international political intrigue, with a great many Nazi agents? And on which side do you think is public opinion mostly?

To which Douglas responded:

I noticed no Nazi agents in Lisbon, though there may have been thousands of them. The few Germans I met were refugees. And the few Portuguese avoided politics like the plague. And the few newspapers were censored, and therefore no guide to the country's political feelings.

While living with Neil Hogg and acutely aware of his indebtedness to him, Douglas came up with an idea for a piece of writing that he could offer as a gift of sorts. It would take the form of an almanac with aphorisms culled from his published books, such as he could locate them in Lisbon, for each day of the year. Once the idea took hold, he developed a routine of working each morning—the flat empty with Hogg at the embassy—walking about Lisbon in the afternoon, and eating with Hogg and others in cafés in the evening.

He had some fifty copies of *An Almanac* printed in Lisbon, and toward the end of 1941 he began sending them off to friends. Nancy Cunard called the one she received a "darling little volume" and noted that "One good thing came out of Lisbon, that collating of thoughts and epigrams from your various books, ascribing one to every day of the year, at random—for such is *An Almanac*. A nicely-worded dedication too: 'To Neil Hogg—Small Return for Great Kindness.'" About the same time the publication was ready for distribution (it would be reprinted in Britain in 1945), Hogg learned of his transfer to England, and Douglas faced the prospect of getting along on his own. Hogg left in early January of the new year, but only a week passed before a place finally opened up for Douglas on a flight to London. He had been in Portugal nearly a year.

★   ★   ★

Polly Peabody shared Hugh Muir's early assumption that Lisbon would be, as she put it, "an ideal reporters' hang-out" since it was teeming with people with stories to tell—and like Muir she soon learned that Portuguese censorship would curb the few trustworthy tales she uncovered. She was only a correspondent-in-waiting, however, and getting the job she longed for meant reaching England and rejoining the war she had just escaped. An American who had spent much of her childhood in Europe and considered it her true home, she had no hesitation in doing so. Her immediate problem was getting a ticket on a flight to London, and after a long delay in Lisbon and with no work to do, she had almost decided to "take out my citizen papers, and be done with it."

In getting to Portugal, Polly Peabody had not followed a typical refugee path, nor was she a typical refugee. When war began in 1939 she was, as her name seemed to imply, a young socialite living contentedly in New York. Unable to ignore what was happening abroad, she at once volunteered as an ambulance driver in France; after she was turned down she funneled her disappointment into helping organize a medical relief committee for Finland. In March 1940 she sailed from New York with the American-Scandinavian Field Hospital, a complete surgical unit with twenty-eight medical personnel, two ambulances, and enough food and supplies to last six months. News stories at the time identified Peabody as one of the five-member committee of the hospital and added that she would be one of two commissioners in charge of supplies and the canteen.

The original plan to work behind Finnish lines abruptly changed with Finland's armistice with Germany, and the ship's destination switched to Norway. Here the field hospital was set up and operated in war-zone conditions until the Nazi advance forced evacuation to neutral Sweden. With the medical operation now blocked by German occupation from relocating in French territory, Peabody set off on her own, hoping to reach Switzerland and then France by making a long journey east from Sweden. To her surprise, she got all the visas she needed to travel by planes and trains from Stockholm to Moscow to Bucharest to Milan to Geneva, where she learned of the Franco-German armistice. Any shred of illusion she had of France as a bulwark in the war was now gone.

She stayed for a time in Geneva on the off chance the International Red Cross could help get the field hospital from Sweden to France. (Never able to leave Sweden, it was eventually packed up and returned to the United States.) Then she decided to enter France herself and try to join some organization working with refugees. While leaving Geneva she happened to see staff members of the League of Nations on their way from Switzerland to Lisbon by bus, and she stored in her mind the possibility of taking that route to safety herself.

Wearing a Red Cross uniform and carrying a duffel bag, she worked her way through escaping refugees and wandering French troops and finally reached Vichy. She stayed for more than a month, helping with the wounded in hospitals and supporting herself by drawing money from the United States, before leaving for Paris in a Red Cross car. Occupied France shocked her: German troops and emblems were everywhere, the troops smart-looking in their uniforms and rigidly correct in their behavior. The road to Paris, on the other hand, was a cemetery of wrecked cars, abandoned artillery pieces, and shattered homes.

In Paris she worked for three months as a Red Cross ambulance driver with the American Hospital in Neuilly, delivering food and clothing to prison camps. When the Germans put tighter controls on ambulances going to the camps, the Red Cross shut down the operation, leaving her without a job and, winter coming on, no coal for heat. The time had come, she realized, to take the Lisbon route.

A train took Peabody to Biarritz, where she stumbled upon a distant cousin who was on his honeymoon and driving through Spain to Portugal to, improbably, deliver the diplomatic Rolls-Royce of the American consul in Le Havre to his new post in Lisbon. Peabody immediately became the third member of the party. The road jam of refugees from St. Jean-de-Luz to Hendaye kept travel to a mile a day, but once across the border the Rolls rolled through Spain loaded down with luggage and cans of fuel.

Lisbon was reached at dusk, and Peabody was introduced to the city's display of light. "The sight of a million lights," she wrote, "blazing in the sky went to my head: it was champagne: it made me dizzy. Lisbon was like a beacon emerging out of the European black-out. It looked like a dream-city." "The whole place," she added, "resembled a Christmas tree. I wanted to blow the trumpets and throw confetti and sing and dance. Light after darkness. It was thrilling!" When she came to her hotel, the Pálacio in Estoril, she had the feeling she was aboard an opulent ocean liner: "In the bar, after the third Martini, I could almost feel the gentle roll of this incredible refugee ship."

Over time the wonders of Estoril and Lisbon receded, revealing the gloom and frustration of refugees searching for visas and transport while worrying if their funds would endure. Portugal was paradise for those living there, Peabody decided, but purgatory for those waiting to get out. Some refugees sold at small prices the works of art they had brought with them to settle hotel bills or buy transport tickets. The same was done with jewelry and cars. Fifty pounds would buy a Rolls-Royce or a Bentley; when a car would not sell for any amount it was abandoned. There were stories of women dangling large sums in front of American sailors in hopes of marriage and American citizenship. For the truly desperate the last chance was always the gambling tables of the Estoril casino.

Waiting herself for transport, Peabody whiled away the time watching the traffic in the busy Lisbon harbor. Ships of various nationalities moved in and out—British freighters with mounted guns and patched hulls, Spanish and American vessels unarmed and painted white—and the docks and warehouses were stuffed with shipments from Portugal's colonies that were difficult to move on to former trading partners because of the British blockade. Seeing a relative off on a New York–bound ship stuffed with passengers caused her to abandon thoughts of going anywhere by sea.

> Nothing, not even wild horses [she wrote], would have induced me to take a trip on one of those refugee ships. They packed the poor refugees on so tight that you couldn't have run a piece of dental floss between them. Truck-loads of mattresses were brought down to the pier before sailing time, and were stacked on the decks. Needless to say, there would never have been enough life-belts or life-boats to take care of all the passengers in case of disaster; as it was there was barely enough food.

Occasionally Peabody reversed course in her Lisbon wandering and went to the airport at Sintra to observe people coming in on British planes. The men, usually outfitted with homburgs and carrying briefcases and umbrellas, hardly seemed to have come from bombed London. When a rumpled figure appeared among them with plaster dust in his hair, she assumed he was an American war correspondent. The more exciting flights to observe were the Clippers arriving and leaving on the Tagus, though Peabody knew from her fellow blocked refugees that the appeal of the flying boats could rapidly fade amid an array of delays. Repeatedly she saw those holding tickets leave their hotels at dawn and drive to the departure area, "only to be back again at noon."

> something always went wrong—the weather was bad at Horta: the mails were too heavy: an important diplomat was awaited by the next plane from London. Once the Clipper didn't go out for three full weeks, and each night of those three weeks each passenger went to bed thinking that he might be called to leave the next morning. At the best of times it would have driven anyone crazy; in war-time, when the majority of the Clipper passengers had a mission to fulfill, the delay was well-nigh unbearable.

To conserve money, Peabody switched from the Pálacio to a small boardinghouse while continuing her wait for a London flight. Back in the war zone in Norway she had developed a connection with the United Press by filing a news story with the wire service's Stockholm bureau, and in Lisbon she had cabled the UP's New York office and learned it would put her to work in England if she could get there. Doing so had come to seem nearly hopeless, leaving her on the verge of remaining in Portugal, when on Christmas Eve a call at last came: she should be at the Sintra airport at four o'clock the next morning.

In England, her thirteenth country reached in wartime, Polly Peabody would set to work reporting on blitzed London.

★   ★   ★

The British writer Ronald Bodley decided he enjoyed Portugal so much he would stay long enough to turn out a travel book about it, though a singular one that would also tell his personal story of refugee flight. That the present market for tourism to Portugal was at best weak was not a consideration. A dashing life of many headlong ventures had already led Bodley from Eton and Sandhurst to an Indian regiment to a wounding on the Western Front in World War I. After retiring from military life as a major, he took his friend T. E. Lawrence's advice to live among the Arabs and spent seven years with Bedouins in the Sahara (giving rise to a *New Yorker* item about him called "Bodley of Arabia"). And along the way he had found time to churn out fiction, biographies, and travel accounts.

In 1939, with war looming in Europe, Bodley had spent the first half of the year in Hollywood as a screenwriter for Charlie Chaplin before leaving for Paris with the idea of trying his hand at a play. All seemed peaceful in France, and he was confident war would be avoided. When proved wrong he was in Biarritz and working on his play in the company of Lorna Hearst, a daughter-in-law of William Randolph Hearst and Bodley's collaborator on a biography of the Arabist Gertrude Bell. After he went up to Bordeaux to see Hearst off to New York on a ship filled with frightened American tourists caught in France, he traveled to Paris to see for himself the situation there.

In the calm of the phony war Bodley found social life unchanged, with the playwright Jean Cocteau a neighbor in his hotel and Colette living somewhere above him. Then the Wehrmacht marched into the Low Countries. With a friend who had a Packard roadster and was going to Biarritz, he set off from Paris, the car carrying the owner's black cook as well as his household silver, books, and enough luggage to see him through six months. Bodley and his friend anticipated a more or less pleasant outing that would include dining in Chartres and a hotel for the evening in

Tours; instead they found themselves in a frenzied sea of refugees. "It was a heartbreaking spectacle," Bodley wrote, "and we drove on in stunned silence, while the negress wept shamelessly."

He spent a tranquil period living with his mother and American step-father in their home near Bayonne until, with German troops south of Bordeaux and his mother and her husband refusing to leave, he set off again, now in the company of three British women, previously unknown, in a car belonging to one of them. The four had passports but no visas. On the bridge between Hendaye and Irun they joined in the snail-paced procession between opening and closing gates. Here fate intervened in the person of a fellow Etonian, now with the British embassy in Madrid; with his help, and after thirteen hours stuck on the bridge, Bodley and the women crossed into Spain with transit visas.

All hotels in Lisbon were filled with refugees and visitors to Portugal's centenary celebration, but another old Etonian, now a military attaché at the embassy, came to the rescue and found a room in Sintra. This the women occupied while Bodley happily settled for a straw mattress in a place above a shop. The next morning, walking about Sintra, he felt an exhilarating sense of being free to do as he wished. Escaping from Paris to Lisbon he had known only apprehension; sight-seeing was the farthest thing from his mind. Now he was liberated "to be a tourist, to rush round and see things, fling myself into the past, gaze at ancient walls and lovely scenery."

With his road companions off to England by air, the first gazing Bodley did was upon his fellow refugees, usually with a highly jaundiced eye. Many he discovered began to "react disagreeably once the danger of persecution [was] no longer imminent"; they turned into "ungrateful hobos" who complained bitterly about their Portuguese hosts. The Americans among them who had lived for years in France now "looked forward with unbelievable horror to being obliged to live in the country [the United States] which had made it possible for them to lead easy existences in Europe." In the American consulate and the Lisbon shipping offices there were unpleasant scenes as refugees tried to gain advantage by "brandishing bribes or telling sob stories."

American consular officials seemed to Bodley hardworking as well as tactful and sympathetic in the daily drama of dealing with mobs of refugees. But skullduggery could go on without their knowing. Bodley told of an attractive woman, a Madame X, who had arrived in Lisbon as a threadbare exile but within a short time was employed by the American consulate to interpret the languages and dialects of Middle Europe. Her wardrobe and appearance rapidly improved, a transformation not entirely accounted for by her linguistic position. Over time her work evolved into that of an informal receptionist, and Bodley, as a "regular ringside spectator" at the consulate, realized that while some refugees waited for days, others Madame X would immediately usher in for an interview with an official. Outside of work, he also saw her dining and dancing with refugees who appeared in "urgent need of American consular assistance." It was obvious to him that Madame X, having found a lucrative sideline, was quite content to stay on in Lisbon.

In a boardinghouse he moved to, Bodley found it possible to live adequately and dine well on little money. For some formerly prominent refugees, their long stays in such crowded quarters had the salutary effect of making them grateful for their good fortune. But for others the boardinghouses were yet another source of loud disappointment: "These would ceaselessly complain, and never miss an opportunity to tell the pension proprietors who could understand them . . . how many baths there were in their homes, and the important people with whom they had been on intimate terms."

Although technically a refugee who needed his passport stamped every month by police while avoiding questions about why he was still in the country, Bodley considered himself an author living in Portugal and gathering material for his combination escape tale and travel guide. From Lisbon he branched out for touring to Coimbra, Porto, and the far north of Minho, then turned about to the country south of the Tagus and reached Algarve. When he returned to Lisbon the city seemed no less congested with refugees, causing him to propose to some who had been waiting months for visas or ship passage that they might follow his example and travel a bit. As he noted, his "suggestions were not even considered, and attributed to a kind of British bluff in moments of crisis."

When after several months Ronald Bodley left Portugal for New York, he chose a Portuguese ship to lengthen as long as possible his link with the country—a mistake, as it happened, since it revealed him to himself as yet another whining refugee. The ship was an ancient liner ("an 8000-ton, 8000-year-old ship which would take twelve days to cross the Atlantic!"), cots had been added to cabins costing extravagant amounts, the food was terrible, and the tablecloths were dirty. The Portuguese explained their illegitimate profiteering by saying they were doing only what other shipping lines did, which was admittedly true. But there was no excuse, as Bodley archly saw it, when they proved themselves unprepared for proper moneymaking by failing to meet the need of "quite a number of optimists" aboard the ship who "wanted to see the New Year in with appropriate toasts," only to find "there was hardly a bottle of champagne to be had and not one lump of ice!"

★   ★   ★

Frederic Prokosch's clandestine Lisbon of fiction was one Marya Mannes knew from experience, if only briefly and at modest depth. She was a late-comer to wartime Lisbon, arriving just three days before the Normandy landings in June 1944. A decade earlier she had given up a promising edi-torial career with *Vogue* magazine in New York to live with her husband in Italy, where he painted and she turned to an earlier interest in sculp-ture. With the war the couple had returned to the United States, where Mannes's husband became a navy pilot and she joined a group gathering information from refugees of occupied countries who were now in New York. She concentrated on those from Germany and Austria, seeing if they might prove useful to the Office of War Information as broadcasters, writ-ers, researchers, or for intelligence work. Dossiers on those who seemed in any way suspicious she turned over to the OSS.

In the winter of 1943 the OSS recruited Mannes for its Secret Intel-ligence Branch, first using her to organize files, later to read intercepted mail. Eventually she was groomed for undercover work, the training tak-ing place in a New York apartment and involving basic spycraft of picking locks, taking secret photographs, breaking codes, and piecing together bits of paper removed from trash. She considered herself so poor at the work that she expected to be dismissed by the OSS; instead she was sent to the agency's Lisbon station. Her cover as a secret agent, ironed out with *The New Yorker* magazine and reasonably plausible given her time with *Vogue*, was that she would write regular "letters" for the magazine from Portugal and Spain, with her payment coming from OSS funds.

In early June 1944 Mannes left New York on a Clipper flight. Aboard on his way to a posting in Moscow was George Kennan, who provided her—so she later noted—with more information about the current state of affairs in Portugal than had come from her OSS briefings. Her Lisbon mission was vague: along with other correspondents she was to linger in hotels, airports, cafés, and local dives, there gathering whatever informa-tion she could about the Germans. Tall, blonde, and glamorous, she hardly faded into her surroundings; nor did she seem, at least to male admirers, believable as a writer for an important American magazine. "What are you doing over here, a beautiful woman like you, alone?" she would be asked, and reply, "Didn't you know, I am an international spy!" Sometimes the candid gambit worked, but at other times more was required to get sources to open up to her. She asked her Lisbon superior about how far she should go in dealing with amorous and aggressive types. "As far as you need," was the unhelpful answer. By her own account, she performed dutifully in this vein, yet on the whole she felt she collected little useful information despite all-out efforts.

With Allied forces moving across Europe, the OSS had less need for operatives on the Iberian peninsula, and after four months abroad Mannes returned to New York. In a final report to the agency she made a point of urging that conspicuous females no longer be sent to Latin countries as secret agents. If her spy work was of admittedly limited value, her *New Yorker* cover was at least productive, resulting in five published letters—two each from Lisbon and Madrid, one from Barcelona.

The initial Marya Mannes "Letter from Lisbon," cabled to New York on June 25, reported that while the concept of neutrality was familiar and understandable, actually seeing it at work in Portugal was unnerving. Germans sitting beside her in restaurants gave her a sense that a filmlike partition had dropped between them: "They are an exhibit marked 'Enemy. Do not touch.'" Unsettling too was the sight of Nazi posters on walls and German publications in newsstands beside stacks of *Collier's, Time,* and *Life*; so was hearing radio broadcasts coming from Berlin and Vichy as well as from the BBC in London. But however extraordinary life there might feel, Lisbon, and Portugal as a whole, had clearly benefited from neutrality. Portuguese men were alive and at home. Lisbon was clean and strikingly attractive. Luxury items filled the shops. New buildings were going up everywhere. There was rationing, but it was hardly noticeable by foreigners—most of whom, with the refugees now largely absent, were members of the diplomatic corps.

How diplomats went about their work and play in the aftermath of D-Day became the subject of Mannes's second Lisbon letter. Although the city had less wartime importance, the diplomatic community was still large. There were roughly a hundred people in the American mission, several hundred in the British, and several hundred more in various friendly missions—which meant, as Mannes wrote, that a diplomat in Lisbon never need fear of dining alone.

This was comforting since Lisbon diplomats, like diplomats everywhere, preferred their own company. Their association with the local Portuguese was usually limited to a few aristocrats and important families. Many of the top-rank diplomats lived in grand style outside the city on country estates, yet wherever they resided they had access to plentiful low-paid household help for entertaining, which was incessant. The elderly minister from Switzerland, Henri Martin, stood out by giving picnics rather than the usual evening dinners. Sundays were his days, and his invitations were sent out in French verse, with replies expected in kind. Guests met at his home at noon for cocktails, then were taken by cars to a beach, where they went swimming while a long wooden table was set with place cards. After a lengthy and elegant champagne lunch, everyone usually took a nap before they were driven home in time to dress for dinner. "In Lisbon," said Mannes of the diplomats, "everyone eats too much and pays for it with either increased girth or 'Lisbon stomach,' an exhausting ailment."

American and British diplomats, Mannes noted, were known for their hospitality. The Spanish ambassador, Franco's brother Nicolás, rarely entertained, but at parties given by others he was a lively guest. The German diplomats had by this time largely vanished from Lisbon social life, as had the Vichy French, and the Japanese had never sought to take part. (If Japan's diplomats kept to themselves, its secret agents were a familiar presence in the Estoril casino. When a new American secret agent was introduced to the casino, a colleague pointed to the Japanese milling about in the gambling room and said, "Again, watch those fellows. Here in Lisbon they receive information about troop departures from seaports on our West and East coasts, which is relayed to Tokyo and Berlin. The Japanese have an excellent worldwide espionage network. They're contacting agents here in the casino, picking up messages, including dates and hours transmitted by the numbers played at the roulette table—right under our noses.") Since Italy's change of sides, the chargé d'affaires of its legation and his wife had become regulars at all Allied evenings. The embassies and legations were also filled with low-level, unattached young men and women, and they were more likely to seek out such Lisbon nightclubs as Nina's and Galgo's or the Wonder Bar of the Estoril casino. On weekends they might even join the ordinary Portuguese at country fairs, bullfights, and at the beaches.

As for official work at most ministries in Lisbon, Mannes reported that it was conducted within a narrow slice of time. Typically diplomats did no business before eleven in the morning, or between one and four in the afternoon, or after six in the evening. The British, a bit more industrious, began the workday at ten. The Americans, in the face of a wall of diplomatic disapproval, held to a scarcely imaginable nine-to-six schedule, with two hours off for lunch.

Mannes's account of Lisbon diplomatic life flowed over into a promised article for *Vogue* on the city's fashions, her last journalistic effort before returning to New York. While the fashion industry in Paris carried on under German rule, she observed that in Lisbon smartly dressed women—a large number of whom were in or associated with the diplomatic corps— "have every stitch they wear made to order," which meant they were far better turned out than the French. Lisbon abounded in superb fabrics, silks especially, and swarms of able dressmakers followed photos in British and French magazines to turn out charming clothes.

With shoes, in Lisbon the ready-made variety were easily found, but for little more money they could be hand made in any color and leather. For women the standard style was a sling-pump mounted on Portuguese cork wedges of different heights—the cork a necessity for maneuvering the city's steep and cobbled streets. Accessories in Lisbon, Mannes found, were not outstanding but of good quality. Gold jewelry, on the other hand, was "something to lust for." Portugal seemed to be overflowing with gold, and skilled craftsmen could work it into highly original designs. Even the country's "junk jewellery" could be ravishing.

Beyond securing fine attire, the main concern of fashionable women in Lisbon was how to avoid getting fat on local meals, which could feature five courses. Exercise was seldom undertaken, with few inclined to walk and even fewer to use the many beaches for swimming. Anyone who had lived in Lisbon long enough, Mannes concluded, knew the reason: "the will to act dies a slow and painless death, thanks to a climate that seems to breed passivity. *It doesn't matter* . . . and *tomorrow* . . . are the two most popular phrases in Portugal."

★   ★   ★

In writing about the constant round of diplomatic social activity in Lisbon, Marya Mannes caustically observed that it often seemed "unpardonably trivial at a time when most of the world is at war. In many respects it is a life as remote from reality as it is from illusion." Colm O'Donovan tried to distinguish firmly between the real and the illusory, at least in reports he sent to Dublin from his diplomatic post in Lisbon, where he had come in the winter of 1941–1942 as the chargé d'affaires of a newly established Irish legation after earlier assignments in Belgium, Germany, and the Vatican. (The columnist in the *Irish Times* who in October 1941 wrote—as quoted in the epigraph to the opening chapter—that Lisbon must be the most fascinating place in the world, had gone on to remark: "I have often wondered, by the way, why Mr. de Valera has not established an Irish Diplomatic Mission of some sort in Portugal, and I can imagine no more interesting job—except possibly my own—than that of an envoy to the Portuguese capital.") At his post in Lisbon, O'Donovan pursued routine ministerial duties—keeping an eye on the trade flow between Ireland and Portugal, attending to the needs of Irish nationals, and defending Irish neutrality against a backdrop of British and American hostility. He was in no sense a secret agent, but he had been given a secondary mission of informing the Irish government about how Salazar's New State truly functioned.

In Ireland at the time, notably in Catholic, conservative, and intellectual circles but also in the popular press, Salazar was receiving high marks. In addition to steering Portugal's neutrality, he had brought financial order and stability, and his vision of a rural and religious nation seemed all of a piece with Eamon de Valera's conception of the Irish state. The Irish view of Portugal generally derived from secondhand information, and in proposing a legation in Lisbon de Valera had told Salazar that "the Irish Government has watched with sympathy and admiration the great work of reconstruction which you have carried out in Portugal and, naturally, it wishes to observe it more closely." Colm O'Donovan and his colleagues in the Lisbon ministry were to do the observing.

Their dispatches back to Dublin did not question Salazar's political skills, nor did they say much about the repressive nature of a regime underpinned by the military and the secret police. But they made an unequivocal case against the New State as a political template for democratic Ireland. O'Donovan quickly grasped that in Portugal "decisions on all matters, even of no special importance are made at the top," and that there existed a vast administrative gap between that elevated point and the next level. Other diplomats told him that Salazar's task of governing was impossible because of a lack of good subordinates and the overall backwardness of the country. A Portuguese religious figure added that the Irish "had nothing to learn here, that there was no country in the world where there was so much poverty." O'Donovan came to conclude for himself that massive poverty was the country's endemic problem, and that the New State was unable or unwilling to address it.

In a wartime situation he was astonished to find that Portugal had not immediately begun rationing essential food items. The government, so he was told, believed the country could produce enough food, oversee its equitable distribution, and prevent smuggling to hungry Spain. But the system that was set up was clearly inadequate, with a black market flourishing and all foodstuffs available at a price. In September 1943 O'Donovan informed Dublin that "there have been many arrests and punishments of firms found to have been hoarding but these measures, though popular, do not tackle the root of the problem, which lies in the failure of the Government to introduce an effective system of rationing." When rationing was finally established, it covered only the purchase of bread, with other items added as the war went on.

In a report in February 1945 O'Donovan contrasted the meager bread ration of poor workers with the well-fed life of the prosperous. In the same year the secretary of the Irish legation, Patrick J. O'Byrne, wrote Dublin that despite the fact that potatoes were in short supply, "it seems phenomenal how . . . large sacks of them come to light from no one knows where to be sold under the noses of the authorities in the city of Lisbon itself at fancy prices." In a subsequent letter the secretary added that the entire food distribution system was "a long-standing joke with the public."

Social unrest was inevitable, and the Lisbon legation alerted Dublin to various protests—an acute embarrassment for a regime obsessed with keeping order. In January 1944 O'Donovan reported a 20 percent pay increase given to civil servants, the military, and local officials with the intent, so he believed, of warding off more dissent caused by inflation and the black market. The pay concessions, he wrote, "were wrung from the government virtually at the point of a pistol, the twice repeated rioting and strikes of the past twelve months and open revolt among the troops in the Azores having forced them to take action." But the boost in earnings could scarcely keep up with higher prices, and he predicted further unrest.

At bottom, the problem was the way the New State functioned. "The war is of course the great alibi of the authorities in regard to everything that is amiss," O'Donovan noted, "but I think it cannot be doubted that a very large part of the difficulties arises from the system." In making their way through it, ordinary citizens resorted to systematic bribery, which in turn resulted in endless prosecutions of businessmen and civil servants but did nothing to stop corruption. The only well-functioning unit of the government, in O'Donovan's sour view, was the propaganda office, which managed to plant in the media a continuing stream of favorable accounts of the regime.

"I leave Portugal with a definite opinion that the present regime will not last," O'Donovan said when he returned to Dublin in February 1945. Although his prediction was more than two decades wide of the mark for Salazar's government, his observations in Lisbon had cast the dictator in a new light. The "sympathy and admiration" that de Valera had expressed to Salazar did not cease in Dublin; Portugal was still admired for its fervent Catholicism and anti-communism. But the Irish government's view of the Salazar era now included reports from the field of poverty, corruption, inefficiency, and unrest.

7

CELEBRITÉ DE PASSAGE

Lisbon always had its current *celebrité de passage*. They came out of the wings, took their bow and passed on again, like the characters in some charity revue.

—Polly Peabody, *Occupied Territory*

Faced with a wartime Lisbon that produced more rumor than news, Hugh Muir fell back on interviewing notable figures passing through the city. There were many possibilities. America's Wendell Willkie, on his way home after visiting England, turned out to be an ideal subject, both congenial and talkative. Britain's Clement Attlee, on the other hand, was glacial in his reserve, and after a half-hour conversation had managed to say nothing. Dorothy Thompson, America's top-paid woman columnist, was good copy but as interested in interviewing Muir about British war attitudes as he was her. H. G. Wells was not copy of any sort since he could be interviewed only through his literary agency, at so much per word. Gracie Fields was returning from singing for the troops in England when she chatted at length with Muir while having her shoes shined. Vivien Leigh and Laurence Olivier were at first unnoticed when they slipped into Lisbon, then for days afterward dominated the attention of the press.

When Noël Coward came in from New York in June 1940 he confided to Muir his irritation with those complaining about his absence from his native England, insisting that all his time away he had been on official war-related jobs. However hard that might have been to swallow for someone with a reputation as a sophisticated entertainer, it was in fact true, though Coward could not fully reveal to Muir or anyone else what he was up to. He recalled in his memoirs of being cornered once by a reporter for London's *Daily Express* whose assignment, as he informed Coward, was to find out "just exactly what war work you are engaged in." Rather than brush him off, Coward solemnly explained that, though he was not at liberty to go into it, he could assure him it was routine activity lacking in mystery. He would be grateful if the reporter would take his word for this and just regard him as an ordinary Englishman rather than a show-business celebrity. The resulting story for the newspaper was so misleading that the British censored it, leaving Coward for once in his life on the side of suppression of information.

The misadventure with the reporter took place in Paris. Even before the war broke out Coward had been recruited to join a group of businessmen and celebrities traveling in Europe to gauge local opinion, the effects of Nazi propaganda, and whatever else seemed worth reporting back to London. With the war he was given a new job of setting up in Paris a propaganda bureau that would operate in conjunction with France's Commissariat d'Information, which was also drawing on the services of such literary figures as André Maurois and Jean Giraudoux. On September 5, 1939, two days after England declared war on Germany, Coward was flown to Paris to start looking for an office. Soon he found a place as well as a flat to live in, then waited out the limbo of the phony war. He dutifully went to the office each morning and did what work there was to do, yet even when the real war got under way he felt he was accomplishing little that mattered, and even this he was unable to communicate to friends and family back home.

In April 1940 he got a reprieve from his Paris assignment in the form of a six-week visit to the United States to report on attitudes toward the war. Coward was delighted to get back to familiar territory, though scurrying away from a war zone to lush neutrality did him no good as far as public comment went.

> The despatch of Mr Noël Coward to the States [wrote one London newspaper] can do nothing but harm. In any event, Mr Coward is not the man for the job. His flippant England—cocktails, countesses, caviare—has gone. A man of the people, more in tune with the new mood of Britain, would be a better proposition for America.

Almost at once, though, the flippant Englishman was having drinks and dinner at the White House and discussions with President Roosevelt. In California he met with British actors working in Hollywood—Cary Grant, Ray Milland, Claude Raines, Charles Laughton, among them—and expressed his view to England's ambassador in Washington that their absence from home in wartime was creating a bad impression in America.

He himself left in early June by way of a Clipper to Lisbon, from where he intended to take rail service Paris to resume his propaganda work. The flight, he recalled, was the "acme of comfort" with good food, drink, and weather. "We might just as well," he added, "have been sitting in a well-appointed bus that had become somehow embedded in the sky." Some of the pleasure fell away when, between the Azores and Lisbon, the pilot informed passengers that Italy had joined Germany in the war.

The news was not unexpected, but what Ambassador Walford Selby said the next morning over breakfast at the British embassy was. Coward had brought his overnight bag with him, expecting to leave directly for the railway station; Selby, however, strongly advised him to stay in Lisbon. The situation in Paris was deteriorating rapidly, with the embassy unable to establish any contact for the past ten days. Coward protested that he had to get back, if only to help with the evacuation of his office staff. The ambassador held firm: if Coward canceled his train reservation he would see to it that he had priority on an air flight to England. Coward reluctantly agreed—and later realized that Selby might have saved his life. The train he intended to take reached Paris just ahead of Hitler's army.

During Coward's wait in Lisbon the ambassador put him to work giving a talk at a hastily organized affair at the Royal British Club before club members and a few journalists. Coward had no time to prepare his remarks, which left him—oddly for a seasoned performer—extremely nervous. He read to the audience a news report from the *New York Times* about the rescue at Dunkirk, talked about British-American relations, and ended up with hopeful comments about the outcome of the war. The *Anglo-Portuguese News* reported that his listeners were deeply moved by the talk—and added, surely to Coward's delight, that he had been engaged in government propaganda work in Paris since the start of the war. Still ahead for Coward before he left Lisbon was propaganda work in the form of a broadcast over local radio and a cocktail party at the British Club for a group of Portuguese journalists.

On Coward's journey to England his plane made a stop in Bordeaux. He went to a café inside the airport, seeking coffee well laced with cognac, and found, with the Germans in Paris, an atmosphere of hysteria. When he returned to the plane it was surrounded by police holding off refugees desperately hoping to become stowaways on what might have been the last civilian flight to touch down in wartime France.

Shortly ahead for Coward was more important and highly hush-hush government work, or so he thought. William Stephenson, the coordinator of British intelligence in the United States, who in the shadow world operated under the code name Intrepid, had offered him—as Coward recalled—"a job which, in his opinion and in mine, would be of real value to the war effort, and would utilise [*sic*], not only my celebrity value, but my intelligence as well." He was again on a Clipper flight from New York to Lisbon when, during the stop in Bermuda, a telegram from Stephenson told him the job was over before it could begin—"nipped in the bud," Coward recorded, "by High Authority in London." He was badly disappointed but, in retrospect, consoled himself with the realization that, had be become one of Intrepid's troops, he might never have written *Blithe Spirit*, the light comedy that opened in London on July 2, 1941—the audience crossing planks over rubble from a recent air raid to reach the seats—and ran there continuously until March 9, 1946.

★   ★   ★

Just after Noël Coward left Lisbon, the Duke and Duchess of Windsor appeared. For the former King Edward VIII and the woman he had given up his throne to marry, the chic American double-divorcée Wallis Simpson, there would be no gatherings or public remarks at the Royal British Club, nor a word about their presence in the *Anglo-Portuguese News*. If Coward was a figure the British were eager to showcase, the Windsors were best kept out of sight until they could be shipped elsewhere as soon as possible.

Coward, who while on duty in Paris had been on the same social circuit as the famous couple, hinted in a letter at the reason for the cold shoulder. While dining with them one evening, the Duke had held forth on the Germans as "awfully dogged and capable of really surprising endurance in the face of practically anything, which is very important." Herbert Pell was more forthright after a similar evening of dining with the Windsors in Lisbon. If the couple had any notion to moving on from Lisbon to the United States, the American envoy wanted his view on record—as he immediately cabled Washington—that their "presence in the United States might be disturbing and confusing" since they "desire apparently to make propaganda for peace."

The Windsors had lived in France since their marriage there in 1937, the same year they visited Germany at Hitler's invitation. When the phony war ended, the Duke held the rank of major general and was acting as the British liaison officer at French military headquarters in Paris. With the

Wehrmacht moving on Paris, he received permission to leave the city and joined the Duchess at their villa in Antibes. There was much dithering about what to do next until the British consul in Nice advised immediate flight. On June 19, 1940, a four-vehicle convoy set out for Spain, the consul in a Bentley with diplomatic plates in the lead, the Duke and Duchess following in a Buick. Bringing up the rear was a hired van carrying the Duchess's maid and the Windsors' voluminous luggage.

At the Spanish border the van's driver was refused transit papers, and he, the maid, and the cargo of luggage turned back to Antibes. The other vehicles ventured on without difficulty to Barcelona and then Madrid, where the Duke and Duchess were taken under the wing of Samuel Hoare. The ambassador was an old friend of the Duke, but his guests would prove troublesome due to the controversy surrounding the abdication and, of more immediacy, the Duke's public association with a policy of accommodation with the Third Reich. The moment the Windsors reached Madrid, German propaganda had gone into high gear, as Hoare glumly informed Prime Minister Churchill.

> Under the pressure of the German machine the Spanish press declared that you had ordered his arrest if he set foot in England, that he had come here to make a separate peace behind your back, that he had always disapproved of the war and considered it an even greater mistake to go on with it etc., etc.

Given the stories swirling about, it was wise to move the couple from Spain to Portugal. So it came as cheering news for Hoare when London told him that a British flying boat was leaving on June 22 for Lisbon, and he was to invite the Windsors to head there at once.

But at this point Salazar intervened. The Duke's younger brother, the Duke of Kent, was about to arrive in Lisbon for the centenary celebration, and the prime minister wanted nothing to draw attention from the importance the royal visitor lent to the event. It would be "inconvenient and undesirable," Salazar told the Portuguese ambassador in London, to have the two royals in Lisbon at the same time, and pointedly added that "if the Duke of Windsor does come while his brother is here, I shall let him know by all means that we should be grateful if he retired for that period to another part of the country." So Hoare was instructed by London to change plans and hold the Windsors in Spain until the Duke of Kent was safely out of Portugal.

Having the couple settled in the Ritz Hotel in Madrid while the Spanish rumor mill kept clanking away was worrying enough, especially when stories circulated that Hoare had joined the Duke in urging a separate peace. But the ambassador also had to confront the possibility that the Duke might dig in his heels and refuse to leave Spain. The British royal family was grimly opposed to having him—and especially "her," as the Duchess was cuttingly known at court—back in England, and as result he had been assigned no new wartime work. Hoare suggested to Churchill that, given the Duke's love of the sea, a naval command of some sort might entice him back. And he added darkly: "If the chance is lost [to get the Windsors back to England], there will be a prince over the water who will be a nuisance and possibly an embarrassment."

Unknown to Hoare and Churchill, the Germans were actively plotting to keep the Duke and Duchess exactly where they were. A Spanish friend of the Duke made it known that the Windsors could remain in the country as guests of Franco's government and occupy a castle in Andalusia. Presumably the Duke had no knowledge of the German hand behind the invitation, but the possibility of wartime exile in a neutral Spain had appeal, especially if no position was forthcoming in England, the royal family continued putting up barriers, and Churchill held to the view that the couple should return home without conditions.

A resolution of the situation was still in doubt when, after nine days in Madrid, the Windsors reached Lisbon on July 3 to find the city overflowing with refugees and visitors to the Portuguese exposition. They did not settle in Lisbon but in the secluded summer villa in Cascais of Ricardo Espírito Santo. Originally they had planned to take rooms in the Palácio in Estoril, but the hotel manager had informed the British embassy that he was short of space and adequate security and had made arrangements for them to go to Cascais. Their host was a young, dashing, immensely wealthy Portuguese banker who was apparently drawn to the social cachet of having the Windsors as guests.

Although Espírito Santo had English connections and had recently entertained the Duke of Kent, he maintained friendly relations with the German minister in Lisbon and was generally thought by British intelligence, where he was referred to as "Mr Holy Ghost," to be pro-German. Whatever the host's political views, they were not enough of a stumbling block to prevent British Ambassador Walford Selby, yet another old friend of the Duke, to be on hand to greet the Windsors at the villa. Selby had reason to hope, in any case, that the couple would spend little time with Espírito Santo since two RAF flying boats had already reached Lisbon and were scheduled to leave within forty-eight hours, as required by Portuguese neutrality regulations. He also had in hand for the Duke a telegram from Churchill, dated July 1, that in effect was a military order to return to England under threat of a court martial. Angry but bowing to the inevitable, the Duke agreed to leave promptly. The travel schedule rapidly put together had the Windsors boarding a flying boat in Lisbon late on the night of July 4 and arriving in Britain the next day.

The arrangement lasted only to the following morning, when the Duke drove to the British embassy in Lisbon and learned that Churchill had changed course. A telegram from the prime minister, dated early that morning, offered the Duke an appointment as governor general of the Bahamas. If accepted, Churchill added, the Windors might leave for the islands directly from Lisbon. Stunned by the sudden development, the Duke went back to Cascias and informed the Duchess; after lunch together he returned to the embassy and typed out a brief reply to Churchill: "I will accept appointment as Governor of Bahamas as I am sure you have done your best for me in a difficult situation." News of the appointment was leaked by the BBC in London on July 9 and made worldwide headlines in morning papers of the 10th.

A planned two days in Cascais now stretched to four long—and, as later would become apparent, perilously uncertain—weeks. British agents and the Portuguese secret police heavily guarded Espírito Santo's villa, and the Duke and Duchess were instructed to leave the residence only in the company of armed escorts. The Duke made a courtesy call on President Carmona, who lived in a former royal palace in Cascais, and he was a regular on the golf course in Estoril. He also managed to attend a bullfight in Lisbon, where he was recognized and applauded by the crowd. But for the most part the Windsors remained sheltered in the villa in the company of embassy figures, Espírito Santo and his wife, and a small circle of friends.

Marcus Cheke, the embassy's press attaché, saw to it that nothing about the couple's activities came to the notice of the British community in the pages of the *Anglo-Portuguese News*. David Eccles, highly placed in the embassy with the Ministry of Economic Warfare (and about whom more in a later chapter), often dined with the couple, his impressions of them swinging back and forth. Following one meeting, he wrote his wife back in England that "I wouldn't give ten shillings for Wallis, she is a poor creature. . . . He's pretty fifth-column, but that's only for you." But in a subsequent letter Eccles acknowledged "being seduced by the Windsors who have made a dead set at me, and by heaven when they turn their united charm on, it is hard to resist. . . . And he has a confiding manner of talking that is dangerous to a degree. Anyway I dine twice a week. They are the arch-beachcombers of the world."

London's advice that the Duke make his own travel arrangements from Lisbon proved easier said than done. The Duchess preferred ships to planes, and the usual sea route to the Bahamas was to take an American Export Lines vessel from Lisbon to New York, then in New York make accommodations to move on to the islands. With the shipping firm's vessels overwhelmed with refugees and others fleeing Europe, sailing arrangements could not be made before August 1. The Windsors had planned on a New York interlude before moving on to the Bahamas, but the British ambassador in Washington stepped in and told London it would be undesirable to have the couple pass through New York since it might set off bad publicity. London agreed and so informed the Duke, which brought forth a furious reply that he had been "messed about quite long enough." Churchill nevertheless kept the door firmly closed. "His Majesty's Government cannot agree to your landing in the United States at this juncture," the Duke was told. "This decision must be accepted." The British government made possible the diversion of the *Excalibur* from New York to a landing in Bermuda by paying the American Export Lines a fee of $17,500. And to try preventing any last minute weakening of the Duke's resolve to board the ship, on July 28 it sent Walter Monckton, his close confidant and legal adviser, to Lisbon to remain with him in the final days.

On July 30 the news blackout surrounding the Duke and Duchess was finally lifted with an announcement of their departure at a press conference in the British embassy. The Duke thanked Portugal for its hospitality and fielded a few innocuous questions before sherry was served. The next day he played his last round of golf, and that evening he and the Duchess gave a large party—a "great farewell to Europe," as the Duchess described it in a letter—at the Aviz Hotel. On August 1 the Duke had a private meeting with Salazar, which had been arranged by Espírito Santo, before heading to the harbor in the company of Monckton and Espírito Santo. The Duchess had boarded the ship earlier, and a news story noted that she, other passengers, and well-wishers on the pier had "tapped their collective heels for forty minutes past sailing time . . . while waiting for the Duke of Windsor."

Unlike the mere mortals packed like sardines on the refugee ships leaving Lisbon, it was still possible in the early period of the war for the Windsors to travel in high style aboard the *Excalibur*. They had to themselves a suite of cabins enclosing a private veranda, where they entertained diplomats and their wives who were sailing home on the ship. Also with them on the vessel were their dogs, fifty-two pieces of luggage, four wicker crates of Madeira and port, and their Buick and a travel trailer.

After reaching Bermuda, a Canadian cargo ship carried them to the Bahamas and a waiting group of American reporters and photographers gathered in Nassau. *Time* magazine gleefully observed about the Duke's new position that the former King of England was now the overseer of "29 islands, 661 cays, 2,387 rocks in the Northern Caribbean"; commander-in-chief of "six officers and 124 men in the native constabulary"; and ruler of 13,000 white subjects, 55,000 black, and a floating population of several thousand tourists—largely American."

★   ★   ★

With the Windsors finally planted in Nassau, the royal family and the British government had accomplished a common aim of getting them safely tucked away for the duration. And the Duke now had an official position, if a demeaningly minor one, in his country's wartime service. But left behind in Portugal was a tale of German intrigue that, up to the very moment of sailing, had sought to subvert just such a conclusion.

What was known to the Germans as Operation Willi, a brainchild of Foreign Minister Joachim von Ribbentrop, was a plot to lure the Duke back to Spain and thereby have him readily available to German power in Europe. In Salazar's Portugal he would be far less so, and in England or Nassau wholly beyond reach. To convince the Duke both of the benefits of residence in Spain and the perils of a journey to the Bahamas, the Germans had dispatched to Lisbon as their emissary Miguel Primo de Rivera, a son of the former dictator of Spain and a close acquaintance of the Duke. How the Duke responded to Primo de Rivera's blandishments is uncertain, but in any case Ribbentrop did not leave the work of persuasion solely to the Spaniard. A rising young SS officer (and later head of the SD, the security and intelligence service of the SS), Walter Schellenberg, was sent to Lisbon with instructions from Ribbentrop that the Duke was in sympathy with the German cause and had to be pried from the grip of the British, by force if necessary. Schellenberg was also authorized to deposit fifty million Swiss francs in a Spanish bank if the Duke would issue a public statement separating himself from British war policy.

In memoirs published after the war, Schellenberg declared that he believed Ribbentrop's project was based on an exaggerated reading of careless remarks made by the Duke together with excessive weight given by the foreign minister—a former German ambassador to London and supremely confident of his knowledge of all things British—to peace sentiment in England. Nonetheless Schellenberg, when he reached Lisbon, loyally set about carrying out his mission. He had an American car brought to Lisbon for his use as well as a faster car for two agents who accompanied him. He procured exact information about the floor plan, servants, and Portuguese and British guards of the villa where the Duke and Duchess were staying. By spreading about ample sums of money, he replaced some of the Portuguese guards with his own people and placed informants among the servants. Within five days of his arrival in Lisbon, he boasted, he "knew of every incident that took place in the house and every word spoken at the dinner-table."

A prime element of the German plan had been to entice the Windsors to leave Cascais for a hunting-party holiday near the Portuguese border, then have them step over—by mistake or with a push—into Spain. Schellenberg soon determined that the Duke was not interested in the invitation, but he believed his annoyance with close surveillance by the British gave Germany another opening for turning him away from his appointment to Bermuda.

Schellenberg had a Portuguese police official tell the Duke that Portuguese guards at the villa needed to be increased because of information that he was being intensely watched by both British and German intelligence agents. Then the German agent organized an evening of stone throwing at the windows of the villa, which in turn brought about a police search of the interior. He followed up by planting rumors that British agents had started the ruckus in order to make the Windsors uncomfortable in Portugal and eager to leave for Bermuda. Finally, a bouquet was delivered to the villa with a note that read, "Beware of the machinations of the British Secret Service—a Portuguese friend who has your interests at heart."

"These things were, of course, fairly unimportant," as Schellenberg rightly acknowledged. But they at least gave him some actions he could report to Berlin, though plainly far more was expected when a telegram from Ribbentrop told him, "The Führer orders than an abduction is to be organized at once." Schellenberg believed the command was ultimate folly—taking the Duke to Spain against his will would surely reduce or eliminate whatever feeling he had for the German cause—and decided he would not carry it out. He arranged that twenty more Portuguese police were assigned to guard the Duke, which caused the British to increase their security as well, and then conveyed to Berlin the information that a stand-off existed in Lisbon and asked for more instructions. Two days later he received an enigmatic telegram: "You are responsible for measures suitable to the situation." Schellenberg's interpretation was that Berlin was backing off the kidnapping plot.

But it did not follow that Ribbentrop was admitting failure. Chief among a flurry of last-minute efforts to keep the Windsors in Portugal was a long telegram he sent on July 31 to Baron Hoyningen-Huene in Lisbon. The Duke was informed about it the following morning by his host, Espírito Santo, but shown nothing in writing. He was told only that the source of the message was an authoritative German. In essence the message informed him that Britain would soon be attacked, and if he remained in Europe and cooperated with Germany a happy future would be available for him. On the other hand, if he went to the Bahamas, Churchill would surely hold him there forever, though it still might be possible to maintain some channel of communication with Germany.

Precisely how the Duke responded to this indirect contact is unknown. In a lengthy report back to Ribbentrop the day after the Windsors left Portugal, Hoyningen-Huene took note of the obvious—"every effort made to detain the Duke and Duchess in Europe . . . was in vain." Yet he passed along the verbal and perhaps self-serving impressions of Espírito Santo that the Duke had shown interest in the message and was open while in the Bahamas to keeping contact with a secret confidant in Portugal, who would be Espírito Santo himself.

Meanwhile Schellenberg, who had had no role in the final effort to reach the Duke, made a last effort to cover himself with Berlin. He planted a story that the British planned to drive home the danger the Duke was in from Germany by planting a time bomb on the ship that would explode a few hours after departure, causing great alarm though sparing the Windsors. Alerted to the bomb's existence, Portuguese police searched the ship several times before it sailed, and security measures were strengthened— further evidence that Schellenberg could put forward to persuade Berlin that kidnapping the Duke was an impossibility. Relieved but still aware he must return to Berlin to face Ribbentrop and Hitler, Schellenberg retreated to a tower room in the German legation and peered through binoculars as the *Excalibur* took the Duke and Duchess down the river to the sea. "The chapter," he stoically reported in his memoirs, "was closed."

★　　　★　　　★

It seemed unlikely that any couple could come near matching the celebrity status of the Windsors, yet less than a year after they departed there appeared in Lisbon another and less decorous combination of royalty and romance whose ongoing lives kept the cable lines humming with news and speculation. Ex-King Carol II of Romania, popularly known as the playboy monarch, and Elena (Magda) Lupescu, his flame-haired Jewish mistress, had begun their flight from war in September 1940 when, in the royal palace in Bucharest and under German pressure, Carol turned over the throne to his eighteen-year-old son Michael and boarded a special eleven-car train headed to Yugoslavia. With him was Lupescu, a royal entourage that included the court chamberlain, Ernest Urdăreanu, and a king's ransom in paintings and other state valuables.

Eventually the royal cars were coupled to the *Orient Express*, which wended its way through Switzerland, Italy, France, and into Spain. At Barcelona the royal cars were uncoupled, and Carol was informed he could remain in Spain but not move on as planned to Portugal. In holding him the Franco regime was presumably bowing to the wishes of Berlin, and despite a torrent of letters Carol sent to gain his release—among them, one to President Roosevelt—his confinement in Spain, and close surveillance by armed police, went on for months. Carol and Lupescu were not, though, living rough. They were allowed to move to the Andalusia Palace Hotel in Seville and occupy an entire floor with a dozen servants and—in a typically detailed press inventory of the possessions accompanying the couple's odyssey—"this property: 152 trunks, a collection of rifles, three automobiles, four Rembrandt paintings, a valuable stamp collection, a big china collection and four dogs."

As time went on, Ernest Urdăreanu traveled to Lisbon to look into possible future arrangements for Carol—and to draw for correspondents a sympathetic portrait of the ex-monarch. "Had Carol been Hollywood's latest discovery," Hugh Muir noted, "he could not have been better served by his Press agent" than he was by the loyal Urdăreanu. The correspondents learned that in food-short Spain Carol existed mainly on cold ham. "I send him a parcel of food each week—tea, coffee, sugar, and sardines," said Urdăreanu. "I can't send him anything perishable, and he's tired of living on ham. Only this morning on the telephone he told me he had asked for chicken, but was told there wasn't any to be had. Not only is he half-starved, but he has to change dollars at a ruinous rate to pay for everything he has."

Each time correspondents saw him, Urdăreanu had fresh stories. An especially dire one was that Carol had decided to go on a hunger strike and die rather than stay on in Spain. "Once his Majesty makes up his mind it is difficult to make him change it," said his spokesman. "I know him intimately, and he is quite capable of carrying out his threat." Other stories involved Lupescu. One had it that Carol wished her to flee to another country to escape the grasp of the Gestapo, but she had refused. "Not long ago I myself pleaded with her to let me get her away to safe hiding," Urdãreanu confided, "but she turned on me angrily and said she would share the King's fate."

The correspondents got wind that Carol's situation in Spain was soon to change when it was learned that a certain Madame X was making frequent trips from Portugal to Seville, each time returning garbed in one of Lupescu's fur coats and draped with her jewelry. The change came on the early morning of March 3, 1941, when Carol and Lupescu went out the side door of their hotel and into a limousine packed with luggage. Carol was behind the wheel, and used his experience with racecars to speed along twisting mountain roads toward Portugal in a carefully arranged flight. Just before reaching the frontier the pair changed to the vehicle of a known smuggler, crawled into a space beneath the back seat, and were unceremoniously delivered to Portugal. The next day Lisbon and Madrid correspondents cabled stories of the sensational escape in which, according to Spanish authorities, Carol and Lupescu had been just fifteen minutes ahead of the hotly trailing police when they reached Portuguese soil. The more probable truth was that Spain, fully aware of Carol's intended escape, had permitted it happily to rid the country of his presence while not openly defying Germany. To rescue from Spain the rest of his luggage, valuables, cars, and dogs, Carol needed only to send an emissary to Seville to pay his $852 hotel bill. Lupescu, so it was said, had phoned Seville to dismiss her chauffeur and maids and tell them their salaries would accompany payment of the bill.

Carol and Lupescu stayed in Lisbon in a home owned by Augusto Lopes Joly, a wealthy Portuguese businessman and friend of the ex-king. Now that Carol was free of Spain, Urdãreanu kept reporters at a distance; not until March 8 did the former monarch give an interview in Joly's home to the Associated Press, the American wire service presumably chosen because Carol had hopes of ultimately entering the country. He said little during the interview beyond thanking Portugal for granting him asylum and the American public for showing sympathy for what he had gone through. He steered clear of political matters, mentioning only that Salazar's policies interested him and he meant to read up on them.

Carol was thin and pale when he reached Lisbon, and it was thought he looked forward to a long rest. Lupescu, on the other hand, was said to be fretful and wished to put the Atlantic between the couple and the Germans, though not before taking a turn at the casino in Estoril. Described by one source as a "plump lady in red lace with a diamond-and-ruby brooch pinned above her monumental bosom," when she won a pile of money at a card game she took no chance of trying to double her gain. Nor did her good luck cause her to linger in Portugal. Fewer than two weeks went by before tickets were bought under assumed names for the *Excambion* sailing to Bermuda and New York. On the afternoon of departure, Carol and Lupescu, wearing dark glasses, slipped on board along with four dogs and locked themselves into a suite.

Their attempt at secrecy did not extend to their luggage piled on the dock, and the press was soon alerted to full details of their journey. (As apparently were the Germans. André David, a French writer sailing on the vessel, claimed its whole civilian crew was made up of Nazi informants.) The luggage was calculated at "about two railway freight carloads plus a mountain of hand luggage and trunks," with the pieces clearly labeled "His Majesty King Carol, Cuba via New York." Ernest Urdăreanu, who was also on board the ship, conveyed to the press a message from Carol thanking Portugal and explaining that he had decided to go to Cuba among other Latin American countries because of its neutrality and favorable climate. "I still need a rest," Carol added through his spokesmen, "and it goes without saying that there will be no political activity on my part while away from my own country."

After arriving in Bermuda, where Carol and Lepescu were given red-carpet treatment and spent several restful weeks before going on to Cuba, intense press coverage resumed. The lovers observed appearances of a sort by refusing to pose together in photographs or newsreels, nor was Lepescu present at interviews given by Carol. When they disembarked the *Excambion* the couple had taken separate carriages to their hotel suite, though later they were seen together in the hotel's lounge. Close attention was paid to how smartly both were dressed—and to Lepescu's plump figure, a matter of long-standing public interest. One woman's reaction upon arrival, "Oh, she's not fat at all," seemed to carry the day, though there was some sentiment that Lepescu was heavier than she appeared due to "tricks" of dress. A reporter sidestepped the issue with a remark that she "looked her reputed age of 41, but no more."

Wisely, Carol in a news conference in Bermuda had waved off any expectation that en route to Cuba he might stop in the Bahamas and pay a call on another former king. The press could only salivate about how an encounter might have gone between the paramour of one and the wife of the other.

★   ★   ★

Hugh Muir observed about Carol that during his time in Lisbon the entire world seemed interested in his fate, but "most of the people [of the city] never knew that he was in their midst." In the same early period of heavy refugee movement—from the summer of 1940 through the spring of 1941—a similar anonymity shrouded the presence of important artists, writers, and intellectuals sent to Lisbon by Varian Fry's rescue group in Marseille. The last thing Fry wanted for his charges was attention from the local press corps. Other notable figures reaching the city through their own efforts or with aid of agents other than Fry kept the same diminished profile, leaving Lisbon largely in the dark about the procession of cultural stars who graced it for a time. They boarded ships as refugees, and across the Atlantic emerged as celebrities.

The Lisbon route taken in their car by the French novelist Jules Romains and his wife was so surprisingly trouble free that they gave themselves time leisurely to inspect the cathedral at Burgos. Once quietly installed in Estoril, they took the electric train into Lisbon to be with friends departing on ships. Their own voyage on the *Excambion*, in the company of such countrymen as the composer Darius Milhaud and the Franco-American writer Julien Green, was uneventful until arrival in New York, where they were set upon by reporters patrolling the docks. "Celebrities Forced to Flee France Arrive Here by Way of Lisbon," announced a newspaper, and in an accompanying story the new arrivals told of their plans for a new life in America.

When three weeks later the same liner again departed Lisbon, it carried the American photographer Man Ray and the composer Virgil Thomson. When Ray fled Paris by train, he had with him two valises and a small camera loaded with color film; expecting to return in a short time, he had placed his car on blocks to save the tires and had drained the battery. Along the way south he joined up with Thomson, whom he had first met in Paris in the 1920s, and the two traveled together. At the Spanish border German guards were suspicious about the luggage of the men: while Ray had little, Thomson had fourteen pieces, including six trunks filled with musical scores he hoped would be performed in the United States. A suspicious guard thought the scores might be some sort of wartime code, but when an inspired Thomson said they were Mozart sonatas, the guard sighed with appreciation—"Ah, Mozart!"—and waived the pair through.

In Lisbon, waiting for space on a ship, Ray and Thomson spent their time sitting in cafés, looking in at museums, swimming on the beaches, and listening to Portuguese music in nightclubs. One night they came upon a local fair with booths attended by pretty girls in native dress, and Ray pulled out his camera and took pictures. One of the girls could speak French and gave him her address so he could send her a print. When ship tickets came through they were for mattresses on the floor of the *Excambion*'s library, and Ray and Thomson departed for New York along with Salvador Dalí and his wife, the French film director René Clair, and scores of American students returning home from European universities. In the cramped conditions Ray slept with his camera under his pillow, but it was stolen nonetheless. The ship's purser thought it might be recovered on landing, but Ray never saw it again. "If the thief had only left me the film," he later wrote, perhaps with the pretty Portuguese girl who spoke French in mind, "I would have pardoned him." When the liner reached New York, Dalí was singled out by the press as the celebrity most worth questioning.

Antoine de Saint-Exupéry, the French writer and aviator, luckily found a hotel room in Estoril after he reached Lisbon. But the nearby casino and the exile throngs within only intensified a feeling of unreality that was rooted in his qualms about leaving France in her darkest hour. The figures at roulette or baccarat—men in stiff shirtfronts, women with glittering pearls—stimulated what he called "a kind of anguish—the same feeling that you experience at a zoo when looking at the survivors of an extinct species." Just as Lisbon and its ongoing centenary celebration seemed to him to be playing at happiness, the exiles played at clinging to their past identities: "They still pretended to be someone. They clung obstinately to some semblance of meaning. They said, 'That is who I am. . . . I come from such and such a town. . . . I am the friend of so and so. . . . Do you know him?'"

Despite his glum mood, Saint-Exupéry went public in Lisbon by giving a lecture at the École Française, where he was said to have wept during his emotional remarks yet afterward was in good enough form to sample vintage port at a reception in his honor. He gave a second talk in Lisbon, this at an engineering school, where he again spoke with deep feeling about various personal ordeals out of which he had forged a fresh definition of life: "To live is to be conscious that you are not dead, second by second, as bombs burst around you, which amounts to an extraordinary anguish." On board the *Siboney* for New York, Saint-Exupéry's cabin mate was the French film director Jean Renoir, who had also reached Lisbon via North Africa. Through the efforts of the American documentary filmmaker Robert Flaherty, Renior had secured a visa to the United States, and Flaherty was on the docks to greet him when the ship arrived. But it was the aviator-writer reporters flocked to, and through an interpreter he responded to a long list of questions about the collapse of France and military tactics. He had nothing to say about his time in Lisbon. When the interview was finished, the interpreter, a young wire-service reporter in awe of Saint-Exupéry, asked him to autograph his interview notes. Veteran reporters present did the same.

★   ★   ★

In the spring of 1941 the writer Kay Boyle and the art collector Peggy Guggenheim languished in close company for several trying weeks in Lisbon while waiting for seats on a Clipper flight. In Marseille both had been members of Varian Fry's Committee of Patrons, with Guggenheim also one of his important financial backers. But their connection had a history that went beyond Marseille to expatriate Paris between the wars—and to the troublesome fact that Boyle's current husband, the American painter and writer Laurence Vail, was Guggenheim's ex-husband. Since Vail had custody of the two teenage children of the Vail-Guggenheim union, Boyle was now their stepmother. For these and other reasons there was no love lost between the two strong-willed women, yet they were brought together in Lisbon by Guggenheim's ability to pay the high tab for their need of eleven spaces on a Clipper.

As was their custom, the women were accompanied by men. With Boyle in Lisbon was Laurence Vail, though their marriage was in shambles. She had fallen in love with a handsome, considerably younger, and moneyless Austrian baron with the imposing name of Joseph von und zu Franckenstein. To get her lover an American visa, Boyle had sought the help of Varian Fry, whom she impressed with her determination and striking appearance. "She was like her books: intense, emotional and very finely wrought," he wrote. "She always wore small white-bone earrings cut in the form of the many-petaled flowers of the edelweiss, and her blue eyes seemed like [the dark-blue mineral] lapis lazuli." Visa in hand, Franckenstein had left Marseille on the ill-fated voyage of the *Winnipeg* to Martinique. When Boyle, now in Lisbon, learned that he had been detained in Trinidad and would not be allowed to enter the United States without $500 deposited in his name in a bank, she approached several people for the money. Laurence Vail's mother, at her son's urging, finally came through, and eventually Franckenstein reached Miami. (In 1943 he became Boyle's third husband.) Guggenheim, who had refused Boyle's plea for financial help, angrily told Laurence Vail: "No, I'll never forgive Daze [Kay Boyle] for the way she acted. . . . And you stood for it. You let her walk all over you. Why you even lent her money so she could get her lover out of France . . . you were an angel to that fiend."

With Guggenheim in Lisbon was her present lover, the white-haired German artist and pioneering surrealist Max Ernst. (Varian Fry, who seemingly had an eye for earrings, wrote of Guggenheim that hers were "long crescents from the ends of which hung tiny framed pictures by Max Ernst.") Later, in the United States, the art patron and the artist would briefly become man and wife, but in Lisbon their affair was seriously complicated by the presence of Leonora Carrington, a dazzlingly attractive young British surrealist painter whom Ernst considered his true love. Carrington was also waiting for transport to America; with her was a Mexican journalist and diplomat whom she would later marry, yet she spent her days with Ernst, who followed by spending his nights carousing in Lisbon with Laurence Vail. Guggenheim was distraught at Carrington's reappearance, but emotional upheaval was a familiar state and she managed to endure this latest episode. One day Ernst and Carrington came to her hotel room, and she had the sense that Ernst was being returned to her. Whether from relief or generosity, when time came to leave Lisbon in the company of Ernst, she said she would also pay Carrington's plane fare to New York. Carrington declined the offer and took a ship.

Along with men, Boyle and Guggenheim had seven children with them, ranging in age from two to eighteen. Six bore the surname Vail, with Guggenheim the mother of the two oldest; the seventh was a teen-aged French girl, a schoolmate of one of the Vail daughters, who was being taken to America to stay with her grandmother in New Orleans for most of the war. (She would be the only member of the traveling group whose Clipper ticket Guggenheim did not provide.) With no schooling or friends to occupy them, the children were bored and restless. After two weeks in Lisbon—Guggenheim in a hotel with the French girl and her son and daughter; Ernst, the Vails, and their children in a pension—the entire party shifted to a hotel near the sea in Monte-Estoril to escape the city heat. Now there were beach outings to help fill the time and jaunts to nearby Cascais and Sintra. But within the confined quarters of the hotel, where the group occupied an entire floor, the crosscurrents of stress and grievances were only increased. "Our life in the hotel was rather strange," Guggenheim said of the time.

Boyle, generally thought a caring mother when not devoted to her typewriter, chose to avoid the strangeness by checking into a Lisbon clinic for what she claimed was sinus trouble. She visited Monte Estoril on Sundays, leaving the bulk of parenting to her husband and Guggenheim but mostly in the hands of the older children. Dinners with everyone around a vast table in the hotel dining room were often the occasion for emotional scenes touched off by Laurence Vail bemoaning to the children his wife's absence. Once in a café he became so angry when one of them defended Boyle that he lifted the top off a table and flung it at the child. He missed, but the infuriated owner ushered everyone from the premises.

To lighten the atmosphere of hotel life for the children, the adults tried stunts meant to be amusing. Max Ernst came to dinner one night with his hair dyed turquoise with mouthwash. Laurence Vail picked up a young prostitute and treated her to ice cream at a café in Estoril. The girl became attached to the group—she was "our only native friend," Guggenheim noted—and each day she was found waiting for them on the beach. For their own entertainment, two of the adults, Guggenheim and Ernst, went swimming at midnight. Once Guggenheim did so in the nude, despite the strict swimwear code enforced by the police, while Ernst—apparently less concerned with her arrest than his financial future—wailed from the beach, "What will become of me if you drown?" After the swim Guggenheim dried herself off with her chemise, following which she and Ernst made love on a raincoat spread on rocks. Thereafter they went to a hotel bar, where she hung the chemise on the bar railing. "Max loved my unconventionalities," Guggenheim remarked of the escapade.

On July 13, 1941, the four adults and seven children at last flew off to New York. Reporters and photographers were on had to greet their arrival, as was Laurence Vail's mother, who earned Guggenheim's gratitude by reimbursing her for the cost of the tickets of her son, his wife, and their children. News stories listed the names and ages of all the children and gave capsule accounts of the adults. Guggenheim, identified as Miss Marguerite S. Guggenheim, and Maxmillian Ernst were said to be traveling with the Vails. It was announced that Ernst, as a German citizen, would be taken to Ellis Island for a hearing. Guggenheim revealed that her collection of modern art, shipped to the United States three months earlier, had apparently reached the country safely. She valued the pictures at fifty thousand dollars.

But most press attention went to the Vails and their flock of children. An Associated Press photographer got all six together for a seated picture, with Laurence Vail holding a pipe and looking remote, and Kay Boyle, in the motherly center of the group with her dark hair setting off her white earrings, holding her youngest child on her lap. Later, Boyle gave a long interview to Robert van Gelder, which appeared in the *New York Times Book Review*. "Kay Boyle, Expatriate," as the headline had it, said that after the struggle of escaping Europe she was anxious to begin writing again, especially short stories for the popular magazines. "While waiting in Lisbon," she noted, "I read all the American magazines," but she acknowledged it might be difficult to fit her manner of writing to the requirements of mass-market editors. "Does my style seem involved?" she asked rhetorically. "It doesn't to me."

★   ★   ★

After the great refugee rush through France and Spain tapered off, most Lisbon celebrities were on their way to or from Britain or the United States or had come to Portugal on goodwill propaganda missions. With the latter, the whole point was to make as much public use of them as possible. When the eminent photographer Cecil Beaton arrived on such a mission in the summer of 1942, however, no one at the British embassy had been told exactly what he was to do.

Engaged in war work for the Ministry of Information, Beaton had come from more than three months in the Middle East, where he had been on loan to the Air Ministry to photograph RAF activity in Egypt and elsewhere. The delicious contrast of Lisbon's security and abundance gave him the feeling of being back on prewar holidays in Spain or the south of France. The British embassy booked him into the Aviz Hotel, which with its thirty-odd rooms struck him as more a magnificently overdone Victorian mansion than a hotel. He basked in the luxury of an ornate bedroom with a balcony, then went for a three-course luncheon in the hushed, rose-tinted dining room. The only suggestion of a world at war was that a shortage of coal for electricity meant the hotel's lights went off after ten o'clock at night, a slight inconvenience that paled when he realized he could send letters from Lisbon to friends—Gertrude Stein, for one—still living in oc-cupied countries. How strange it was, he also noted, to realize "one could even have written to an enemy if one wished."

Beaton spent his unhurried days on taxi tours of the city with the knowledgeable British press attaché Marcus Cheke as his guide. One memorable trip was up into the Alfama along, as Beaton recorded in his diary, "huddled streets hung with balconies, bird-cages, morning glories and washing." From the heights of the ancient area of Lisbon, the jumbled roofs below seemed to Beaton's artist's eye "like a patchwork quilt with the texture of coarse weaves." An excursion to Sintra and its "Cinderella-like" structures gave him the different sensation of coming upon a "startling display of architectural fireworks."

When word finally came that London wanted him to photograph Salazar and Carmona, other major government figures, and a host of local grandees in an effort to enhance pro-British feeling in the country, Beaton finally had his mission. He set about making the complex arrangements for sittings, with embassy figures cautioning patience, and then more patience. Over time, as he noted in his diary, an unvarying ritual developed when he at last approached his subjects: "first the production of cards, then a short delay, long corridors, at last effusive welcomes." Following his final sitting—an admiral who commanded the Portuguese navy—Beaton dropped his Rolleiflex on a stone staircase. Unwisely, it was the only camera he had carried with him when he went to the Middle East—and thus a convincing sign, so he decided, that he should return to England. He was back in London when in December 1942 fifty-six of his Portuguese portraits were exhibited at a Lisbon studio.

★   ★   ★

Rose Macaulay's stay in Lisbon a few months later also resulted in productive work in the form of research for an historical account of the long record over eight centuries of journeys to Portugal by her British countrymen. Beyond absorbing some feeling for Portuguese life as the traveling English might have known it and looking into local research material, there was no vital need to make a dangerous wartime effort to follow in their wake. London libraries held nearly all the material she needed. But Lisbon offered something she herself badly required at the time: a respite from bombed London and personal grief.

On the night of May 10, 1941, a German bomb destroyed the building in London where Macaulay had a much-cherished flat. "I now have nothing," she wrote a friend. "I came up from Liss [a village in Hampshire where one if her sisters had a home] at night to find Lux [Luxborough] House no more—bombed and burned out of existence, and nothing saved. I am bookless, homeless, sans everything but my eyes to weep with." It was her bookless state that seemed most cruel. At age sixty, Rose Macaulay, with some twenty novels as well as works of poetry, essays, and criticism behind her, was a notable figure in British literary circles. Books were her life, and though she could and did find another London flat, her large library of some fifteen hundred volumes, most dating from the sixteenth to eighteenth centuries, was hard to replace.

A more painful and enduring blow came in July of the following year with the death of Gerald O'Donovan, the great love of her life. Irish born, a former Catholic priest, a minor novelist, and married, O'Donovan and Macaulay had met while both were British civil servants during World War I, and their relationship continued off and on until his death. An intensely private person despite leading an active social life, Macaulay chose to keep the relationship hidden, and much that is believed about it comes through hints in her letters and her fiction. What is certain is that she was deeply affected by the death of the man who, in a letter to a friend, she acknowledged as "the dearest companion."

> He died on July 26th. I had spent the day before with him, and he knew me and talked to me, and had been asking for me, but was only partly there. Then, late in the evening, he became unconscious and died next morning. I wasn't there then, but didn't want to be. I feel empty and dead, and without purpose. I'd like to get right away—to Portugal if I could. . . . I think an entire change of scene would help me begin life again.

The desire for a change of scene was understandable, but why flee to Portugal? The obvious explanation was that travel to the country, which she had never visited, was the focus of her planned book. Another reason was that Portugal was accessible in wartime. Switzerland was equally neutral, but Macaulay noted in a magazine article written shortly after her return from Lisbon that in contrast to Portugal it was a "a moated fortress, impregnable, enemy-barred, without approach." Since her book subject tied into the extended history of Anglo-Portuguese relations, Britain's Ministry of Information considered her a goodwill ambassador, and space was found on the London-Lisbon air route. Before she set out on the journey, Portuguese censorship reared its head with a requirement that books she was taking with her had to be brought to the embassy in London to be read (in theory) and sealed. Amused, Macaulay considered including a work that might cause a modest flap.

She arrived in Lisbon in early March 1943 and stayed until May. She settled into a modest hotel on the Avenida da Liberdade, one she later recommend to her friend E. M. Forster, and was given morning work space in a room at the British Institute. The Institute held the collection of the Lisbon branch of the Historical Association of Great Britain, which had gathered material on the British in Portugal. She was helped in her work, and in negotiating Lisbon, by a young staff member, C. David Ley, who spoke and read Portuguese, frequently contributed articles on literature and history to the *Anglo-Portuguese News*, and would become a close friend. Another important contact in Lisbon was Susan Lowndes, a well-known member of the local British community and married to the editor and publisher of *APN*, Luiz Marques. Lowndes was equally well connected in England. Her father, Frederick Lowndes, worked for the London *Times*, and her mother, Marie Belloc Lowndes, was the elder sister of the prolific man of letters Hilaire Belloc and a successful author herself.

An avid bicyclist in London, in Lisbon's tilted streets Macaulay did her touring on foot and on the yellow trams, which struck her—as she wrote in an article for the *APN* contrasting Lisbon and London—as pretty as wasps humming on their way. Compared to London's monotonous gray, Lisbon from every street was a riot of color:

> golden ochre, rose-pink, terra cotta, the clear deep delphinium blue which is the blue of Lisbon, torrents of mauve wisteria cascading over a white wall, orange trees on the terrace above it, banners of gay garments pennanting a steep street from balconies of wrought iron. . . . And always sudden glimpses, down the steep slant of a street, of the Tagus, dull green, steel-blue, golden brown, grey-laced with jade green currents . . . and, faintly or deeply indigo beyond it, the line of the Setúbal peninsula.

Climbing with her into twisting lanes of the Alfama and to the heights of St. George's Castle, Susan Lowndes thought Macaulay "looked not unlike the typical Englishwoman in a French farce: tall and very thin, her face crowned by a flat straw hat." With David Ley as a guide, Macaulay also went to Sintra to see where Byron, among the British travelers she was writing about, had stayed. In Porto she did some poking about in archives, and she also visited Caldas da Rainha, where a few refugees were living while awaiting permanent resettlement.

"Portugal was lovely!" she wrote in a letter when she was back in London in May. "I had two months there, and enjoyed it all the time. Very interesting architecture; glorious weather; charming towns; wine, fish, and lots of material for my Great Work on the English in Portugal." Ahead for her were two years of unceasing research before the manuscript was delivered to her usual publisher, William Collins, and promptly turned down, as she anticipated might happen, as far too long. Jonathan Cape then agreed to publish if the manuscript were radically cut. In September 1946 roughly half the work, more than four hundred pages, appeared as *They Went to Portugal*. Although the book sold surprisingly well, the second half did not see print until 1990 as *They Went to Portugal Too*.

★   ★   ★

While Rose Macaulay was in Lisbon the British Institute had given a reception for her and two other prominent visitors from England, Harold Spencer Jones, the Astronomer Royal, and Leslie Howard, the film actor, causing her to quip that one looked at the stars and the other *was* the star. The slender, urbane Howard, who in 1939 had played Ashley Wilkes in *Gone with the Wind* and appeared in *Intermezzo* with Ingrid Bergman in her first American screen role, had left Hollywood in August of that year to direct, produce, and perform in inspirational films in his native Britain. In April 1943 he was persuaded to fly to Lisbon at the behest of the British Council to begin a lecture tour of Portugal and Spain that was meant to bolster the Allied propaganda effort in the two neutral countries. Accompanying him was Alfred Chenhalls, his accountant and financial adviser.

From Portella airfield the two were driven into Lisbon, the city unusually warm for April and Howard suffering in his English tweeds. Following a press reception at the local office of the British Council, Howard and Chenhalls switched their lodging from the Aviz Hotel to the Atlântico in Estoril. Here the air was cooler, and Howard had a room with a view of the beach and the sea, the setting reminding him of California. Dictating to a secretary, he began work on a scheduled lecture about film; more demanding was a second talk, to be given at the National Theater before an audience of professors and critics, on *Hamlet*. In addition to these and other appearances, Howard was the center of attention at a whirl of receptions, parties, and such special events as the showing at the British embassy of *Pimpernel Smith*, the anti-Nazi film he had made in Britain. At one gathering he met the British violin virtuoso Philip Newman, who had fled to Lisbon in 1942 and stayed on to become professor of violin at the National Academy of Music.

From Lisbon, Howard and Chenhalls went to Madrid for another round of talks, film showings, and receptions that went on for nearly two weeks. Back in Portugal, the pair returned to the Atlântico for a period of rest and sun before returning to England. When it was learned that Howard's film *The First of the Few*, considered one of his best, had never been seen in Lisbon, the interlude was lengthened while a print was shipped from London and invitations hastily went out for a private screening at Estrela Hall of the British embassy. The film was intended to add final luster to the propaganda value of Howard's Lisbon-Madrid tour, all the more so since one of those attending the showing would be the present Portuguese propaganda chief, Tavares d'Almeida, who afterward would host a dinner in Howard's honor at the Aviz.

To ready themselves for the flight home, just before the film screening Howard and Chenhalls moved from their Estoril hotel to the Aviz. On the morning of June 1, 1943—after the film had been shown the previous evening, the dinner party given, and Howard received a gold medallion from Tavares d'Almeida for the best film of 1942—Howard and Chenhalls left for the airport and their return flight to England. The British airliner they flew, the *Ibis*, was shot down over the Bay of Biscay, with all passengers and crew lost.

In a front-page story the *New York Times* reported that the aircraft "was apparently the victim of German planes on unusually active reconnaissance along the seldom-molested air transport lane from neutral Portugal." It was generally understood, the story added, that commercial liners flying between Lisbon and London carried only civilians, so it was unlikely the plane was mistaken for a military transport. Later information revealed that a swarm of eight German Junkers flying from Bordeaux had deliberately attacked the unarmed liner. "I am being followed by strange aircraft," the Dutch pilot had reported over the radio. "Putting on best speed. . . . We are being attacked. Cannon shells and tracers are going through the fuselage. Wave-hopping and doing my best." On two previous occasions the *Ibis* had taken fire from the Luftwaffe, but this was the first, and would be the only, fatal attack on the Lisbon-London route.

That the plane's wreckage and the bodies of its passengers and crew were never found only intensified the question of why the scheduled and clearly marked airliner flying a daylight route had been targeted. The attack could have been simply a mischance of war. One of the German airmen that day gave weight to the possibility when, well after the event, he recalled the anger of the Luftwaffe group upon returning to their base in France:

> On our return, we were told that we had shot down a civilian aircraft with VIPs on board. I can still remember quite clearly that we were all rather angry particularly because no one had told us, before, that there was a scheduled flight between Lisbon and the UK. If we had, it would have been an easy thing for us to escort the DC-3 to Bordeaux.

A glaring omission in the explanation was that the Germans were fully aware that for nearly three years there had been regular civilian flights between Lisbon and Britain.

But what eventually turned a puzzling situation into a mystery, one enduring to this day, was a famous political actor suggesting that he played a role in the death of the famous film actor. Winston Churchill, in his memoirs of World War II, wrote as follows about his return with Anthony Eden to England after his discussions in North Africa with General Eisenhower and other military leaders about the invasion of Sicily.

As my presence in North Africa had been fully reported, the Germans were exceptionally vigilant, and this led to a tragedy which much distressed me. The daily commercial aircraft was about to start from the Lisbon airfield when a thickset man smoking a cigar walked up and was thought to be a passenger on it. The German agents therefore signaled that I was on board. Although these neutral passenger planes had plied unmolested for many months between Portugal and England and had carried only civilian traffic, a German war plane was instantly ordered out, and the defenceless aircraft was ruthlessly shot down. Fourteen civilian passengers perished, and among them the well-known British film actor, Leslie Howard.

Churchill added that the Germans were impossibly stupid if they believed that "with all the resources of Great Britain at my disposal I should have booked a passage in a neutral plane from Lisbon and flown home in broad daylight."

The thickset man in Churchill's account was presumably Alfred Chenhalls, who bore some physical resemblance to the British leader and smoked cigars. But subsequent investigations of the loss of the *Ibis*—especially in books by the British journalist Ian Colvin in 1957, by Howard's daughter Leslie Ruth Howard in 1959, and by his son Ronald Howard in 1981—set out other and more detailed explanations for what took place. Among them was that Leslie Howard was the focus of the attack because of his anti-Nazi filmmaking and the possibility that during his speaking tour of Portugal and Spain he was also gathering information for British intelligence. Another was that other passengers were the targets: a British wolfram expert; Tyrell Shervington, general manager of Shell Oil in Portugal, who had been a source of information to British intelligence in Lisbon; Wilfrid Israel, a German Jew who had been in Portugal and Spain as part of an effort to transport young Jewish refugees to Palestine (about whom more in the following chapter); and a British inspector general of embassies whom the Germans might have mistakenly identified as a military general. (When toward the end of 1943 Aline Griffith, a newly trained OSS agent on her way to the Madrid station, took a Clipper flight from New York, she was surprised it was going to Lisbon by way of Bermuda. She had thought the flight was traveling through Brazil and Morocco. "The route is changed for extra precaution," explained an American four-star general aboard the flight. "The Germans attack everything crossing the Atlantic. Not long ago, they downed a plane from Lisbon with Leslie Howard aboard. They were after a friend of mine, an English general. Unfortunately, he was a friend of Howard's, too. We suspect the German agents were able to trace his whereabouts because of the movie star's publicity.")

The most astonishing explanation was that those aboard the *Ibis* were sacrificed to keep a precious wartime secret. In his book about the flight, Ian Colvin noted that at the time of the attack the Luftwaffe was in a state of day-and-night alert over the Bay of Biscay—and the only reason for doing so, in his opinion, was Churchill's intended flight home. Although they might only have been part of a deception campaign, rumors had been widespread in Lisbon that Churchill would be passing that way. "It would not have been possible," Colvin wrote, "even with the best intelligence, to clock his departure and pinpoint his aircraft. So a wide net was spread in those days, and a high state of alert maintained." While there was no evidence that the Germans had issued a "Kill Churchill" order, Colvin leaned in that direction. Nonetheless he switched in his book's final pages to an entirely different explanation by relating a story attributed to an Allied intelligence officer who in late 1944 had been sent to Australia to lecture military figures about the necessity of secrecy in event of an invasion of Japan. To make his point, the officer told of an airliner shot down the year before, after leaving Lisbon.

As Colvin related the officer's story, British intelligence had intercepted a message from a German transmitter in Lisbon giving Berlin names, obtained by German-paid agents watching Portela airport, of passengers flying from Lisbon to London on June 1, 1943. Such messages were not uncommon, but with Churchill flying home at the same time this one drew special attention. The British could remove passengers named in the message from the plane or cancel the flight altogether, but doing so might alert the Germans that their coded messages were being read by the Allies. "That would lead," Colvin wrote, "to enemy wireless silence in Lisbon, the picture would become blurred, the mastery of intelligence might be lost." And he added: "It was decided at the top, so I am told by an officer who was present at the lecture [in Australia], that no action was to be taken." So the *Ibis* was allowed to fly to guard the all-important secret that the Allies were penetrating German radio traffic.

Colvin closed his book with the reservation that he could not officially confirm what he had related about the Australian lecture. In 2005 the American historian Douglas L. Wheeler maintained, in a brief newspaper account, that the plane carrying Leslie Howard had indeed been sacrificed to shield the Allied intelligence program known as Ultra, operating from Bletchley Park in England, which decoded German messages. From information provided by former intelligence officers, Wheeler concluded that for several years intelligence figures from the United States, Britain, and Australia were taught that Britain had intercepted a German radio message that suggested the plane would be attacked. But to keep the Germans both from learning about Ultra and to protect Churchill, who was making a return flight to England at the time, "the British"—as Wheeler wrote—"did not warn, cancel or divert" the flight of the *Ibis* "but let it take off to its doom."

8

HOLDING OUT HOPES

The world is at war and I am comforting refugees, holding
out hopes which, when I hold them out, I myself am almost
convinced cannot be fulfilled.

—Howard Wriggins, *Picking Up the Pieces from Portugal to
Palestine*

When Varian Fry flew into Lisbon in August 1940 to begin his secret
rescue assignment, one of his fellow passengers on the Clipper was
Alexander Makinsky, a Rockefeller Foundation medical doctor on his
way to the Unitarian Service Committee's recently opened office in the
city. Passing through Portuguese customs, Fry, with Emergency Rescue
Committee money attached to his leg, stayed close to Makinsky, hoping it
would appear they were both visiting dignitaries and thus be given the same
casual inspection. Neither had any difficulty, and for Fry it marked the start
of a period in which he often leaned for help on figures associated with the
Unitarian Service Committee (USC). Before leaving for Marseille, Fry ac-
quainted himself with such other Lisbon aid organizations as the Red Cross,
the YMCA, the American Friends Service Committee, the American Jewish Joint Distribution Committee, Catholic Relief Services, and HICEM,
the merged name of three Jewish immigration societies. Yet both in Lisbon
and Marseille his tie with the Unitarians would have special importance.

"In those days Rescue was our work," Charles R. Joy of the USC's
Lisbon office wrote of his group's mission, the capital letter perhaps only
a matter of emphasis—or calculated to distinguish the Unitarian task from
what most established charities typically characterized as refugee relief or
assistance. In origin the USC was modeled on the Quakers' American
Friends Service Committee, and while cooperating in the work of this

171

and other such aid efforts, it had a particular concern with rescuing illegal refugees and anti-Nazi figures wanted by the Gestapo. More broadly, what set apart the USC, and helped make it a dependable collaborator for Fry's work, was an open commitment to the Allied cause at a time when most relief workers went about their duties under a protective umbrella of war-time neutrality. When the Quakers launched a program of widespread food distribution in France, the Unitarians voiced strong opposition on grounds the supplies would surely end up in German hands. As the war progressed there would be other displays of partisan action that distanced the USC all the more from colleagues in other humanitarian endeavors. In an interview given in the 1960s, Elisabeth Dexter, who with her husband, Robert Dexter, directed the USC's Lisbon office following Charles Joy's tenure, made emphatically clear the distinctive position of the USC:

> We rather specialized in illegals for two reasons. One was that the illegals on the average were outstanding people. . . . Then, also, we specialized in illegals because neither the Joint [the Jewish Joint Distribution Committee] nor the Quakers who both had offices there [Lisbon] liked to work with illegals. They did at times, but it was really against their principles because both felt that they could help more people in the long run if they did not go counter to the laws of the country. . . . I know that sometimes they helped people when they weren't supposed to, but they were very glad indeed if we could take them off their hands.

The Unitarian project in Europe had begun in early 1939 when a young minister and his wife from Massachusetts, Waitstill and Martha Sharp, came to Prague to work with the Czech Unitarian Church and assist in refugee movement to the United States and other countries. The Sharps returned home with the start of the war, but their overseas work was carried on with the formation in May 1940 of a service committee based in Boston, with William Emerson as chairman and Robert Dexter as executive secretary. In June a Lisbon office was opened as European headquarters, and the Sharps returned to take charge. When they learned that among the refugees now streaming south through unoccupied France there was a great shortage of food and especially milk for infants, they devoted their first weeks in Lisbon to getting condensed milk shipped by rail to Marseille. They traveled to Marseille themselves to arrange for the distribution, with Martha staying behind to continue the work in France after Waitstill returned to Lisbon to set up aid activity with refugees who had reached the city. The Unitarian office soon became Fry's Lisbon connection by supporting his clients as they arrived and helping locate ocean transport. As Waitstill Sharp recorded, involvement with Fry turned into a routine part of his duties:

> The days defy description. They were filled from seven o'clock in the morning until midnight, and sometimes after, with interviews, searches for persons about whom the Emergency Rescue Committee had cabled from America, or their agent [Fry] had cabled from Marseille; appeals and interventions at the American Export Line, the Pan American Airways, the French Consulate, the [Portuguese] International Police . . . the British Embassy, and, daily, at the American Consulate.

Waitstill Sharp's link with Fry would also extend to taking a personal hand in helping get his troublesome client Lion Feuchtwanger out of France and into Portugal. As Fry's stellar guide Leon Ball led the writer and his wife over the Pyrenees, Sharp, on his own way back to Lisbon after another trip to Marseille, took their luggage by rail across the border into Spain—as Fry himself had earlier done with the luggage of Heinrich and Golo Mann and Franz Werfel and his wife. Then on the train from Barcelona to Lisbon, Sharp handed Feuchtwanger his briefcase to carry, the large Red Cross emblem on it meant to provide a measure of disguise on the journey. As it did. In a railway bathroom, a Gestapo officer in an adjacent stall spotted the briefcase at Feuchtwanger's feet and initiated a brief chat but otherwise ignored him. At the Portuguese border, however, an American journalist called out Feuchtwanger's name as he waited in a customs line, causing others to take notice. Sharp firmly told her to keep quiet, which she did after complaining she was only looking for a scoop.

Sharp had one more role to play in the extended drama of getting Lion Feuchtwanger to safety. In Lisbon in late September 1940 the two boarded the *Excalibur* together, the writer using Martha Sharp's return ticket since no others were available, while his own wife waited for another ship. In New York, press reports noted that Feuchtwanger was accompanied by Waitstill Sharp of the USC, who had obviously been part of a "thrilling rescue" but, unlike the talkative literary celebrity, was saying nothing about it to reporters.

With her husband in America, Martha Sharp returned to Lisbon to continue the work of getting milk and food supplies out to children in unoccupied France. She also began the frustrating labor of satisfying immigration requirements for getting a select number of refugee children and adults from Marseille to Lisbon and finally to the United States. When she found transport for herself to New York in early December

1940, she brought with her two children and four adults; when another ship docked on December 23, she was there to greet the rest of her refugees. A press story the following day reported that among the *Excambion*'s 185 passengers were "twenty-five refugee children of five nationalities, the first group of its kind to come here since the war began." Martha Sharp was left unmentioned, though it was noted that the children, ages three to thirteen, had come under the joint auspices of the Unitarian Service Committee and the United States Committee for the Care of European Children, and that representatives of the two organizations had met the ship.

Martha Sharp continued working with the USC in the United States as a member of its board of directors and an effective fund-raiser for the organization. In February 1945 she returned to Lisbon to take over the USC office temporarily after the current directors, Robert and Elisabeth Dexter, suddenly resigned following a dispute with officials in Boston. (Waitstill Sharp had earlier taken a position with a relief agency in Cairo.) After learning that Portugal had asked the American ambassador to close down the office as a "friendly gesture to Portugal"—presumably a reaction to the USC's long involvement with illegal refugees—she went to work trying to patch up relations with the Salazar regime.

Another chore was negotiating with the secret police to get Spanish Republican refugees, who at the time made up the largest number of the USC's Lisbon clients, out of Portugal to permanent settlement in Mexico and Venezuela. She also visited refugees held in Caxias, the ancient fort-turned-prison outside Lisbon, where upgrades to first- and second-class cells were available for inmates able to pay for them, with third class—often with dirt floors and without beds or mattresses—the freely provided accommodation for everyone else. Other visits were made to USC clients in Caldas da Rainha, a three-hour ride from Lisbon aboard a wood-burning train, where she found that the thousand or so refugees still there had formed a hospitality center in a pink farmhouse surrounded by flowers but lacking any plumbing. Although classes were offered in the center, and books and magazines were available, the atmosphere of idleness was stifling since no one, regardless of prior training or education, was allowed to work while awaiting resettlement. Before leaving Lisbon for good in September 1945, Martha Sharp managed to get all of her clients freed from the town, with more than half of them off to permanent destinations.

★   ★   ★

When Charles Joy followed Martha and Waitstill Sharp in the USC's Lisbon office, he expanded ties his predecessors had formed with Fry's group in Marseille, and developed as well USC efforts to get medical supplies into unoccupied France and operate medical and dental clinics for refugees. The work with medical supplies was so successful that the International Red Cross began using the USC as its distributor of such material throughout southern France. In time it became apparent to the Lisbon office that its increased involvement in Marseille required an office there and a resident director overseeing operations.

Through Donald Lowrie of the International YMCA, Joy learned of Noel Field, a tall, lean, attractive American who had been raised in Switzerland, graduated from Harvard (as had Joy), worked for the U.S. State Department, and in 1936 left government service and came to Geneva with the League of Nations. During Spain's civil war he had served as a League representative in the country, and later he had an active role in repatriating foreign fighters who had joined the Republican cause. That Field had a Quaker background was no disqualification in Unitarian eyes, and Joy's superiors in Boston were delighted to find an American with Field's experience who was fluent in French and German and already located in Europe. Unknown to Joy, the USC leadership, and many others who knew him, Noel Field had for some years led another life as a dedicated Communist.

After Field and his wife, Herta, were hired to run the new Marseille office with a joint yearly salary of $5,750, they took an apartment in a shabby furnished house and plunged into the work. Both to the Lisbon office and to Unitarian officials in Boston, the couple seemed motivated wholly by selfless devotion to refugee assistance. That Noel Field was known to give away his ration tickets and spend part of his salary taking hungry exiles for meals in black-market restaurants only added to their appeal in USC eyes.

A continuing chore of the Marseille office was purchasing medical supplies from French pharmacists, as required by Vichy, and getting them to a free clinic operated in Marseille, to a hospital in Toulouse, and to infirmaries that had been set up in area concentration camps. When concern surfaced in Boston that medical supplies sent to the camps might wind up in German hands, a Unitarian minister from Staten Island, Howard L. Brooks, was sent to Marseille on a temporary mission to work with the Fields while also checking on the distribution process. After reaching Lisbon, Brooks spent some time observing Charles Joy's USC operation— and enjoying a city he found colorful, vibrant, and given over to pleasure yet tense with rumor about an imminent Nazi invasion. German tourists roamed the streets, though few believed they were really tourists, and there was repeated talk of Panzer divisions poised on the Spanish border, even an armored division in Spanish Morocco prepared to set sail for Portugal. A U.S. Coast Guard vessel lay in the Lisbon harbor to evacuate up to two hundred Americans in event of a German incursion.

In Marseille Brooks found that medical supplies for the camps were delivered by car by a refugee medical doctor on the USC staff, René Zimmer. When Brooks accompanied him on a two-week tour, he found that the supplies indeed reached those they were intended for, though frightful conditions in the camps created an urgent need for food and clothing as well as medicine. Back in Marseille, Brooks joined the USC staff in a host of other ongoing chores.

> There were [he noted] the education projects in the concentration camps. Also, there was a rehabilitation program for Lorraine refugees at Puycelci [a village in the south of France] which required much time and thought. Finally, there was the intricate package system whereby we sent to internees the permitted 500 grams of food, whenever possible, as provided by our Lisbon office. . . . One of Mr. Field's important duties was to check constantly that these parcels were properly delivered.

Brooks also found time to get involved with Varian Fry in work that, due to his committee's covert tactics, caused him to be "ostracized by other relief workers who secretly admired his work." Brooks went beyond admiration by spending time each day at the CAS office so, as he put it, "at least one American would be working there." Dangling at the time between waiting for a successor who never arrived and Vichy authorities preparing to expel him, Fry would remember that he "tried to get one or two of the other American relief workers to step into my shoes, but with the exception of Howard Brooks of the Unitarian Service Committee, no one would, and Brooks could do so only for a very short time—after that he had to return to the States."

When Brooks finally did go home, he brought with him a favorable opinion of Noel Field, both personally and as head of the USC's Marseille office. He apparently had no awareness that Field was a Communist, and for good reason. After Brooks met with a destitute German Communist and gave him money, Field had chided him for dealing with a political figure and thereby putting the USC at risk in the eyes of Vichy authorities. Nonetheless some in Marseille had begun wondering about Field. Donald Lowrie was told by Czechs he had known in Prague that Field had ties to Communists, and he passed on what he heard to Hugh Fullerton, the American consul. Members of Fry's committee had also noticed Field's interest in Communists and had gotten into the habit of referring those who came to them to the Unitarians. But there was no firm knowledge about Field's political loyalties, and in Marseille at the time more pressing matters claimed attention.

In fact, while Field was running the USC office he was also deeply caught up in Communist activity. He made frequent trips to Switzerland for meetings with party members from various countries and became involved, among other things, in sending Unitarian food parcels to German comrades held in concentration camps and helping German Communists in France make illegal escapes to Switzerland. Under instructions of a Communist leader in Marseille, Field also sent Unitarian parcels and money to people the local party was caring for, afterward carefully listing the names so he could make proper accounting to headquarters in Boston.

Through his various activities Field learned of Communist undergrounds in Western and Central Europe, information that had value for the Allied wartime effort. Just as Charles Joy had found him for the USC in Marseille, another Unitarian leader came forward to draw him into American intelligence operations. Robert Dexter, who while serving as the USC's executive director was now running, in conjunction with his wife, the group's Lisbon office, was also secretly working with the American OSS and reporting to Allen Dulles, the agency's European chief based in Bern under the cover of special assistant to the American ambassador. Elisabeth Dexter later disclosed that her husband's work for Dulles "was to carry a large sum of money for the OSS to a well-known labor leader in France, and do several other errands, and he was to contact OSS men in Madrid and in Marseille for further information and to make reports." Others in the USC hierarchy may have known and approved of Dexter's cooperation with the OSS. There was no question, at any event, of the USC's position in the war effort.

Robert Dexter was seemingly unaware of Field's ties to Communists, but he knew that Field's work with refugees in Marseille had given him contacts that might interest Dulles. He took Field to Bern to meet the spymaster—the two had first met during World War I when Dulles, then doing intelligence work in Zurich, often visited the home of Field's father, an eminent expatriate biologist, and his British mother—and Field signed on with the OSS. The decision apparently caused him no ideological conflict since the agency and the Communists were united in the fight against Nazi Germany. Nor apparently did it matter to Dulles, given the Allied alliance with Russia, that Field might also be receiving orders from Moscow. Field seems never to have been on Dulles's payroll, though he was given money that in turn was passed on to Communists; his main effort was as a middle-man bringing potentially valuable people to OSS attention.

When the Allies landed in North Africa and German troops poured into unoccupied France, Noel and Herta Field made a hasty retreat from Marseille to Geneva. (American relief workers who stayed behind in Marseille were told by the Germans to leave for Lourdes, from where they were moved to Baden-Baden in Austria and interned until, early in 1944, they were exchanged through Lisbon.) With permission of the USC, the Fields set up a Unitarian office in Geneva and were back in business as a relief center, working now with refugees in Switzerland. At the same time Noel Field carried on his involvement with Communist groups and with the OSS. With the Normandy invasion at hand, he helped organize French Communists in support of the military thrust. Later, following the liberation of France, the USC opened a Paris office while Field remained in Geneva with a new and challenging position of European director of the entire Unitarian service program.

After the war ended Field went to Boston to report to USC leaders on his prolonged period of European relief work. There was great pride in what he had accomplished, and admiration for how little he had asked for himself. Questions arose about his zealous aid of Communists—at their most extreme, they asked whether as director of European operations Field had in reality turned the USC into what amounted to a Communist-front organization—but nothing at the time seemed genuinely serious or could not be explained as the carping of scattered individuals. Eventually, however, concern about Field, heightened by furor in the United States over Communist affiliation, reached a point where the USC sent a representative to Europe to investigate. Nothing was proven to full home-office satisfaction, yet Field was eased out of the USC by the closing, in October 1947, of the European director's office. He was offered a position in Boston but declined, and in 1949 he vanished behind the Iron Curtain.

*   *   *

If Noel Field had a polar opposite it was Howard Wriggins. A member of the pacifist Society of Friends, Wriggins had sought and received conscientious objector status after graduation from Dartmouth in 1940, then entered a four-month training program with the Quakers' American Friends Service Committee (AFSC), an honored nonsectarian organization with roots extending back to World War I. Another four months followed as an apprentice with the group's refugee division in Philadelphia before Wriggins, age twenty-three, was sent to Lisbon in May 1942 to replace a man moving on to a Quaker post in Marseille.

The AFSC's Lisbon office had opened a year earlier, in the spring of 1941, the refugee flood off its peak but still high. The office director, Philip Conrad, was an older man, fluent in Spanish and Portuguese and with long relief experience. Wriggins operated as his assistant, the two working along with a secretary and a Portuguese errand boy in a converted apartment on a steep hillside above the Tivoli Hotel on the Avenida da Liberdade. The new man's first task was familiarizing himself with the specialties of Lisbon's other agencies so he could direct refugees turning up at the Quakers' door to the best place for help. With limited financial means, aid groups cautiously doled out their services no matter how compelling the stories brought to them. At times, as Wriggins soon understood, a sympathetic hearing was the best he could offer.

Especially trying were his monthly visits to Caxias prison to meet with refugees held for illegal entry into Portugal. He could do little for them beyond trying to connect them with a consulate, if their native country had one in Lisbon, and issuing scraps of clothing and food. His regular trips to Caldas da Rainha were only slightly less draining. Refugees could live anywhere in the city they could find housing but had to report daily to the local police; visits to Lisbon for any reason required a day permit, with return that evening. Wriggins's task was get to know the thirty or so families there receiving Quaker aid and gauge funds needed for the following month. "The evidence for making a decision on how much a person needs," he wrote of the work, "is very slight . . . hunch, guesswork . . . nothing you can be sure of. But a decision must be made and on the spot. At the end of a day of interviewing I quietly prayed to myself that I had done the best I could."

He also tried to help clients with decisions about the future, which meant appearing hopeful in order to maintain their spirits yet realistic about when and where they might be relocated. Time dragged on while papers to immigration officials were mailed back and forth. Transatlantic telephone calls for civilians were nearly impossible while telegrams were expensive and required getting typed messages to the post office in Lisbon. "The world is at war," Wriggins recorded of the humanly demanding work,

> and I am comforting refugees, holding out hopes which, when I hold them out, I myself am almost convinced cannot be fulfilled. And the next time I see this person I may have to slap down one hope and

substitute another to give them enough strength to go on. And it all must be done gently, since they are near the edge already, and a shock would be the last shove over the lip.

In his refugee advocacy Wriggins dealt with two governments—Portugal as host country, the United States as favored overseas destination. His transactions with Portugal were largely a matter of maintaining good relations with both the local and secret police, and giving assurances that the Quakers' clients would not become financial drains on the state. Although officials he met with were invariably polite and proficient in English or French, Wriggins was always aware that he was in an authoritarian state, that he was probably being watched, that phones could be tapped, that continuing his work required going about it with constant awareness of his situation. At times, though, his involvement with Portugal simply meant standing back and observing incidents of its stiff behavior as a neutral nation. At the dockside one day, seeing off some of their refugees, Wriggins and Conrad realized that a young couple they had worked exceptionally hard for could not be seen. They had entered Portugal illegally and been kept in separate jails; the AFSC had managed to get them papers, provide ship tickets, and persuade the police to transport them to the dock. Ultimately Wriggins and Conrad learned the couple were already safely aboard the ship but confined to the brig until departure because the police were unwilling to take responsibility for allowing them to leave the country.

American authorities were equally polite yet inflexible about immigration matters. Even when national quotas allowed the issuing of visas, the procedure crept forward due to changing conditions before a passport was actually stamped. Prospective immigrants needed FBI clearance that could take months to get as well as affidavits from relatives in America or well-connected citizens offering a job or otherwise certifying they would not become public wards. The local consul issuing the visa could then weigh whether the affidavit was, in his view, sufficient; if not, the process began all over again. The renewal process for an expired visa was treated the same as a new application. In case after case, as Wriggins later became aware, he had witnessed in operation a State Department policy of intentional delay in granting American visas.

The hindrance only increased with American entry into the war due to deepened security concerns that the Nazis might use refugees to infiltrate spies and fifth columnists into the country. Wriggins encountered the worry firsthand when he paid a courtesy call on George Kennan, then counselor of the Lisbon legation. At the end of Wriggins's conversation with the "civil but severe" official, Kennan caught his visitor off guard by saying, "Of course you realize, Mr. Wriggins, that the activities of your committee and the others are tearing a hole in the security of the United States. You have no way of really knowing about the identity of the people you are helping. You have their stories but you have no way of confirming their veracity." Wriggins answered: "Sir, if you sat listening to their stories the way I have, and saw the fear and anxiety in their eyes, I think you would be able to make some distinctions."

Following Operation Torch in North Africa and reduced concern in Portugal about a Nazi invasion, Wriggins found a slight easing of the country's neutral stance. Earlier, refugees who had come to Portugal illegally would tell him their stories while peering anxiously out his office window to see if the police were arriving to arrest them. A French refugee now came to the Quakers with a story that illustrated a change of attitude, at least on the part of the police. After reaching Portugal illegally, he had made his way to a main Lisbon square to blend into the crowd, unsuccessfully it turned out since a policeman took him by the arm and asked if he had proper papers. The refugee admitted the truth, then asked for directions to the French consulate. The policeman told him the consulate, under Vichy direction, would only send him back to France, and added: "You'd better go to the Quakers; they're most likely to help you." The policeman knew the address and gave the refugee directions.

An unexpected effect of the North Africa landings put an ongoing program of the AFSC in jeopardy. In October 1942 it was learned that some thirty American women, all professionally involved in work for children, were coming from New York to Lisbon on a Portuguese liner to escort back to America a thousand French children who had been granted emergency visas through the efforts of the United States Committee for the Care of European Children. Once the children were across the Atlantic, the women would help establish them with foster families for the duration of the war. But with the North African invasion and subsequent German occupation of the south of France, the escape door for the children abruptly closed, leaving the women with nothing to do after they landed in Lisbon.

To occupy them the AFSC's office secretary showed them the sights of Lisbon and the beach communities, yet energetic and with duties back home, the women had not come to Portugal for touring. For one of them, the idle period was unbearable. Wriggins recalled a quiet, gray-haired lady who appeared at his office one afternoon and asked if she could speak with him; busy at the moment, he made an appointment to see her early the next morning. She did not appear, and later her shoes were found on a cliff above the sea. The Lisbon police reported finding a handbag on a rock in the wide crater of Boca do Inferno, Mouth of Hell, near Cascais, and said it was possible the owner—identified as Hazel Helen Mackay, who was on leave of absence from the Children's Welfare Foundation of New York City—either fell into the sea or was overtaken by a wave.

Eventually an idea was spawned of how to put the women to work. In Caldas da Rainha some parents had considered sending their children overseas even if they themselves were unable to go. There was understandable fear, though, of never reuniting with them. Would the United States open itself to immigrants after the war? Would the children, after their lives with foster families, want to be back with their parents? The American women began meeting with the families to respond to such concerns and gather information about the children. Medical histories were taken, and after police permission was granted the children were transported to the Lisbon consulate for medical exams and the voluminous paperwork needed for immigration. In the end, twenty-two children from Caldas da Rainha were among the three hundred who sailed for America aboard the *Serpa Pinta*, with the majority coming through Spain from refugee families interned there for illegally entering the country.

In weekend breaks from his AFSC work, Wriggins took in the usual pleasures of Lisbon. He went swimming on the Estoril coast and snacked on sardines roasted on beachfront charcoal fires. There were long walks in the Lisbon hills with their striking views of the shipping and ferry traffic on the Tagus. Narrow side streets near the docks smelled of fish and were vivid with baskets of flowers hanging from windows. And always there was the spectacle of light: shifting tints on buildings during the day, the war-defying brilliance of avenues at night.

Late in the summer of 1943 Wriggins left Portugal for an AFSC post in North Africa. As a Quaker, one of his goals had been to resist generalizing about the refugees he worked with and treat them as unique individuals; nonetheless large thoughts now came to him about Lisbon's particular brand of exiles. Removed from their pasts and faced with beginning a new life, while stuck in Lisbon they were in a fretful limbo—"rather like a patient with an unknown disease," as Wriggins thought of the state, "who waits anxiously for an unknowable diagnosis." Caught between accepting the condition with patience or trying to do something about it, in both cases the exiles were nagged by guilt for having reached Lisbon when others had not. The demoralized whiled away their days in cafés; others, responsive still to the effort or luck or connections that had carried them this far, compulsively competed for an edge—a document, a signature, a ticket for a ship—that would open the door to further movement. Perhaps the most fortunate among them, Wriggins decided, were women who calmly filled their days knitting sweaters and vests for winter.

"In Lisbon," he wrote of his own situation and that of other relief workers, "we had a more than ringside seat to the war." From the exiles they learned daily of shattered lives and heard stories of men and women suddenly removed from French camps and shipped off to Poland and elsewhere in Eastern Europe, presumably to work as forced labor in military industries. Rumors of extermination camps also trickled into Lisbon, though they tended to be discounted on grounds the Nazis surely would not spend energy and resources on nonmilitary pursuits. From the Portuguese, their attitudes about the war varying with the military news, they were made aware that radically different postwar futures were at stake. His contacts with the war caused Wriggins to question his position as a conscientious objector: "Was I really a 'pacifist' when I saw what a disaster it would be for all the people I was helping, even for the Portuguese, if the Nazis should come to control Portugal? Even worse would be a Nazi victory." Yet just as Lisbon brought the implications of war close, it also held off Wriggins's doubt. Work overtook reflection—work that fit within the Quaker tradition of affirming humane values while remaining apart from the struggle for power. In that sense, he told himself, Lisbon had not challenged his belief so much as offered a unique opportunity for putting it to action.

★   ★   ★

While in charge of the Quakers' Lisbon office during a four-month home leave by Philip Conrad, Howard Wriggins had turned for help and encouragement to Joseph J. Schwartz, the head of the local office of the American Jewish Joint Distribution Committee—to most, simply the Joint. Tall, black-haired, and with what struck Wriggins as a sad face marked by an endless burden of work—Wriggins suspected he rarely slept—Schwartz was a rabbi with a doctorate from Yale who had turned to social work. In Europe when the war began, he was caught up in the refugee exodus to Lisbon, and in June 1940, with the Salazar government allowing Jewish relief groups in occupied territory to relocate in Portugal, he established in the city the Joint's European headquarters.

In the war's early period Nazi policy continued to encourage the mass migration of Jews, and the overriding task for Schwartz and his group was housing and feeding them after they reached Lisbon, then finding and paying for overseas transport. With American Export Lines favoring American citizens returning home, the Joint relied heavily on a half-dozen Portuguese liners of medium size. With American visas granted only to those with proof of booked tickets, the Joint bought berths, then waited to see if its clients would turn up in Lisbon in time to occupy them. Later in the immigration process the shipping companies shifted from booking individual berths to securing block space and entire vessels, and costs soared accordingly. Yet money could be raised in the United States and elsewhere; the greater problem for the Joint was always a shortage of ocean transport. "A ship goes off," an official wrote in late 1940, "but what we need is a bridge—a bridge that hundreds of thousands could cross—like over a rainbow—from despair to hope or even to despair with dignity."

In its Lisbon work the Joint drew on the support of the resident Jewish community, which in Portugal was small—perhaps about a thousand, including some 650 Jews who had arrived before the war—but ably organized under a notable university professor, Moses B. Amzalak, and with a relief committee headed by a young medical doctor and author, Augusto d'Esaguy. The two men had developed a working relationship with the police, and the Joint supported the local Jewish group with funds for distribution to refugees in Caldas da Rainha and other holding centers.

The number of Jews who passed through Lisbon in the early war years is uncertain. In November 1940 the Joint put the number of Jewish refugees actually in Portugal at 10,000. In February 1941 Augusto d'Esaguy estimated that 32,000 went through the country in the first months after France fell. Another estimate has it that about 40,000 Jews moved through Lisbon in 1940 and 1941. Given the difficulties of obtaining overseas visas and transport, Lisbon is thought to have had a shifting population of some 4,000 Jewish refugees throughout the entire wartime period.

When the United States joined the war and widespread removal of its citizens from Europe began, the work of all Lisbon-based American relief groups was in doubt. "Believe entire staff should be evacuated immediately," New York cabled Schwartz after Pearl Harbor. The Joint's director agreed, and a three-month budget was set and Moses Amzalak appointed to look after the agency's local interests. But Schwartz could not leave his post quickly since large numbers of Jews with valid overseas visas were still caught in Lisbon, and aid money coming in from Jewish contributors in the United States was increasing. In the end, the Joint removed its workers from everywhere in Europe except Lisbon, though a volunteer in Switzerland, Saly Mayer, maintained a JDC office there and grew in value as a collaborator of Schwartz through the rest of the war.

From his Lisbon location Schwartz found he could continue such European operations as sending aid parcels and gathering information on Jews still trapped in occupied territory as well as monitoring overseas shipping. A persistent concern was the situation in neighboring Spain, where stateless Jews and Jews without transit visas were confined along with other refugees in overcrowded camps and prohibited from making outside contact. In Schwartz's view, the newly appointed American ambassador, Carlton Hayes, failed to mount a vigorous intervention on their behalf.

Together with Philip Conrad of the Quakers, Schwartz joined in a proposal to Hayes to place a relief agent within the embassy to represent both the Quakers and the Joint, thereby getting around the Franco government's opposition to having non-Catholic relief groups working on Spanish soil. Hayes agreed, and in early 1943 David J. Blickenstaff, who had a background of relief experience with the Church of the Brethren during Spain's civil war, arrived in Madrid and was recognized as the representative of American relief organizations. Blickenstaff and his co-workers—the group enlarged to include the Unitarians and a Catholic organization—eventually moved to offices near the embassy, with expenses contributed by the Lisbon relief agencies. Needed food, clothing, and medical supplies were brought in from Portugal, though only with permission of Portuguese authorities and often after lengthy bureaucratic delays.

When the Quaker office in Lisbon discovered that five tons of clothing sent to it from Philadelphia had been sitting for months in a warehouse by the Tagus, it was able, with dogged effort, to arrange a transfer to Blickenstaff in Madrid. (Goods waiting in Lisbon for one reason or another was a familiar headache for the relief groups. In early 1941, Reverend Clayton Williams of the American Church of Paris spent several weeks in Lisbon seeking railway transport through Portugal and Spain for two carloads of clothing and medical supplies held for half a year in the city. It took him, so it was said, eighty visits to officials in Lisbon and Madrid to get the cars moving to France.) And when Blickenstaff pried loose refugees from Spanish camps, they had to be met by relief workers at the Lisbon train station, then provided with food and lodging during the time that elapsed before departure on a ship. After he was able to get the release of three hundred stateless men from a camp—by arguing that, since they lacked nationality, they would not be drafted into military service by the Allies if set free—they were placed in a holding center similar to those in Portugal, with the Joint in Lisbon covering most of the costs.

*   *   *

Joseph Schwartz had enough on his hands at the Joint without conflict with another Jewish aid figure. An especially testy situation arose with Isaac Weissman, a Turkish-born Polish Jew and ardent Zionist who had come to Lisbon as a refugee in June 1940 and labored zealously for fellow exiles without discriminating between legal and illegal entrants. Apparently through his contacts with the Portuguese police, Weissman was able to get some two hundred illegal Jews released from prison and placed in Ericeira, a small fishing port on the Atlantic just north of Lisbon. When he asked the Joint to support them, Schwartz said help would be available but distribution would not come through him.

Moses Amzalak and others in Lisbon's Jewish community were already wary of Weissman's unbridled rescue methods, believing they threatened the status of all Jews in Portugal. Weissman kept going about his work as he saw fit, eventually becoming the Lisbon representative of two Jewish aid groups, the Committee for Relief of the War-Stricken Jewish Population and the World Jewish Congress. Not surprisingly, a key associate in his rescue work was the Unitarian Service Committee.

Weissman was considered for yet another Lisbon post, the representative of the Jewish Agency for Palestine, until opposition from the Joint and the local Jewish community blocked any possibility of his appointment. For some time the group had been looking for someone to facilitate the movement of stateless Jews to Palestine, and it was not until January 1943 that it finally settled on Wilfrid Israel as its agent. He was still in an early phase of carrying out his assignment when, in June of that year, he was among the passengers who perished in the shooting down of the *Ibis* on its flight from Lisbon to London.

★   ★   ★

From a prosperous Jewish department store family in Berlin, Wilfrid Israel—he had been born in Britain and held a British passport—had fled Germany for London in May 1939. He left behind a sterling record of efforts to relocate Jews in the period of Nazi policy directed to emigration rather than extermination. With the aid of the Quakers and British Jews, he had overseen the movement of ten thousand children to England. He and his co-workers also packed Jews into ships leaving Germany for Shanghai, where few if any travel documents were necessary; for destinations where they were required, he purchased passports, visas, and residence permits that were openly on sale in Germany. From the Gestapo he ransomed the release of hundreds and perhaps thousands of Jews held in internment camps. After his flight to England, he returned to Berlin once more, in August 1939, to get a last contingent of Jewish children across Holland to England and to aid the departure of some of his parents' friends. When through the American embassy in Berlin he heard stories that all those with dual national identities were about to be interned, he finally abandoned Germany for good.

Although the family fortune was lost, Israel himself was financially independent. Yet rather than settle into life as a prosperous and cultivated English gentleman, he chose to view himself as a refugee with continuing responsibilities to others who had escaped Nazi Europe. Like Isaac Weissman, he was also committed to the Zionist cause, and in the early spring of 1940 he traveled to Palestine by way of Trieste to observe developments there. He had been in the Middle East before and was a co-founder of a movement known as Youth Aliya, which as early as 1932 had sent Jewish children to resettlement in Palestine. What he saw now was deeply pleasing: young pioneers had transformed a barren environment into fertile and thriving communal societies. He gave thought to living in a kibbutz himself, perhaps resuming work as a sculptor, a career path he had once thought of following.

Israel was still in Palestine when Germany invaded the Low Countries. He immediately returned to England and to the refugees, working now as a middleman between British officials and Jewish and non-Jewish aliens who had been rounded up and placed in improvised camps for fear they were enemy agents or fifth columnists. At the same time he lobbied for refugee rights, he retained his concern for Jewish children, especially those of the Youth Aliya movement, now caught in what had become occupied countries. In early 1941 he wrote to a friend urging Jewish groups to mobilize to get them out of Europe though Portugal: "I maintain that Jewish organizations should be working in Portugal saving as many youngsters as possible from Central Europe and France, in close touch with the Joint and Hadassah [a Jewish women's group in the United States and one of the financial supporters of Youth Aliya]." With the fate of Jews in Europe still unclear, some Jewish aid organizations resisted the many perils of transport operations in wartime conditions.

Late in 1941 Israel tried to join the RAF but was turned down for age—he was over forty—and health reasons. In November of that year he took a position at Oxford University as a consultant in the German section at the Foreign Research and Press Service of the Royal Institution of International Affairs (widely known as Chatham House). It was a paid job—five pounds a week—and Israel enjoyed Oxford's monastic atmosphere and high-table dining as well as the intellectual work of research and report writing. He rose quickly from the fringes of the group to its center, yet the yearning to settle in Palestine stayed with him. He took up the study of Hebrew and sought and received an immigration certificate from the Colonial Office.

In January 1943 he was asked by a London official of the Jewish Agency for Palestine to go to Lisbon to—as Israel loosely outlined in a letter the appealing nature of his task—"help in salvage work, refugee selection, or something on that line." The refugees he would try to save were Jewish children, and several new developments had given that long-standing ambition fresh possibility. Israel wasted no time in obtaining a two-month leave of absence from his research position and arranging a March air flight from England.

His brief from the Jewish Agency was to distribute two hundred immigration certificates among the thousands of Jewish refugees gathered in Portugal and Spain, to plan for their transportation to Palestine, and to look into chances of rescuing some one thousand children still caught in occupied France. He hoped to accomplish even more, but plenty of doubt attached to even this challenging agenda. Transportation was a main problem. In the midst of war he could not expect to use Allied ships to move refugees, and commercial shipping was severely limited and expensive. Even if ships could be found, there was a question of the route to take through the war zone of the Mediterranean.

Since the number of certificates he had to allocate fell far short of those needed, Israel was careful to inform the Joint in Lisbon before leaving England to "on no account give any binding undertaking to individuals concerned. Do not wish to face any faits accomplis or raise false hopes." In a letter to an old friend in rescue operations, he tried to tamp down hopes for his mission by noting he was not "coming to the Iberian peninsula as a *deus ex machina*" to "save the situation." Perhaps with awareness that his air flight to Portugal was inherently risky, he took the precaution of making his will before leaving England. Among many bequests was that of a collection of paintings, drawings, and sculpture to the Hazorea kibbutz in Palestine.

In Lisbon, Israel knew he needed the cooperation of the relief agencies, and especially Jewish groups such as the Joint, yet he also realized he had to keep some distance from them in order to independently make his immigration selections from the enormous number of possibilities. He went alone to inspect the refugee centers in Caldas da Rainha and Ericeira, and came away with a view that Jews in Portugal were in a more secure position than those he was likely to find in Spain. He also made the rounds of Lisbon's embassies and legations, explaining his mission and his added hope of rescuing a large portion of an entire generation of young Jews—he set the ideal age for immigration as between fourteen and sixteen—from throughout occupied Europe.

As soon as a visa for Spain came through, Israel left for Madrid, where he found, as expected, Jewish refugees held in wretched camps. He learned about the work of David Blickenstaff on behalf of Jewish internees, using funds supplied by the Joint and other Lisbon relief groups, and he set up his operation in Blickenstaff's office. He met with British ambassador Samuel Hoare, whose prime concern was getting Allied prisoners of war out of the camps but voiced sympathy with the plight of all interned refugees; and he tried to make contact with those able to guide groups of Jewish children out of France across the Pyrenees. Most of all, he knew, he needed more immigration certificates at his disposal, and in cables he bombarded the Jewish Agency in London with requests. Only a few more came his way.

During a reception arranged by the British embassy in Madrid in May, Israel was introduced to Leslie Howard as someone who had been making tours of refugee camps in Spain and had ideas about resettlement in Palestine. As the two sat together during a luncheon, Israel told the famed actor: "This persecution has left many of the older people quite aimless and broken. My hopes are in the young people, but we must get them to Palestine, to Eretz—Israel. It's wrong that they should fester in camps and *domiciles forcées* here, as if they were still in the hands of Hitler." To which Howard responded: "But you *are* the Scarlet Pimpernel. I've only played the part."

Back in Lisbon on May 25, Israel was again besieged by the great number of refugees wanting his certificates. He could tell them only that he would press for more when back in Britain. With a short time left on his leave of absence, he met with the Joint's Joseph Schwartz—whom he told in confidence that, in his view, the only way of getting large numbers of young Jews out of France was over the Pyrenees—and with the USC's Robert Dexter. He spent his last evening in the city, a typically long, sun-warmed, twilight period of the Portuguese spring, by seeing an acquaintance to her home and asking her to return a Baedeker he had borrowed from a bookshop in the Avenida da Liberdade run by a man he had known in Berlin in the 1930s. The next morning he again met Leslie Howard, the actor now distracted by a crowd of well-wishers come to the Lisbon airport to see him off on the *Ibis*.

Some five months after Israel's death, a colleague from England, Fritz Lichtenstein, came to Lisbon as the Jewish Agency representative. Using lists of names compiled by Israel, he began the work of filling the first of what eventually would be four refugee ships destined for Palestine. With the North African campaign over, the *Nyassa* crossed the Mediterranean without difficulty and reached Haifa in January 1944. Lichtenstein did not pursue Israel's grand hope of illegally moving Jewish children from France. Later that year, however, a rescue effort was mounted with the help of Schwartz and the Joint, and a few hundred children were brought across the mountains, though at a cost of several lives lost due to the grueling physical demands of the journey.

★   ★   ★

A relief endeavor run from Casa Verde, a small villa in Estoril, was an entirely amateur effort but no less important to those on the receiving end of its mixed bag of largesse. When Louise Campbell's husband, a British officer, was captured in France in 1940, he wrote her from a prison camp that he needed woolen underwear to endure the German winter. In her reply, Louise Campbell, an American, asked what else he needed, and wondered in a postscript if she could get something for his fellow prisoners. She got back requests for pipes, earphones, books, phonograph records, a mouthpiece for a clarinet, all of which she found and sent on.

Word spread rapidly among British prisoners that a certain woman back in England would supply special needs if you wrote her. Cards and letters began pouring in, and soon Campbell found herself with a mail-order operation so large she decided to move it to Lisbon, where she had never been before, to improve her lines of communication. After leasing Casa Verde, she set to work with a band of helpers. The requests kept coming, and in time the Portuguese Red Cross gave Campbell use of an old Lisbon palace. From there in January 1941 she used a letter to the London *Times* to respond to hundreds of messages from relatives of prisoners, who were likewise seeking help for the captives. "As I am unable to deal with these letters at once," she wrote, "may they consider this as an answer, and be reassured that I am trying to carry out their wishes to the best of my ability."

At war's end Louise Campbell was honored for her work at a party in London's Claridge's Hotel attended by the American and Portuguese ambassadors. She was presented with a piece of Georgian silver, a check for a thousand pounds sent in her name to a new plastic surgery wing of the Queen Victoria Hospital, and a bound book with the signatures of former prisoners who had subscribed to a fund for the gifts.

★   ★   ★

The Red Cross likewise moved to Lisbon in the sense of making the city its central storage and distribution point for a large-scale program of food packages sent to prisoners of war. Over the war's course the British Red Cross sent about 20 million packets to European camps, each weighing an average of 11 pounds, with the food meant to arrive three times within every two-week period following an initial package to a newly captured serviceman. The American Red Cross sent 27 million packets to Europe, and like British shipments they were of uniform size and weight and meant to supplement often minimal prison fare. Along with the food parcels, both national Red Cross groups, and those of British Commonwealth countries, sent parcels with clothing, toiletries, and medical supplies.

After packages were put together at vast sorting centers in England, the complex logistics of transportation loomed. Usually the packages were sent by post to ports and loaded on ordinary merchant vessels bound for Lisbon. After they reached the city the packages were transferred to rented warehouses, then to trains for shipment across Portugal, Spain, and France to Switzerland.

With railway transport slow and unreliable, the Red Cross eventually switched to chartered ships—owned and manned by neutral countries, brightly lit, and bearing Red Cross markings but liable to be stopped and searched at any time—that moved along the Portuguese coast, through the Straits of Gibraltar, and arrived at the French ports of Marseille or Toulon for train delivery to Geneva. From Swiss warehouses the parcels were finally shipped to railway sidings near the camps, where they were often unloaded by prisoners. After Germany occupied all of France in late 1942, the Marseille-Toulon route was briefly terminated, then resumed by the British Red Cross virtually to the end of the war. In December 1942 the American Red Cross began bypassing Lisbon by sending parcels directly from Philadelphia to Europe, using Swiss-flagged ships on safe-passage routes.

The food packets were so critical, with ex-prisoners often testifying they were what saved them from starvation, that any interruption in delivery was cause for alarm. When in September 1944 CBS radio recorded a Swiss broadcast about a temporary delay in shipments to American prisoners in Germany, the Red Cross in Washington put out a nationwide statement maintaining that war packages were still reaching Europe, and provided full shipping details. Two ships carrying packets were said to have just reached Sweden, and the exchange ship *Gripsholm* would arrive at the same port with additional supplies. Aboard the three ships were a total of one and a half million food packages, all destined for prison camps in Germany.

9

GLORIOUSLY NEUTRAL

> Portugal is gloriously neutral; that is its gift from the gods and
> to Europe; a gift never, one hopes, to be snatched away.
>
> —Rose Macaulay, *The Spectator*, July 9, 1943

In the same period Red Cross food parcels were flowing through Portugal, food shortages were cropping up within the country. "It would be a mistake to suppose that Portugal to-day is a country almost without a trouble in the world, a country flowing with milk and honey in the midst of devastated Europe," said the London *Times* on September 8, 1943, marking the war's fifth year. Meat had become hard to find, and there were days when butter and potatoes were unavailable. Limited fuel supplies led to unequal distribution of food that did exist in ample quantities.

Added to food scarcities in some areas, the financial windfall to Portugal from the deluge of refugees and wartime trade with both the Allies and the Axis had sparked inflation, and this coupled with higher charges for imports and a limited number of ships to carry them brought a sharp rise in the Portuguese cost of living. Traditional fish stocks of dried cod and sardines more than doubled in price over the war. Food shortages and high prices encouraged smuggling, black markets, and hoarding, abuses the government tried to combat through a constant round of prosecutions, with limited success. Portugal remained an alluring haven in the midst of war, yet for its ordinary citizens it was no longer the land of ease and unbounded plenty that greeted awestruck new arrivals. "We are not directly engaged in the struggle," Salazar told his country in a speech in the early autumn of 1943, "but we are in the war like the rest."

For the transients streaming in and out, that Portugal was not in the struggle was the central wartime fact about the country. Its external neutrality eclipsed concern with food supplies, prices, or all other internal matters. Portuguese neutrality might be imagined as a glorious gift, as Rose Macaulay lightly characterized it, yet in actuality it was held in place by a complex diplomatic dance that was hedged with uncertainty for much of the war period. And uncertain not only because at any moment the Allies or Axis might choose to upend it. Like a character in Arthur Koestler's 1943 novel *Arrival and Departure*, Portugal in effect went through the war as a neutral while openly displaying a toy British flag in its buttonhole.

In Koestler's story, in which Portugal is thinly masked as a country named Neutralia, a university student and radical from Central Europe takes the Lisbon route as a stowaway in a ship's hold. With the vessel anchored in the dark offshore, he leaps from the deck and swims to a small bay with a cluster of bathing cabins on the beach. When he wades ashore he races to the nearest cabin, instinctively hiding though no one is present to notice him. The time is three o'clock in the morning in the spring of 1941, and the young refugee, Peter Slavek, is twenty-two years old.

In the cabin Slavek changes clothes from an oilskin bundle brought with him from the ship, smokes a cigarette, and in the warmth of the darkness falls asleep. He awakens to bright sunshine, and when he leaves the cabin sees a toy flag that had once topped a child's sandcastle. In the country he has come from, "the possession of this flag meant high treason and death; here children were allowed to stick it into their castles." When he leaves the bay he inserts the flag of Britain—the country never named but easily identified—into his buttonhole, knowing there is no danger in doing so since "this was Neutralia, the land without blackout."

He walks a long distance into an unnamed city that is manifestly Lisbon with its white buildings, clanking trolleys, cafés with tables spilling across sidewalks, and bright awnings shading the hard light of the sun. He has money to last a fortnight, which will be long enough to conduct the business that has brought him to Neutralia; after that he will be "far from here, across the water, in a tidy uniform with a tilted cap." His business, in other words, is to present himself at the British consulate, obtain a visa, and enlist in the country's military.

In a café he has a huge breakfast and talks with other refugees who have been waiting months for overseas visas. Easy conversations, he realizes, are normal in Neutralia since "the exiles here were tied together by their common fate—travellers on the same caravan path huddled around the oasis well." The exiles follow well-worn passageways in the city and consequently keep running into one another; many had already crossed paths on their flight to Neutralia.

This shrunken world sparks a plot in which Slavek falls in love with Odette, a young girl he first sees in the café, and comes to stay in the apartment of Sonia Bolgar, a psychotherapist he had known in his university days who is practicing in Lisbon while awaiting an American visa. The story leaps ahead, weeks passing during which Slavek keeps calling at the British consulate in hopes of a visa. He has a short, torrid affair with Odette, and on the day she leaves Neutralia, her American visa come through, he learns that his to Britain has been granted.

When he suffers a strange nervous breakdown that causes paralysis in a leg, Sonia becomes his analyst and talks him through episodes in childhood and the experiences of Nazi brutality that have darkened his life. Health at length regained, he is granted an American visa (he has relatives in the country who offer him a job) and a place on a departing ship. He has boarded the ship, about to leave for assured safety, when he realizes he cannot ignore his earlier plan to join the war. "I want to go back," he tells himself. "I have never been on the winning side."

At the last moment he leaves the ship and goes to the British consulate to see if his visa is still valid. In a final scene the story comes full circle, shifting to Britain as Slavek parachutes from a British plane, just as in the opening scene he had leaped from a ship. Earlier in the consulate, seeing about his visa, he had outlined for an official what he might do for the British cause: "I have been told that people who know local conditions [in occupied Europe] are trained for special tasks. Some are even dropped by parachutes. . . ."

★   ★   ★

Peter Slavek's sense of duty in wartime trumps his desire for freedom from war. Failure to join the cause on Britain's side would burden him with guilt; in an America still outside the war, his throat would "be dry and thick with loneliness." On the other hand, choosing Britain and the comradeship of war may be a suicidal gesture. While he wrestles with his decision on the ship about to leave for America, Sonia Bolgar's imagined voice cautions him, "He who offers himself for the sacrifice will be accepted. So better lie back on your bunk. . . ."

In Slavek's rejection of Sonia's advice, *Arrival and Departure* is finally a statement of personal nobility. At the same time, in naming a refugee's country of arrival Neutralia the novel draws attention to the larger public matter of Portugal's wartime neutrality. Within the story the country's sole importance for refugees is its freedom from the war, hence its fictional name. The Portuguese people exist only as ghostly background figures. To the waiting exiles they seem like "silent members of the chorus in an operetta . . . performed in the midst of the Apocalypse." Or as a character more simply remarks about the "natives": "They are nice and polite, but they live in another world." Britain's glory is its engagement of the evil enemy, unnamed but obvious. In a shop window Slavek sees its symbol: "There it spread, with its scarlet foundation, the thick black ring, and in the middle of it the cross with its broken limbs turned into a spider." When refugees hear rumors that Neutralia may be invaded, they have no doubt who the invader will be.

In casting his lot with Britain over America, Slavek aligns himself with what he understands is the sole force standing in the way of the Third Reich adding Neutralia to its string of victims. Private fiction here mirrors international fact since Europe's oldest diplomatic pact joined Portugal and Britain in a bond of mutual support. First signed in Saint Paul's Cathedral in London in 1373 and reinforced with a second treaty in 1386, the Anglo-Portuguese alliance required that—in the agreement's language—if one member "need the support or succour of the other, and duly apply to the other Party for such assistance, then the Party so applied to shall be obliged to afford such help or succour to the requiring Party, in as far as is compatible with the dangers threatening himself, his Kingdoms, Lands, Dominions, and Subjects." Over the centuries there were periods of friction and varying interpretations of what had been assented to. But the alliance held. It formed the centerpiece of Portugal's foreign policy, led to major British investment in Portuguese finance and infrastructure, and opened the way to a long and rewarding trading partnership.

For Portugal, the far smaller and weaker party, the importance of maintaining the tie with Britain could not be overstated. "If for London the alliance was a diplomatic instrument whose obligations were only taken seriously when Britain's vital interests were at stake," wrote a Portuguese historian, "for Lisbon it was nothing short of essential for Portugal's survival as a state." For Salazar's regime, as for every Portuguese government in the first half of the twentieth century, the alliance was the fundamental guarantee of the country's mainland and colonial sovereignty. Consequently Portugal's neutral status in World War II was from the beginning yoked to an ancient union with one of the warring powers.

★   ★   ★

Portugal was in the same divided position at the start of World War I. When London invoked the alliance by requesting confiscation of German merchant ships that had sought refuge in Portuguese ports, Lisbon complied, and in response Germany declared war in March 1916. At British invitation, Portugal subsequently joined the Allied cause and dispatched an expeditionary force of more than fifty thousand to the Western Front while also placing troops in its African possessions to defend against German colonial expansion. War involvement cost the country some seven thousand dead, thirteen thousand wounded, and scores of lost ships.

Immediately after the Nazi invasion of Poland in 1939—bringing from Salazar an indirect rebuke in the form of praise of "the heroic sacrifice of Poland"—Portugal both announced its neutrality and acknowledged "the duties of our alliance with England." The government's statement read in part:

> Fortunately, the duties of our alliance with England—which we do not fail to confirm in such a grave moment—do not force us to abandon our situation of neutrality in this emergency. The government will consider it as the highest service and the greatest gift of Providence to be able to maintain the Portuguese people in peace and it hopes that neither the country's interests nor its obligations and dignity will impose on itself any deviation in this determination.

Of course declaring neutrality was not the same as having it observed by the belligerents. Hitler's position was rhetorically straightforward: those not for Nazi Germany were against it. In practical terms, Portugal's freedom ultimately rested on the perception of both Berlin and London that having the Portuguese out of the conflict was of more benefit than having them in.

The British wished for a position of benevolent neutrality under the alliance but accepted that Portuguese neutrality in any form was better than having the country in league with Germany or needing protection under the alliance at a time when Britain, fighting for its own life, was in no position to provide it. (With the fall of France and German troops on the Spanish border, Britain's ambassador to Portugal, Walford Selby, realized he "could not appeal for assistance of any kind from home." He could only advise members of the large English communities in Lisbon and Porto to stay put and "in no circumstances add to the alarm and confusion by flying about in all directions in search of refuge and escape." He also pointed out that, owing to Nazi Germany's lack of respect for diplomatic immunity, the embassy could not be regarded as a safe house "if the worst happened.") The British also hoped that Portuguese neutrality might also aid in keeping Spain clear of the conflict, a consistent British and Anglo-American wartime policy.

For the Reich, neutrality was acceptable if it was what Foreign Minister Ribbentrop termed "impeccable neutrality," Germany's important trade with mainland Portugal and the colonies remained open, and Portugal did not appeal to the British alliance. The day before the Nazi invasion of Poland, Ribbentrop instructed the German legation in Lisbon to stress to the Portuguese government that Germany would not allow any such appeal. In his dissembling response to the German minister, Salazar maintained that the pact placed his country "under no obligation whatever to render assistance, not even in the case of a defensive war," and he could not see "the slightest reason which might compel Portugal in the future to render assistance." At the same time he was bowing to Ribbentrop, Salazar was assuring the British ambassador in Lisbon that Portugal's neutrality would be benevolent toward Britain, and shortly thereafter he publicly proclaimed Portuguese "friendship and complete fidelity to the English Alliance."

★   ★   ★

With the fall of France and German divisions at the Pyrenees, Spain was the immediate threat to Portugal's neutrality. Among the ways Salazar promoted his country's noninvolvement was with the idea that Europe at war needed zones of peace since, as he stated, "it will be with such peace reserves that future peace will be built." In the early years of the war he apparently believed there would be no clear-cut winner or loser. The end would come with a compromise settlement followed by a postwar European realignment in which the Iberian peninsula, as one of the peace zones, could be in position to play a central role.

This assumed Franco also stayed outside the war. He had declared neutrality after the German invasion of Poland, but a decided tilt toward the Reich—among other things, Spain would allow the resupplying of German submarines from her ports—left Portugal wondering how long Spain would stay even technically uninvolved. The two countries had signed a friendship and nonaggression treaty after the Spanish Civil War and an added protocol in 1940 in which Madrid and Lisbon pledged to consult in the event of security threats. Spain's abrupt switch to "nonbelligerence" in June 1940—a wartime status not recognized by international law but effectively a step toward support for the Axis—added fuel to Portugal's concern. (In October 1943, the winds of war now favoring the Allies, Spain returned to a formal position of neutrality.)

Salazar had kept a neutral stance during the civil war, though his un-yielding opposition to the Soviet Union and international communism had allied him with Franco and the Nationalist cause. When Hitler intervened on the Nationalist side in July 1936, Portugal quickly and openly became a supply depot for German arms on their way into Spain. The Reich's post–civil war influence in Spain had, however, disturbing implications. Germany's swallowing up neighboring Austria was a particular warning of what might be in store for Portugal from German-backed Spain.

Following the defeat of France and the meeting of Franco and Hitler in October 1940 (Salazar and Hitler never met), Mussolini's Italy invaded Greece. Subsequently the prospect of parallel war emerged in Madrid. French Morocco beckoned, but Hitler had ruled out a Spanish incursion. That left Portugal, as the historian Stanley G. Payne has put it, as "Spain's Greece." Hitler had not opposed an attack that, presumably, Madrid could at least initiate with its own military capability.

A plan set out in a 130-page study ordered by Franco called for a swift assault to reach Lisbon and the Atlantic coast. The cover for this obvious act of aggression would be a statement from Madrid about a "delicate situation" existing in Portugal that was being exploited by Britain and required Spanish action. The invasion would trigger the Anglo-Portuguese alliance and bring into the situation British air and sea power, negating Spanish troop superiority and requiring Axis military aid, which might or might not be forthcoming. In the event of success, it also demanded of Spain the continuing defense of Portugal's Atlantic coastline.

The planned conquest of Portugal never went beyond the paper of the report, and if a plan at all it was part of broader Spanish ambition that embraced British Gibraltar and French Morocco. While the scheme was still being put together, the Italian attack on Greece turned into a quagmire requiring German intervention, and for the moment Spanish military ac-tion on all fronts was held in check.

Still, there remained the possibility of German intervention in Portugal with or without Spanish involvement. Soon after meeting Franco at Hen-daye, Hitler signed off on Operation Felix, a plan meant to drive the British out of Gibraltar, close the Straits, occupy French North Africa, and effectively turn the Western Mediterranean into an Axis-controlled lake. At a later stage of the operation, a German armored division and a motorized infantry divi-sion would screen off Portugal from Spain and, if required, invade the coun-try. At the time, press reports out of Washington said Germany was clearly "telegraphing" the drive, and headlines blared that the "Nazi Iberian Drive Is Expected Soon" and that "Berlin Push Through Spain and Portugal into French North Africa Forecast."

When Franco resisted joining the operation and Hitler's attention turned to the east and Russia, Felix was shelved and ultimately abandoned. A less ambitious German plan in May 1941, Operation Isabella, called for the occupation of important Spanish and Portuguese ports to forestall possible British landings on the peninsula intended, among other things, to enhance the range and efficiency of its air and naval forces. A following plan, Ilona, excluded Portugal but called for German occupation of nearby northern Spanish ports to protect the Atlantic coastline. Well into the wartime years Portugal remained wary of German intentions. But with Hitler's thrust into Russia in June 1941 (of which Salazar heartily approved, though not to Franco's high point of collaboration in putting his so-called Blue Division of some 45,000 troops into the conflict, of whom some 5,000 were killed), and with Italy now on German hands, the threat of any offensive incursion was reduced.

With the Anglo-American landings in North Africa in November 1942, and especially the British victory at El Alamein in Egypt, the perceived threat to Portuguese neutrality switched from a Nazi attack to Allied operations extending to the Iberian peninsula and German defensive responses. Although the war had now come close, both Churchill and Roosevelt assured Portugal that the country's neutrality would not be broached, nor would Spain's. Yet as late as the summer of 1943 top-level American military officers had discussed with Roosevelt the merits of invading Europe through Portugal and Spain rather than across the English Channel. Admiral William D. Leahy, Roosevelt's chief of staff, thought the "Iberian route might be less expensive in casualty lists as well as in material." But with the landings in Sicily that same month, Salazar could begin to have confidence that the peninsula had no place in Allied invasion plans.

Hitler, on the other hand, clung to the possibility of the Allies opening a second European front in Portugal. American experts had long been reading diplomatic traffic between Berlin and Tokyo, and in early 1944 they recorded an exchange between the Japanese ambassador to Germany, Hiroshi Oshima, and the Führer about the front's likely location:

OSHIMA: Does your Excellency have any idea where they might land?

HITLER: Honestly, I can say no more than that I do not know. For a second front, beyond any doubt, the most effective area would be the Straits of Dover, but to land there would require great readiness and its difficulty would be great. Consequently, I don't think the enemy would run such a risk. On the other hand, along the Bordeaux coast and in Portugal, the defenses are relatively weak, so this zone might be a possibility.

OSHIMA: When you say Portugal, do you have any basis for suspecting something there?

HITLER: No, only I consider it a theoretical possibility and we Germans are preparing for any event, with air bases and submarines. We Germans have plenty of plans, and listen, I don't want you to say anything about them to a living soul.

★   ★   ★

Wartime developments on the battlefield brought inevitable shifts in Portuguese public opinion about who would come out on top, with the country's management of its neutrality shifting accordingly from collaboration with the British to something more evenhanded to, for a brief while, a swing toward Germany. At the same time wartime events opened long and bitter disputes within the Anglo-Portuguese alliance, deeply straining the relationship. A continuing irritant on Portugal's side was Britain's enforcement of the sea blockade, which obliged Portuguese exporters (and those of other neutral nations) to apply to British consuls for navicerts that certified ships were not carrying contraband cargo. Vessels intercepted at sea without the documents were liable to be seized as prizes of war. Portuguese imports were equally controlled by the navicert system, which allowed needed domestic supplies to enter the country but tried to prevent a buildup of stores that might be reshipped to the enemy. Despite repeated Portuguese cries that the blockade infringed on both its neutrality and sovereignty, it remained in place.

A notable low point in Anglo-Portuguese relations came in December 1941 when an Allied force of about 350 Dutch and Australian troops entered the island possession of Timor in the Far East to resist a presumed Japanese invasion. War had made the island, divided between the Dutch and the Portuguese, strategically important, and Dutch and Australian troops were already stationed on the Dutch part of the island. After the Japanese attack on Pearl Harbor, the Dutch chargé d'affaires in Lisbon offered Portugal the aid of the troops, and Salazar, ever mindful of Portuguese neutrality, responded that Portugal would accept help only after the Japanese struck the island. The troops did not wait, and over objection by the governor of Portuguese Timor the possession was occupied.

After Salazar complained that Portuguese sovereignty had been breached, Britain expressed official regret over the Allied action and said troops would withdraw if Portuguese reinforcements arrived. Portugal mustered a force of some seven hundred men at Lourenço Marques, but before it could arrive Japan settled the issue by invading both Portuguese and Dutch Timor. The Japanese minister in Lisbon explained that the action was necessary to drive out "foreign troops"; Japan's troops, in any event, held the island for the duration of the war. Hugh Muir reported that German legation and consular officials in Lisbon were downcast that Salazar's irritation over the violation of Portuguese rights in Timor had not reached the boiling point of ending the alliance with Britain.

A greater challenge to Portugal's neutral-yet-Allied status arose over British and, after the United States joined the war, American use of the string of Portuguese islands some 800 miles out in the Atlantic and a third of the way from Lisbon to New York. Collectively known as the Azores and an integral part of Portugal rather than a colonial possession, the nine volcanic outposts, mountainous but with lush fertile areas and 250,000 inhabitants, had strategic air and naval importance and were coveted by both warring sides.

Following the landings in North Africa and Sicily, and with the cross-Channel invasion ahead, the Allies stepped up pressure on Portugal for military use of the islands. Britain led the way in negotiations through its ambassador in Lisbon, Ronald Campbell. Salazar repeatedly deflected his requests, typically distinguishing between the British actually invoking the Anglo-Portuguese alliance or only appealing to its spirit. Difficult enough in themselves, the Azores talks were conducted against a background of the prime minister's lingering annoyance over the Timor incident.

In the United States the State Department supported the British effort for base rights in the Azores during talks with the Portuguese ambassador to Washington. In April 1943 the United States also assigned Vernon A. Walters (later an army lieutenant general, deputy director of the CIA, and holder of many diplomatic posts, including ambassador to the United Nations) to accompany two Portuguese military officers on a two-month inspection tour of American wartime production facilities. The officers had recently visited the Eastern Front in Europe and were much impressed by German military might. The purpose of the journey with Walters, who had a command of the Portuguese language, was to put what they had seen in perspective by showcasing American capability and, by implication, how use of the Azores would enhance it. One of the officers doubted the Allies could successfully invade Europe through Germany's Atlantic wall until, at the Curtiss-Wright factory in Buffalo, he saw C-46 aircraft on the production line, all with tail hooks to tow gliders. As Walters recalled, the officer "looked at me, startled, and said, 'Now I see you are going over the Atlantic wall.' 'Over and through,' I replied. These hooks greatly impressed him, and he never challenged the fact that we would land in Europe."

Finally in June 1943 Britain made unmistakably clear that it was invoking the alliance. Prime Minister Churchill had favored a British-American invasion of the islands if the Portuguese failed to turn them over—"simply taking the Azores one fine morning out of the blue and explaining everything to Portugal afterwards," as he said in a letter. But Anthony Eden, his foreign secretary, and Clement Attlee, a member of the war cabinet, had argued for the alliance as the wiser course, and Churchill had reluctantly gone along. "Salazar's temperament being what it is," Eden and Attlee told him, "he is less likely to give way to an ultimatum. We feel it would be better to invoke the Alliance and state our case. If he rejects that he will have shown that the Alliance is of little value."

For both sides, invoking the alliance was understood as a solemn measure with grave consequences. If Portugal refused the British request, the long record of friendship would be over; if it accepted, it might well be cast into the war on the Allied side. As it turned out, Portuguese refusal was never a possibility, though long and hard bargaining went on before an agreement was reached ceding the bases to Britain in return for guarantees of military aid if Germany retaliated, supplies of war materiel, and protection of Portuguese shipping. The secret talks were concluded in August 1943, but the deal went into effect in October, when British forces entered some of the islands to prepare the military installations.

In the interval there was fear that if news leaked out, Germany would not only loudly protest but also begin attacking Portuguese ships at sea. British vessels bringing troops to the islands would also be vulnerable to assaults by submarines and surface raiders. Such concerns, in any case, kept the Azores agreement from public awareness until four days after the first troops landed. Churchill, informing Parliament on October 12, used a bit of theater to underscore the astonishing endurance of the old agreement that had brought about the accord. In his multivolume history of World War II, he was still savoring his performance that day.

"I have an announcement," I said, "to make to the House arising out of the treaty signed between this country and Portugal in the year 1373 between His Majesty King Edward III and King Ferdinand and Queen Eleanor of Portugal." I spoke in a level voice, and made a pause to allow the House to take in the date, 1373. As this soaked in, there was something like a gasp. I do not suppose any such continuity of relations between two Powers has ever been, or will ever be, set forth in the ordinary day-to-day work of British diplomacy.

★   ★   ★

The American counterpart to Ambassador Campbell during the Azores negotiations was George Kennan. After passing through Lisbon as part of a diplomatic exchange with Germany and then a two-month vacation at home, Kennan was reassigned to Lisbon as counselor of the legation. The American minister at the time, Bert Fish, was a political appointee from Florida who seldom left his Lisbon residence for appearances at the legation's offices. Kennan's morning meetings with him were usually held in Fish's bedroom, where in an armchair the minister spent his time listening to BBC broadcasts and receiving visitors. Despite Fish's confined life, Kennan found him remarkably well informed about Lisbon events and personalities.

After Fish suddenly took ill and died in July 1943, Kennan became chargé d'affaires of what wartime conditions had elevated to a key diplomatic post. (Fish's funeral service in Lisbon was conducted with full diplomatic honors, the casket draped with an American flag and borne from the legation to the English Church of St. George on a gun carriage escorted by cavalry and given a seventeen-gun artillery salute. Among the mourners in the accompanying procession to the church were Salazar and high Portuguese officials. Fish's burial took place in Florida.) Over the next year and a half a major issue facing Kennan was American involvement in the Azores accord, a task complicated by the surprising fact that despite United States entry into the war there had been little political contact with the Portuguese government. "Ah ain't goin' down there and get mah backsides kicked around," Fish had replied when Kennan urged a direct meeting with Salazar. "He's too smaht for me." When Kennan tried to move the State Department to greater interest in Portugal, there was no reaction from Washington.

During the secret negotiations over the Azores, Kennan and W. Walton Butterworth, who was directing American economic warfare activities on the Iberian peninsula under the aegis of the government-operated United States Commercial Company, were both kept informed of developments by the British embassy. They in turn informed Secretary of State Cordell Hull, but their messages brought no response, leaving Kennan and Butterworth to assume that the government on some other level was consulting with the British. Then, three days before the British landings in the islands were to begin in October 1943, the State Department told Kennan to assure Salazar that the United States would respect Portuguese sovereignty in all its overseas possessions, but only to do so if directly asked by the prime minister. Since the matter had not come up with the Portuguese, Kennan did nothing.

When on the day of the landings another message came telling him to give the assurances without waiting to be asked, Kennan sped to the Ministry of Foreign Affairs to arrange a meeting with Salazar, and learned he was out of town and would return only for serious reason. Kennan hinted at the reason by recalling a similar important situation when he and Bert Fish had asked to arouse President Carmona in the middle of the night to tell him of the North African landings. The hint was strong enough that Salazar, contacted by telegraph, agreed to return and meet Kennan at his private quarters at ten o'clock on a Sunday morning.

On the appointed date, only minutes before leaving for the meeting, Kennan received a coded message now telling him not to give assurances but providing no explanation. What was he to do? He had brought Salazar back from a journey on a weekend and now had nothing to tell him. In what he recalled as "black despair," he went to the dictator's modest residence and vaguely confessed to some last-minute change of instructions. Was it possible, though, they might use the time to generally discuss the neglected matter of Portuguese-American relations? A puzzled Salazar agreed, and a wide-ranging discussion followed. When Kennan reported to Washington on the conversation there was, once again, no response, and he wondered if assurances were being withheld because, somewhere in the vast chain of government, plans were afoot to seize some piece of Portuguese territory.

After the presence of British troops in the Azores finally came to light, Germany responded with what Kennan called a "menacing diplomatic note," and in subsequent weeks Portugal held its breath in expectation of attack. *Time* magazine maintained that with the agreement "Portugal was a neutral no longer; she was a participant." She had "half-stepped into World War II." Lisbon had become, the magazine also noted, the destination of the moment for war correspondents. Civil-defense exercises took place throughout the city; anti-aircraft guns were stationed in Eduardo VII Park; windows were taped; air-raid wardens watched skies from rooftops; some families moved to the countryside for safety. Trying to calm the storm, the newspaper *Diário de Lisboa* told readers, "the present moment is not for panic but for precaution against the repercussion of events." At the American embassy in Madrid, the Azores accord seemed a rerun of the crisis that had followed Operation Torch in North Africa. In the event of a German move on Portugal through Spain, all consulates in Spain were told to be ready to destroy confidential material and make plans to rush personnel by automobile to Gibraltar or Lisbon. (The embassy's concern, as it turned out, was unfounded. The Spanish foreign minister told the German ambassador that Spain remained loyal to its neighbor while Franco informed the Portuguese ambassador in Madrid that Portugal's back door would be "guarded by Spain.")

Roosevelt and Churchill had engaged in correspondence about a military response should Portugal be attacked. Roosevelt wrote that "we must expect Germany to launch concentrated air and submarine attacks upon Portugal as retaliation and in order to impress neutral nations." He considered putting into Portugal a defensive force that included an infantry division, anti-aircraft battalions, fighter-plane and anti-submarine squadrons, and various support troops. Churchill cautioned that Portugal would resist having Allied ground forces in the country—and that sending them might only increase the probability of a German attack. He also thought a German air attack on Lisbon and Porto unlikely. "By so doing," Churchill wrote, "they would blot out a valuable listening post and enable us to base air squadrons in Portugal. . . . They would also lose their vital wolfram." Nonetheless he added that if asked by the Portuguese, Britain was ready to send a hundred anti-aircraft guns and two daytime and one nighttime fighter squadrons to defend the two cities.

German retaliation turned out to be nothing more than diplomatic demands. Portugal should remain otherwise neutral by agreeing not to carry Allied supplies on Portuguese vessels going to the islands, by continuing trade relations with the Axis, and by refusing the United States the same use of the Azores as the British. The latter proved another thorny issue for Kennan when he was instructed by order of President Roosevelt to seek an interview with Salazar to request American military facilities on the Azores far greater than those Britain had been granted under the alliance. What the request amounted to, as Kennan grimly saw it, was "a virtual takeover of the islands by our armed forces for the duration of the war and the ruination of the culture and traditional mode of life of the inhabitants."

He knew Salazar would not agree. The prime minister had already fulfilled what he understood the Anglo-Portuguese alliance demanded of him, and in so doing had stretched Portuguese neutrality to the limit. Kennan also thought he now grasped why he had not been allowed to give Salazar assurances that the United States would guarantee Portuguese sovereignty in its possessions. Salazar would now believe, Kennan assumed, that America was telling him to allow full use of the Azores or they would be seized. In that case his response might be to turn the coin of the alliance and remind the British that he had honored it, now it was their turn to do so by protecting him from the Americans. Or he might, as Kennan noted, "have picked up his hat and gone back to the University of Coimbra . . . and said, 'If I have brought my country to a place where it is necessary to negotiate under the threat of violence, I am not the man to handle its affairs. Somebody else will have to do it.'" He would surely not, in any case, agree to American demands under what was plainly a threat. Kennan felt he had no choice but to challenge the presidential order.

There followed a standoff between Lisbon and Washington that resulted in Kennan being recalled home. After a painfully useless meeting with Secretary of War Henry Stimson and a roomful of top military brass— none of whom, the Lisbon chargé d'affaires concluded, knew nearly as much about Portugal as he did—Kennan found himself (after he had been closely vetted by Harry Hopkins, President Roosevelt's chief adviser) in a one-on-one meeting with the president. Roosevelt heard him out and said to return to the White House the following day to get a personal letter to present to Salazar. And then, added the president, "you just go ahead and do the best you can." Although elated by Roosevelt's confidence in him, Kennan still brought up his meeting at the War Department where those present seemed to have a different course in mind. As Kennan recorded his response, the president—"with a debonair wave of his cigarette holder"— said, "Oh, don't worry about all those *people* over there."

In his letter to Salazar, Roosevelt appealed for American use of the Azores on the grounds of shortening the war and saving British and American lives—and, in a chatty personal aside, recalled that as undersecretary of the navy in World War I he had visited bases in the Azores used by the Allies. After the war, when American forces had withdrawn, the president said he had "personally inspected everything, and the relationship at that time between Portugal and the United States was on a basis of mutual confidence and great friendship." The implication was that Portugal could expect the same total and efficient withdrawal from the islands once the current conflict ended.

In reply, Salazar observed that Portugal's situation was different now due to "well-known circumstances" of, presumably, his country's World War II neutrality. He had been "able to satisfy the desires of England" for use of the Azores bases because of the alliance. And "those concessions," he added in diplomatic-speak but with clear meaning, would also go "some distance towards meeting the requirements which we know exist on the part of the United States." The Azores agreement, in other words, was with the British; America's appeal for use of the bases as Britain's ally, and hence friends to friends of Portugal, would be allowed only under the umbrella of British authority. As the Lisbon ministry later set out the situation for Washington, Salazar was permitting "our immediate use of existing British facilities provided external appearance of adherence to existing British agreement is maintained." When an American naval air squadron began operating from an island airfield in 1944, the crews would maintain that appearance by wearing insignia of both Britain and the United States.

★   ★   ★

Full details of the Azores pact were yet to be worked out when in late 1943 a new American minister was appointed in Lisbon. A former ambassador to Peru, R. Henry Norweb was a career diplomat whom George Kennan liked and was pleased to serve under, but he stepped aside to let Norweb finish the arrangements. (While in Peru, Norweb had negotiated rights to military bases, leading the German press to announce about his present appointment that a "famous American base stealer" had been posted to Portugal.) After Kennan returned to the United States for reassignment, Norweb—with the rank of ambassador after the American legation was designated an embassy in June 1944—quickly recognized what dealing with the Portuguese was like. "We must remember," he wrote Secretary of State Hull, "that even if we can once overcome the qualms of principle in Dr. Salazar's mind we will still have to face the usual Portuguese proclivity for horse trading over details." (Kennan's version of the same view: "Salazar was a cautious man. All Portuguese are. They are the damnedest traders in the world. They can think of more reservations and little details.")

The fondness for bargaining over minutiae was again evident when the United States sought to build and operate a new air base on Santa Monica Island in the Azores. Norweb handled the trying talks in Lisbon that, without British involvement and the possibility of appeal to the alliance, inched along until Salazar finally consented in November 1944, some five months after the Normandy landings.

10

WAR WITHOUT GUNS

> For here too men were at war. A war without guns. A war of
> speculations, betrayals and secrets.
>
> —Frederic Prokosch, *The Conspirators*

Portugal came through the struggle over military use of the Azores with
the Union Jack ever more visible in its buttonhole yet its neutrality otherwise intact. But a second and more severe test, this involving Allied and
Axis demands for one of the country's few abundant natural resources, was
already in the making. Well before either defining challenge to its status,
however, the country knew war by other means in the form of intense
hearts-and-minds competition waged by the belligerents' propaganda machines. While all European neutrals were targets of propaganda, Portugal's
strategic assets—Atlantic location, open port, overseas possessions—made it
an especially contested battleground.

At the war's start Germany held the stronger hand. Following the
Spanish Civil War its firms had penetrated Portuguese commercial and
investment areas while the government exploited Salazar's fear of communism, a two-pronged approach that reminded British Ambassador Walford
Selby of Nazi tactics in Austria, his previous posting before Lisbon. When
the war began Germany also had in place Joseph Goebbels's well-oiled
propaganda apparatus. "Nazi Germany believes propaganda is as powerful
as Panzer divisions," Hugh Muir wrote of the Reich's Portuguese ambition, "and in Portugal Hitler's propaganda machine is geared to give its
maximum output."

Britain quickly formed a parallel organization, the Foreign Publicity
Directorate (FPD) within the Ministry of Information, and set to work

utilizing its strength of broad Anglophile feeling among the Portuguese people, usually calculated over the course of the war at some 80 percent of the population. In the long run, success for the British in the word war was largely a matter of holding the allegiance it already had. In practice this first meant assuring the Portuguese that Britain would survive the shooting war; later, that the outcome would be total Allied victory rather than a compromised peace; finally, that Britain would hold a leadership position in the postwar world.

Yet for both warring parties Portugal proved a troublesome propaganda market. Salazar's rigid interpretation of neutrality required equal treatment of the Axis and the Allies, Russia excepted, and his regime censored anything that seemed to tilt the balance, or that it simply found displeasing. The New State from the beginning had tightly controlled what its citizens could read and hear through a system of prior censorship set up to scrutinize books, magazines, and newspapers as part of a national—as an official decree had it—"labor of reconstruction and moral cleansing." A highly generous interpretation was that the dictator believed a nation with at least half its population illiterate needed protection against opposition voices promoting confusion and disorder. The society would be brought along with patient, fatherly care to see what was best for it. Savvy consumers, at any event, soon learned that Portugal's constrained media were at any moment a fair measure of the government's thinking.

In Antonio Tabucchi's brilliant short novel *Pereira Declares*, set in Lisbon in 1938, an aging journalist named Pereira—overweight, a widower, a University of Coimbra graduate and literary minded—is the culture editor of a minor newspaper called *Lisboa*, where he mostly writes advance obituaries and excerpts work from French writers but still must contend with censorship. When he translates for the paper a nineteenth-century story by Alphonse Daudet that ends with the phrase "Vive la France!", an acquaintance reminds him the government might not allow it to appear: ". . . there's the state censorship and every day, before your paper appears, the proofs are examined by the censors, and if there's something they don't like don't you worry it won't be printed, they leave blank spaces. . . ."

As it happens, the government censor allows the Daudet story to appear, but Pereira's boss, the paper's editor-in-chief, lectures him on the need for care in the future. Since the story concerns the Franco-Prussian War, it might give offense to Germany, which the editor points out is Portugal's ally. Pereira objects that the country has no alliance with Germany, but the editor insists it has "strong sympathies, we think along the same lines as Germany does." When Pereira falls back on the fact that the censor passed the story, the editor cynically instructs him on the role of self-censorship:

> The censors are a bunch of illiterate boobies . . . the chief censor is an intelligent man, a friend of mine, but he cannot personally read the proofs of every newspaper in Portugal, the others are just officials, common-or-garden policemen paid not to let through subversive words such as socialism or communism, they could scarcely be expected to understand a story by Daudet ending with the words "Vive la France!," it is we who must be vigilant, we who must be cautious, we journalists who are versed in history and culture, we have to keep a watchful eye on ourselves.

The censorship of Pereira's prewar period intensified in the neutrality of wartime, with the added concern now of giving no offense to the belligerents as well as the government. Space allotted to military accounts in Portuguese publications was finely calibrated to give the Allies and Axis equal space. Certain loaded words—"rout" to describe a battle result—were removed. Newspaper advertisements about shortwave broadcasts coming from London, Berlin, and the United States were restricted to identical size. When the journalists Reynolds and Eleanor Packard reached Lisbon on the exchange train from Italy, they were briefly able to transmit uncensored news dispatches until, as they later wrote, "the corrugated-iron shutters were dropped. . . . We had lunch with the chief censor and asked him about the change in censorship, and he replied: 'You sent your best material, didn't you? Now we have to placate the Axis. Remember, we are trying to be neutral.'"

William L. Shirer and Edward R. Murrow broke off their leisurely reunion in Estoril long enough to put together a radio broadcast from Lisbon, schedule it with CBS in New York, and submit their script to Portuguese censors. By telephone a censor politely told them he had translated two of the ten pages; he thought it possible he could finish the rest by the following week, after which the broadcast could take place. Murrow and Shirer argued their case until nearly airtime before concluding the censor would not speed up his pace.

In early 1940 the British embassy in Lisbon believed the Portuguese chief censor was so dazzled by Nazi combat success that he even restricted references to the Anglo-Portuguese alliance and what it required of both nations. At year's end, W. E. Lucas, the Lisbon correspondent of the London *Times*—and during 1940 listed on the masthead of the *Anglo-Portuguese News* as its director and proprietor—was given forty-eight hours to leave the country after authorities objected to uncensored stories he had written for the New York newspaper *PM* (and described in this book's opening chapter). Hauled before the secret police, Lucas defended his work, but a report found that "without the slightest regard for the country whose hospitality he benefits from, he did not hesitate to twist or make up facts, writing not just nonsense but also untruths which clash with national pride and which falsify Portugal's international stance." Although he apologized to the head of the secret police and the propaganda chief, Lucas's stay in Portugal was only slightly extended, and he left the country in early January 1941. Soon thereafter the government dispelled an Italian journalist, thereby rebalancing its treatment of Allied and Axis newsmen.

While newspapers and other media coming into Portugal from abroad were dutifully inspected, the effort was inconsistent because of divided attitudes within the secret police and the Salazar government. There was also inherent difficulty in the censors' guessing in advance what might offend the warring nations. One response was to assume anything might, so when newsreels of war events were shown in theaters, a notice on the screen asked for no expressions of sympathy for any of the belligerents. Pro-Allied audiences circumvented the prohibition by stamping their boots on the floor when Hitler appeared, having coughing fits when it was Mussolini, and shouting out "Viva Benfica!", the name of a Lisbon football club, for Churchill.

The sheer mechanics of monitoring the content of internal and external media were also daunting. Books were examined by a panel of censors, most of them military officers, while in Portuguese newspaper offices censors were permanently in place. Surprisingly, given Portugal's high rate of illiteracy, Lisbon in wartime had six daily morning newspapers and two evening papers, and in the country as a whole there were hundreds of newspapers and periodicals. An army of censors was needed, and they had to be given broad instruction about sensitive or dangerous subjects, then be able to apply what they were told to specific stories.

With foreign publications, even getting hold of material to inspect could prove difficult. When the head of Portuguese press censorship, a Colonel Alvaro Barreto, found he lacked funds to buy foreign newspapers, he ordered news agencies to provide them free. Then, overwhelmed by the number and variety of English-language papers, he decided that only some foreign publications would undergo censorship, with the list changed periodically. Since this meant that many non-English papers would also escape inspection, the British embassy's press attaché, Marcus Cheke, complained. Colonel Barreto's supposedly serious rejoinder was that since he and his workers could read only English in addition to Portuguese, there was no point of bothering with publications in other languages.

There was difficulty too in keeping absolute control of newspapers and magazines brought into the country by Portuguese fishermen (who could turn a tidy profit by buying them at sea from British fishermen, then reselling them when they returned home), merchant seamen, and passengers arriving on foreign ships and air flights. Nazi agents hunting for uncensored information staked out Lisbon's wharves and landing facilities and were known to pay as much as sixty dollars for a copy of the *New York Times*, with a single copy of *Life* magazine going for double the amount. Such publications were often badly dated by the time they reached enemy hands—a problem the Germans got around with American newspapers when they learned that the State Department furnished the Lisbon ministry with several current papers that were typically sent in microfilm form to save space and weight on Clipper flights, with a Lisbon photographer then enlarging the film. The Germans merely paid the photographer for extra sets and sent them winging off to Berlin.

★   ★   ★

In the war's early period Germany's newspapers and magazines overflowed Portuguese newsstands, and its radio broadcasts commanded the airwaves. Nazi pamphlets were routinely placed in trams, cafés, hotels, barbershops, hair salons, and the waiting rooms of doctors and dentists. The popular illustrated fortnightly magazine *Signal*, published in Portuguese and other languages and sold cheaply throughout Europe, had a wide audience for accounts of Nazi military triumphs and lavish picture displays of contented populations in conquered countries. When the British photographer Cecil Beaton leafed through some of the German propaganda magazines in Lisbon, he was struck by the high quality of the illustrations.

> Their photographs of the war [he wrote in his diary], both in colour and black and white, are so much more original than ours. Not only do they know the value of restraint in colour, but their attitude is so bold. They show dramatic blurs—pictures taken in semi-darkness, in smoke, in rain or fog that create a tremendous dramatic effect.

There was a bewildering contradiction, Beaton noted too, between the "contemporary spirit" displayed in the magazines and the constant Nazi railing against degenerate modern art.

Portuguese newspapers and radio stations could save the costs of subscribing to news services by accepting what Germany's Deutsches Nactrichtenbüro (DNB) provided free of charge. The news agency's Lisbon bureau recruited many of its staff from among Portuguese journalists, in return gaining an advantage in placing favorable stories in local newspapers and magazines. As for photographs, Portuguese publications could get British pictures by asking at the embassy while the Germans passed out theirs without waiting for requests. For journalists wanting them, the Germans provided language courses without charge. Bookstore windows in Lisbon and elsewhere in Portugal displayed stacks of Hitler's *Mein Kampf*, the copies given away to the shops or sold at small cost. Accompanying the media blitz were German "tourists" and "commercial travelers" who fanned out across the country with whispering campaigns of how much Portugal stood to benefit from a Nazi victory and, the bleak other side of the coin, how a British triumph would surely mean the end of Salazar and the dismantling of the overseas empire. For the Portuguese academic, business, and government elite, junkets to Germany were arranged to show at firsthand the achievements of national socialism.

The British counterattack against German intriguers, as they were known in the London press, was slow to get off the ground. Lecture tours of Portugal by public men, arranged by the British Council, were believed an effective tool—as noted in a press report of a series of talks in early 1940 by Lord Harlech on such carefully orchestrated subjects as Portuguese and British monuments and English university life—for forging "cultural relationships." But the report acknowledged that the Germans made a stronger propaganda drive to "force sympathy for their cause and ideology" by flooding Portuguese schools with attractive literature of all sorts. Hugh Muir, while he was working as the *Continental Daily Mail* correspondent in Paris when German troops reached the city gates in June 1940, reported that British propaganda at the time consisted of little more than readings over a local radio station of *Pride and Prejudice* and articles on cricket and India's trade figures. In Lisbon, British propaganda continued on a largely cultural course by promoting accounts of English life presumably appealing to Portuguese taste—sport, royalty, rural affairs, military figures, famous men such as Churchill. It backed away from political matters considered sensitive in the country—discussions of democratic society, for one—as well as overt anti-Italian or anti-German declarations.

The Duke of Kent's appearance at the Portuguese centenary celebration of 1940, extensively covered by the Portuguese press and recorded in movie newsreels shown about the country, was considered a major propaganda triumph. So too on the exposition grounds in Belém was the Hall of the Anglo-Portuguese Alliance, which the British had adorned with documents, portraits, and banners highlighting the age-old links between the two nations. Favorable treatment of the centenary in the London *Times* was duly reproduced by Lisbon papers. Victory of another sort came in June 1941 when a group of Oxford dons traveled to the University of Coimbra to present Salazar with an honorary doctorate, the degree bestowed with an address in Latin and Salazar replying in kind. Earlier the dictator had steered clear of the award since he had turned down honorary degrees from German universities. The event was "first class propaganda," the British ambassador in Lisbon gleefully informed London. "The Germans are livid."

Still, unambiguous propaganda triumphs were few and far between, leaving great swaths of time in which—as David Eccles concluded from his position within the British embassy—the "demented atmosphere in Portugal played into the hands of the Germans." He decided "the best personal reply an Englishman could make was a show of exuberant confidence in our ultimate victory." What this meant in daily life was the pleasant duty of taking attractive women to the best restaurants and either giving or attending a party nearly every evening. When Eccles invited a woman he met on the beach to lunch and she turned out to be the daughter of a German military attaché, the news got back to Salazar—who passed it off by saying it seemed Eccles was enjoying Lisbon society, and offering him use of a rose-colored palace in the event he was thinking of giving a ball. "He approved our confidence in ourselves," Eccles decided about the incident. "The Germans could not compete in light-heartedness and, although some members of the British colony were shocked, the social bravado paid off."

In time Britain challenged Germany in more typical propaganda fashion by producing an illustrated magazine distributed throughout Portugal, subsidizing Portuguese publications, providing increased funding for its Exchange Telegraph's cable news service in Portugal, introducing Reuters news service into the country, and through broadcasting the BBC's Portuguese-language news programs. A grant from the British Council enabled the *Anglo-Portuguese News* to shift from fortnightly to weekly publication for the duration of the war, while Marcus Cheke led groups of Portuguese journalists on tours of England.

After the British began enjoying some military success in North Africa in 1941, the Lisbon propagandists finally had some war stories to boast about—and surveys showed British accounts getting more play in local newspapers and on radio stations than German reports. This reversed an earlier trend in which DNB and the Vichy-controlled French service Havas had been dominant. Theater showings of British feature films began making some headway against Portuguese censorship, though a plan to send traveling film vans into rural areas was scrapped out of concern the Germans might do the same and the government would put a stop to both.

Overall the British may have gained a measure of sympathetic media treatment simply as a reaction against the Reich's insistent bluster about ill treatment by the Portuguese. As early as the summer of 1940 the German minister in Lisbon was firing off sharp protests about pro-Allied stories, the failure of many Portuguese periodicals to carry German propaganda, and a similar failure of the government to close down publications considered offensive. Between June 1940 and June 1944 Germany submitted more than a hundred formal press protests compared to nine by Britain.

A persistent problem for Lisbon's British propagandists, on the other hand, came from accounts in London publications that Portuguese authorities viewed as critical of Salazar—and British writers and journalists defended as simply factual reporting about how his repressive regime functioned. Marcus Cheke, on the receiving end of a stream of Portuguese complaints, pleaded for a softer tone from London, even occasional flattery of Salazar and his works. (Cheke's scholarly 1938 biography of the figure whose imposing statue stands at the head of the Avenida da Liberdade had carried a blunt title: *Dictator of Portugal: A Life of the Marquis of Pombal, 1699–1782*.) He kept pointing out that, for his propaganda efforts in Portugal to go forward at all, a working relationship with the government was a basic need. In London the Foreign Office mildly cautioned the British press to treat the Portuguese regime at least with some care.

BBC radio broadcasts from London equally drew Portuguese ire. A particular issue arose over the presence of what the government considered anti-Salazar broadcasters slanting the news service coming into Portugal. Removing one of them, António Cortesao, a Portuguese, became a heated demand, and under pressure from the regime as well as Lisbon's British embassy the BBC sacked him. A further irritant was the BBC's favorable treatment of Britain's wartime alliance with Russia, though here—as in most printed and broadcast disputes—London officials refused to wholly tailor their work to fit Portuguese attitudes. In July 1942 *The Economist* pointed to an evident lack of balance in Salazar's renewed complaints, during a radio address to the Portuguese people, about the Allied blockade and the Anglo-Soviet relationship. In speaking of the blockade, said the magazine, the prime minister should take into account the German U-boat campaign, which had also helped turn shipping into "the one great intractable problem of the war effort. Portugal, as a maritime Power, cannot expect to be totally unaffected by it." As for the Soviet alliance, at a time when Russia on one side of Europe and the Anglo-Saxon powers on the other stood between Portugal and "the most ruthless, godless and soulless tyranny mankind has ever known," the "terrors of Bolshevism might with rather more realism be allowed to fade a little." Beyond this, the magazine went on, Russia would be a major postwar power regardless of the pact with Britain, and it was in the interests of Portugal and other nations to look ahead to drawing it into a peaceful new Europe rather than walled off in hostile isolation.

Nonetheless Nazi insistence that the British blockade harmed the economy—that free of it Portugal would rank among the richest of countries—remained throughout the war a potent weapon of German propaganda. Equally telling was the belief pushed by the Nazis that the Allied war aim of overthrowing dictators in Berlin and Rome also extended to Salazar in Lisbon—and that the allegiance with Russia meant that, with an Allied victory, a Bolshevik wave would sweep across Europe. When Germany invaded Russia in June 1941, some members of the Portuguese Legion, a voluntary adult militia formed by Salazar in 1936, were vocally eager to join the Wehrmacht on the eastern front. Since Spain raised the Blue Division for combat, German circles expected that Portugal would follow suit. But when the German minister in Lisbon called on him, Salazar skirted the issue by saying he would give consideration only to a demonstration by the Legion in support of the German effort. According to a report to London by the British ambassador, when the German military attaché in Lisbon asked Portuguese authorities for direct aid in putting together a Legion force for Russia, he was declared persona non grata.

The closest Portugal came to joining the struggle was to send a young military officer as an observer with German forces. His reports to Lisbon, so it was said, strengthened Salazar's commitment to neutrality by convincing him the German cause was hopeless. Still, British propagandists had to keep hammering home to the Portuguese that, despite the Anglo-Russian alliance, a steadfast political distinction existed between English democracy and Soviet communism. An unexpected ally in moderating Portuguese attitudes toward Russia appeared in the spring of 1942 when the Catholic Patriarch of Lisbon, Manuel Conçalves Cerejeira, instructed the country's clergy that while preaching to their congregations they were not to identify Communist ideology with the Russian nation. Nor should they, on the other hand, identify anti-communism as the crusade of any great power. According to press reports, in his directives Cardinal Cerejeira was trying to halt parish sermons that had become so anti-Russian as to be effectively anti-British and pro-German.

★   ★   ★

Some small-scale British efforts to counteract German propaganda were easily arranged yet could have disappointing consequences. When the British matched the Germans with war-photograph displays in shop windows in Lisbon and elsewhere—an attempt at getting around media censorship of military news—the London *Times* judged the pictures so dull, static, and insignificant that no Fleet Street photo editor would bother looking at them, let alone the passing Portuguese. By contrast, the "thrilling action pictures" of German displays were said to "hold the unwilling attention of everybody, and there is a bustling crowd round them all day long." The differing appeal of the displays was made all the more galling by the newspaper's disclosure that Britain had gotten window space usually without rental charge while Germany had to pay at high rates.

In a controversy over wearing military badges in public, on the other hand, the British effortlessly carried the day. When the government bowed to German protests and declared that Royal Air Force badges could not be worn on Lisbon streets, the order was not enforced. Yet when Germany began a Luftwaffe campaign, police confiscated the badges. The unequal treatment, as British propagandists explained it, was the result of government fear that other Portuguese would rip off the German badges. Early in the war an American correspondent reported seeing RAF emblems everywhere in Lisbon but noticed only a single Luftwaffe symbol, this worn by a newspaperman in the office of what he considered the pro-German *Diário de Notícias*.

German black propaganda (by one definition, propaganda masking its true origin, as against white propaganda which acknowledged it) was employed as readily in Lisbon as the white variety, with the usual mixed bag of results. A German-produced edition of London's *Daily Mail*, sent to Lisbon by air, was an exact replica of that day's paper save for an article labeling the Portuguese army as cowardly. Meant to strike a blow at the Anglo-Portuguese alliance, the forgery backfired when British officials quickly publicized it, thereby bringing it to the attention of Portuguese who had never seen the paper. A German deception that had the desired effect was an announcement placed in a Lisbon newspaper about well-paying jobs for men, and giving the address of the British consulate. When a large number of applicants showed up, the consulate was left trying to explain that it knew nothing about the openings. The same trick played on the American consulate brought the same result. Another successful German scheme was to buy up and hoard basic foodstuffs, then let it about that the shortages were due to the Allied sea blockade.

Yet despite making inroads here and there, German propaganda over the course of the war was unable to seriously erode broad popular support for Britain within Portugal. If anything, the Reich pushed its agenda too tenaciously, trying to force rather than cajole the Portuguese into Nazi arms. A notable instance came in September 1942 when the German legation invited movie critics and other Lisbon residents to a first showing of a propaganda film about the disastrous failure of an Allied raid at Dieppe on the northern coast of France. The Associated Press reported—and got through censors—that critics in the audience were unimpressed by the curtly titled *How We Dealt with the British at Dieppe.* Augusto Fraga, one of Lisbon's leading film critics, believed the Germans had doctored the work. "In order to produce this film," he reported, "they had to bring in a lot of clever studio work and make-ups, which no longer pass unnoticed by movie fans." He went on: "The only real things actually shown were British prisoners being marched in the streets—some in underwear—and the tremendous destruction the raiders did until their re-embarkation." Fraga was equally critical of a figure who commented on the film: "He meant to help the poor show by joking about each scene. . . . Such statements, aimed to make the audience laugh . . . found no or little response." About one scene, called by Fraga the most impressive in the film, the commentator said nothing—and the critic came away with a feeling of his own that was clearly the reverse of the unalloyed German triumph the film intended to convey. The scene revealed the

> gloomy sight of scores of [Allied] men—probably hundreds—who fell dead on barbed-wire fences. The commentator did not explain how they were killed, but the general impression was that the barbed wire carried a strong electric current, because some were holding the wires tight with both hands.

The Germans overreached in another and equally apparent way when they remodeled a Lisbon building for use as a tourist agency and began operating it following the Allied invasion of North Africa. The Portuguese, hardly taken in by a tourist agency with some twenty young "clerks" when there was no tourism, referred to the refurbished building as the "second front." They delighted in dropping in and innocently asking if vacation trips were available to Hamburg or if they might buy tickets to Stalingrad. Such inquiries were reportedly met with a courteous and deadpan no.

Gradual Allied success on the battlefield also deflected the impact of German propaganda aimed at the Portuguese, and may even have weakened previously tight Nazi control over the prewar German colony in Portugal. As early as the summer of 1941 the Lisbon correspondent of the London *Times* reported that though attendance at National Socialist meetings, financial contributions, and acceptance of some tasks were still expected of them, local Germans who only passively approved of Hitler were now treated with less bullying, even with a measure of kindliness. It was as if, the correspondent speculated, the Germans in Portugal, both the leaders and the led, were "subconsciously trying to pick up again former contacts unconnected with Nazi ideas—old German and neutral friendships, old hobbies and interests, all those things which can continue and develop when the Nazi regime has passed away."

★   ★   ★

Together with its propaganda endeavor within Portugal, Britain used the country as a launching pad for black propaganda aimed at occupied nations and the German heartland. In the autumn of 1941 David E. Walker arrived in Lisbon with just such a psychological warfare mission. An agent of Britain's Special Operations Executive (SOE), a secret sabotage, subversion, and black propaganda group formed after the fall of France for action in neutral and enemy countries, Walker had behind him wide experience with British intelligence operations in Switzerland, Romania, and the Balkans. His cover for the clandestine work had been that he was a freelance journalist sending reports to the London *Daily Mirror*, in reality his former employer. He was back in London and working as a journalist when he was recruited by the SOE and sent to Portugal with the cover that he was now a staff correspondent for the *Mirror*, which in fact he was.

Lisbon was rich turf for Walker's deception assignment, given its population of Axis nationals who mingled in bars, cafés, and hotel lounges in the guise of businessmen or stranded exiles, and eagerly soaked up information to relay to Berlin or Rome. Axis diplomats offered fertile ground as well, and it seemed wholly natural for a journalist to seek them out for seemingly routine conversations. Walker cultivated his territory with a cadre of troops he engaged and sent into action with London's consent. The stories they planted, all hatched in London and known in the trade as Sibs—short for sibilant, a hissing sound, a whisper in the ear—were calculated, as a British source delicately put it, "to inconvenience the enemy" to the extent, in accumulated form, of weakening his will to continue the war.

Once a week an attractive woman met Walker in one of Lisbon's coffee houses. They sat and gossiped, then the woman left and Walker stayed behind to pay the bill—and pick up a newspaper the woman had left behind. Inside was a piece of paper with some unrelated words on it—to all appearances, the sort of random notes a journalist might make as reminders for himself. For Walker the jottings were Sibs to set in word-of-mouth motion.

His first Lisbon effort involved planting a markedly low-level Sib aimed at the enemy's economy. Among the ways the manufacturing behemoth I. G. Farben propped up the German war machine was by acquiring foreign currencies through its sales, with aspirin one of its humble but profitable overseas products. Since sexual prowess was everywhere important to men and, so it was believed, mightily so in Latin counties, the Sib whispered about in Lisbon was that German aspirin, taken regularly, led to impotence. That men did not speak out about the unwelcome condition was explained as normal reticence about intimate matters. Certainly, as the Sib went on, Farben would correct its aspirin problem, but the necessities of German war manufacturing might slow the process. In the meantime, the wise course was to buy other brands.

The most effective Sibs were those with at least a modest factual basis. After Hitler attacked Russia in June 1941, physical conditions facing the Wehrmacht in winter offered many possibilities. The Sibs simply helped spread accounts given out by returning troops of typhus, frostbite, compulsory delousing, and overwhelming physical filth on the eastern front. London always sought confirmation that launched stories were reaching their intended targets, with the come-backs, as they were known, the tool used to evaluate SOE agents in the field. Reports from intelligence agents in occupied Europe indicated that accounts of physical misery in Russia had indeed gotten back to German troops preparing, with evident lack of enthusiasm, to go into action. Whether a successful Sib had been initiated in Lisbon or in such other neutral sites as Stockholm, Cairo, Buenos Aires, Dublin, Madrid, Berne, or Ankara, London never disclosed.

Of course some Sibs, possibly most, never got off the ground at all. Some were so obviously senseless they were never tried. At times, though, it was possible to give a jolt of life to a feeble story by stressing that it was obviously false. "Have you ever heard such bunkum?" Walker would say. "Some damned Italian here from Rome claims that Himmler has been dead three months—killed on Hitler's orders. They're using a stand-in until they make the news official." In theory Walker was not to initiate stories himself, though opportunities that came his way were hard to resist. "Never in my life, before or since," he wrote, "have I had so much to say, so many things to tell people, as during the Lisbon interlude."

Most of his work was done through his dissemination team of various nationalities and language abilities and with contact lines to several enemy groups. The essence of the job was to fit his workers into places that were plausible settings for what they were selling. Some Sibs were best initiated by waiters in restaurants, others by seamen in the bars and brothels along the Tagus waterfront. Sibs of a higher order were more at home in diplomatic receptions and garden parties. Nightclubs were always good starting points since recent Axis arrivals, enlivened by Lisbon's lack of blackouts and ample food and drink, were determined to enjoy the evenings—and likely to carry back home what they had overheard in the unguarded atmosphere. For Walker's purposes, the best of the Lisbon nightspots was the Nina Bar, packed each evening with Britons and Germans, Free French and Vichy French, Greeks and Italians, all sitting side-by-side at tables and brushing shoulders on the dance floor. The owner of the bar, a dapper young Austrian, circulated among the partygoers each night, dispensing the latest London Sibs.

To carry on with his undercover operation, Walker had to maintain his cover as a *Daily Mirror* correspondent, and in this he was innocently aided by *Time* magazine naming him and quoting a report he had written about neutral countries having reason to worry about Hitler's intentions. "Germany's most dangerous secret agents are at work in Portugal," Walker wrote. "One of them is an old enemy of mine. He is notorious and wears a monocle. I was personally depressed last night to see him in Lisbon. The last time I saw him was in . . . Bucharest, just before the occupation of Rumania, and in . . . Belgrade, before the attack on Yugoslavia." *Time* commented that "such E. Phillips Oppenheimish apprehensions were commonplace realities last week among Europe's chief neutrals." By the spring of 1942 Walker was doing his newspaper work from an office in an area of Lisbon where few foreigners lived. The building also housed the office of a correspondent of the London *Daily Herald*, and on the ground floor was a printing operation, both adding to the picture that he was just another working journalist. He seemed all the more so when he began reporting for the *Christian Science Monitor* and the London *Times* as well as the *Mirror*. The *Times* position—a choice job since the paper was held in high regard throughout the Portuguese government—came about when its Lisbon man, W. E. Lucas, was expelled from Portugal and Walker was appointed acting correspondent.

While workaday activity as a journalist formed Walker's Lisbon cover, so too did spending his free time blending into the background as a British expatriate—a task, as he later wrote, that "was certainly not arduous." He found the Portuguese friendly, living costs cheap, and the Salazar dictatorship nothing to be greatly upset about. The contrasts between life in battered London and bountiful Lisbon caused him only passing pangs of conscience. On sunny days Lisbon seemed to him to rise away from the Tagus like a wedding cake, tier upon tier of beauty; at dusk it took on a rose coloring, and by moonlight it looked Athenian. "Despite all the poverty and squalor hidden by its superficial charms," he noted, "the city was meticulously clean; and there were very few who did not fall under its easy-going, noisy, garrulous spell." One day on a tennis court he met a woman recently arrived from London and fell under *her* spell. In May 1943 they married and spent their honeymoon on a farm near Caldas da Rainha—more evidence, if more was needed, that he was just another Brit comfortably at home in Portugal.

With the war elsewhere, the British community went about keeping up the national rituals of tennis and cricket at Ajuda, golf in Estoril, pink gins at the Royal British Club. They went native to the extent of eating octopus or dried cod done in various ways, drinking the country's tart green wine, attending bullfights—in which, in the Portuguese manner, the bull was never killed in the ring—and in nightclubs listening to the mournful laments of fado ("the immensely sad songs of Portugal," as Walker described them, "that had everybody weeping, except the English who could not understand them"). During cocktail parties in villas along the Sun Coast there would now and then come the distant sound of explosions at sea from bombs falling on convoys. "We were sitting on the edge of the war," Walker recorded of life in Portugal, "with our feet dangling over the side."

As Lisbon took on more diplomatic and intelligence-gathering importance, the British colony swelled. In addition to the ministerial staff, the embassy had three military attachés, a press office with a staff of forty, various departments engaged in economic warfare, and a large number of young women busily encoding and decoding the cable traffic between Lisbon and London. There were also staff members for the consulate and passport office as well as the British Institute, the British Council, and the British Red Cross. And there was always a flow of English transients traveling under false identities of a sort. Once the naval attaché introduced Walker to a Mr. Mountain, and the three went out on the town for drinks. Oddly for a wily secret agent and inquisitive newspaperman, weeks went by before Walker learned that Mr. Mountain was Louis Mountbatten.

As the war evolved with the Japanese attack on Pearl Harbor and Allied landings in North Africa, Walker and his collection of agents had better material to work with. With it now certain that the next stage of the war would be a direct assault on Europe, Sibs arrived from London at a rapid rate—and there were "mid-week specials," as Walker called them, that were to be pushed immediately to aid some tactical military maneuver. Stories were planted about corruption within the German homeland, Hitler's sanity, what foreign laborers in Germany might be doing behind the backs of the troops, America's immense economic power, the lawless nature of Russian soldiers, and what to expect when Allied bombing went into high gear. As the Italian campaign progressed and attention shifted to the cross-Channel invasion of France, the SOE's deception work in Lisbon and elsewhere pulled out all the stops in a major campaign to disguise the Normandy beaches as the landing site.

After the eventual breakthrough from the beaches and the Allied drive across France, Walker's work in Lisbon was essentially over. London agreed he could replace a *Daily Mirror* correspondent who had been killed on D-Day, and in the summer of 1944 he resigned from the London *Times* and the *Christian Science Monitor* and closed up his deception section of SOE operations in Portugal. His team of devoted workers—Walker resisted an impulse to have a group photograph taken as a souvenir—faded back into their other lives, and he left from Portela airfield for London. By autumn he was attached to the American Ninth Army on its way from Holland into Germany.

★   ★   ★

American entry into the propaganda war with the formation of the Office of War Information (OWI) in June 1942, under the direction of the popular radio commentator Elmer Davis, had given Britain's FPD both a powerful partner and fresh problems. The two propaganda organizations were closely and effectively linked but inevitable strains arose over aims and means. The Americans typically combined propaganda with political aims while the British tended to keep the two separate. And the Americans came with piles of money for the services of local workers and a seemingly endless supply of Hollywood films, which the British could only hope to match with better quality. The British generally felt that any major American propaganda venture within Portugal was wasteful duplication since the country was already pro-British. Still, Marcus Cheke reported to London that the Americans "appear to have ambitious plans" for Portugal, and he wondered whether "a major reduction in our propaganda services is now desirable on political grounds."

A prickly conflict arose when the OWI provided radio equipment to the BBC in return for use of time slots on its European Service, with the result that broadcasts to Portugal were cut back and replaced with programming by Voice of America. A British official protested—the American offerings were said to be poorly designed and the announcing "unpleasant"—and after the State Department intervened the OWI agreed to follow the BBC's wealth of experience in broadcast matters. The British were also annoyed with the sheer size of the American propaganda project. By the end of 1943 the OWI's Overseas Branch, operating from a base in London, had some 300 workers in the city; soon after the Normandy landings the number ballooned to more than 2,500 people churning out publications, leaflets, films, and radio programs destined for the Continent.

For all its size, OWI London was only part of the American propaganda effort abroad. In 1943 a second organization appeared with the formation of the Office of Strategic Service's Morale Operations Branch (MO), with a mission of vigorously pursuing black propaganda warfare against Germany. Modeled on Britain's SOE, the MO came late to the war and was always a much smaller organization than that put together by the OWI. Yet during a brief existence from 1943 to 1945 its no-holds-barred approach to covert operations—as one historian described its achievements—"implemented campaigns of a scope and level of sophistication beyond any propaganda ever practiced by the Nazis."

An early MO undertaking was a profile of Hitler written by Walter C. Langer, a Harvard psychologist who later became head of the OSS's Research and Analysis Branch. It drew on interviews with such German exiles as Ernst Hanfstaengl and Otto Strasser and was meant to provide the basis for a sweeping rumor operation directed against the Führer. Set in motion by undercover agents, radio broadcasts, leaflets, forged documents and letters, black newspapers, and plants in genuine newspapers, such psychological ploys were a favored MO style of attack—and judged as hitting their target if they were repeated in other media as legitimate information or angrily denounced by Nazi officials. An example was the League of Lonely German Women, dreamed up by the MO to prey on the anxiety of soldiers about the behavior of the women they had left behind. A widely circulated leaflet told the troops to display a small red heart when they were on leave in restaurants or bars, the badge marking them for members of the League, all of whom were eager to lift morale by bestowing sexual favors. Stories about the leaflets subsequently showed up in American and other national publications, and numerous captured German troops carried with them both a leaflet and a red badge of hopeful encounters.

Radio was one of the MO Branch's more effective means of spreading deceptive material. Among its varied efforts was cooperation with the British in running a station supposedly broadcasting from Calais, France, while actually transmitting from Woburn, England. As the station expanded its popular programming—so popular that the Germans repeatedly warned against tuning in, though it was said that Goebbels did so—of news, music, and propaganda aimed at civilians and enemy troops, the MO drew on the services of Hollywood writers, an orchestra, film stars like Marlene Dietrich, and singers from the New York Metropolitan Opera for its twelve-hour-a-day schedule. After the failed attempt to kill Hitler in July 1944, the station carried the names of those possibly involved in the plot, trying in the confusion of the moment to eliminate a wide spectrum of German leaders. Reports after the war showed that the Gestapo took an active interest in the names.

As British and American bombers began making regular appearances over Europe, so too the Continent was bombarded by Allied radio broadcasts, with the Voice of America bridging the Atlantic by having its shortwave broadcasts picked up in England and sent on by British transmitters. Only just before the Normandy invasion did the OWI install its own medium-frequency transmitters in England for American broadcasting directly into Europe. After Operation Torch, new stations were set up in North Africa to penetrate Europe by radio from the south. But from whatever angle broadcasters took, they were up against the obstacle of unrelenting German jamming—and the threat of arrest or worse for those in the Reich or occupied countries caught listening to programs that did get through. The extensive and costly jamming effort was considered evidence that Germany believed Allied radio was a vital wartime tool, a view corroborated after the war by a study showing that roughly half of German adults said they had heard foreign broadcasts.

The written word joined the spoken in forms ranging from leaflets to books, which agents from England smuggled into occupied territory or were dropped by planes. From the start of the war the British conducted "confetti raids" on their high-altitude nightly bombing missions, and American flyers eventually mastered the techniques of dropping leaflet bundles by parachute and at lower levels during their daylight raids. For informing the French in the unoccupied part of the country about the Allied war effort, American OWI propagandists developed a four-page weekly newspaper, *L'Amérique en Guerre*, printing five thousand copies a week and sending them by air to Lisbon, from where they went into a diplomatic pouch carried to the American ministry in Vichy and the consulate in Marseille.

The producers acknowledged that the paper was "a dowdy little sheet about half the size of a tabloid" and a small instrument of war at best; but the ministry kept welcoming the paper until Germany occupied Vichy France and the American diplomatic corps was interned. With the Vichy outlet closed off, *L'Amérique* went on to bigger and better things. In November 1942 the British dropped a new airborne edition of 250,000 copies on Paris and northern French cities. The paper was still a four-pager but carried three columns of news on each page and had illustrations. In January 1943 page size was increased; it now bore an American flag on the masthead, and it carried four-color maps and illustrations. When American planes joined in dropping the paper, circulation sometimes reached a spectacular seven million copies a week. OWI's Overseas Branch also put together a miniature weekly for Spain, *Carta de America*, in an attempt to balance favorable German treatment in the Spanish press. Like *L'Amérique*, the paper reached Lisbon by air and was sent on by diplomatic pouch to Madrid.

The OWI's favored publication directed to friendly and neutral nations was *Victory*, an illustrated magazine printed on slick paper and both offered for sale and given away to barber and beauty shops and to hotels. Writing in *The New Yorker* in 1944, Marya Mannes reported that despite the volume of free copies in circulation, *Victory* was snapped up from Lisbon newsstands the moment new issues appeared.

★   ★   ★

Following the cross-Channel invasion, disagreements surfaced among Allied propagandists in Portugal and elsewhere over American psychological warfare tactics, which the British found overly aggressive. With Allied forces now in enemy territory, the American view was that propaganda efforts should not only assist the military machine but be out in front of its progress. An OWI directive set out the new policy: "From now on our propaganda offensive will run boldly in advance of our military offensive. We shall proceed on the implicit assumption that the German will to resist can be broken and will be broken by next December."

To that end American propagandists, working on the assumption that the attempt on Hitler's life in July revealed the presence of a large peace movement in Germany, appealed to the populace through leaflets and radio broadcasts to take acts of passive resistance, pushed rumors of the Führer's worsening health, and promoted the surrender of German troops. With the last, the propaganda effort had some success, as it had in the earlier military campaign in Italy. Anthony Eden revealed in the House of Commons that 77 percent of German prisoners captured after D-Day said they had heard or seen appeals to surrender, and 40 percent had leaflets with them when they did so.

Another aspect of American propaganda tactics with the war's end in sight was directly to challenge neutral countries to support the Allied cause. This meant no longer giving material aid to Germany but also actively cooperating with the Allies; continuing on the sidelines, it was made clear, would be a postwar liability. In Portugal the British, always better attuned to Salazar's inclinations, realized the country would not wholly abandon neutrality under pressure. While it would move closer to the Allied cause, there remained, among other divisive issues, the large obstacle of the Communist Soviet Union and the prime minister's less than enthralled view of Americans and their hard-charging methods. But the British also understood that American propaganda aimed at Portugal, considerably increased after Normandy, had had the effect of enhancing the United States in Portuguese eyes at the expense of Britain. In a memorandum from Lisbon in September 1944, Marcus Cheke offered London a clear-eyed, if rueful, assessment of American propaganda at work:

> The inflated staffs of the U.S. Mission go about their business in the latest and most flashy of American cars, which are expressly reserved for U.S. officials abroad, and whet the appetites of the Portuguese, planning a brave new world to come. . . . It is reasonable to suppose that so long as the U.S. is to play a part in Europe, Portugal, with its Atlantic seaboard, will be a country of prime importance to them. However this may be, this intensive propaganda is having some effect in turning the minds of the Portuguese toward America and therefore away from Britain. I submit that it would be dangerous complacency to assume that their effort is a mere flash in the pan and that we can afford to live on the capital of sentimental ties, goodwill, and trade connections accumulated in the past.

His country's best bet, Cheke added, was to concentrate its attention on Salazar, whose bond with Britain was strong, and who was inclined to believe the British could serve to balance American as well as Russian power in the Europe to come.

Disagreements and rivalries aside, with the push across France into Germany the Allied propaganda machines found themselves flush with success in Portugal. The Salazar regime now leaned so far to the Allied cause that editorials in Portuguese newspapers anticipated a swift Nazi defeat, and newsreels of the Normandy landings and the liberation of Paris were shown to cheering audiences. Tributes to Churchill and the Anglo–Portuguese alliance were everywhere in newspapers and magazines. Use of Reuters and Exchange Telegraph by the Portuguese press now far eclipsed that of Germany's DNB. A news bulletin put out by the British embassy's press office reached a monthly circulation of 74,000 copies, and British and American feature films were shown in cinemas throughout the country with few restrictions.

Perhaps the most telling sign of the propagandists' triumph was that the Salazar regime came around to acknowledging Russia's participation in the war. Newsreel footage of Stalin was allowed in cinemas for the first time in February 1945, causing Stephen Lockhart, who had replaced Marcus Cheke as the new British press attaché, to note that "in all cases the reaction [of the audience] was the same, a gasp of surprise and astonishment whenever he appeared." Salazar's explanation for allowing the newsreels was clipped and pragmatic: "Since Stalin existed it was no use behaving as if he did not!"

11

THE SEETHING CAULDRON

> . . . the already seething cauldron of espionage and counter-
> espionage that wartime Lisbon constituted.
>
> —George F. Kennan, *Memoirs, 1925–1950*

When he became counselor of the American legation in Lisbon in the late
summer of 1942, George Kennan had more than routine diplomatic
duties to deal with. As he later revealed, his "real mission . . . was the co-
ordination of American intelligence in Portugal," and taking on the chores
of legation counselor was necessary to preserve his cover. Intelligence operations in Portugal had "gotten rather fouled up," he further noted, and
he was charged with "trying to disentangle things." In another context he
said that, privately and informally, he had been asked to "straighten out
the dreadful confusions which our various intelligence people had created,
among themselves and with the British. . . ." Kennan did not to disclose
the particular nature of the confusions, leaving it that they were caused by
efforts of American secret agents to "insert themselves," belatedly, into the
"seething cauldron" of Lisbon's spy war.

During wartime and in later accounts, the city's shadow world encouraged metaphors. "Great clearing house" of spying was common, as in
an editorial in *The Economist* in 1942: "The place [Lisbon] has become a
great clearing house for international information, a centre of espionage and
a meeting place where thousands of invaluable contacts can be developed
or maintained." Others depicted the city as a crossroads, ant heap, hot
bed, skulking place, playing field, nerve center, listening post, and so on,
of clandestine activity. But Kennan's hackneyed, thriller-fiction image of a
seething cauldron stands out for its suggestion that Lisbon's spy stew was a

mix of agents and double agents, amateurs and professionals, the comically furtive and the deadly serious. That Kennan may have intended such a thickly layered view is supported, perhaps, by his going on to say about his intelligence task that he accomplished it, but "not without the usual lurid byplay—sometimes (and usually) laughable, sometimes fantastic, sometimes hair-raising."

Rather than metaphor, the British journalist and author Phillip Knightley used an apocryphal story to portray the amusing side of Lisbon spying. A small-time Portuguese agent—call him X—contacted the British in Lisbon and offered to sell them a new German codebook for $100,000. After some deliberation the British forked over the money. Then X contacted the Germans in Lisbon and said he had valuable information that he would sell for $100,000. When the Germans agreed, he told them he had sold their new codebook to the British. Rather than responding angrily, the Germans realized they could use the code to plant false information that would have the British running in circles. Then X went back to the British and told them he would tell them something *really* valuable for another $100,000—which was that he had told the Germans about selling the codebook to the British. At this point the British had had enough and told X to expect a very serious accident in the near future. But before the accident could take place the British received a call from the chief of the Portuguese secret police, who simply said, "I understand you people have been threatening my partner."

All neutral countries had the same magnetic pull for spies as they did for propagandists. Yet here again Portugal, with its open port of entry and exit and its evenhanded neutrality, offered a particularly enticing field for both Allied and Axis intelligence operations. In his 1957 novel *The Case of the Four Friends*, Britain's highly placed wartime spymaster J. C. Masterman (about whom more below) has a character explain Portugal's importance for agents of both sides:

> Portugal was neutral, and so to Portugal came the agents official and unofficial of many countries and countries on both sides. It was not possible to learn in Berlin what was happening in London, but it might well be possible to hear, or guess, or deduce in neutral Portugal what was happening in both. And further, it might be possible to spread information (and make it appear credible) of what was *not* happening in London or Berlin and yet have it believed in the other place. And so Lisbon became a kind of international clearing-ground, a busy ant-heap of spies and agents, where political and military secrets and informa-

tion—true and false, but mainly false—were bought and sold and where
men's brains were pitted against each other.

All told, it is estimated that as many as forty to fifty foreign intelligence
services were at work in wartime Lisbon. But nationally formed groups occupied a high end of espionage activity—a level at which, as Masterman's
novel has it, men's brains were pitted in competition. Far below was a vast
outcropping of watchers, informants, and freelance agents whom the journalist Jack Alexander, writing in the *Saturday Evening Post* in 1943, crisply
evoked by quoting an unnamed Portuguese: "Everyone in Lisbon make
espionage." Only slightly less bold, American military intelligence in the
same year reported that "a remarkably high proportion of the inhabitants
[of Portugal] are working for one or more intelligence services." And the
same report added: "Espionage has become a national Portuguese racket."

Harvey Klemmer, in his *National Geographic* article, questioned the
importance of intelligence gathering when conducted as a mass occupation:
if "the suave young men and the beautiful young women who loiter about
the hotels" were truly dangerous agents, "they would take more pains to
hide their identity." This seemed equally true of spies who invariably hung
about in bars. Klemmer told of meeting one night with an American businessman at the bar of the Palácio Hotel in Estoril and cautioning him that
there were Germans present. "Don't worry about them," the man replied.
"They're just a bunch of leg men. The one on the left tells Musso [Mus-
solini] who's here. The big fellow does the same for Himmler. The little
guy keeps Goebbels supplied with English newspapers."

The leg men and women, the bottom feeders of the spy trade, were
found everywhere in Lisbon and along the Sun Coast, using their eyes and
ears and not infrequently only their imaginations to earn their keep from
the intelligence services, or simply an evening meal. These paid informers,
typically Portuguese but also refugees and others washed up in Lisbon by
the war, were so ubiquitous that they gave rise to what Hugh Muir called
an "epidemic of spy fever" in which those not in the game suspected everyone else was. Women, in Muir's estimation, were especially susceptible
to the scourge. He told of an attractive American who at bridge in a hotel
lounge invariably lost because her eyes kept darting from the table. "Sorry,"
she would say after playing a wrong card, "but I was looking at that guy
like Trotsky in the corner. Says he's American, American my foot!" And
another woman told him with absolute conviction that German agents had
poisoned her husband. "They talk by signs," she insisted, "and make the
swastika by crooking their little fingers and linking them together."

Unattached women were invariably labeled spies, though Alice-Leone Moats suspected that many were really down-at-the-heels workers in an equally old profession. Those she happened to meet struck her as "so abysmally stupid that I couldn't believe any government would really pay them good money to gather information." Polly Peabody told of a strange woman who said she was Swiss and spent her days in the sun growing darker and more mysterious, leaving observers positive she was a spy but with no idea for whom. Then there was a group of four Germans who regularly sat in the lobby of the Palácio, spaced about in the corners of the room. Now and then they merged to talk, then hurried back to their corners. One of them, a man, carried a raincoat despite the lack of rain. Another was Hollywood handsome. A third—bald, thick-necked, a scar across his forehead—had the look of a dime-novel spy. What could they all be but spies? "It became quite absurd in the end," Peabody concluded, "but one could never completely get away from the spy-mania, because there were quite a number of real ones around."

Howard Wriggins of the American Friends Service Committee regularly had an elderly retiree of the British Foreign Service drop by to ask in diffident fashion for his impression of certain refugees the Quaker relief office was caring for. When Wriggins assured him they were indeed refugees and truly in need, the man always apologized for his questions—leaving Wriggins to suppose he was trying to connect shreds of information picked up from other sources. In one instance, the fellow inquired about a German woman who had gotten permission to live in Lisbon rather than the refugee containment town of Caldas da Rainha. Apparently that was enough to raise suspicion. Another Englishman was always seated at the bar of the Tivoli Hotel at lunchtime. When Wriggins sat beside him they would chat amiably, the man revealing about himself only that he was in the import-export business. Was he actually a spy—and the Tivoli bar his daily listening post?

The bars and brothels of Lisbon's waterfront were assumed to be settings where more useful wartime information might be picked up. The German Abwehr was known to own or control some brothels, and they trained the workingwomen in methods of drawing information from seamen about sailing dates and routes of convoys. The British countered by lining up a string of brothels of their own. One day in the British embassy, John Beevor, a secret agent working undercover in the embassy (and about whom more below), was shown a card in which, in English, a certain madam cordially invited the bearer to her home for "a jolly good time and dancing too."

Shipping, railway, and airline offices were regularly patrolled for the names of those coming and going from Lisbon. Possibly more than that turned up at the flying boat landing port on the Tagus River after the Pan American Clipper crash in 1943. Aline Griffith, an OSS agent based in Spain, was told by a fellow agent in Lisbon that Japanese operatives were first on the site of the downed plane—"cruising the wreckage before anyone could get to the scene, picking up pouches destined for Allied embassies, leaving wounded passengers to drown while salvaging top-secret documents." The main Portuguese secret police figure at the port, one Corte Real, was also in the pay of the Germans and reportedly turned over to them parts of the plane and possibly some mail. (Amazingly, some seventy thousand letters were salvaged from the crash, with most addressed to American troops. Mailbags of sodden letters were transferred from Lisbon to Britain's General Post Office, where after reconditioning some 95 percent were in shape for delivery.)

It was common belief that maids in hotels routinely sifted through wastebaskets for sellable material. Likewise, stewards and other workers aboard transatlantic ships and planes were assumed to be agents or informers. In one known instance, Rene Mezenen, a steward in the Clipper service, was used by German intelligence as a courier between Lisbon and the United States, for reporting on convoy sightings and for smuggling platinum into Portugal. After his arrest in New York, he pleaded guilty to all charges and went to prison. In another case a Portuguese citizen living in New York, John Da Silva Purvis, was arrested on a charge that, while working as a stevedore aboard neutral ships, he transported maps for his German handlers. Roberto Vallecilla, a native of Colombia, chose letters rather than ships as his means of transmission. When arrested in Washington, where he was employed as a government translator, he was charged with beginning work with the Germans in 1940 while a student in Lisbon. After training, he was sent to the United States to provide information about aircraft production and other matters by means of invisible writing on the back of letters.

★   ★   ★

While clearly of a higher order than leg workers trolling for information, Real, Mezenen, Purvis, Vallecilla, and their like were minor players in the spy game, given narrow tasks to perform and paid accordingly. (In the charge against him, Vallecilla was said to have received $2,900 for his secret letter writing.) Well above them was the realm of prized agents who were trained or self-trained for undercover work and given the trickiest and most dangerous assignments—the James Bonds and George Smileys of spy lore. If ever they emerged from the shadows, it was not in news accounts of the time but, as government secrecy restrictions eased and documents became available, well afterward in memoirs, histories, and scholarly studies. Ordinarily such tales were success stories—the agents had at least survived to tell their deeds or have them told—though the likelihood of failure and its possibly unhappy consequences were always intimately part of the spy genre.

For John Beevor, failure on a large scale came at the very start of his undercover career. Like David Walker, Beevor was an agent of Britain's Special Operations Executive—or the Baker Street Irregulars, the informal name attached to SOE operatives due to the group's London headquarters in Sherlock Holmes's Baker Street—and also like Walker he was sent on a secret mission to Lisbon. His assignment was not spreading the Sibs of black propaganda but laying the groundwork for sabotage operations within Portugal. Specifically he was charged with forming a local resistance organization to go into action in the event of a Nazi invasion of the country by attacking roads, bridges, mining operations, and oil facilities along the Tagus estuary.

The background of the lightly organized operation—Beevor, a lawyer in civilian life, had been given only brief training and spoke no Portuguese—was earlier British advice to Salazar to make only token resistance to a German incursion and shift his government to the Azores. Anglo-Portuguese discussions about countering an invasion had, however, eventually bogged down over conditions that would require evacuation of the government, levels of resistance on the mainland, and British involvement in defense of the Azores. In sending a secret agent to Lisbon without informing the Portuguese prime minister, SOE was taking the matter of resistance into its own hands.

Beevor's cover as assistant military attaché in the Lisbon embassy was arranged by Ambassador Ronald Campbell, one of the few at the embassy who knew of his undercover mission. Since Beevor had been told that a German attack within months was a strong possibility, he quickly went about building a postoccupation group. The only problem he found in recruiting pro-British Portuguese was their high level of enthusiasm for the work, which made the keeping of secrets difficult. He left the actual dealing with them to regional organizers, whom he supplied with money to dole out for services rendered.

When the German invasion of Russia reduced the likelihood of a Nazi move on Portugal, Beevor returned to London expecting new directives.

"Hitler might be in Moscow by the end of 1941," he was told, "and if so he might switch forces back to Iberia in 1942. So continue as before but with the utmost discretion." Beevor returned to Lisbon with a gnawing sense that at any moment something could go wrong with his mission.

Something did. Through a Portuguese crackdown on pro-Allied propaganda early in 1942, two of his organizers came to police attention. Then police learned that an apartment Beevor had unwisely leased in his own name had been used, with Beevor's equally unwise consent, by an agent of Britain's MI6 to interview a man in a location away from the embassy. Salazar then indirectly raised with Ambassador Campbell the possibility of someone in the Lisbon embassy secretly preparing to resist a German occupation.

Campbell in turn informed Beevor that, since his diplomatic contacts with Salazar depended on mutual candor, he felt compelled to reveal the name. Beevor protested, but Campbell went ahead; sabotage work in an occupied Portugal was not as important as London maintaining cordial relations with the country, especially with negotiations over the Azores just ahead. Infuriated that he had been kept in the dark about the British action, Salazar demanded Beevor's recall. Beevor's response was twofold: he prepared a report the ambassador could show Salazar, emphasizing that the sabotage plans were in Portugal's interests; and with the help of the MI6 in Lisbon he put together another report that set out German illegal actions in the country, which already surpassed anything he had been planning. The second report, cleared by London, revealed the Abwehr's infiltration of government departments, bugging of the foreign ministry and possibly Salazar's office, widespread bribery of officials, and the extent of German informer networks within Portugal.

Impressed and possibly surprised by the reports, Salazar considered allowing Beevor to stay on in Lisbon. Ultimately his fate was left to Campbell, and in June 1942, a year and a half after arriving in Lisbon, Beevor was removed from the embassy and brought back to London for a new SOE assignment. Left behind was a secret mission in shambles. Portuguese police had already arrested or deported scores of Beevor's agents, including employees of Shell Oil in Portugal, members of the country's Communist party, and others in Salazar's political opposition.

As for the counterintelligence report on German secret activity in Portugal, Salazar was in no hurry to act upon it or fully comprehend what it revealed. Six months after receiving the dossier, Campbell reported him as saying, "He intended to do it himself, but it was a long job and he simply had not had the time." It was the spring of 1943 before the Portuguese took action against the Nazi spy ring. In the meantime four Lisbon propaganda distributors were arrested, presumably as a warning to Portuguese citizens to avoid giving aid to the British, and in June 1942 Salazar in a radio address attacked foreign propaganda for dividing his people. To the mild satisfaction of the British, he included Axis as well as Allied propaganda. Nonetheless a frustrated Campbell pushed British propagandists to get the prime minister to open his eyes "to see on which side his bread is buttered" in the contest between Britain and Germany.

★   ★   ★

At the same time John Beevor was setting up his SOE postinvasion sabotage operation in Portugal, his MI6 colleague operating from the British embassy in Lisbon, Philip Johns, was puzzling over how to get all the figures under his command—agents, informers, staff members—to safety if the Germans rolled across the border. After much discussion with other attachés and the ambassador, it was decided the best hope of escape would be by sea to North Africa, on a ship that would hold Johns's personnel and others in Lisbon who might be on the Gestapo's wanted list—in all, some one hundred passengers. London approved the idea and the funds needed, and Johns set about looking for the right vessel, which turned out to be an oceangoing tug moored in Porto. After it was acquired for eight thousand pounds, brought to Lisbon, and named the *Johan*, it seemed wise to conduct a test run. Since having it fully boarded by the intended escapees and loaded with fuel would alert both the Portuguese police and the local Germans, only a few members of the embassy and Johns would make the run, and it would be only a twenty-mile weekend ride up the Tagus to the town of Vila Franca de Zira, where on Sunday an annual festival was to take place.

The upriver journey was uneventful, and the shipmates spent Saturday night on board. During the festival the following day, the town jammed with people, adorned with flags and banners, and booming with music, a bull run took place through the streets. In the evening a giant barbecue was held in the town square, the *Johan* party at a reserved table, and afterward there was dancing and consumption of local wine until the early hours. At dawn the next day the vessel turned down the Tagus, and the passengers returned more or less ably to Monday work.

Johns counted the test a success and the festival a "wild and unforgettable party for war-time Portugal." Never needed at sea, the embassy got rid of the *Johan* after the war, though before that it had had some effect on Philip Johns's career. Due to irritation with what he thought was confused direction coming from headquarters in Britain, he lodged an official complaint, and London sent another MI6 officer to investigate the Lisbon station. When Johns, who had led the station for nearly two years, learned that the inquiry included looking into the expense incurred on the river trip, he decided he was being purposely undermined and asked for a new assignment elsewhere. After future MI6 assignments in North and South America, he transferred in 1943 to the SOE.

★   ★   ★

While John Beevor was still dangling in Lisbon after the exposure of his secret operation, the assistant military attaché at the American legation in Lisbon, Robert A. Solborg, urged Washington to take up his cause—understandably so since he was engaged in similar undercover work. An agent of the newly formed Office of the Coordinator of Information, soon to be renamed the Office of Strategic Services, Solborg had arrived in Lisbon in February 1942 as the first OSS operative based in mainland Europe.

The background he brought to the work was, to say the least, varied. Born in Warsaw and the son of a Polish general, Solborg had served as an officer in the tsarist cavalry in World War I. After a severe wound he was sent to New York on a Russian military purchasing mission. When Communists took power in Russia, he returned to the United States, this time to become a citizen, and later enlisted in the army. Following service as a military attaché in Paris, he went into business with Armco Steel, and when war broke out in 1939 he was the firm's managing director in Britain and France. In December 1940 Solborg joined American military intelligence, and the next year he was recruited by the dynamic head of the OSS, William J. ("Wild Bill") Donovan, for the Secret Intelligence Branch of his new agency and sent to London to study the operations of Britain's SOE before his posting to Portugal.

Under Solborg the OSS Lisbon station was soon using paid agents for surveillance work and developing plans for sabotage against German-owned or -leased mines should the Nazis march into Portugal. The Lisbon station also had the unglamorous task of providing OSS's Research and Analysis Branch back in Washington with a steady supply of German newspapers, journals, and books to pore over for intelligence value. (British intelligence was supplied with the same material through Lisbon, giving rise to a local story that, since British and German civilian planes flew from the same airport and at similar times, Portuguese workers simply transferred bundles of material brought in by planes of one country to planes of the other.)

In 1941 Solborg had toured North Africa for eight months, officially as an Armco executive but gathering information for military intelligence on French resistance figures. Afterward he made journeys through Portugal and Spain, reporting back that he could detect nothing indicating a likely German invasion of the Iberian peninsula. In Lisbon the following year, and against Donovan's instructions, Solborg went to Casablanca to meet with a French officer about a plan to form a pro-Allied government in French North Africa. He had told John Beevor the trip was cleared with American intelligence at the level of the War Department, and he would fix it up with his OSS boss later. Donovan did not wait for an explanation. "It was agreed between us (you gave your promise) that no activities were to be carried on in North Africa," he informed Solborg. "You are directed to stop immediately whatever you may be doing, go to Lisbon and await orders." From Portugal, Solborg flew to Washington to appeal his case in person. Donovan refused to see him and subsequently fired him for insubordination, though Solborg stayed on in Lisbon as a military attaché reporting to the War Department.

He was still in the position in April 1945 when he was drawn on to assist the American deception effort against Japan. With important channels to the Japanese in Germany and Argentina now closed, military attachés in the European neutral centers of Bern, Stockholm, and Lisbon were asked by military intelligence in Washington to locate agents with lines of communication to Tokyo. Solborg in Lisbon came up with four such types. One of them he identified as the director of the Portuguese secret police, whom he called "a clever man of independent financial means, blindly devoted to Salazar and the totalitarian regime." The others on his list were a former press attaché of the Hungarian legation in Lisbon; a Turkish woman who had been the mistress of the Japanese military attaché in Lisbon; and a Portuguese army officer. Throughout the late spring and summer of 1945 Solborg was given weekly lists of disinformation items for his channels to convey to the enemy—and he reported to Washington that on his end the operation was proceeding smoothly.

★   ★   ★

At the time of the Allied landings in North Africa in 1942, Donovan's OSS was well supplied with operatives on the Iberian peninsula. For the American ambassador in Madrid, Carlton Hayes, this produced more aggravation than comfort. As he saw it, the agents were both too energetic and too unskilled. American ministers in neutral countries were generally opposed to OSS activity in their territory, but Hayes left diplomatic language aside in setting out his hostility. Washington was told that Donovan's agents were "notoriously uneducated, indiscreet, and intemperate," and that their secret antics were endangering the Anglo-American policy of keeping Franco in the neutral camp. Hayes distinguished between the experienced foreign-service officers and military attachés on his embassy staff and OSS men "whose missionary zeal outstripped their judgment." Along with some of their superiors back home, the agents failed to understand that their mission was to win the war against the Axis, not overturn the Spanish government. Hayes proposed to Washington that the OSS in Spain either be placed under the authority of the military attaché in Madrid or removed from the country altogether. In a lengthy response, Donovan rejected both plans but admitted Spain was a problem for the OSS, with many of the men it sent overseas "virtually amateurs" due to the hurried buildup in the size of his agency.

In June 1943 the rift in Madrid between the ambassador and Donovan's organization was temporarily overshadowed by what had the appearance of a major OSS blunder in Portugal. Earlier the American legation in Lisbon had intervened with Washington to prevent, as George Kennan recalled, "various eager beavers in General Donovan's OSS from developing plans for a revolt against Portuguese authority on the part of the inhabitants of the Azores." The Azores matter may have been part of the "dreadful confusion" that Kennan said he was asked to straighten out in his diplomatic post. In any case, the background for the scheme was American distrust of Salazar—in some quarters, Kennan noted, he was considered "a dangerous Fascist and in league with the enemy"—and impatience with British efforts to secure military use of the Azores. A rebellion by the islands' inhabitants, so it was imagined, would undermine Lisbon's rule and prepare the way for an American takeover.

The Azores revolt never left the planning stage. With the trashcan burglary in the early summer of 1943 the OSS was less fortunate. A Portuguese employed by OSS Lisbon and placed inside the Japanese embassy as a messenger in the office of the naval attaché removed some crumpled sheets of paper from a wastebasket and turned them over to agents. The pages had numbers and Japanese characters on them, leading the Lisbon station to believe the writing might represent a cipher. The sheets were delivered to the OSS in Washington, which in turn sent them on for analysis. When it was determined the writing was indeed a cipher but one used for low-level communication and, beyond that, one already known to American code breakers, the papers were filed away as useless.

Then in July the American military read messages moving between Tokyo and its embassies in Lisbon and Madrid that indicated the Japanese had learned from Italian sources that Americans had entered the Lisbon embassy and possibly gained access to its codes. The Japanese ambassador in Lisbon was ordered to report back at once on security measures while the ambassador in Madrid was told to dispatch an officer to examine the Lisbon embassy's procedures.

The flurry of messages among the Japanese set off alarms in Washington. A major secret of the war was that the United States had broken Japan's cipher machine used to encrypt high-level diplomatic communication. Known as Magic, the decoding operation gave the Americans vital access to Japanese military planning since much of it was revealed in diplomatic traffic among embassies and consulates. If Japan believed one of its diplomatic ciphers had been compromised in Lisbon, it might well change all its coding systems.

General George V. Strong, the powerful chief of military intelligence in Washington, launched an investigation that forced the OSS to turn over records of the Lisbon operation. Strong and Donovan had clashed before, partly as bureaucratic rivals, partly because Strong was determined to keep intelligence matters in military hands. The purloined papers offered him a choice opportunity to reduce Donovan's authority, and he was soon firing off memos to General George C. Marshall, the army chief of staff, denouncing OSS activity as "ill advised and amateurish" and a "menace to the security of the nation." Strong also informed Marshall that George Kennan had confirmed to him that OSS Lisbon agents were complete amateurs who should have known that their sources within the Japanese embassy (there were two, the other, also Portuguese, located in the office of the military attaché) were surely double agents who also informed on the OSS.

In his defense, Donovan launched a campaign that maintained that the Portuguese who removed the cipher material had acted entirely on his own initiative. The orders to both figures inside the Japanese embassy were only to "pick up any available information as to Japanese official activities and to report on any callers or conversations." Donovan also pointed out that Strong had been given advance notice of the existence of the two informers, as had British intelligence services and George Kennan in the American legation. According to Donovan, Kennan had in fact "congratulated the agent [who took the material] on the operation and encouraged further activities."

Eventually it was learned to American satisfaction that the Japanese concluded there had been no lapse of security in Lisbon and consequently no need for changing codes. When the dust finally settled on the trashcan affair, Donovan had been weakened, but OSS Lisbon was still in business. The OSS's Iberian operations, however, were curbed to the extent that agents were ordered to stay clear of cipher material and to pool information with American military intelligence groups at work on the peninsula. At the time of the Normandy landings in 1944, the OSS had forty-four agents operating in Spain, Portugal, the Azores, and Madeira, and its Secret Intelligence Branch at work in Portugal had a staff of seven together with three hundred subagents.

★   ★   ★

The top rung on the spy ladder belonged to double agents, the bold specialists who were capable of working both sides of the intelligence street and sustaining the appearance of leading two entirely separate lives. Of those who performed the perilous feat in or through Lisbon, none did so better, longer, or with more imaginative zest than Garbo. J. C. Masterman, who was well positioned to know, believed him "something of a genius." And added: "Connoisseurs of double cross have always regard the Garbo case as the most highly developed example of their art."

Known to the Germans under the code name Arabel and to the British as Garbo, the double agent was Juan Pujol, a Spaniard from Barcelona who during the civil war had, in a foreshadowing of his future spy career, participated on both sides. One day in January 1941 he appeared at Britain's embassy in Madrid and let it be known he was a fervent anti-Nazi and immediately available as a British secret agent. After he was turned away, he decided more preparation for spy work was in order before contacting the British again, and so he offered his services at the German embassy in Madrid.

Here he met with some success. An interview process began with an Abwehr officer, but while it was still under way Pujol took another tack. He developed a story that his father had funds in Britain and necessary documents for them were in a safe deposit box in Portugal. With the Spanish government badly in need of foreign funds, Pujol was granted a passport and a visa for Portugal and left for Lisbon. He took a room in a hotel and registered with the Spanish consulate as a resident living permanently abroad. He was trying for a visa for Britain when his plans took yet another turn. Staying in his hotel was a fellow Galician who showed Pujol an imposing document said to be a special Spanish diplomatic visa to Argentina, where he planned to go as soon as he got a ticket for South America aboard a Clipper. After several evenings out on the town as his compatriot's guest, Pujol took him to a hotel in Monte-Estoril for a gambling venture at the nearby casino, ostensibly to repay him for his generosity but also to photograph the visa, which he did with a borrowed camera after complaining of stomach problems and returning alone from the casino to the hotel.

Back in Lisbon, Pujol had the photo enlarged, an engraving plate made, and a printer ran off copies. His hazy scheme was to use the printed visas, in doctored form, to impress the Abwehr about his ability to leave Portugal for Britain. After his return to Madrid, his talks with the German agent dragged on until Pujol spun a story that he had been asked by a section of the Spanish police to go to Britain to look into a currency racket involving Spanish pesetas and Portuguese escudos. After allowing the agent a glimpse of one of his printed visas—Pujol's name now filled in and his diplomatic assignment shown as London—he was equipped by the Abwehr with a bottle of invisible ink, a code book, three thousand dollars, a Madrid address for his reports, and was dispatched to England as an agent with the code name Arabel.

He went no farther than Lisbon. He meant to again contact the British, reasoning that the ink and codes the Germans had given him would clearly demonstrate his capacity for work as an agent. Still, his efforts to reach the British failed, leaving him mystified why the country he wanted to serve was aloof while the Nazis were welcoming. His best option, so he concluded, was to add to his clandestine résumé by setting up as a freelance operative.

With money the Germans had supplied him, Pujol bought a map of Great Britain, a Blue Guide to England, a Portuguese publication about the British fleet, and an English-French vocabulary of military terms and began studying them along with British magazines and reference books he located in Lisbon libraries. In October 1941, while living in a room in a fisherman's house in Cascais, he felt himself sufficiently armed to begin sending Arabel's invisible-ink reports to Madrid via an imaginative mechanism in which a KLM employee, paid to serve as a courier on flights between London and Lisbon, delivered his London-written letters to an Abwehr address in Lisbon and collected replies from a safe deposit box at the Espírito Santo Bank, which Pujol had rented under what he hoped was the thoroughly British name of Mr. Joseph Smith Jones. Despite the large limiting facts that Pujol had never been to England and spoke no English, the entirely fictional scheme worked to perfection. The Abwehr was convinced it was dealing with a secret agent diligently at work in Britain.

In subsequent reports Pujol spun increasingly notional—in the language of spycraft—stories of being offered a job by the BBC in London, of a convoy of ships that had left Liverpool for Malta, of recruiting subagents throughout England. When the Abwehr sent requests for specific information about troop movements, military installations, and British morale, he was quick to respond with lengthy detail—and an often wildly inaccurate grasp of English life and locations (about Glasgow: "There are people here who would do anything for a litre of wine"), which the Germans seemed not to notice or passed off as the Spaniard's natural naiveté in his new location. Yet after a time Pujol began to wonder if he could continue keeping all his balloons in the air. He considered giving up the spy game and leaving Europe, but only after another attempt to double-cross the Germans.

In early 1942, the United States now in the war, Pujol went to the American legation in Lisbon and asked to speak to a military or naval attaché. After being searched by a Marine on duty, he was brought to the naval attaché, Kenneth Demorest, and told in broad terms his full story, beginning with his initial rebuff by the British in Madrid. Intrigued, the attaché asked for some proof, which Pujol supplied, then asked for time to look further into his story—and gain time to inform his British colleagues of an alleged German operative astonishingly willing to turn over invisible ink and a code book given him by the Abwehr.

The British subsequently contacted Pujol and a meeting was arranged with an MI6 officer, Eugene Risso-Gill, a Briton with important connections in Portugal. When they got together in a seaside villa of Risso-Gill's family midway between Lisbon and Estoril, the agent was polite, affable, and apparently wholly at ease with Pujol's story. Almost at once he began plotting to remove him from Lisbon—it seemed miraculous to the British that Pujol had evaded detection as long as he had—without alerting German informants or the Portuguese secret police. Meanwhile, Pujol was to hand over the ink and code book to Risso-Gill, who in turn would forward them to London, and prepare to leave Portugal immediately.

What Pujol could not know was that he had long been a figure of interest to the British. Due to the genius of Bletchley Park and the Ultra system in decoding German messages, his reports to the Abwehr in Madrid and forwarded by wireless to Berlin had been read in England, prompting questions about Arabel's identity and how he had gotten into the country. Among the officers of MI5 (the British Security Service operating within the United Kingdom) searching for answers was Tomás Harris, the son of a British father and Spanish mother, an accomplished artist who had studied as the Slade School of Fine Art, and a successful art dealer before the war. To Harris and those working with him, it eventually became clear that Arabel, rather than an agent in Britain as the Germans believed, was a Spaniard in Portugal. Then it appeared clear that Arabel and the Spaniard who had offered his services to the British embassies in Madrid and Lisbon, Juan Pujol, were one and the same. Although MI5 also understood that the information the agent supplied the Abwehr was wholly fabricated and contained obvious blunders (as well as intelligence that, incredibly, was nearly on target), it had been accepted without question. Ultra intercepts confirmed that Arabel was seen by the Germans as a major asset.

Left unanswered was whether he should be recruited as the double agent he claimed he wanted to be and brought to Britain. Leaving him in Lisbon was unwise since physically monitoring him would be difficult, while in Britain, with his evident credibility with the Germans, he would be invaluable. On the other hand, if he was a German plant, as a triple agent he could put at risk Britain's already highly successful counterespionage program.

When a German invasion of Britain seemed certain following the fall of France, the Abwehr had increased its number of agents in England. MI5 had captured and turned nearly all of them—some coming over voluntarily, others under threats—and developed an extensive ring of double agents operating under the direction of the XX or Twenty Committee. From his formal position as the committee chair, J. C. Masterman—a tall, spare history don at Christ Church, Oxford, who wrote mystery stories and was a skilled cricket player—coordinated the work of what came to be known as the Double-Cross System. The overall head of the operation was Guy Liddell, MI5's director of counterespionage throughout the war. From 1943 onward, the committee had a Yale University literature professor now attached to OSS London's counterintelligence or X-2 Branch, Norman Holmes Pearson, as an American delegate at its weekly meetings and privy to all its secrets. (Pearson would later salute the British as "masters [of the double-cross game] and whatever Americans did similarly in the European and Mediterranean theaters stemmed from British direction and example.") While Masterman's group oversaw the work of the double agents and pro-vided, through liaisons with governmental agencies, the accurate or partly accurate information they could transmit to the enemy, individual MI5 case officers guided their operations. (Masterman may have never actually met any of the double agents since there was no necessity to do so.) Over time, Britain came to believe that through the efforts of the Twenty Committee they effectively controlled the entire German espionage system within the British Isles.

What helped swing the debate inside British intelligence in favor of recruiting Juan Pujol was his notional report about the British convoy bound for Malta. Messages decoded by Bletchley Park indicated that the

German military, operating on the information, intended a coordinated attack in the Mediterranean using U-boats and Italian warplanes. When the convoy failed to appear, no blame was directed to the Abwehr or to Arabel. If such self-generated invention could so manipulate the Germans, the British reasoned that Pujol could do far greater damage as part of an artfully scripted deception effort.

Just at the time London decided that MI6's Eugene Risso-Gill should locate Pujol and persuade him to switch from a freelancer in Lisbon to a controlled double agent in Britain, he had revealed himself at the American legation. The British in Lisbon operated a secret fishing-boat shuttle to Gibraltar, but having Pujol use it to begin his journey to London might end the service if, after all, he turned out to be a German plant. Finally he was smuggled aboard a merchant ship going to the Mediterranean and taken as far as Gibraltar.

At the Rock he was led through passport control by a British agent, taken for a large English breakfast in a restaurant, given money to purchase new clothes, and put up in a room from which he could come and go as he pleased. Shortly thereafter Donald Darling, the MI9 agent in Gibraltar working with evaders and escapees, got him space on a military flight to Britain. Since Darling had not been given a code name for Pujol, he chose one himself: Bovril. When he stepped off the British plane in Plymouth, finally in the country he had notionally been working in from July 1941 to April 1942, Pujol was met by two MI5 officers. One of them, Tomás Harris, spoke perfect Spanish.

After an intense debriefing, which finally satisfied everyone concerned about Pujol's credentials, he went to work with the equally inventive and industrious Harris in a close relationship that would last for the rest of the war. He was given cover as a translator for the BBC; his wife and young son were brought from Portugal to England; and his code name was changed from Bovril to Garbo, a reflection in British eyes of his ability as a top-notch actor. Since Pujol had already recruited a network of subagents in England, Harris decided to continue the notional operation with added agents—creating notional networks put together by the notional agents—while enriching the deception steadily fed through them with bits and pieces of accurate information. At its height, Garbo's spy ring numbered some twenty-seven imaginary sources—among the lot, a Greek seaman, a Royal Air Force pilot, an American sergeant, an employee in the Ministry of Information, a Welsh nationalist, a South African in the War Office, a German-Swiss businessman, a Portuguese commercial traveler, a Venezuelan living in Glasgow, and a seaman who carried documents and espionage material to Lisbon that, in reality, arrived in a British diplomatic bag. "The one-man band of Lisbon developed into an orchestra," J. C. Masterman wrote of Pujol's expanded efforts, "and an orchestra which played a more and more ambitious programme."

A notably bravura performance by the team of Pujol and Harris came when it was necessary to remove from duty the notional subagent who lived near Liverpool (and had reported the Malta convoy) since he was in position to observe the genuine convoys assembled in the Mersey estuary for the invasion of North Africa. If he failed to report them, the Germans—in retrospect—would surely question his usefulness and possibly his existence. So to take him out of the picture he was stricken with cancer and simply ceased sending in material. But Garbo took the matter further by notionally hurrying to Liverpool to discover, as he informed the Germans, that the agent had died. An obituary notice was duly placed in the *Liverpool Daily Post* and passed to the Germans, who responded with an expression of sympathy to the widow. To tie up the story all the more, the notional widow, short of funds, asked to work for Garbo and, as Widow, was brought to London to assist with his hefty burden of work.

In actuality, Pujol's days were spent commuting to Harris's office in London's Jermyn Street and drafting his uniquely ornate and long-winded cover letters with wide gaps between the lines for insertions in invisible ink, the work always carried on under tight security measures guarding what he could do and know. (Obviously crucial was that Pujol be kept wholly in the dark about the existence of the deciphering system that allowed the British to monitor German reaction to his messages.) While notionally continuing to reach the Germans through a courier on the London-Lisbon air route, the letters were now carried by diplomatic bag to Lisbon and posted by MI6 to cover addresses in the city, from where they were sent on by the Germans to Arabel's case officer in Madrid, an Abwehr official named Karl-Erich Kühlenthal. Replies and generous payments for Arabel and his network from their satisfied employer were collected by MI6 from the safe deposit box in the Lisbon bank and turned over to MI5 in London. In time, some German payment came directly to Garbo through a complex method of bank transfers of pesetas from Madrid that were exchanged for British pounds in London. By agreement with MI5, Pujol was allowed to keep 25 percent of his payment from the Germans; from the British came a monthly salary of a hundred pounds and occasional bonuses.

Beyond his scores of letters sent to Madrid, eventually a system was created whereby Pujol could contact the Germans by wireless through coded messages sent to Madrid. These were transmitted, so the Germans believed, by a leftist radio enthusiast who had built his own set and thought the messages were from Spanish exiles to their colleagues in Spain. Over the course of his work in England, Pujol would send the Germans some two thousand wireless reports.

Pujol's activity by letter and wireless took on added importance with Operation Fortitude, the massive deception campaign about the place and timing of the cross-Channel invasion. In late July 1944, just after the landings in Normandy, Madrid informed Arabel that he had been awarded an Iron Cross Class II, the Germans thereby certifying their confidence in him as a star performer despite recent intelligence lapses. As it happened—and the British learned through intercepts—the award was never presented due to bureaucratic objection raised in Berlin about the agent's Spanish citizenship. This was no obstacle for the British, who shortly before Christmas 1944 bestowed on Pujol an honorary award of Membership of the Order of the British Empire (MBE). For obvious reasons the honor was not made public at the time, though the medal was presented at a private luncheon attended by some MI5 members who knew of Garbo's work. (In June 1984, the fortieth anniversary of D-Day, Pujol wore the medal at Buckingham Palace when the Duke of Edinburgh thanked him for his wartime contributions.)

With the war's end, MI5 arranged Pujol's "escape" from England for a new life in South America. But before he vanished from view he made a journey back to Madrid at the behest of the British to meet Arabel's handlers, this in an effort to detect any postwar German planning. Pujol's guise for returning to Spain was the possibility of starting a new spy ring to penetrate the Soviet Union. He found Karl-Erich Kühlenthal, a figure he had never met and knew only under an alias, cowering in Avila in fear of the Allies repatriating him to Germany. They spent some three hours together, the emotional case officer indicating his undiminished trust in the agent while bemoaning his own fate. Finally Pujol announced that if he could no longer be of service to the Germans he would leave Spain for Portugal and eventually for South America. Perhaps pondering a move to Portugal himself, Kühlenthal inquired how he planned to cross the border from Spain. "Clandestinely," said Pujol, playing the role of Arabel to the end. In truth he crossed the border openly and with no difficulty, and after he reached Lisbon he flew to London to report to MI5 on his Spanish visit, his final act as Garbo.

12

ONE WORLD TO ANOTHER

It was an Alice in Wonderland experience, passing from
one world to another, except in this case both worlds were
abnormal.

—Dusko Popov, *Spy/Counterspy*

Some of Garbo's long run of success as a double agent was thanks to
the shortcomings of his German handlers and the Abwehr itself. From
the start of the war Admiral Canaris and many key aides in the service's
divisions had distanced themselves from the Nazi cause. "The Abwehr as
a whole," observed a British historian, "became notorious as a haven for
dissidents from the regime"—"a group of men," as an Abwehr defector
further identified them, "who do not like the Nazis and do not want to
go to war."

Beyond its ideological wavering, the Abwehr in neutral countries such
as Portugal and Spain operated as independent and often competing units
working under diplomatic cover and with little central control from Berlin. In recruiting and running secret agents, the units often seemed to act
in a fog of disinterest, scrutinizing them with little care, monitoring them
loosely, failing adequately to evaluate or even read raw data in their reports.
Corrupt station chiefs supplied just enough information to hold their positions while enhancing their standard of living through padding expense
accounts, taking "commissions" on money paid to agents and informers,
and currency transactions. (J. C. Masterman noted that after the war information came to light indicating, as the Twenty Committee had surmised,
that Abwehr officials intentionally ignored suspicions about German agents

in Britain. "They thought it better for selfish reasons," Masterman wrote, "to have corrupt or disloyal agents than to have no agents at all.")

After Hitler replaced Canaris as head of the Abwehr in early 1944, the service was absorbed into the SS under Heinrich Himmler. In London the new leadership and organization of a presumably more formidable German intelligence system was a serious concern for the Twenty Committee. But if Britain could no longer count on the Abwehr's lack of rigor, it now—the Normandy invasion near at hand and the war about to enter its final phase—had fortunate timing on its side. "If the changes had been made earlier," Masterman acknowledged, "it is probable that the new brooms would have swept away much that we were concerned to preserve. Once again, the margin of safety for our double-cross system was very small."

The luck of timing was again evident in the spring of 1944 when an Abwehr officer in Lisbon, Johann Jebsen—a flamboyant figure who lived in a villa in Estoril and shuttled back and forth to Lisbon in a Rolls-Royce—went to the German legation for what he understood would be the presentation of a medal. Instead he was overpowered by an officer of the SD, the security service of the SS, rendered unconscious with drugs, put in a metal trunk fitted with air holes, placed in a sedan with diplomatic plates, and driven to France. (In another version of what took place, Jebsen was invited to tea at the legation, knockout drops were put in his tea, he was given an injection, and then removed to France; in still another, he was simply kidnapped from his villa.) Transferred to the custody of the Gestapo, he was later moved to a concentration camp in Germany and executed.

To the British, Jebsen was a recently acquired double agent working on the Continent under the code name Artist. When it was learned in London that he had been taken by the Gestapo, there was hope that he was suspected only of illegal currency transactions; nonetheless under questioning he might betray crucial information about the double-cross system—in particular about the work of Dusko Popov, a Yugoslav whom early in the war Jebsen had recruited for the Abwehr and the British had come to value, as a double agent with the code name Tricycle, nearly as highly as Garbo. While Garbo encountered his German case officer in Spain only after the war, Tricycle in wartime often traveled from Britain to Portugal for face-to-face meetings with his Lisbon-based handler, putting himself and the entire British double-cross system in jeopardy.

★   ★   ★

Johann Jebsen and Dusko Popov first met in 1936 at Freiburg University in Germany and became fast friends. With the war, Jebsen, from a prominent Hamburg shipping family and now an anti-Nazi member of the Abwehr, came to Belgrade and proposed that Popov, a charming and supremely confident commercial lawyer, work as a German operative in Britain. Popov immediately revealed all to the British embassy in Belgrade, which in turn put him in touch with a local MI6 agent. After getting instructions from England, the agent told Popov to accept the German offer but say he needed to get to London for business reasons—and add that while there he would try to recruit a friend who might also agree to work for the Germans. In reality the British wanted Popov in England to make certain he was on the Allied side and not setting himself up as a triple agent.

The Germans agreed to the London trip, and in November 1940 Popov was sent on a journey that took him first to Rome and then to Lisbon, the usual training point and launching site for inserting German agents into Britain. Following a convoluted set of deception maneuvers, he was brought to the Moorish-style villa in Estoril of a tall and elegant figure who was the Lisbon head of the Abwehr's intelligence section. Under the name Ludovico von Karsthoff, he would serve as Popov's case officer through nearly all of his time working for the Germans. Over drinks that first evening they discussed methods to be used in future meetings: Popov—known by the Abwehr under the code name Ivan—would always be taken by car to the attached garage of one of Karsthoff's residences, lying flat in the back seat to avoid notice; on return, lying flat again, he would be dropped off within walking distance of his hotel, the Aviz.

In those future meetings Karsthoff personally handled Popov's spy education, instructing him about codes, mail drops, and how to take photos of installations with a girl posed in front so they looked like tourist snapshots. (The officer had a special fondness for the cloak-and-dagger aspects of spying. During their long relationship one of the ways he had Popov get instructions was by code while watching Elizabeth Sahrbach, Karsthoff's secretary and mistress, at roulette in the Estoril casino, the numbers she played indicating the place, date, hour, and minute of a meeting. "It was an expensive code," Popov dryly noted. "She rarely won.") Karsthoff also let Popov know that a certain Fritz Kramer, head of Abwehr counterintelligence in Lisbon, would be keeping an eye on him while he was in Portugal.

In late December 1940, after several weeks in Portugal, Popov took a commercial flight to England, the prized ticket seemingly coming in normal fashion but in fact arranged by MI6 in Lisbon. A car and driver were waiting at the airfield near Bristol, and Popov was transported to the Savoy Hotel in London for a meeting with an MI5 officer and Twenty Committee member, T. A. (Tar) Robertson, who took him for beer and sandwiches. Later, from his hotel window in the Savoy, Popov got his first taste of the London blitz.

Four days of tough grilling by various intelligence officials followed—among many uncertainties about Popov was his well-earned reputation as a playboy who favored, as he admiringly said of himself, sports cars and sporting women—before he convinced his interrogators that he was thoroughly anti-Nazi. Working in his favor was his refusal to accept any money for his services from the British (though he would allow, as it turned out, MI5 to come to his rescue when he was in trouble with debts, as he often was) while expecting to be handsomely compensated by his German masters.

Popov was given the code name Scout and linked with a robust Scot, using the cover name Bill Matthews, as his case officer. Popov's own cover, entirely genuine, was that he was a businessman with an office in Imperial House in Regent Street, from where he represented a group of Yugoslav banks which were allowed to purchase goods that were not vital to the war effort. While he was still in Lisbon, the Abwehr had given Popov a list of questions to pursue, and to be on solid ground when later quizzed by the Germans, he traveled about England and Scotland in the guise of his business work. Matthews accompanied him and used the time together to put to rest any lingering doubts about Scout's authenticity.

Some of what Popov supposedly gleaned was sent back to Karsthoff in secret writing in letters directed to accommodation addresses in Lisbon, with Popov's office secretary mixing the invisible ink given him in Lisbon by the Germans and drafting coded letters that he copied in his own hand. The bulk of what he gathered, however, would always be passed along in person during business trips to Lisbon. Along with occasional truths and half-truths, he fed the Germans deception material that, at the early stage of his double-cross work, largely dealt with British morale and military readiness. To this were added choice tidbits of rumor and gossip he picked up as a prosperous man-about-town in London who, under the guidance of a social mistress provided by MI5, had entrée to elite English society.

Another mission Popov was given came personally from MI6's chief, Stewart Menzies. "It is an important game," Menzies said of Popov's work with the Twenty Committee and MI5, "but we mustn't let it reduce the possible crop to a limited field. My department wants to profit by your talents and your circumstantial position as well." Popov was instructed to gather in Lisbon information about Admiral Canaris and other top Abwehr figures, using his friend Jebsen as a main source. Menzies was trying, as Popov understood the assignment, to prepare himself for direct communication with Canaris or those around him about removing Hitler from power. "I am handling this matter myself," Menzies emphasized. "All information you pick up is to come directly to me with no intermediary." He added: "One last thing. All MI6 representatives abroad will be instructed to give you unlimited assistance, but limit your contacts with them to emergencies only."

Carrying a briefcase filled with papers about Yugoslav deals for the purchase of Portuguese tin and turpentine, Popov made his first visit to Lisbon as a double agent in early January 1941. "It was," he later wrote, "an Alice in Wonderland experience, passing from one world to another, except in this case both worlds were abnormal. War-torn London to an artificial Lisbon, crowded to the bursting point with refugees and competing secret services superimposed hodgepodge on this city of medieval appearance and archaic mentality." But he was doing more than moving into a sharply different atmospheric situation, for when he exchanged London for Lisbon he was knowingly placing himself at the mercy of the Abwehr. "Each time Dusko went back to Lisbon to report to the Germans," said a British official after the war, "he was warned his life was in their hands and we could do nothing to help him if things went wrong." Menzies had been blunt, warning him that "one false step and you'll bugger everything, yourself in the lead." Popov also understood that if he were exposed as a double agent the Gestapo would surely take retribution against his parents, two brothers, and other relations living in Yugoslavia.

After a meeting with Karsthoff that went well despite the Abwehr officer's close questioning about his espionage work in England, Popov traveled to Madrid for a meeting with Jebsen, who brought him a ten thousand dollar bonus from Berlin for his stellar London efforts. The money was welcome—to the Germans it was always clear that Ivan was in their employ solely for the money—and it was good to see his old friend, though Jebsen maintained the outward appearance that he was a dedicated Abwehr officer, and Popov that he was a dutiful Abwehr agent. Back in Lisbon, Karsthoff suggested that since some of Popov's contacts in London were proving so valuable, he should try to recruit them as independent agents—an idea, Popov knew, that would both greatly delight the Twenty Committee and add to his prestige in the eyes of the Abwehr. Soon he was running, in Britain, Balloon and Gelantine, the latter in reality his MI5 social mistress, and the service switched his code name from Scout to the more fitting, for an agent with two notional channels of misinformation, Tricycle. (In the authorized history of MI5, the name is said to have had an even more apt origin: Popov's "fondness for three-in-a-bed sex.")

Popov continued to move routinely back and forth between London and Lisbon. Often in Lisbon he met with Jebsen, who came in from Berlin, and through him he was able to obtain for Menzies and MI6 the names of important Abwehr figures in Germany as well as lists, with code names and private addresses, of the main Abwehr officers in Lisbon and Madrid. But with the German invasion of Yugoslavia in April 1941, abruptly ending the possibility of shipping goods into what was now occupied territory, Popov had to come up with a new explanation for his Portuguese visits. He proposed to the Germans that if a Yugoslav government-in-exile were set up in London, following the lead of the French, Poles, and other occupied nationalities, he might pull strings and get himself a ministerial position. The Germans leaped at the possibility since it provided excellent cover for a new use of their valued agent.

When Ulrich von der Osten, the German intelligence specialist for the United States, was struck and killed by a taxi in New York, Popov's Abwehr handlers chose Ivan as a successor. On their end, the British agreed to loan Tricycle to the FBI, and in early August 1941 Popov, with the imposing title of Delegate of the Yugoslav Ministry of Information to the United States, left for Lisbon to await a Clipper flight to New York. Karsthoff gave him a thorough questionnaire listing information the Abwehr wanted from America, though this time the material did not have to be memorized. The Germans had developed microdots in which the questions were easily concealed, with Ivan the first secret agent to use them (and also, as Tricycle, to provide a copy to Philip Johns, the MI6 station chief in Lisbon). Karsthoff was so pleased with the arrangement and Ivan's capacity to build an intelligence operation in America that champagne was popped to celebrate—and Popov given an advance of some forty thousand dollars to be deposited under a false name in a New York bank, with more to come as needed from a bogus Portuguese company in the United States.

On August 10, 1941, Popov left Lisbon for New York on the *Dixie Clipper*. In his briefcase he carried seventy thousand dollars in cash (the advance from the Germans, money of his own, and money from a bank in Yugoslavia for goods that could no longer be delivered); eleven German microdots for his use; a phial of crystals for making invisible ink; a list of ten addresses—eight of them in Lisbon—as mail drops for his letters; a copy of Virginia Woolf's novel *Night and Day* to use for coding radio messages; and half a business card to identify himself to a German agent who would present the other half. If such a carry-on load of money and spy paraphernalia caused him any unease, it was not apparent. After an excellent meal of fresh fish in the Azores, Popov slept the rest of the way to Bermuda, where a British intelligence agent joined him for the journey to Port Washington. A room had been reserved at the Waldorf Astoria, and after a shower and a room-service sandwich Popov took a leisurely stroll about New York, where he had never been before. In a car showroom on Broadway, a new Buick convertible with red leather seats caught his eye. He had to buy it, and did—the start of an American style of lavish living he meant to fully savor while, as Ivan, keeping his German paymasters satisfied.

An unseen obstacle in the way was the FBI under J. Edgar Hoover. The British believed the best use of Tricycle was to continue on American soil the clever deception work he had done in London. Hoover had something else in mind: using him to entrap real German spies in the United States, who could then be prosecuted in a blaze of publicity. In addition to this major difference, there was the stumbling block of Popov's persona. The officers of MI5 had shrugged off Popov's unrestrained playboy manner, largely going along with his self-serving view that it was an established part of his cover with the Germans. The puritanical Hoover was not as flexible. Popov's spending was offensive—after taking delivery of the Buick, he leased a New York penthouse, had an interior designer decorate it, hired a Chinese manservant, and shelled out some twelve thousand dollars for furniture, books, a hi-fi system, and stacks of records—and his obsessive womanizing annoyed Hoover all the more. Within a month of his arrival in New York he and a young Englishwoman were lovers and spending long weekends together on Shelter Island.

Yet this was only the start of a long American trail of high living and heated romance. After breaking up with the Englishwoman, Popov leased a weekend retreat on Long Island, complete with gardener and domestic staff, and revived an affair with the glamorous French film actress Simone Simon, whom he had known in Paris before the war. Not surprisingly, by the end of February 1942 Popov was running short of money and demanding more from the Abwehr, which was not immediately forthcoming since he had sent little useful information. Neither had he pleased the FBI by leading them to German agents operating in the country.

Popov stayed more or less at work in the United States through the summer of 1942. But by then he had gone through all his money, was in debt to the FBI, and had transmitted so little material that the British feared the Abwehr had grown suspicious. Facing up to what had become a bad show on both sides, MI5 and the FBI mutually agreed to cancel the loan of Tricycle.

★   ★   ★

J. C. Masterman remarked that Tricycle's key strength as a double agent was always his "ability to impose himself and his views on the Germans when personal contact could be made." This capacity was put to the test when Popov returned to Lisbon in the autumn of 1942. The sight of the sparkling Tagus filled him with confidence—"I felt alive again seeing it as the Boeing glided in. I was back in the game again"—and he quickly turned the tables on Abwehr concerns about his poor performance in America by maintaining it was their fault: they had failed to provide Ivan with enough money to properly perform his duties. Popov did not know that Berlin had ordered Karsthoff to end all contact with him, and presumably arrest him, if he failed to explain adequately his American failure. But after long questioning, Popov's ploy of continued harping on money was successful. By the time he was ready to leave Lisbon for London, he was fully back in Karsthoff's good graces and carrying with him $25,000 in Abwehr cash, 6,000 escudos to cover his Lisbon expenses, and a promise of a future payment of $2,500 a month if he produced good work.

At his office in Imperial House, Popov was put through a lengthy debriefing by an MI5 team. Soon thereafter his new questionnaire for Britain arrived from Lisbon—in the form of a microdot attached to a message—asking for information about the effects of German bombing on England, details about searchlights, and much more. The Twenty Committee at once began preparing answers, both true and false, for Ivan to forward to his new cover addresses in Lisbon. Plainly, Tricycle was also back in full accord with the British.

At the end of November Popov shifted his residence from the Savoy Hotel to Clock House, rented quarters with a maid in a fine part of Knightsbridge, though on a street where few homes were undamaged by bombs. He was now running new double-cross agents along with Balloon and Gelantine as well as writing his long and laborious letters to Lisbon. He was properly attending to his romantic needs as well as his clandestine obligations, but the sedentary nature of his espionage left him restless for a more active role.

He soon found one in the form of a deception scheme that he presented to MI5 in May 1943. As he also laid out the plan to the Abwehr in Lisbon in the summer and autumn of 1943, with the authority of the

Yugoslav government-in-exile in London he would set up an escape route for Yugoslav military officers languishing in Switzerland after escaping from occupied territory. The benefit for the Abwehr, who would actually create the "escape" route, was that it would enable them to infiltrate the Yugoslavs with agents who would eventually reach Britain—figures whom MI5, as of course the Abwehr did not know, would immediately apprehend or turn into double agents for Tricycle's network after winnowing them from genuine officers. The escape route would be through France, using false documents provided by the Germans, then into Spain where Popov himself would meet the "escapees" and direct them to British officials in Madrid and finally to Gibraltar before transport to England.

To Popov's delight and surprise, Karsthoff and his superiors in Berlin bought into the plan without hesitation, and the Yugoslav escape route—the slipping-out plan, as Masterman called it—went into operation. Masterman would later acknowledge that Popov "successfully carried out the greater part of his scheme." Popov himself estimated that about 150 men were moved from Switzerland, some reaching London, others going no farther than Paris. An added benefit for Popov was that the escape operation reunited him with his older and much admired brother, Ivo, a medical doctor who was working for British intelligence in Yugoslavia under the code name Dreadnought. Popov had hoped the slipping-out plan might involve Ivo, but neither brother had been aware the other was a British double agent.

Popov was also now reconnected with Johann Jebsen. While in charge of the Madrid end of the Yugoslav escape route for the Abwehr, Jebsen had become alarmed that the service would no longer be able to shield him from the Gestapo. Given the way the war was going for Germany, no doubt he was also pondering his own future. In Lisbon he contacted an MI6 officer and set up a meeting in Sintra, where he arrived nattily dressed in a pin-striped suit and announced: "I recruited three people to spy for me against Britain. I knew them to be pro-British and knew they would double-cross me. I am pleased you are running my agents. Now run me."

Masterman simply recorded about Jebsen's change of sides that "by the end of September [1943] he had agreed to participate actively with us in order to further his professed anti-Nazi views." For Popov, the official turnabout of his close friend was "like a baptism—three and a half years late." In his new role as Artist, Jebsen informed the British about Abwehr agents within England, among them the figure well known to them as Garbo. He also came up with information about German weapons systems, including the V-1 flying bomb, which was passed along to the current MI6 station chief in Lisbon, Cecil Gledhill. London came back with long lists of technical questions for Artist, with the queries eventually so detailed that specialists were sent to Lisbon to talk with him.

About the time Artist began working for MI6, Popov's presence in Lisbon paid off for American OSS operatives in the city. Stretched out in the back of a car one night while being transported to a meeting with Kartshoff, Popov overheard the two Abwehr secretaries driving him refer to a "der Dicke Alois" who had trouble maneuvering his ample behind into the car. Popov knew of an Austrian political refugee called Fat Alois who had a low-level job at the American embassy yet the means to live at the Palácio in Estoril, where Popov preferred to stay himself. Intrigued, he followed Alois one evening when he went to the cinema in the casino building, then after ten minutes left—an old spy gambit to gain an hour or two of secret time. Popov trailed him in darkness from the casino to the coast road to Lisbon, where a car Popov recognized as an Abwehr vehicle picked him up. The next day he reported what he had seen to MI6, which passed the information to the OSS. Fat Alois quickly confessed to selling secret documents to the Germans, then in an effort to save himself denounced a young Portuguese servant working in the American embassy who was also in the Abwehr employ. When taken into custody the servant was found to possess a newly made key to one of the embassy safes.

Popov's relationship with his Lisbon case officer remained close, so much so that he spent Christmas of 1943 at Karsthoff's farm in Colares, a few miles from Sintra, where champagne was consumed and carols sung despite the general gloom of German guests about the direction of the war. The recently acquired farm and a new Cadillac were fruits of money Karsthoff regularly skimmed from Berlin's payments to Popov and his notional network in England. While Popov was a money machine for the Abwehr officer, he was also inadvertently the recipient of his protection. Since Karsthoff's own fate was tied to Berlin continuing to believe Ivan was a top agent, pursuing possible cracks in that façade was never in the officer's interest.

Popov's last Lisbon visit took place at the end of February 1944. For the Germans he was there to organize another group of Yugoslav escapers; for the British he was delivering to the enemy deception information about the Normandy invasion in June. It was a measure of MI5's confidence in Tricycle that he was allowed at this critical juncture in the war to continue his intimate contact with the Germans—questioned by them, socializing with them—while other double agents were kept in England writing letters and sending wireless messages. With Canaris's dismissal from the

Abwehr and the shakeup of the organization, Popov's formal interrogation in Lisbon was now handled by an SD officer, Alois Schreiber, rather than Karsthoff—a two-day grilling that Popov survived without incident. Ultra intercepts later indicated that Berlin had accepted Ivan's deception material as confirming its own overall view of Allied invasion planning.

During the Lisbon trip Popov was reunited with his brother Ivo, who, at Ivan's insistence, had been sent to Lisbon to discuss with him the Yugoslav escape route. After Ivo appeared as a passenger in Jebsen's Rolls-Royce, the brothers repaired to the Palácio for room service and talk. MI6's Lisbon station chief later arranged a secret dinner in Dreadnought's honor, afterward reporting to Britain that the agent had revealed "a seriousness and depth of feeling which contrasts with Tricycle's expansive bonhomie."

As for Jebsen, his work for British intelligence as Artist continued to have high value, yet with D-Day drawing close there was also high risk in keeping a double agent on the Continent and beyond reach of immediate protection. The Twenty Committee had ceased sending to Portugal and Spain seamen double agents—always a prime means of contacting the Germans and Japanese—but had nonetheless left Artist in place despite intercepted messages indicating he was in trouble with Berlin. Abruptly pulling him out of Portugal, it was argued, might alert the German to the existence of Ultra at a time when its continued operation was essential.

The decision would prove a source of lasting regret among some in MI5 when, in the spring of 1944, Jebsen was taken into custody in Lisbon and eventually moved to Gestapo control. He had a wealth of information that could harm Allied interests, but whatever he might reveal would come too late to matter. Once again, Masterman would write, "we were saved by time and fortune. D-Day arrived before the Germans had succeeded in unraveling all the tangled skein of the Artist case, and presumably there was little opportunity after the invasion for patient research into such matters in German offices." (Even had such research been possible at the time, it would have revealed—as was learned following the war—that Jebsen, whose kidnapping had involved currency dealings, apparently disclosed nothing about British double agents.) Nonetheless, with Artist now beyond any control, the Twenty Committee took the precaution of shutting down the work of Tricycle and his ring of subagents.

Popov first learned of Jebsen's desperate situation on May 7, when he returned to Clock House and found two MI5 officers waiting for him. He was told only that Artist had not been seen at his Estoril villa and had failed to keep an appointment with his MI6 control in Lisbon, but Popov had no doubt that his friend was under arrest, nor about what awaited him. His immediate response was to write angrily to the Germans in Lisbon that if Jebsen were not released he would cease all Abwehr work. In the Abwehr shakeup Karsthoff had been removed from his Lisbon post and transferred to Austria (eventually he was captured and executed by the Russians), leaving Popov to deal with new spymasters of the German SD. But even had Karsthoff still been in place in Lisbon, Popov knew it was unlikely the letter would have any effect since Jebsen was in Gestapo hands.

Shortly thereafter, the fighting in Normandy now intense, Popov was invited to what he thought was a small dinner at London's Hyde Park Hotel. It turned out to be a surprise gala attended by nearly everyone he knew in MI5. There it was announced that Tricycle had been recommended for a British honor, an OBE, in recognition of his work for the intelligence service. Popov was moved and embarrassed, though he could not keep concern for Jebsen from intruding on his thoughts.

It helped to some degree that Ivo had escaped German arrest in Yugoslavia and had been moved to England by MI6. The brothers took adjoining rooms in the Savoy—Clock House had been damaged by a V-1 bomb—and enjoyed another reunion. But Dusko's concern for Jebsen would not let him rest. In the fall of 1944 he began a long effort to locate where Jebsen was being held—there was some reason to believe he was still alive—by following Allied troops across previously occupied territory, doing what he called "de-Nazification" work for military intelligence while also searching for Jebsen. He reached Paris and then Zurich, but his inquiries led nowhere, and around Christmas he was back in London and was told Jebsen was dead. While trying to escape from Oranienburg concentration camp near Berlin, he had been shot—an overworked euphemism, Popov understood, for execution. He went back to his mopping-up work for intelligence on the Continent while now also searching for Jebsen's killer.

In August 1945, the war over, he found him, a man named Walter Salzer who was in hiding on the outskirts of the nearly destroyed German port city of Minden. He had been a member of the SD, and when confronted by Popov about his actions he gave the standard explanation: he had followed the orders of superiors. Popov drove Salzer to a remote area, meaning to shoot him with a pistol. When he could not, he beat him with his fists, then left him crumpled on the ground and drove away.

After the war Popov declined to return to a Yugoslavia under Communist rule. Although he eventually settled in France, in 1946 he became a naturalized British citizen. Late the following year he was presented with his OBE. Since MI5 was far from ready to showcase its former double-cross figures, the typical ceremony of awarding the decoration was moved from

Buckingham Palace to a location that seemed suitable for someone like Tricycle. The chosen venue was the bar of the Ritz Hotel in Piccadilly.

★   ★   ★

While still active as a British double agent in Lisbon in 1943, Johann Jebsen had uncovered the existence of Ostro, the code name of what he thought was an Abwehr spy ring in the city that was passing the Germans information derived from subagents in England and America. Dusko Popov remembered his friend telling him, "Ostro is run by someone named Paul Fidrmuc von Karmap, but I haven't much of a line on him. I don't know his background and I don't know if that's his real name, although I rather doubt it." When Popov asked how long Ostro had been at work, Jebsen told him, "Don't know. The Abwehr has been keeping Fidrmuc under cover. Even von Karsthoff and Kamler [Abwehr officers in Lisbon] don't have any control over him. They have orders only to collect his information and send it by special courier to Berlin."

Jebsen and Popov did not know that British intelligence had been aware of Fidrmuc since at least early 1942, and believed, or later determined, that he was an Austrian who had fought in World War I and for several years had been working for the Abwehr in Denmark and Italy before entering Portugal in the summer of 1940. With his Danish wife he settled in Estoril under the cover of a businessman who was a partner in Brucker-Traus, a Lisbon firm exporting Portuguese products to Germany. Furthermore, Ostro was his code name and he had no string of agents communicating with him, as he claimed, by secret writing in airmailed letters to Lisbon. The material he was feeding the Germans was a concoction put together from reading Allied publications, contacts with prominent Portuguese figures, and straight out invention that was as magnificently bogus as Juan Pujol's during his Lisbon period. Nonetheless, the reports, as Jebsen had discovered, were considered so valuable by the Germans that they bypassed analysis by the Lisbon Abwehr and were sent on to Berlin by radio or special courier.

Further evidence of Ostro's standing in Nazi eyes came from knowledge that high-ranking officials visited Lisbon to consult with him, and that the Germans richly rewarded him for his services with cash and art objects he put up for sale. Ostro had no hesitation in also seeking additional funds. With the end of the war in sight in the spring of 1945, he suggested to the Germans that he and his network receive three-months' advance pay to protect the operation against what might soon be an interruption in their endeavors. Ostro also expected that his German masters treat him with full awareness of his importance, as an American military intelligence report in 1943 had stressed:

> This officer, who lives in Lisbon but is responsible direct to . . . Berlin, has for the last two or three years professed to maintain an immense network of agents in all parts of the world, who report back to him by air courier. FIDRMUC has contrived to get himself regarded by the Abwehr as a wayward genius who produces the goods but must on no account be flustered. There are, however, grounds for believing that his network is wholly or chiefly imaginary, and its reports invented in Lisbon.

The Twenty Committee in London equally believed that Ostro's reports were inventions, but there was concern that through chance, educated guesswork, or picking up a Lisbon story with some credibility he might convey dangerous information, especially in the period before the Normandy landings. By use of British controlled double-cross channels it was possible to correct or confuse anything Ostro transmitted, yet worry persisted. Given his authority with the Germans, his Lisbon reports were likely given closer attention than those sent by Abwehr agents at work in England. The concern was realized when Ostro, in a report also containing much incorrect information, hit home with a prediction that the invasion would take place on the Cherbourg peninsula, and gave as his supposed source a British officer on the staff of Field Marshal Bernard Montgomery. Seemingly one of the major intelligence feats of the war, the report had no noticeable influence on German planning, though it brought Fidrmuc a note of congratulations shortly after the June 6 assault took place.

In February 1945 an Ostro report correctly noted the transfer of Canadian troops from Italy to the front in northwestern Europe, prompting fresh anxiety by the Twenty Committee. Finally, as J. C. Masterman wrote, a "variety of schemes" were "put forward for the elimination of Ostro." He did not elaborate on the character of the proposals, adding only that none succeeded and Ostro continued as an Abwehr agent in Lisbon and thorn in the Allied side to the end of the war. At the time of Ostro's Canadian report, Guy Liddell noted in his diary that MI5 should "buy him up or bump him off." (Philip Johns, the former head of MI6's Lisbon station, on bumping off: When a highly wanted figure who had infiltrated escape lines and turned over names to the Gestapo was located in Lisbon, he asked London for permission to dispose of him. The signal that came back said "KILL

HIM REPEAT KILL HIM." Johns subsequently noted that "there was no lack of volunteers to take drastic action and the man disappeared without trace!") According to one account, Stewart Menzies of MI6 resisted elimination in favor of an effort to turn Ostro to the Allied side, but the war ended before an approach to him could be made.

Just shortly before the war ended, Fidrmuc left Lisbon for Barcelona, from where in March 1945 he submitted his final report to the Germans. The following year he was taken into custody by the American military, moved to internment camps, and interrogated over a period of several months. Since he was not a Nazi party member and fit no arrest category as a war criminal, he was eventually released. Much of what is believed about him stems, in addition to that learned by Allied agents in Lisbon and through Ultra intercepts of radio traffic between Lisbon and Berlin, from his recollections under questioning.

Among the deeds he recounted was a futile attempt on his part to recruit Frederic Prokosch as an agent after he learned that the American writer, living in Estoril in 1940-1941, was returning to the United States. When in 1943 Prokosch passed through Lisbon on his way to an Allied propaganda post in Sweden, Fidrmuc advised the Abwehr to make contact with him, but he believed nothing came of this effort as well. Fidrmuc cast himself in a more successful light in a strange story involving Britain's ambassador Ronald Campbell. In August 1943 Fidrmuc was alone on the beach near the Setúbal when a boat appeared with three people aboard, one of whom he recognized as Campbell. After the party went swimming, their boat was stranded by the outgoing tide, and Fidrmuc helped them launch it. When asked to watch their belongings on the beach while they explored a nearby cove, he agreed and used the opportunity to search their pockets. In Campbell's he found a small diary with coded messages, which he memorized and later reconstructed. Fidrmuc showed his notes to an Abwehr officer, and the two decided they had something to do with an important meeting between an Italian general and Allied military officers. Fidrmuc wrote up a special report for Berlin, yet learned in response only that he should have stolen the diary.

The final American interrogation report on Fidrmuc made mention of the British view that much of the intelligence he forwarded to the Germans was "erroneous," but it took no firm position on whether or not it was wholly or partially invented. The report left it that since his stream of reports throughout the war had satisfied top Nazi figures, Fidrmuc had to be considered "one of the most successful and potentially dangerous German agents of the war." Walter Schellenberg of the German SD, during his postwar interrogation, gave added weight to this view by calling Fidrmuc the best source of military intelligence the Nazis had in Portugal, and among the top four of all German agents.

While the British took Fidrmuc seriously enough to want him removed, they were convinced he had worked alone in Lisbon and that his reports were not only inventions but often amusingly mistaken. A British intelligence agent remarked in a memorandum about Ostro that his messages supposedly coming from subagents in England "have been, with the exception of a tiny percentage, not only false, but *fantastically* so." A similar near-comic edge in phrasing with regard to Ostro also appeared in the name British intelligence agents in Lisbon pinned on Fidrmuc, who as it happened was a skilled oarsman. They called him "the canoe man" because, as it was explained, he was always "hanging about the sea around Lisbon. We thought he was looking out for U-boats." In Michael Howard's official study of British deception work, an Ostro report is quoted to illustrate both how wrong, even almost humorously wrong, his inventions could be. Describing panic caused by V-bombs striking central London, Ostro wrote: "Acute anxiety among the people has not been relieved. More evacuation is expected. The Plutocratic families in particular are leaving London."

★   ★   ★

Lily Sergueiev's service as a British double agent was finished before the war ended, though the Germans had good reason to think otherwise. She was based in England and transmitted disinformation in secret writing, which in turn was passed on to a handler in Paris, an Abwehr officer named Emile Kliemann. Early in 1944 her double-cross work abruptly changed when she was asked by MI5 to arrange a meeting with Kliemann in Lisbon, during which she would provide him with valuable information and he would give her a wireless radio transmitter and frequencies to reach the Germans directly. Letters were taking too long to get through and the British, with D-Day looming, wanted to step up the pace of the deception campaign. Known to MI5 as Treasure, Sergueiev agreed to the move even though she feared blowing her cover in a face-to-face meeting with Kliemann. Early in her recruitment by the Abwehr he had told her, "If I thought that you were betraying us, I'd shoot you here and now! But you won't ever betray us because your parents have remained in Paris. In *Paris*."

The Russian-born Sergueiev indeed had parents living in occupied Paris, and she understood the leverage the Germans had over her. But she was used to a life of risk. Tramp, her German code name, well described early travels that had taken her from Paris to Warsaw, Berlin, Beirut, and Indochina. Back in Paris after the fall of France, she was sought out by the Abwehr due to her ability with English as well as French, and the fact that she had relatives in England and Portugal and a sister in North Africa. The Germans trained her in spycraft, including the use of Morse code, and regularly paid her salary but were in no hurry to assign her a mission. With delay following delay, which included Kliemann's inability ever to be on time for meetings with her, she worried the war would be over before she accomplished anything.

Finally in the summer of 1943 she was told to go to Lisbon to keep an eye on the local British community while waiting to get to England through the help of a cousin living in Cambridge. Once there, her cover would be that she was a refugee who had managed to escape Europe by buying the necessary documents and now wanted to help the Allies liberate France. As an Abwehr agent, she would visit friends living in the village of Wraxall near Bristol and report by invisible ink on everything coming and going in the bustling area on the Mouth of the Severn.

On her way to Lisbon, Sergueiev stopped in Madrid, went directly to the British consulate, and offered her services as a double agent. After initial interrogation, the British arranged for her to travel under a false name to England via Gibraltar—Portugal had refused her a visa, presumably because of her Russian name—with the ostensible purpose of visiting her relative in Cambridge. She had one nonnegotiable demand: her cherished dog Babs had to make the journey to England as well, though without going through an ordeal of six months of quarantine. The British told her they would see to it. As for the Germans, they were delighted to have their agent bypass Lisbon and go directly to England. Kliemann came from Paris to Madrid to supply her with funds to last for six months and with jewelry she could sell after she arrived.

She expected to spend only a few days in Gibraltar, but weeks passed. When questioned about the delay, the British told her there were problems with Babs. An American pilot she met on the Rock said he could get a friend to fly the dog to London, thus skirting all controls. Sergueiev agreed to leave Babs with the pilot, but only after the British, informed of the plan, agreed to transports Babs if the pilot failed to come through.

In London there was the usual period of rigorous interrogation before Sergueiev met with her MI5 case officer, Tar Robertson, who explained the importance of her work for Britain, took custody of the money and jewelry the Germans had provided, and said she would be paid 50 pounds each month plus traveling expenses. Sergueiev agreed to the money but noted to herself that the Germans had valued her services at the equivalent of 250 pounds a month. Money, she also reminded herself, was not why she was now helping the British. In aiding them she understood she was aiding France.

As she recorded in a diary, the information subsequently given to her by Robertson and his aides and fed to the Germans made little sense: ". . . bits of conversation mentioning rank and badges; trains supposedly seen in stations; information obtained by chance through overhearing conversations in the train." But it seemed to add up to something since the Germans heartily praised her work. Her life in England, though, gave her little comfort; she felt isolated, and the people she worked with were efficient but cold and unemotional.

Her only close relationship was with Mary Sherer, the day-to-day contact assigned to her by Robertson. The pair often ate together and went to films, yet Sherer carefully kept a professional distance. A continuing irritant, as Sergueiev let Sherer know, was British failure to keep their word about bringing her dog to England. Shortly before her mission to Lisbon she learned from her sister in North Africa that Babs, who had been taken there from Gibraltar by an American pilot, had been killed in a road accident. "Everything is indifferent to me now," she confided to her diary about the loss. "The circle of loneliness has closed around me; I am alone, absolutely alone."

The cover MI5 arranged for her in Lisbon was nearly impossible for even Sergueiev to take seriously. Through her English cousin, the story went, she had found a position in the cinema section of the Ministry of Information, which was preparing a series of films for showings in liberated countries. There was urgency about the project because the Americans were doing the same and had more capacity for turning out propaganda films. She had offered a suggestion that, in order to make the MOI films more realistic, someone should talk with experienced filmmakers who had escaped from occupied territory to neutral places such as Lisbon. Since she spoke French, she had proposed herself as the one to contact exiled French screenwriters about working on the films, and her MOI supervisors had agreed. Despite doubts about the flimsy story, Sergueiev cabled Kliemann that she was coming to Lisbon and bringing him information. He in turn was to provide her with a transmitter, a code to use, and money.

She flew to Lisbon in early March 1944, took a room in the plush Avenida Palace Hotel, and learned at the British embassy that a figure the MOI had supposedly sent her to meet, the chief of the film section in the embassy's press attaché office, was away in London. Her handlers in MI5 had never considered that possibility. Knowing the Germans would check all details of her Lisbon mission, Sergueiev quickly developed another explanation for her presence in the city, which was that she now understood that most French refugees were going to North Africa via Spain and Gibraltar, so she would write the press attaché in Madrid for help in locating scriptwriters there. This would take time, as would a letter to the MOI in London asking for instructions about a journey to Madrid or the possibility of sending screenwriters to Lisbon rather than Gibraltar. The wholly notional process would buy her about a month for staying on in Lisbon. With her new cover story Sergueiev put on her other hat and tried to contact Kliemann, only to learn he was still in Paris and apparently had no idea she had come to Lisbon. Two weeks passed before he reached the city, and for their first meeting he was smartly turned out in a dark blue suit and a felt hat but late as usual. When she spun her far-fetched account of film work for the MOI, he simply said, "You are very clever. Very, very clever."

Over the following days a technician taught Sergueiev how to operate as well as take apart and reassemble the transmitter Kliemann had brought her. Then she had to learn to build by hand a Morse key because it seemed too chancy to include a keyboard with the transmitter on her return to England. A story she had invented for the British, as she told Kliemann, was that the transmitter was actually a secondhand radio bought from a Frenchman and could be shipped in the diplomatic bag due to her work with the MOI.

Just before she left Lisbon, Kliemann took Sergueiev in a hired car on a sightseeing idyll to Sintra, where she used a camera with an automatic shutter to take snapshots of the two of them. When the photos were developed, she gave Kliemann three prints and the negatives, keeping another set for herself and one for Tar Robertson. On the drive back to Lisbon, Kliemann told her he would happily escort her to the casino in Estoril for a fine dinner but realized it would not be wise to be seen together in such a den of international agents and double agents.

Meeting in Lisbon the following day, they took a ferry across the Tagus for lunch in Cacilhas, where Kliemann gave her fifteen hundred pounds, the money all in one-pound notes and wrapped in a large parcel. "You find it a bit bulky?" he asked her. "*A bit!*" she exclaimed, and insisted the funds had to be exchanged for larger notes. Before separating that day, Kliemann said they must agree on a secret message which would indicate to him that the British had found her out and were forcing her to work for them. She suggested a simple repeated stroke in Morse code. "That's excellent!" Kliemann responded, and noted the signal in a notebook.

At their final Lisbon meeting Kliemann gave Sergueiev 500 pounds in ten-pound notes—all he had been able to exchange in local banks for British currency—and the rest of the money in Portuguese escudos. He also presented her with a bracelet with forty-two diamonds set in platinum that he had bought for 69,000 escudos. As they parted, he told her to be very cautious when she returned to England, then bent over and gallantly kissed her hand.

Dank and dreary London gave Sergueiev a feeling that she had never really been away, but when Mary Sherer saw the bracelet on her wrist and asked her to describe what Lisbon had been like, she sketched the city in affectionate detail. "I wish I could have gone too," Sherer replied dreamily. Then she resumed her MI5 role and took from Sergueiev her photos of Kliemann and the bank notes and bracelet she had been given and put everything in an envelope to send on to Robertson.

When contact with the Germans was made with the transmitter, Sergueiev was again in the business of sending disinformation messages, now at a rate of six a week. On weekends she left London and went to her friends near Bristol, and from there took imaginary journeys that allowed her to harvest imaginary information. In reality there was furious activity in the area, with convoy after convoy arriving and a constant flow of armored vehicles and trucks carrying British and American troops. With the air heavy with a sense that the invasion was about to take place, Sergueiev's workload increased to as many as three messages a day. From the Germans came anxious requests for added detail.

On June 2, 1944, Sergueiev recorded in her diary a conversation in which she was asked by Sherer to explain a remark she had made earlier about her ability to "ruin" the work she was doing for the British. She had said exactly that in one of her recurring periods in which overwork, her loneliness, and continuing bitterness over the loss of her dog surfaced in vengeful awareness that she had a lever of power at her disposal. With two strokes of her Morse key she could tell the Germans she was no longer a free agent. "There is a security check," she told Sherer, but did not disclose what it was. Sherer, she knew, would have to inform Robertson.

A week after the Normandy invasion Sherer and Robertson appeared at Sergueiev's flat, and Robertson informed her that because of the security check she had arranged in Lisbon with the Germans she was no longer considered trustworthy. Consequently her work was over. She would have a fortnight to vacate her flat, and he would provide her with transportation either to Paris or to her sister in Algiers. If she made any difficulties or spoke to anyone about her work, she would be jailed and then handed over to French authorities.

While Lily Sergueiev was through with the British—though Treasure, with someone else operating the transmitter in London, continued to contact the Germans—she was far from done with the war. She told Robertson she would return to France but without his help. In the process of doing so, she had to be interrogated by an agent of French intelligence, and to this end MI5 furnished the service with a dossier that said British intelligence had organized her journey to England and that she had worked there under the authority of the War Office until June 14, 1944. As a recruit of the French army, Sergueiev returned to liberated Paris at the end of August 1944, finding her parents alive and well.

Later J. C. Masterman wrote that from the Twenty Committee perspective, Treasure "turned out not to belie her name." And with justifiable pride in the machinations of the British double-cross system, he added that after Paris was freed

> we allowed TREASURE . . . to return to France in the French ATS [women's auxiliary army]. In August the German Abwehr officer who ran the case [Kliemann] was captured and was brought to England as a prisoner of war. TREASURE was therefore in France and her spymaster in England; but wireless communication continued as though TREASURE was still here and her spymaster in Europe!

★   ★   ★

With equal reason for pride, Dusko Popov remarked in a memoir of his spy career that "Ian Fleming said he based his character James Bond to some degree on me and my experience. Could be." The possibility stemmed from an encounter with Fleming that, according to Popov, had taken place in Estoril just before he left to work with the FBI in the United States. One evening he became aware of Fleming—whom he believed, incorrectly, was an MI6 agent—observing him in the lobby of the Palácio Hotel, later in a restaurant, and finally in the casino, where Popov was involved in a masterly performance at the baccarat table. An explanation for the watchfulness was that Popov was carrying with him a hefty amount of Abwehr money for deposit in a New York bank, though in fact to be turned over to the British, and Fleming was protecting the funds for MI6. But in Popov's estimation this was not likely, and he believed that Fleming really had his eyes on him as a potential fictional character. "Perhaps," Popov wrote, "he developed what happened that night into a Bond adventure."

The Bond novel Popov had in mind was Fleming's first, *Casino Royale*, in which Agent 007 out-duels the sinister Le Chiffre at the baccarat table.

Whether Popov actually inspired Fleming's novel is uncertain, though the two could have crossed paths in wartime Portugal. In May 1941 Fleming, a commander in the British navy and now a member of naval intelligence, arrived in the country on a flight from England. With him was his boss, Admiral John Godfrey. While waiting for a Clipper flight to New York to begin coordinating British intelligence work with their American counterparts, the two stayed at the Palácio. After dinner one night they went to the casino, where the only gamblers present were a few Portuguese businessmen. Fleming gambled and lost, and when leaving the tables said to Godfrey, "What if those men [the Portuguese gamblers] had been German secret service agents, and suppose we had cleaned them out of their money; now that would have been exciting."

Although Popov might well have, he did not suggest that a more illustrious British novelist made imaginative use of Tricycle. Juan Pujol could have floated stronger claims for Garbo, and Paul Fidrmuc even stronger ones for Ostro. All three agents would have come to the attention of Graham Greene when he returned to England in early 1943 after fourteen months in West Africa as an MI6 operative. Greene was taking up a new post with the secret service, first at a country facility in St. Albans, later in an office building in central London's Ryder Street, where one floor was occupied by the American X-2 group under Norman Holmes Pearson.

Greene was attached to Section V of MI6, and his immediate boss was Kim Philby, the future defector to the Soviet Union. Philby ran the section's Iberian Department, which monitored operations in Portugal, Spain, Gibraltar, and North Africa, and Greene was put in charge of the Portuguese desk. He knew little about the country and nothing about the language, but with Portugal swarming with undercover figures the new post was clearly a promotion in the spy business. In his other business as a novelist, Greene already had behind him the enduring achievements of *Brighton Rock* and *The Power and the Glory* together with the superb thrillers *This Gun for Hire* and *The Confidential Agent*.

To prepare for the work with Philby's group, Greene put together a handbook listing names and activities of all known Axis intelligence agents in Portugal. Doing so meant going through an existing card index and sorting out true and false information, a slogging task given that the confirmed names of some two thousand enemy agents were on file together with another two hundred Germans living in Portugal who had intelligence involvement. Greene also had to contend with some forty-six business firms in the Iberian peninsula considered covers for German clandestine activity.

With this large preliminary task finished, Greene's everyday duties were those of collecting and filing intelligence reports from agents in Portugal as well as intercepts from Bletchley Park, and sending coded instructions back to MI6 agents in Lisbon. In later accounts of the work, Greene downplayed its importance. He told a biographer, "It was an office job really. . . . Giving directions to our man in Lisbon." And he wrote himself: ". . . it was a question of files, files, endless files." Philby remembered him working "quietly, coolly and competently" as a deskman, and for writing "terse, sometimes devastating marginalia" on correspondence coming from the field. "Poor old 24000, our Man in Lisbon," went one example, "charging around like a bull in a china shop, opening up vast vistas of the obvious."

Routine or not, the Portuguese desk gave Greene intimate knowledge of Lisbon's shadow world and allowed him to take part, under Philby's direction, in a broad effort in 1943 and 1944 to turn German agents in Portugal to the Allied side. Some were abandoning what by now was clearly a sinking ship, and came over on their own accord, Artist among them. Others needed a shove.

An agent of MI5 introduced Philby to an ideal man for the shoving, Jona von Ustinov, a cosmopolitan figure (and father of the actor Peter Ustinov) who went by the name Klop Ustinov. In World War I he had served in the German army, and before World War II had worked in London as a press attaché at the German embassy. Now connected with British intelligence, Ustinov was said to have an unerring eye for distinguishing Nazi and anti-Nazi elements within the Abwehr. Sent to Lisbon with the excessively British cover name of Middleton-Pendleton, he chose figures at the German legation—top officials but also clerks and secretaries—whom he believed were anti-Nazi and sent them messages beginning "Greetings from Klop" and suggesting a rendezvous at some remote spot or lunch at a flat he shared with an MI6 agent. "Yes," Klop often reported afterward. "He's willing to work with us."

On the Portuguese desk in London, Greene would have duly noted Ustinov's achievements. His work also involved him, in indirect fashion, with the Abwehr's Admiral Canaris, as Greene recalled when he later reflected on Kim Philby's Communist affiliation. During Canaris's appearances in Portugal, Greene had sent telegrams to the police that informed them about the spymaster's movements, all in an effort to annoy him. Had Philby allowed the provocation because it actually served Russian interests?

[T]he thing which I have always wondered [Greene wrote] was whether Kim Philby smiled up his sleeve when I arranged to have

Admiral Canaris, head of the Abwehr, harassed. I had him harassed, when he went to Portugal, by giving the police information about the meetings he was holding and so on. My telegrams had to be passed by Kim and he didn't prevent it and everyone knows *now* that Admiral Canaris was on our side. He was anti-Hitler. But there was talk on the German side of a separate peace which the Russians were very much afraid of. I wonder whether Kim knew this and was letting me harass him because the Russians feared a separate peace.

Just before the Normandy invasion in June 1944, Greene abruptly resigned his position with MI6 and took a new post with the political intelligence division of the Foreign Office for the remainder of the war. More than a decade later, and after publishing *The Heart of the Matter* and *The End of the Affair*, he turned back to his time on the Portugal desk for the comic spy novel *Our Man in Havana*. About the origin of the tale Greene recorded that, shortly after the war ended, he was asked to write a film script and thought about "a Secret Service comedy based on what I had learned from my work in 1943-4 of German Abwehr activity in Portugal."

Nothing came of the film, but as late as 1956 Greene was planning a similar film treatment set in wartime Portugal, and intended to go to Lisbon to gather local atmosphere. As it turned out, he chose to write a novel with Havana as the setting in the period in which Fidel Castro's guerrillas and the Batista regime were locked in a struggle for control of Cuba. Published in 1958, *Our Man in Havana* was quickly followed by a film version (with the screenplay by Greene) shot in Havana with permission of the triumphant Castro.

In the story Jim Wormold, a feckless, longtime English vacuum-cleaner salesman in Cuba, is recruited by a British secret service agent named Hawthorne (played in the film by Noël Coward) to be their man in Havana (agent 52900/5). Wormold shrewdly rises in spy stature—and income to provide for his beloved and crafty young daughter—by dint of invention. With a map of Cuba, copies of *Time* magazine, and various government publications he fabricates a spy ring made up of characters with useful fields of expertise—an engineer, an economics professor, a drunken pilot. Back at headquarters in London, Wormold's superiors accept the information his subagents supply, delightfully erroneous, at face value.

When crude drawings of parts of a vacuum cleaner are submitted along with a report of the engineer, London concludes it might be a diabolical weapon under construction by someone (rebels, Americans, Russians, Germans, and so forth) in the Oriente hills. When "they" ("the others") learn

of the drawings, and learn too that British intelligence believes them important, they also take Wormold and his work seriously, so much so that they
decide to poison him. The attempted murder fails, but "they"—an agent
in the form of a pipe-smoking rival English vacuum cleaner salesman—take
revenge by killing Wormold's valued German friend Dr. Hasselbacher. The
comedy now turns less comic, and Wormold, so to speak, turns with it. He
seeks out the murderer and, after an exchange of gunfire, kills him.

The truth out at last about the notional drawings and the notional
ring of agents, Wormold is recalled to London, expecting to be sacked
or possibly even hanged. But doing either would amount to admission of
incompetence by intelligence officials. So, in a return to the novel's full
comic mode, the top official—a figure known simply as "Chief"—informs
Wormold that his intelligence post in Havana will close but he will be kept
on in England with a position on the training staff ("Lecturing. How to
run a station abroad. That kind of thing"). And, naturally, he is in line to
receive a British honor, an OBE.

13

WOLFRAM BY DAY

> Your stories are good. Wolfram by day and fornication by
> night—your colleagues must eclipse in gallantry all other
> competitors in Dr Salazar's raffish capital.
>
> —Letter of Sybil Eccles to David Eccles, 1942

J im Wormold's surname might simply have been a witty reversal of "old
worm," but it could also have been suggested by a prized Portuguese
mineral. On MI6's Portugal desk in London, Graham Greene could hardly
have avoided incessant talk about the vital wartime need of wolfram, or
wolframite, and possibly the odd name of the ore stuck with him when
he came to write his story of the inept vacuum cleaner salesman become
honored British spy. In any case, wolfram had a way of getting inside the
minds of both Allied and Axis officials. "I think I never heard of wolfram
before I went to Spain," confessed Ambassador Carlton Hayes. "I soon
learned, however. In fact, all of us at the Embassy in Madrid had perforce
to make it a topic of daily conversation and some of us dreamed about it
at night." From Lisbon in 1942, David Eccles wrote his wife in England
about the British ambassador to Washington "penning wolframic messages"
to Secretary of State Cordell Hull, with Hull then sending back bewildering
instructions to Lisbon's American legation that left everyone there help-
lessly begging the British embassy's aid in drafting coherent replies.

From the start of the war Portugal's neutrality coexisted with the intent of extracting as much commercial benefit to the country as possible.
In a radio address to the nation in 1942 Salazar effectively acknowledged
the dual aim by remarking that "the desire for neutrality cannot be superior
to the interests of the nation." In the economic sphere of trade he wielded

neutrality as a national resource, which allowed him to conduct through most of the war a flourishing business with both sides. Portugal imported its needs of wheat, oil, steel, and military materiel and exported its staples of cork, wine, wool, olive oil, canned sardines, turpentine, tin, and—of overriding importance—wolfram, the mineral from which tungsten is derived, used in military production to harden steel for tanks, airplanes, and armor-piercing shells.

The Allies could draw on wolfram supplies in the United States and in South America. Germany's wolfram came mainly from China and Burma until the war closed down ship routes and rail transport across Russia. The Third Reich then turned to abundant deposits in Spain and especially Portugal. From 1942 forward, Portugal was Germany's main source of wolfram, and following the fall of France the Reich had secure land routes for moving the ore from the Iberian peninsula. (Portugal did not supply wolfram to Mussolini's Italy on grounds it could end up in Germany, throwing off the balancing act of equal treatment of the belligerents.) The trade with Portugal was so essential for Germany that always there was fear, actual and rhetorical, that if denied wolfram the Wehrmacht would come and take it—or German submarines would attack Portuguese shipping on the high seas as a warning of what might befall the country.

In December 1941 the Portuguese merchant ship *Corte Real* was sunk by a U-boat while on its way to the United States with, so Germany later claimed, a cargo of wolfram that, had the ship landed, presumably would have been sent to Britain. After the attack David Eccles noted in a letter written from Lisbon that the "wolfram business goes from bad to worse, the Germans have now sunk a Portuguese ship carrying wolfram to the USA to warn this wretched little country . . . that they mean to stop at nothing to secure wolfram for themselves and to deny it to us and America. We are getting near a shooting war as you can see." Eccles later added to his letter that "we find it untrue that the ship had any wolfram."

★   ★   ★

In the early period of the shooting war David Eccles was a central figure on the Allied side in the long and intense contest over Portuguese wolfram. He had flown into Lisbon from England in April 1940, just before the fall of France, and would be based there off and on for more than two years. He was on the wartime staff of the British Ministry of Economic Warfare (MEW), made up of businessmen and civil servants with a mission of limiting trade between neutral countries and Germany while bolstering it for Britain. Spain and Portugal were of prime importance, and Eccles's assignment in Lisbon was to head the commercial side of the embassy. His business experience in the Iberian peninsula was considerable since he had been chairman of a British company that had built and operated a railway across northern Spain.

He found the small Lisbon staff of MEW squeezed into rooms in the ambassador's residence, and his first task was to set up new offices where he could conduct business with Portuguese officials. The only one who ultimately counted was Salazar, and the ambassador, Walford Selby, turned over to Eccles much of the direct contact with the prime minister and his staff. By his own reckoning, Eccles got along well with the dictator, whom he considered handsome, dignified, intelligent, and thoroughly informed. Salazar frequently called on him about matters of finance, the British sea blockade, and virtually all else involving Anglo-Portuguese relations.

They spoke together in French in Salazar's office in São Bento Palace, with Eccles feeling he had to be prepared for any subject, as if back at Oxford during a tutorial. Now and then their conversations drifted off weighty matters. After deciding on the Portuguese decoration to be given the Duke of Kent during his appearance in the summer of 1940 at the centenary celebration, Salazar asked Eccles, "What about yourself? Would you like a decoration?" When Eccles politely declined, Salazar turned to a window and mused, "Look down there at the homes of my people. I have their respect. Perhaps also their love. That is the only decoration worth having."

Eccles routinely sent letters to his wife in England about his life and work in Lisbon. The day he arrived in the city he informed her that "Lisbon at first sight—the streets and wall-gardens—seems more like Italy—Naples or Sicily—than anything I've seen in Spain. Flowers everywhere. Oranges and reds predominate, but as I look closer I expect I shall find every sort." Later he found Lisbon "the most adorable place. The combination of blue skies and sea, the colours and the gardens, have gone straight to my heart." Although the embassy where he had a suite was sunk "in a slum where dogs bark and cocks crow almost all night," he dined regularly with the ambassador in a "life of luxury": "We breakfast on the terrace in an embrace of flowers, the orange juice is the best in the world. A superb chef sends exquisite lunches and dinners to be eaten with the finest silver and linen under the gaze of George V and Queen Mary."

The countryside beyond Lisbon, as seen on weekend drives and long walks, was as engaging as the city. "Fields of maize and vineyards and patches of pine trees," as Eccles described the scene. "The houses white with browny-red tiles. . . . Any man, after a hard life, would be glad to come to rest in such a place." Accounts of his economic work, on the other hand, came with an emotional roller coaster of success and failure. In October 1940 he wrote:

> I am disappointed here. The relations we established with the Portuguese Government in May-July were really good. Now they are quibbling and crotchety. It's a one-man show and that man [Salazar] is so complex and gifted that he takes handling. Well, there we are, after three months of air battles [with the Luftwaffe over England] he doesn't seem (I haven't seen him, this is what I gather) to believe in us as much as he did in July.

But abruptly Eccles turned from his troubles with Salazar to the consolations of living and working in Lisbon: "The harbor reflects the blue of heaven, there go half a hundred ships, with or without navicerts, who cares, they look so quiet and confident riding on the Tagus. I love Lisbon, but hate to think of the chances we miss here."

Late in November 1941, believing his efforts in Lisbon finished, Eccles returned to London and a new post within MEW. But with the new year and America in the war, he had to return because "the wolfram negotiations in Portugal turned sour" and the British embassy in Lisbon thought he might soothe "Salazar's bloody-mindedness." America in the war meant that negotiations about Portuguese wolfram shipments were now a three-nation affair, and all the more difficult. Still, the diplomatic life was not all unrelenting labor. Eccles acknowledged to his wife that "if we work late at night in Lisbon it is certainly not wolfram that engages our attention," and went on to disclose "here [the Lisbon embassy] the most frightful scandals. Everyone sleeping with everyone else and being catty about the others. What a nuisance sex is! Why can't we mind less? I mind very much, but I also see the point of celibacy." To which his wife deftly responded: "Wolfram by day and fornication by night—your colleagues must eclipse in gallantry all other competitors in Dr Salazar's raffish capital."

While wolfram negotiations remained problematic for Eccles, some trade deals went smoothly in that they involved disputes only over price. "I am up to my neck in buying 750,000 cases (100 tins each) of sardines," he noted. "What a job it is as the [British] Ministry of Food only want to pay £3 a case against the ruling intra-Blockade price of £6 upwards." Eccles also found himself queried for advice when Portugal began thinking of food rationing. He asked the Ministry of Food to supply literature on its program in England, then realized Portugal could not follow the system since so many of its citizens were unable to read and write. One day a boy had mistakenly brought to his flat a parcel addressed to someone living above him. "Don't you read?" Eccles asked him. "Not every day," the boy replied, without a trace of humor.

★   ★   ★

Throughout the war Britain enjoyed a significant advantage in securing Portugal's wolfram since British-owned companies controlled the most productive Portuguese mines and had long practice in extracting and exporting the ore. Germany owned or controlled mines as well but had to buy from Portuguese or other producers to meet increasing annual requirements as the war went on. A further and equally significant British advantage was that Portugal allowed its oldest ally to buy on credit while Germany paid with Portuguese escudos. By war's end the British debt for wolfram and other Portuguese products caused the two countries to reverse their historic financial positions, with Portugal now the creditor nation.

Germany's need for cash payment was eased by complex money arrangements with Portuguese banks whereby German and Swiss currency was exchanged in Lisbon for escudos. Germany also exchanged monetary gold for escudos, and there was some payment in the form of imported German steel, fertilizer, and military equipment. A 1945 study by the American embassy in Lisbon found that Portuguese companies and government ministries also advanced escudos to Germany to facilitate purchases. Perhaps as a last resort to gain local currency for buying wolfram, the Germans offered for sale in Portugal and Spain a half-million bottles of high-quality French champagne and some twenty tons of pâté de foie gras.

Britain in 1942 had intervened in the scramble for wolfram in Spain and Portugal by denying it to Germany through preemptive buying—purchasing more than needed and outbidding on price—through its MEW-formed United Kingdom Commercial Corporation. America joined in the fray through its wartime economic arm, the United States Commercial Company. Combined Anglo-American buying caused the price of ore to skyrocket. Portuguese wolfram going for about a $1,000 a ton in 1941 reached $6,000 a ton the following year, which included a steep $1,200 government export tax. By 1943 prices had soared to 775 percent above prewar rates, lifting the wolfram business to a $100 million-a-year industry. Preemptive buying went on for other Portuguese products imported by Germany—sardines especially, and one winter the British scored a coup by snapping up nearly every sheepskin in Portugal to frustrate the Wehrmacht's need for them in the Russian campaign—but wolfram remained the primary focus, and in the mining areas escalating demand created fevered conditions.

Wolfram mines were mainly in the northern province of Beira Alta, a historically poor mountainous region of small villages and granite block homes. Grossly underpaid farm laborers and miners abandoned their work and went prospecting for themselves with picks and shovels for chunks of "black gold." These were often near the surface, outside the control of the mines, and could be sold or smuggled across the border into Spain, where prices were even better. During an inspection tour of a British mine high in the mountains, David Eccles was struck by panoramic views that "rival any in Europe," but he lamented the effect of the new entrepreneurship on ore output:

> Before the war there was plenty of hungry labour in the surrounding villages. . . . The men walked over the hills to Panasquiera, brought a week's food on their back, slept on bare ground, were paid 2s.6d. per day, and deserted whenever they felt like it. Now the great rise in the value of wolfram has made a hundred other ways of working more remunerative than coming to our mine on the old conditions. Down went our labour force and our production.

At the height of the wolfram frenzy some 100,000 people were employed in mining and distribution, and the Portuguese national coffers were vastly enriched through ore sales and tax revenues. But boom times also brought with them inflated costs for basic goods, labor shortages in both agricultural areas and—as Eccles had pointed out—established mining regions, and general social unrest. In Lisbon the term "wolframistas" was born to describe sardonically those who tossed off routine lives in the free-wheeling rush for new riches. The *Anglo-Portuguese News* mildly defended those so mocked by suggesting they were no different than others caught up in the excess of national gold rushes. Moreover, added the newspaper, since many of the "more blatant *nouveaux riches*" had barely earned a living as rural laborers, it was hardly unexpected that sudden wealth had gone to their heads.

In February 1942 Salazar stepped in and established the Metals Regulatory Commission to bring order to what had been light government oversight of the wolfram business. Now all ore legally mined in the country was purchased by the government commission, then resold to the belligerents at a flat rate under a quota system which allowed them to export a certain amount of production from their own mines together with a fixed percentage from the yield of independent mines and individual prospectors. But what was intended as equitable regulation of the wolfram trade turned out to be fraught with difficulties. Neither warring side was satisfied, and heated squabbles broke out when one or the other appeared to receive favored treatment.

★   ★   ★

In 1942 and again in 1943 Allied-Portuguese relations were severely stressed by a series of wolfram agreements between Lisbon and Berlin. David Eccles had preached the need for patience in all dealings with Salazar, though, as he well knew, the virtue was hard to apply. He had lamented to his wife: "When you have a man like Salazar who says, 'I would rather my people starve then give you a guarantee not to export olive oil to the Germans, not because I like the Germans but because I will not compromise my right to trade with any other country,' what is one to do?" When at the beginning of August 1942 Eccles was recalled to London to take up a new position in the Ministry of Production, he dismally characterized the present wolfram dealings with the Portuguese as all "dust and bitterness." "We have lost all benefit of the doubt," he continued. "If the Germans say, 'A is true about business,' and we say, 'No, B is true,' the Portuguese incline to A. That's a handicap I never imagined I should have to carry."

A Portuguese trade agreement with the Germans in the spring of 1943 was particularly infuriating. It caught the Allies unawares, with an unapologetic Salazar blithely explaining to the British ambassador that Berlin had simply accepted his terms for more than two thousand tons of wolfram plus half of available ore from independent mining operations. To the Americans it seemed evident that Salazar was employing wolfram not only for the huge sums it brought him but also as a main bargaining chip for securing a variety of required Portuguese imports. In supplying such needs the Germans displayed their legendary efficiency. "The fact is," the American minister informed Washington, "that while German deliveries of a wide range of commodities seem to be maintained with reasonable punctuality and involved no strain on Portuguese shipping transportation, difficulties have nullified to a considerable degree the effect of supply concessions which we made to the Portuguese in the present agreement." Put simply, Germany was better than the Allies in supplying Portugal with what it wanted, and supplying it on time on overland routes through France and Spain. The new deal called for Germany to provide Portugal with steel, railway cars, artillery and ammunition, and military trucks, all at good prices.

Anthony Eden, usually willing to go the last mile with Salazar, noted that his behavior in the latest agreement with Germany was incomprehensible in an ally. From Washington came talk of reprisals, possibly in the form of restricting oil shipments to Portugal. "Oil is our key card," Secretary of State Hull told the Lisbon ministry. "Neither shipping nor supply limitations obscure our ability to control its flow." But at this point the Azores accord intervened and the latest wolfram crisis was defused, the Allies now with reason to be grateful to Salazar. It was possible that keeping Germany supplied with wolfram had even played a role in moderating its response to the pact. Churchill reportedly said that a continuing flow of wolfram to the enemy was all right if it quieted Hitler's response to the Azores. And keep flowing it did. Despite Allied pressure through preemptive buying, some sabotage actions, and threats to limit Portuguese imports, the Reich, at least through mid-1944, was able to satisfy its needs for Portuguese wolfram.

★   ★   ★

After the landings in Normandy, land routes for moving wolfram and other exports across the Pyrenees and through France rapidly closed. Well before that development the Allies had begun pressing Portugal for a total end to wolfram shipments to Germany on grounds they were prolonging the war. Salazar countered with a string of delaying arguments: wolfram was a doubtful factor in continuing the war; in fairness Germany should be allowed production of mines it owned; Portugal had already signed wolfram agreements with Germany, which morality required he must satisfy; it made no sense to restrict Portuguese wolfram without a similar arrangement in Spain; and, finally, a reduction in shipments might be considered but a complete embargo was out of the question. When it suited his purposes, Salazar ended all dispute by vanishing for a time. In February 1944 Ambassador Norweb explained to Secretary of State Hull that he had been *trying* to meet with the prime minister.

> Inability to see Dr. Salazar in regard to the wolfram matter is not due to any lack of perseverance on my part or the part of my British colleague who has been equally assiduous in endeavoring to follow up this pending problem. It appears though that the Doctor, like Br'er Rabbit, is lying low pending developments in Spain.

The Americans and the British also disagreed among themselves about how hard to push for the embargo. The United States believed the Anglo-Portuguese alliance caused Britain to give Salazar too much leeway, the

British that the Americans did not appreciate his importance as the leader of a neutral nation and the chaos that would follow if he were removed. Yet since invoking the alliance had worked in gaining access to the Azores, the overall Allied strategy put Britain in the lead in discussions about the wolfram embargo.

In the meantime Britain and America intensified preemptive buying of wolfram in Spain and Portugal, with press reports in early 1944 estimating that they were getting up to 75 percent of Spain's ore and the lion's share of Portugal's. And they tried pressuring Salazar with personal letters favoring an embargo from Churchill, Roosevelt, Eden, and other leaders. The ambassador of Brazil informed him that Portuguese wolfram going to the German war industry was being used to kill Brazilian troops fighting for the Allies in Italy, a message that, so the American ambassador believed, took Salazar by surprise and had special effect since it came from a "daughter nation—a member of the family."

Finally on May 29, 1944, Ambassador Campbell delivered a message to Salazar appealing in the name of the Anglo-Portuguese alliance for a total ban on wolfram exports to Germany. When Salazar asked if he could fulfill an earlier agreement to ship Germany a hundred tons of ore, Campbell said no. A week later—aware or sensing that his own regime was at stake, and against a background of Spain agreeing on May 2 to sharply restrict but not end the wolfram trade with the Reich—Salazar banned not only wolfram shipments to Germany but to all countries, and closed down the mines. (Britain had earlier announced it would stop purchasing Portuguese ore once the German embargo was enacted.) Salazar's order went to the printer on the day of the Normandy invasion, and on June 7 the official announcement appeared in Portuguese newspapers:

> In view of the fact that the Government of His Britannic Majesty in the name of the Anglo-Portuguese Alliance made an appeal that we should put an end to all exports of wolfram as a means of contributing to the shortening of the war, the Government has resolved to accede to this request and has decided henceforth to cease the exportation of this mineral.

In the House of Commons, Anthony Eden announced the ban to a cheering assembly and added that it matched in importance the Azores agreement. When a question was raised about the Portuguese government having taken a "long time" to act, Eden agreed but referred again to the great contribution of its Azores action. From the State Department came word that the United States had been "active in the negotiations," though Ambassador Norweb in Lisbon, reporting back to Washington, was certain where the bulk of the credit belonged. He wrote: "In reviewing the course of the wolfram negotiations . . . it appears to be undeniable that it was the invocation of the Anglo-Portuguese Alliance which finally carried the day."

For Portugal, upholding the alliance provided a means of bowing to the Allies—as a member of Salazar's government frankly put it to him during deliberations over the embargo—"without humiliation." But preserving national pride did nothing to ease the upheaval in the Portuguese economy caused by ending the wolfram trade. Many thousands of men were thrown out of work, and tax revenues plunged. *The Economist* magazine, summing up the damage, also pointed to "mines wrecked by ruthless methods, miners too enriched by clandestine profits to return to the service of the reputable concerns, and a price level of some 26 escudos . . . per kilo as against 650 at the wartime peak." Mining would resume in peacetime, but the heady days of Allied-German competition for supply together with Anglo-American preemptive buying were gone for good. Remaining behind was immense national wealth amassed by the wolfram trade—and linked to it, a developing history of Allied aggravation with the Salazar regime and later Portuguese governments that reached far beyond the end of the war.

★   ★   ★

Before the wolfram embargo went into effect the Allies were aware of the role of gold in financing German purchases of the ore as well as other Portuguese products—and equally aware that, with the exhaustion of Germany's own gold reserves by the end of 1942, the monetary gold used for the transactions had been looted from the central banks of occupied countries. Germany deposited plundered gold mainly in the Swiss National Bank, from where it took the Lisbon route to German accounts in the Bank of Portugal. Thereafter it was exchanged for Portuguese escudos and credited to German accounts in two private banks in Lisbon, where it was available to finance trade arrangements as well as Nazi propaganda and intelligence activity. Some looted German gold also arrived in Portugal via direct purchase from Switzerland. In the latter part of 1944, according to one report, Swiss banks were embarrassed by the amount of Nazi gold accumulated in their vaults and began making secret sales to neutral countries. In turn, Portugal disposed of some of its gold by secret sales to countries in the Far East through its colonial enclave of Macao.

Smugglers likewise moved into Portugal considerable amounts of looted nonmonetary or so-called victim gold, which could be exchanged for currency or reworked into gold bars with Portuguese markings. After the war, when the Allies took control of Nazi assets in Portugal, they discovered within the German legation in Lisbon five thousand gold sovereign coins, which presumably had come into the country under diplomatic cover. In an incident three weeks after the Normandy invasion, Allied agents reported that a German plane had landed in Lisbon, and couriers carrying four diplomatic bags were met by a car from the legation. Each bag, it was later revealed, held four kilos of gold.

As German military fortunes waned over the following weeks, additional gold transfers took place in Lisbon and other neutral countries, causing the British Foreign Office to wring its hands in frustration. "This tendency of the Germans," said an official, "to transfer nest eggs to their Legations in neutral counties needs watching. But I do not see what more we could do to prevent it." As well as gold, the nest eggs the Germans were secretly moving were made up of legal wealth and the spoils of massive pillaging in gems, art objects, securities, patents, and all else of value.

In the period leading up to D-Day, Washington had grown concerned that such shifting of assets to neutral safe havens was meant to create a basis for the Reich's postwar renewal. And not only Washington. The dark possibility of a rekindled Reich had enough wider wartime currency to become, in 1943, the stuff of thriller fiction in Frederick Hazlitt Brennan's novel *Memo to a Firing Squad*. A former newspaperman in St. Louis and a prolific writer for popular American magazines as well as film and television, Brennan set his story in Lisbon, where Axis figures have gathered to plot future world conflict from the new Nazi stronghold of Argentina.

The tale is told by Stephen McGibbs, a jaded but—by his own estimate—right-thinking American correspondent who, after losing his position for too much warmongering before America was in the war, has escaped from occupied territory with the help of a resistance group known simply as "the movement." Now in Lisbon, McGibbs is tied in with the group's multinational local band, who live and scheme as servants in the nether reaches of the castle of a fascist Portuguese general. When it is learned that an agreement has been signed in the general's quarters by high military figures from Germany, Italy, Japan, and Argentina to carry on the war after making peace under the idealistic cover of a plan to convert the world to a single and pacified united nation, the movement must get hold of the signed agreement—known as the Lisbon Pact—and expose its evil contents to the world.

The feat is accomplished after much letting of blood, and McGibbs, through the aid of a British secret agent, is taken by ship to London to cable a great scoop. He knows that revealing what he calls a "complete blueprint for World War III" will cause a worldwide sensation and bring him instant fame. Yet he is also cynically certain that both will quickly fade into the Allies blind preoccupation with winning the war. There are other messages in Brennan's preachy melodrama, but the central one informs Americans that the Axis powers, knowing their cause is doomed, will seek to squeeze victory from defeat.

Back in Washington's actual world, efforts to block perceived German postwar ambition led to the creation in May 1944 of the Safehaven Program, and with it a mission to Lisbon and other neutral capitals by Samuel Klaus, then a member of the Foreign Economic Administration (FEA). As Klaus described his self-designed undertaking, he intended to look into "German attempts to frustrate anticipated controls over a defeated Germany by safe havens in neutral countries." Just earlier, delegates of forty-four countries meeting at Bretton Woods in New Hampshire to develop a postwar international financial system had, in a resolution, called on neutral nations to freeze German assets in their countries and turn them over to the Allies. Subsequently the U.S. State Department conveyed the resolution to all its neutral missions in Europe.

A multilingual lawyer in his early forties, Klaus had been a special assistant to the general counsel of the Treasury Department and was considered a tough and persistent investigator, qualities not always found congenial by Washington colleagues. From the start his European journey was plagued by turf disputes among the FEA, Treasury, and the State Department together with the feeling in some quarters that Klaus was plunging ahead without due preparation and authority. "I made it perfectly clear . . . didn't I," Treasury Secretary Henry Morgenthau, Jr., reminded his staff after Klaus departed for Europe, "that I didn't know what he was going for, and that he would not go as a Treasury Representative, period. . . . What is he going over for, anyway?"

In London Klaus realized that the Safehaven Program's success required full cooperation by the British, but the government, though informed by Washington of his mission, had yet to declare its participation in the American-led venture. Another obstacle was that the mission had become public knowledge after a report in a London newspaper, with the result that Klaus and a State Department representative traveling with him, Herbert J. Cummings, were—as Klaus put it—"marked men in any neutral capitals which had taken notice of the publicity." While Klaus and

Cummings were still in London the State Department had alerted neutral ministries in Europe about their journey but told them the Safehaven project was to be kept secret.

The first stop for Klaus and Cummings after a flight from northern Scotland was Stockholm. As Klaus saw it, the pair were mainly concerned with learning what fact-finding about Nazi safe-haven activity was already under way in neutral ministries, not unearthing new facts, and in Stockholm they were encouraged by the American embassy's actions. In Madrid they encountered a stone wall. Ambassador Hayes made clear his embassy was not doing, and would not do, any investigation of what the Germans were up to beyond the normal information gathering of a diplomatic mission. Equally plain was that, given Hayes's firm stance, the Madrid OSS station would not be helpful. Lisbon, however, turned out to be as cooperative as Stockholm. Ambassador Norweb was in full sympathy with Safehaven and placed the embassy's effort under the general direction of the commercial attaché. Specific investigations of German activity were handed over to the financial attaché.

Given Portugal's authoritarian government and some high officials assumed to be partial to the Axis cause, Klaus considered the country a prime location for German efforts to transfer assets. This was especially so in the financial arena, where the country's unregulated money market made it possible for Germany to move gold and currencies through local banks to locations elsewhere. Publicizing such financial transactions would have little effect, Klaus concluded, since "the Portuguese commercial community is alleged to be less idealistic and more venal than similar communities in other countries." On the other hand, the bank he considered the primary collaborator with the Nazis, the Espírito Santo Bank, had business dealings beyond Portugal and might be vulnerable to Allied pressure, assuming the Americans and the British could agree among themselves on how to proceed.

After leaving Lisbon, Klaus and Cummings stopped in Tangier before returning home in early October without having visited, as planned, Switzerland and Turkey. Events on the battlefield in Europe were rapidly moving forward, and Klaus acknowledged in a final report about his journey that the main thrust of the Safehaven Program would be with control groups working in occupied Germany after the war's end. The task left for ministries in neutral countries would largely amount to locating and recording German assets, and he called for local mission chiefs to assert their authority in setting legal attachés and OSS agents to work.

(Among the Reich's assets were human resources. When after the war the first group of esteemed German scientists was brought to the United

States under what was known as Project Paperclip, with a blind eye turned to their possible Nazi pasts, their visa applications were submitted by the air force and—high irony—reviewed at the State Department by Samuel Klaus, now working with the department and still dedicated to the Safehaven principle of denying German assets secure locations abroad. Klaus turned down all the applications. For Paperclip to succeed, as it did, future visa submissions had to be reviewed by others.)

In the postwar period Safehaven work in Portugal was replaced by an Allied joint commission made up of representatives of the American, British, and French ministries in Lisbon and charged with liquidating German government property in the country and recovering monetary gold and other looted assets. In the fall of 1946 the Salazar government reluctantly entered into negotiations with the group. That part of the talks dealing with gold soon bogged down over exactly how much tonnage the Portuguese would have to turn over, if any. Portugal's position was that its gold reserves, which had soared during the war from $93 million to $433 million, were the fortunate result of demand for wolfram and other products. Moreover, if it could be demonstrated that the gold it had received from Germany had indeed been looted, it expected compensation for whatever it turned over to the Allies since the acquisitions had been made as payment for legitimate trade.

Exasperating back-and-forth discussions staggered on for more than a decade. The Allies, concerned with continued military use of the Azores and with linking Portugal to the West in the cold war realignment of Europe, steadily cut back on the amount of gold they demanded, originally forty-four tons, and Portugal just as steadily resisted. In October 1958 an agreement finally was struck for turning over just under four tons, a trifling amount valued at the time at about $4.5 million. In October of the following year the deal went into effect, and the gold, for which Portugal was ultimately reimbursed by the Federal Republic of Germany, was delivered to an Allied gold pool.

★   ★   ★

While the matter of Portugal's restitution of looted monetary gold had reached a conclusion, a comprehensive historical analysis of the country's wartime economic cooperation with Nazi Germany would wait another forty years. Over time, growing scrutiny of the financial transactions between Germany and all the neutral nations had developed to a point where, in early 1997, the *New York Times* could headline an article "The (Not So)

Neutrals of World War II"—and pointedly take note in a subhead about the accumulation of "Profits on the Sidelines." In the United States the inquiry culminated in a study commissioned by President Bill Clinton and appearing in separate volumes in 1997 and 1998. Written by a number of government historians and coordinated by Stuart E. Eizenstat, who at the time of the second volume was an undersecretary in the State Department, the work—in all, some four hundred pages—became known as the Eizenstat Report.

In a foreword to the first volume, Eizenstat described the study's overall aim as tracing the history of "confiscation by Nazi Germany of an estimated $580 million of central bank gold—around $5.6 billion in today's values—along with indeterminate amounts in other assets during World War II." He went on: "The picture which emerges from these pages, particularly of the neutral nations, is often harsh and unflattering. Many profited handsomely from their economic cooperation with Nazi Germany, while the Allied nations were sacrificing blood and treasure to fight one of the most powerful forces of evil in the annals of history."

As summarized in the report, Portugal's main role in serving German interests was through supplying a "variety of vital mineral resources for the Third Reich's war machine, including ore for tungsten, a key additive used in the production of weapon-grade steel." The usual explanation of the neutrals for trading with the enemy, said the report, was the threat of Nazi invasion or reprisals, but with Portugal this had little validity since among Continental neutrals it was the country which "had the least reason to fear a German invasion, particularly once it became clear that Franco's Spain would not join the Axis." As for later Allied efforts to recover looted Nazi gold, the report glumly noted that "discussions dragged on through the 1950s because of Portuguese resistance," and it was not until the very end of the decade that gold was actually handed over to the Allies.

The issue of compensation to individual victims of looted Nazi gold and other assets was also a core feature of the report, with Eizenstat ending his foreword to the second volume with a call to action while war survivors were yet alive. "The approach of the new millennium offers a clear window of opportunity to act," he wrote. And added: "By completing the unfinished business of the middle of this century by its end, we can enter the new millennium having attempted a moral accounting of this lingering ledger of grief."

In the wake of the Eizenstat Report, an official commission in Portugal determined in 1999 that no such moral accounting was due. After sifting through public records, the six-member panel—named some two years earlier by a post-Salazar democratic government and headed by Mário Soares, a former prime minister and two-term president of the country—found that Portugal was under no obligation to compensate Holocaust and other Nazi victims since it had not knowingly dealt in plundered gold. As its leaders had insisted at the time, gold had been acquired in good faith during a wartime period in which the country was free to trade with both sides. Newspapers around the world carried brief notices of the report under headlines reading "Panel Clears Lisbon on Nazi Gold Trade" and "Portugal Didn't Launder Nazi Gold, Report Finds." Also mentioned in some accounts was that the World Jewish Congress had immediately dismissed the report as a "whitewash of the Salazar regime and a betrayal of the Portuguese people."

14

WHERE TO SPEND ONE'S HOLIDAY

Among the many post-war problems, most of which will give
grounds for anxiety, there will be at least one of a pleasurable
nature—that of where to spend one's holiday.

—*Anglo-Portuguese News*, September 30, 1943

When news came on May 8, 1945, of the end of the war in Europe, the
only decision confronting Mário Soares was how to free himself from a
student lecture hall at the University of Lisbon. After a friend in the corridor
signaled the long-awaited event, Soares leaped to his feet and called for an
end to the class session. At once a Nazi sympathizer among the students protested that, as a neutral nation removed from the war, Portugal had nothing
to celebrate. A heated argument followed in the classroom, with the professor
at last timidly suggesting that the students consult a higher authority about
ending the rest of the lecture. His proposal was not popular, and when the
debate dragged on Soares and a half-dozen other students walked out.

Soares's father had been deeply involved in opposition politics, spending many years in prison or exile, and Mário Soares would follow a similar
path in the slow progress to Portugal's "Carnation Revolution" of 1974.
During his early university days he had resisted the Salazar regime's strict
neutrality and lobbied for the Allied cause by getting tickets from cultural
attachés for private film showings at the British embassy's cinema and dis-
tributing them among classmates. From the American legation he procured
a projector and films and conducted viewing programs in small working-
class clubs. With the war ended in the Allied favor—and the time come,
as Soares and some of his fellow students ardently hoped, for Salazar's removal—he was not about to miss the great victory festival.

Waving flags of the Allied nations, Soares and his cohorts strode from the university to Rossio Square in the heart of Lisbon. A cheering throng greeted them, as did a force of police spaced about the square that sought to manage the crowd, though in an unusually civil manner. When a huge Portuguese flag materialized, the national anthem was sung to what Soares recalled as electrifying effect: "Within seconds there was a press of people around us clamouring for a triumphal march to foreign embassies. It was a sea of people, thousands upon thousands of them, chanting 'Victory! Victory! Liberty! De-mo-cra-cy!'" On the main thoroughfare of the Avenida da Liberdade that giddy day, an estimated 500,000 joined in celebration. Among them might have been some of the 1,000 refugees still housed in Portugal.

Rejoicing went on for several more days, but for Soares and his growing band—schools and colleges were closed and it seemed the whole of Lisbon was in the streets—the next morning brought a more strident political element to the war-end elation. They marched to the Allied ministries with cries of "Death to Fascism!" and "Free the political prisoners!" Allied envoys were handed messages, which they received, as Soares recorded, with "purely formal thanks and acknowledged the cheering in a chilly sort of way." The subdued response was an early sign for those wanting political change of the disillusionment that lay ahead.

★   ★   ★

A succession of church services and public events had led up to VE-Day. With the Allied landings in Normandy, the British and American colonies in Lisbon conducted an Anglican prayer service in the Church of St. George. Somber diplomats from both nations joined representatives of the Brazilian, Dutch, Polish, Norwegian, Greek, Belgian, and Free French missions. Outside the church Portuguese onlookers stood in bright sunlight while news of the invasion circulated among them. Boys selling newspapers in the city squares were mobbed, and all editions of the local papers were snapped up.

Less than a year later, on April 14, 1945, a memorial service was held at St. George's following the death of President Roosevelt. Among the dignitaries and diplomats met at the door by the newly appointed American ambassador, Herman B. Baruch, were Salazar and many members of his government. At the end of the service the national anthem of the United States was played.

With news of Hitler's suicide on May 1—reports from Bremen and Hamburg coming over Portuguese radio said he had died in action—Salazar leaned sharply in the other direction by ordering three days of national mourning and Portuguese flags flown at half mast on official buildings. While reaction was not expected from the controlled local media, reports coming from Madrid said Spaniards were so surprised by the Portuguese action that they suspected it was a hoax, or at least an exaggeration. Even the ultra-nationalist Falange Party, it was pointed out, had not offered official condolences to Germany. The lone other neutral nation to stage a similar show of respect was Ireland, where Eamon de Valera in Dublin went to the home of the German minister and extended his sympathy (much to the puzzlement, it was said, of the minister). With the war's end de Valera stood alone among neutral leaders in rejecting Allied requests for a public policy statement refusing asylum to fleeing Axis war criminals. Salazar had bowed to the request, though only after Sweden and Switzerland had done so.

On May 6 Portuguese radio announced that the government had informed the German minister in Lisbon that the legation and all consulates in the country were to be closed immediately and staff members considered persona non grata. Portugal held control of German buildings and their contents until early June, when they were handed over to a joint Allied commission charged with liquidating enemy property in the country. On May 14 Portugal enacted a decree freezing all German assets in the country, and on May 23 it was extended to include the Portuguese colonies. The German minister in Lisbon was not caught unawares by the rapid wave of such developments. On May 1 he had hosted a farewell cocktail party for some seven hundred of his countrymen and informed several hundred workers for German propaganda that their services were no longer required.

★   ★   ★

On VE-Day Salazar solemnly addressed the national assembly, thanking God for keeping Portugal "in the margin" of the conflict and expressing joy that Britain was in the vanguard of the victors. Other Allied nations went unnamed. In the early evening a British thanksgiving service was held in St. George's, with the British and American ambassadors in attendance and the national anthems of both countries sung. The official British memorial service, ordained by the King and the Archbishop of Canterbury, was conducted five days later at St. George's, with Salazar present together with the Allied diplomatic corps.

Ten days after his national assembly speech Salazar again addressed the group, now about Portugal's future. In the area of foreign policy, he said he meant to strengthen the alliance with Britain while keeping friendly relations with the United States and France. Although Portugal's position during the war had been what he termed collaborative neutrality, in any future European war his country could not and should not attempt to remain neutral. As for Portugal's corporative-style economic system, it would not be abandoned. "We hope," said the prime minister, "that cleansed of some abuses and excesses, it will return to the purity of its principles from which, to some extent, through war-time circumstances, it had departed."

Those friendly relations with the United States and France as well as Britain were challenged in the immediate postwar period by the vexing issue of repatriating German state personnel. Portugal staked out a position with four main points: it wanted assurance from the Allies that German nationals would not be sent to the Russian zone of occupied Germany; it would assist in repatriating only those Germans who wanted to return home; it would allow those who refused repatriation to stay in Portugal as political refugees; and it would force repatriation only in cases where it was proven that an individual was a war criminal or dangerous to Portugal. All of this the Allies, not surprisingly, found unacceptable. Their common position was that they would draw up a list of those they wanted returned to Germany and demand their repatriation. Ambassador Baruch told Washington that Portugal had to be reminded that the "German surrender was unconditional and the Allied nations therefore must have the right to prevent Germans throughout the world from again putting themselves in a position to renew their harmful activities against the Allies and civilization in general."

The specter of German postwar rebirth taking place in Portugal was raised by an American military intelligence report in July 1945. After noting that Nazis working in the country before the war ended were still freely moving about and had large sums of money and connections with Portuguese sympathizers, the report turned to a group calling itself the "Iron Nazis." The ringleaders were said to be three "dyed-in-the-wool" Hitlerites who had been active before the collapse and were trying to revive the party in Portugal, though so far their efforts had amounted to nothing more than meetings with fellow Germans.

By mid-August 1945 repatriation matters were still unresolved, and Baruch was complaining to Washington that the "position of ex-German officials [in Portugal] is becoming an open scandal and detrimental to Allied prestige." Later in the month Robert Solborg, winding up his duties as the military attaché of the Lisbon embassy, reported that he had a list of six hundred Germans for repatriation, with eighty considered such dangerous figures that the Portuguese government had placed thirty of them in a restricted residence in a small town in northern Portugal until they could be sent home. (OSS's X-2 files in Lisbon listed nineteen hundred enemy agents and two hundred enemy officials in Portugal at war's end.) Those Germans remaining in Lisbon, Solborg added, were able to come and go as they wished, had ample money, cars, and gasoline, and possessed "influential Portuguese friends and . . . the notorious International [secret] Police agents give them a great deal of protection." Finally, on September 25, the American embassy reported that Portugal had designated a captain of the secret police to work with the Allies on a repatriation program and that transport was ready to fly the Germans from Lisbon to Paris. (How to get them on to Germany was still unsettled.)

But in March of the following year the second secretary of the Lisbon embassy, H. L. Rose, would tell Washington that though progress had been made—recently a ship, the *Highland Monarch*, had left Lisbon carrying Germans—he had followed State Department instructions by expressing American displeasure to the Portuguese foreign minister over the country's failure "to seize every opportunity to deport obnoxious German nationals" who had been involved in espionage and sabotage operations. In a personal aside at the end of his dispatch, Rose noted that the foreign minister had "left no doubt in my mind that we may expect no further assistance from the Portuguese Government in the repatriation of German nationals."

★ ★ ★

In many ways Portugal was in an enviable position among European nations at the war's end. Its cities were unscathed, its young men were alive, its war-related business had enriched it with private and public capital, and its colonial possessions remained intact. The wolfram trade would never be the same, but now Portuguese agricultural products and fish were in demand by war-ravaged populations. In the area of diplomatic activity, the end of the war stimulated increased American engagement with Portugal—in part because of the drawn-out negotiations over German repatriation and the recovery of looted German gold, but also due to the cold war need for continued military use of the Azores, Salazar's unrelenting opposition to the Soviet Union (which Moscow met by blocking, until 1955, Portugal's admission to the United Nations), and the country's eventual integration into NATO.

The appointment in 1945 of Herman Baruch, the brother of the financier and presidential adviser Bernard Baruch, as ambassador was considered strong evidence of a new level of American-Portuguese relations.

Another indication was a dramatic display of U.S. military might put on before Baruch, Salazar, and Carmona in August 1946 during air-and-sea exercises off the mouth of the Tagus. More than a hundred planes from the new aircraft carrier *Franklin Roosevelt* staged a mock attack on the ship and its escorting destroyers, the vessels responding with simulated gunfire.

Yet despite these and other areas of good fortune, Portugal had some reason for apprehension about the future. No glory clung to it as a victorious nation, nor had it experienced a joyous release from occupation. With the war's end it slipped back to its unassuming stature as a small European nation with a heavily illiterate population, a vast gulf between the few rich and the many poor, and a magnificent port city now no longer the hub of the Western universe. That the country remained under the thumb of an authoritarian government, still censoring what citizens could read, see, and hear, still enforcing order with the secret police, set it strikingly apart from the democratic thrust of a new Europe. Rumblings of discord appeared—demonstrations by workers, strikes organized by the banned Communist Party of Portugal, unrest in the universities and the military. Salazar responded with such cosmetic gestures as characterizing his country as an "organic democracy" and holding elections, yet fundamentally his repressive regime would carry on unchanged for the next two decades.

Time magazine in 1946 fastened on the outmoded character of the government in a hugely unflattering cover story about the Portuguese leader. "The real news from Portugal," said the report, "was that another European dictatorship had failed, though it might hang on for years. . . . Not only was Portugal at a new low point, it showed every sign of changing for the worse, perhaps slowly, perhaps by violent upheaval." The regime reacted to the story as the magazine in effect predicted it would (". . . Salazar distrusted news. He suppressed and distorted it for the good of the Portuguese who, he believed, were unfit for facts"): *Time*'s Lisbon correspondent was expelled from the country; distribution and sale of the offending issue was halted; police were told to confiscate copies in private hands and record names of those possessing them (black market copies were said to be selling for up to twelve dollars); and the magazine was temporarily added to a list of forbidden foreign publications.

As early as the autumn of 1943 the *Anglo-Portuguese News*, anticipating a spectrum of unnamed postwar problems "which will give grounds for anxiety," had looked ahead for a new role for the country. What it envisioned in an article called "After the War" was an adaptation of Portugal's wartime position as a refuge from the conflict: now the country could promote itself as a rest cure for the worn and weary survivors. Since *APN* was directed to the local British community, the visitors the newspaper had mostly in mind were countrymen back home. With ships, planes, and trains again ready to serve them, what better destination for holidaymakers than the ancient ally? France, which had once claimed many of them, would not be in shape for some time to serve as host, while Portugal—with "dream-like beauty" yet also "clean, spic and span"—was ready and willing. The British tourist would find much in the country to remind him of England, especially if he lingered in Lisbon before heading out to the provinces, yet even more that was distinctive. He would, in any case, return home feeling "that he *really has* had a holiday away from the beaten track."

Portugal as a postwar tourist destination was not a fresh idea. Ronald Bodley had had something of the sort in mind in his 1941 book *Flight into Portugal*, as a reviewer in London's *Times Literary Supplement* noted when mildly praising the work as a "token of gratitude to Portugal and a lure to visitors after the war." Four months before *APN* glimpsed the future, the paper had carried Rose Macaulay's short article "Lisbon Day, London Day." Promoting tourism was not Macaulay's intent, nor was she thinking ahead to the war's end; but her clear implication was that any Londoner able to get there should not miss Lisbon.

> You would know blindfold [she opened the article], at any hour of the day or night, which of these two capitals you were in: the voice is differ-ent, the smell, the whole rhythm. Open your eyes, and the cities might be two planets. The one has light, colour, radiance, pale luminousness, a precipitous slant, a lilting jangle and blare of noise; the other darkly and impersonally hums, waves of sound swell and die, as if winds beat on a forest.

In 1947 Macaulay became a tourist herself, though of Spain more than Portugal. "I think when the war is over," she had told her Lisbon friend David Ley in 1943, "I shall try and visit Spain. . . . I will get the ancient Morris that is mouldering in a garage, and fling it across the Channel." The journey became possible when a London publishing house proposed a travel book as part of a series treating lesser-known cities of the world. Macaulay drove by herself the length of the Spanish coast from the Pyr-enees to Portugal, a journey of some four thousand miles, skipping familiar inland cities in favor of coastal communities and finally ending her account in Sagres on the southwestern tip of Portugal.

The same year her *Fabled Shore: From the Pyrenees to Portugal* was pub-lished, 1949, saw the appearance of *The Selective Traveller in Portugal* by Ann

Bridge and Susan Lowndes, a thickly detailed hardbound guide to both remote and familiar regions of the country. The two women had strong backgrounds for the task. Lowndes, as previously mentioned, lived in Lisbon and was married to the editor of *APN*. Mary Sanders O'Malley—Ann Bridge was her writing name—was a popular novelist (the year before the guidebook came out she published *The Portuguese Escape*, her sixteenth book and a novel dense with information about Lisbon and aristocratic country life in Portugal) and the wife of Owen O'Malley, who in 1945 had taken over as the British ambassador to Portugal.

The Bridge-Lowndes guidebook made prominent mention of the Catholic shrine of Our Lady of Fatima, located in remote hill terrain some eighty-five miles north of Lisbon, where in 1917 the Virgin Mary had appeared to three peasant children. Over the years the site had developed into a center of international pilgrimage—the Lourdes of Portugal. Although the war interrupted the flow of visitors from abroad, the Portuguese had continued to flock to the shrine, especially in May and October of the year, and typically going on foot the entire distance from their homes. News reports in May 1941 said that despite unusually bad weather in the country there had never been larger crowds of Portuguese pilgrims at the shrine. In April 1942 the statue of Our Lady of Fatima was for the first time removed from the shrine and carried through the streets of Lisbon for a week of prayer devoted to keeping the country free of the war and to future world peace. In May, the statue back in Fatima, a hundred thousand pilgrims gathered to mark the twenty-fifth anniversary of the apparitions. Portuguese bishops holding a retreat at Fatima and cut off from world events when the war ended were startled when they emerged to find thousands from throughout the country gathered in gratitude for peace.

In March 1946 Cardinal Francis Spellman, on his way home from Rome, where Pope Pius XII had just elevated the Archbishop of New York to the College of Cardinals, stopped in Lisbon for local sightseeing and a visit to Fatima. At a luncheon afterward, arranged at the Aviz Hotel by Ambassador Baruch and with Salazar among the guests, Spellman, in remarks quoted in press stories, said: "I was really touched when the choir sang in our own language 'The Star Spangled Banner' when I said mass in Our Lady of Fatima Church this morning and I must say that Fatima is a real inspiration to us." For American and other Catholics uncertain about the authenticity of Fatima, the cardinal's favorable comment was presumably a boost for including Portugal in their travel plans.

APN's "After the War" had not mentioned pious believers as candidates for peacetime tourism, though presumably they were as welcome, as were the escudos they would leave behind, as ordinary holidaymakers. Nor had the paper taken into account transients who had passed through wartime Portugal and, for one reason or another, might choose to come back. Spellman was in fact a former transient who returned. In the fall of 1943 he had come to Lisbon from New York on the first leg of an overseas tour in his role as military vicar of the American armed forces. He had a whirlwind of meetings with the American minister Bert Fish, various clerical figures, and Portuguese officials. One of the officials left him with a sense that, despite neutrality, the country was tense with worry. In his office they spoke in person and had nothing important to share, but the official had taken the precaution of disconnecting his telephone from the wall socket.

Spellman recalled his time in Lisbon as short but concentrated, and his postwar visit was the same. Other wartime figures lengthened their stays, as Rose Macaulay had when she came back to write a travel book. And at least two former transients, ex-King Carol II of Romania and Elena Lupescu, stretched their returns into permanent residency.

★   ★   ★

VE-Day found the famed couple in Brazil, where they had come after long exile in Mexico and where they had recently been married in a civil ceremony. At once they applied for Portuguese visas, which were quickly granted, and booked ship passage to Lisbon. But at this point the American and British governments intervened, and Portugal agreed to a request to cancel the visas. The Allies' concern was that Carol, back on the Continent, might meddle in a current Romanian crisis involving the Communist-controlled government and the slim possibility that Carol could be restored to the throne. With events in Romania smoothed over, the visas were restored, and Carol and his wife reached Lisbon in October 1947 with their usual mountain of belongings—"112 pieces of baggage, six dogs and a canary," said a press report—and settled into a spacious villa in Estoril among a circle of deposed royalty and their retinues. Living close by was Ernest Urdăreanu, still seeing to it that court protocol was maintained.

The Portuguese government allowed Carol to have diplomatic plates on his cars, though the diplomatic community kept a cautious distance from him. His local activity was largely limited to dining out, going to movies, the opera, and the casino, and playing an occasional round of golf. At the villa he occupied himself with his valuable stamp collection and was now and then seen puttering about the garden. He and Lupescu—with their marriage Carol had given her the title of Princess Elena of Romania—took trips to Paris and

London, often to meetings of stamp collectors. Although the press no longer hotly trailed them, in 1949 rumors began appearing in the tabloids that the couple was getting a divorce. Perhaps to put them to rest, an Orthodox priest was brought from Paris to conduct a religious ceremony in the villa before only a few friends, Princess Elena draped in white silk and Carol in white tie and tails.

In 1953 Carol died of a sudden heart attack at age fifty-nine. Urdăre-anu saw to the funeral arrangements, which had Carol lying in state for several days in the villa. Since a distant grandmother of his had been a member of the Portuguese royal family and there was no Orthodox priest or church in Portugal, the government permitted him to be buried in the Royal Pantheon of the Monastery of São Vicente, the interment place of Portuguese kings, and a military escort was provided for the long proces-sion of funeral cars. Princess Elena, so distraught at the service that she was nearly carried from the monastery, would live almost a quarter-century before she was buried beside Carol.

★   ★   ★

Calouste Sarkis Gulbenkian had no need to return to Lisbon because, after reaching it as one of the war's exiles, he never left.

Born in Armenia to a prosperous trading family and educated in engi-neering at King's College, London, Gulbenkian had become a naturalized British citizen in 1902. Shortly thereafter he helped arrange the merger that created the petroleum giant Royal Dutch Shell, the start of a career in oil exploration and development, primarily in the Middle East and Latin America, that made him one of the world's richest men—and gained him the nickname "Mr. Five Percent" for the stake he typically retained in oil companies he organized. At the same time he was amassing a fortune, he was acquiring a private art collection of high quality.

When the war began Gulbenkian was living in Paris, partly with his wife, Nevarte, and his art collection in an elegant home in the Avenue d'Iéna, partly by himself in the Ritz Hotel, a pattern of dual residence he had also followed in London with a suite at the Ritz. When France fell he followed the government to Vichy. While still in Paris he had used his con-nections in the Middle East to become Iran's (Persia) commercial counselor in Paris, a diplomatic position he later held in Vichy—at a cost of losing his British citizenship as an enemy alien and the confiscation of his interest in Britain's oil ventures in the Middle East.

After Iran was occupied by British and Russian troops and declared war on Germany in late 1942, Iranian ministers left Vichy, and the Gulbenkians departed with them. They first considered going to Switzerland but finally determined that Portugal, with Lisbon's open port and access to the United States, was the wiser choice. While Calouste Gulbenkian took a suite in the gold-filigree luxury of the Aviz Hotel, with another suite in the hotel for his secretary of long standing and a room for his valet, Nevarte Gulbenkian chose to live with her maid in the Palácio in Estoril. The couple, it is said, often journeyed back and forth for visits, and they appeared together at social events along with Portuguese officials and members of the American and British embassies.

Although Calouste Gulbenkian's British citizenship was restored after he left Vichy, he never returned to England. He conducted his oil business entirely in Lisbon, and without need of an office beyond his rooms in the Aviz. Even in the heat of summer, when most of Lisbon's rich moved to places outside the city, he remained in the hotel. When it was necessary to go out, he went by hired car, seeing no reason to maintain a limousine and chauffeur. The war curtailed but did not halt his art collecting. In 1943 he was approached by Baron Henri de Rothschild, living in exile in Estoril, about buying some of his collection. Long negotiations followed, with Gulbenkian drawing on professional advice from Kenneth Clark, at the time director of the National Gallery in London, before the sale was completed.

For the British, Gulbenkian was considered a key source of intelligence information. Before Philip Johns left London to take command of MI6's Lisbon station, he was told to develop an association with the new resident of Aviz, and brought with him a letter of introduction. The two men met frequently, at times over lunch at Gulbenkian's reserved corner table in the hotel's dining room. Johns thought him far from imposing—"a small, grey, wizened and stooping individual, completely unremarkable except for his bird-like piercing eyes"—but there was no question of his deep knowledge of the oil business. What the British especially wanted from him was all he knew about Russian and Romanian oil production that might be available to Germany, and this Gulbenkian willingly supplied.

With the end of the war Gulbenkian made frequent trips to France to revisit his Paris house and collection, both of which had survived the occupation. But he continued to keep his home in Lisbon. (Nevarte Gulbenkian eventually returned to the Paris house and died there in 1952.) When the popular Armenian-American writer William Saroyan stayed at the Aviz in the spring of 1949, Gulbenkian invited him to lunch, and they spoke at length in Armenian, though Gulbenkian was fluent in English. Saroyan found his host wholly agreeable, though meeting him was not the reason for his Lisbon stay. During a European swing Saroyan, a veteran gambler, had tried his luck in Venice, Monte Carlo, and Aix-en-Provence before reaching Lisbon. At the Estoril casino his fortunes swung up and down, but finally completely down. He was broke when he finished and had to sell a gold coin purchased in Marseille to settle his hotel bill. "A very high-tone hotel," he wrote in the Aviz's visitor book. "There are flies in the room. They are very plain and apparently do not know they are at the Aviz. Bravo." On his way to Paris, Saroyan paused briefly in Biarritz, and at the casino, using what was left of the sale of the coin, lifted his stake to $125.

According to a source who knew Gulbenkian well during his Lisbon period, it was Portugal's benign climate and stable social order that held him in the country. His art collection, however, he considered shifting to permanent quarters in London or Washington, though finally he decided to keep what was an eclectic accumulation of paintings, sculpture, books, coins, carpets, and tapestry together in Lisbon. After his death in the Aviz in 1955 at age eighty-six, much of his vast fortune went to the Calouste Gulbenkian Foundation, based in Lisbon, which funded an array of cultural, educational, and social programs in Portugal and elsewhere. In 1969 his art collection found a permanent home in Lisbon's Museum of the Calouste Gulbenkian Foundation.

As *APN* had ardently hoped in 1943, a flow of holidaymakers would eventually help fill the economic void of the war's end. But in the enduring value it brought to Portugal, nothing would overshadow the bountiful legacy of the oil king who came during the fighting and stayed into the peace.

ACKNOWLEDGMENTS

I owe special thanks to these libraries and archival centers: Hesburgh Library, University of Notre Dame; Christopher Library, Valparaiso University; Franklin D. Roosevelt Presidential Library; Library of Congress; National Archives of the United States; National Archives of the United Kingdom; Arts Library of the Calouste Gulbenkian Museum; United States Holocaust Memorial Museum.

My thanks also to these individuals who responded generously to my inquiries: Douglas L. Wheeler, Ellen W. Sapega, Nigel West, James Fry, Pierre Sauvage, Isabel Soares, Filipe Ribeiro de Meneses, José António Barreiros, Rui Araújo, Jenny Wriggins, Gregory Pfitzer.

As always, Pat Weber read every page of every draft. And once again Ivan Dee was a superb reader and editor.

The book's dedication is to the four adventurers who first joined me in taking the Lisbon route.

NOTES

References to the text are indicated by the last words of a passage or by key words within a passage. Some references to newspapers and magazines are incorporated into the text and consequently not included below.

PREFACE

ix   "wait and wait": Howard Koch, *Casablanca: Script and Legend* (Woodstock, N.Y., 1973), 31. Koch was one of three writers credited with the screenplay.

x   "collapse of France": Demaree Bess, "American Strategy Pains Portugal," *Saturday Evening Post*, August 30, 1941, 19.

x   "resident population": Hugh Muir, *European Junction* (London, 1942), 30.

CHAPTER 1: HUB OF THE WESTERN UNIVERSE

3   referred to Service: Mário Soares, *Portugal's Struggle for Liberty*, trans. Mary Gawsworth (London, 1975), 23–24.

3   "the whole truth": Howard L. Brooks, *Prisoners of Hope: Report on a Mission* (New York, 1942), 52.

5   "place in the world": *Irish Times*, October 23, 1941, 4.

5   "international limelight": *The Times* (London), December 3, 1940, 5.

5   its port city: *New York Times*, December 25, 1940, 19.

5   "Nazi scourge": *The Times* (London), October 15, 1940, 5.

5   swamped with work: *New York Times*, July 28, 1940, 4.

5   "becoming a prison": Lilian Mowrer, "Fiesta in Lisbon," *The New Yorker*, July 20, 1940, 36.

6   six to eight million: Michael R. Marrus, *The Unwanted: European Refugees in the Twentieth Century* (New York, 1985), 201.

6   four million: Hanna Diamond, *Fleeing Hitler: France 1940* (New York, 2007), 2.

6   splitting the nation: For further detail on the division of France and a map showing the demarcation line, see ibid., 108, 121.

7   "circle of madness": Erich Maria Remarque, *The Night in Lisbon*, trans. Ralph Manheim (New York, 1964), 186.

7   lifeline of freedom: Denis de Rougemont, *Journal d'une époque, 1926–1946* (Paris, 1968), 437.

7   its own truck: Carlton J. H. Hayes, *Wartime Mission in Spain, 1942–1945* (New York, 1946), 49.

7   "on the move": Mowrer, "Fiesta in Lisbon," 41.

7   on many fronts: Spain's lingering intent to join the conflict is discussed in Stanley G. Payne, *Franco and Hitler: Spain, Germany, and World War II* (New Haven, Conn., 2008), 269–270.

8   "leaving no trace": Quoted in Marrus, *The Unwanted*, 260.

8   aimed mainly: Marrus, *The Unwanted*, 261.

8   considered a feature: On this point, see Payne, *Franco and Hitler*, 217.

8   the new regulation: A full account of Sousa Mendes's work for refugees is given in José-Alain Fralon, *A Good Man in Evil Times*, trans. Peter Graham (New York, 2001). I largely follow this work for my account below. See also Douglas Wheeler, "And Who Is My Neighbor? A World War II Hero or Conscience for Portugal," *Luso-Brazilian Review*, 26:1 (1989), 111–139; Harry Ezratty, "The Portuguese Consul and the 10,000 Jews," *Jewish Life*, September–October 1964, 17–20; and the section on Sousa Mendes in Mordecai Paldiel, *The Righteous Among the Nations* (New York, 2007), 263–268.

9   "ones they had": Quoted in Fralon, *A Good Man in Evil Times*, 53–54.

9   Chaim Kruger: The rabbi is identified in some accounts as H. Kruger and Haim Kruger.

9   "conscience tells me": Quoted in Wheeler, "And Who Is My Neighbor?," 123. A slightly different version of the nephew's recollection is given in Fralon, *A Good Man in Evil Times*, 60.

10   "maintain order": Quoted in Ezratty, "The Portuguese Consul and the 10,000 Jews," 19.

10   "seen him do before": Quoted in Fralon, *A Good Man in Evil Times*, 61–62.

10   "let them through?": Ibid., 95.

11   crippling retirement: Filipe Ribeiro de Meneses, *Salazar: A Political Biography* (New York, 2009), 239. In 1967 Israel's Holocaust memorial at Yad Vashem declared Sousa Mendes a Righteous Among the Nations.

The Portuguese government remained silent until 1988, when he was posthumously reconnected with the foreign service and compensation paid to his family. In the same year he was made an honorary citizen of Israel. For more on the belated recognition that came to the consul, see Fralon, *A Good Man in Evil Times*, 145–160, and Wheeler, "And Who Is My Neighbor?," 130–131.

11   booked weeks ahead: *New York Times*, June 21, 1940, 14.

11   journey to Lisbon: *New York Times*, June 26, 1941, 15.

12   comfortable quarters: *The Times* (London), July 1, 1940, 3.

13   "*left* by air": *New York Times*, August 19, 1941, 4. Emphasis added.

13   overseas transportation: *New Horizons*, May 1942, 18.

13   about 100,000: David S. Wyman, *Paper Walls: America and the Refugee Crisis, 1938–1941* (Amherst, Mass., 1968), 150. The same number is given by Marrus, *The Unwanted*, 265.

13   nearly a million: Wheeler, "And Who Is My Neighbor?," 122, 134 n19.

13   "many refugees": Tom Gallagher, *Portugal: A Twentieth-Century Interpretation* (Manchester, UK, 1983), 105.

13   "the European continent": Marrus, *The Unwanted*, 263.

13   "Continent's surface": Arthur Koestler, *Scum of the Earth* (New York, 1941), 275.

13   "poisoned stomach": Ibid., 279.

16   "In his autobiography": Eric Sevareid, *Not So Wild a Dream* (New York, 1947), 181. In a biography of Sevareid, Raymond A. Schroth notes that when Sevareid returned home from Portugal he tried to get Adam an American visa but failed because Adam was a Communist. *The American Journey of Eric Sevareid* (South Royalton, Vt., 1995), 121, 179.

17   from the government: *New York Times*, March 14, 1941, 3.

18   as the PVDE: For the many functions of the PVDE, see Douglas L. Wheeler, "In the Service of Order: The Portuguese Political Police and the British, German and Spanish Intelligence, 1932–1945," *Journal of Contemporary History*, 18:1 (1983), 3–5.

19   the financial pie: T. J. Hamiton, "Turbulent Gateway of a Europe on Fire," *New York Times Magazine*, March 23, 1941, 13ff.

19   and Long Island: "Rich Refugees," *Fortune*, February 1941, 81ff.

20   official sources: Samuel Lubell, "War by Refugee," *Saturday Evening Post*, March 29, 1941, 12ff.

23   "United States itself": The text of the speech was printed in the *Washington Post*, May 28, 1941, 1–2.

23   "of the moon": *The Times* (London), May 31, 1941, 3.

23   "fight for them": Bess, "American Strategy Pains Portugal," 18ff.

23   still pending: W. E. Lucas, "Hitler Eyes Portugal," *The Nation*, April 26, 1941, 495–496.

25   "the rain began": Mark Schorer, "The Little Door," *The New Yorker*, September 20, 1941, 31–33. The story is collected in Mark Schorer, *The State of Mind* (Boston, 1947).

CHAPTER 2: TRAMPING FORWARD

27   emergency relief: *New York Times*, February 17, 1941, 1; *The Times* (London), February 18, 1941, 3.

27   "audacious pageant": *Time*, June 17, 1940, 36.

28   "at its height": *The Times* (London), June 3, 1940, 5.

28   "What we will celebrate": Quoted in Ellen W. Sapega, *Consensus and Debate in Salazar's Portugal: Visual and Literary Negotiations of the National Text, 1933–1948* (University Park, Pa., 2008), 24. The ideological ambition of the exposition is explored in this work and in David Corkill, "The Double Centenary Commemorations of 1940 in the Context of Anglo-Portuguese Relations," in *The Portuguese Discoveries in the English-Speaking World, 1870–1972*, ed. Teresa Pinto Coelho (Lisbon, 2005), 143–166.

28   "plainclothes dictator": A. J. Liebling, "Letter from Lisbon," *The New Yorker*, July 6, 1940, 32. The letter is reprinted in Liebling's *World War II Writings* (New York, 2008), 111–112.

28   nationalist dictatorship: The designation is John Lukacs's in *Blood, Toil, Tears, and Sweat* (New York, 2008), 10. The "prime incarnation" of the form, Lukacs notes, was National Socialist Germany.

28   New State: For the theory and practice of the New State, see especially a recent study by Filipe Ribeiro de Meneses, *Salazar*, 83ff. For earlier works, see Hugh Kay, *Salazar and Modern Portugal* (New York, 1970), 48ff., and Gallagher, *Portugal*, 62ff.

29   "country at heart": *Anglo-Portuguese News*, May 11, 1940, 1.

29   "modern times": *The Times* (London), June 3, 1940, 5.

29   "guiding light": *The Times* (London), June 4, 1940, 7.

29   for two days: "Portuguese Primitives," *Time*, September 2, 1940. 48–49.

30   two hundred people: Diamond, *Fleeing Hitler*, 43.

30   "always fiesta": Mowrer, "Fiesta in Lisbon," 42.

31   "voracious appetite": Antoine de Saint-Exupéry, *Wartime Writings, 1939–1944*, trans. Norah Purcell (San Diego, Calif., 1986), 103–104.

31   Atlantic for home: Ben Robertson, *I Saw England* (New York, 1941), 5–6.

31   "laid down for her": *The Times* (London), December 2, 1940, 5.

32   new master: Rougemont, *Journal d'une époque*, 437, 446. The translation above is Colin W. Nettelbeck's in *Forever French: Exile in the United States, 1939–1945* (New York, 1991), 14, 19.

33   Gallagher's story: Wes Gallagher ["See You in Lisbon"], *Free Men Are Fighting: The Story of World War II*, ed. Oliver Gramling (New York, 1942), 239–242; *Reporting World War II*, Part One (New York, 1995), 190–192.

34   "Artist from Prague": *We Escaped: Twelve Personal Narratives of the Flight to America*, ed. William Allan Neilson (New York, 1941), 58–75. I follow this work for the account below.

35   "Catholic Writer": *We Escaped*, 152–186. I follow this work for the account below.

37   Louis B. Harl: *New York Times*, May 23, 1942, 5.

37   opposite decision: Eric Hawkins and Robert N. Sturdevant, *Hawkins of the Paris Herald* (New York, 1963), 219–227. I follow this work for the account below. A portion of the story of Hawkins's flight from Paris appears in Ronald Weber, *News of Paris: American Journalists in the City of Light Between the Wars* (Chicago, 2006), 281, 286–287.

39   living in Paris: Koestler's *Scum of the Earth* is the main source for his European escape, and I largely follow it for the account below. Daphne Hardy is called G by Koestler. His recollections are amplified, and in some instances corrected, in David Cesarani, *Arthur Koestler: The Homeless Mind* (New York, 1998), and most recently in Michael Scammell, *Koestler: The Literary and Political Odyssey of a Twentieth-Century Skeptic* (New York, 2009).

41   water was chilly: Edgar Ansel Mowrer, *Triumph and Turmoil: A Personal History of Our Time* (New York, 1968), 310–314.

42   discharged in Casablanca: Scammell, *Koestler*, 189.

42   "right to exist": Arthur Koestler, *The Invisible Writing* (New York, 1954), 423.

42   at the same time: Rupert Downing, *If I Laugh: The Chronicle of My Strange Adventures in the Great Paris Exodus—June 1940* (London, 1941), 61. I follow this work for the account below.

44   different stripe: Otto Strasser and Michael Stern, *Flight from Terror* (New York, 1981; orig. pub. 1943). I follow this work for the account below.

47   chose Canada: Strasser's period in Portugal and his later long sojourn in Canada are related in Douglas Reed, *The Prisoner of Ottawa: Otto Strasser* (London, 1953).

47   German intellectuals: Franz Schoenberner, *The Inside Story of an Outsider* (New York, 1949). I follow this work for the account below.

48   had fainted: Lisa Fittko, *Escape Through the Pyrenees*, trans. David Koblick (Evanston, Ill., 1991), 24.

50   "I know *Simplicissimus*": Schoenberner recounts his work on the publication in *Confessions of a European Intellectual* (New York, 1946).

CHAPTER 3: WHATEVER WE CAN

53   Varian Fry: The basic source of information about Fry's rescue work is his memoir, *Surrender on Demand* (Boulder, Colo., 1997; orig. pub. 1945), and I largely follow it for the account below. The work is supplemented by two biographies, Andy Marino, *A Quiet American: The Secret War of Varian Fry* (New York, 1999) and Sheila Isenberg, *A Hero of Our Own: The Story of Varian Fry* (New York, 2001).

54   "*get* them out": Quoted in Marino, *A Quiet American*, 44.

54   figures needing rescue: For many of the names on Fry's list, see ibid., 53–55.

54   selected exiles: For an account of the emergency visa program, including sharp dispute within the State Department, see Wyman, *Paper Walls*, 142–151.

55   "Dr. Sedgwick": For Hansfstaengl's intelligence work, see Joseph E. Persico, *Roosevelt's Secret War: FDR and World War II Espionage* (New York, 2001), 191ff.

55   "Hissed Film": *New York Times*, July 26, 1935, 8.

55   "this continent": Quoted in Rosemary Sullivan, *Villa Air-Bel: World War II, Escape, and a House in Marseille* (New York, 2006), 191.

55   Germany "Eloise": Marino, *A Quiet American*, 58.

56   "One just doesn't": Quoted in ibid., 89–90.

56   "take everything": Ibid., 105.

56   "only marry geniuses": Ibid., 62.

57   Hiram (Harry) Bingham: For a recent magazine account of Bingham's work in Marseille on behalf of refugees, see Peter Eisner, "Bingham's List," *Smithsonian*, March 2009, 50–57.

57   "played his part": Lion Feuchtwanger, *The Devil in France*, trans. Phyllis Blewitt (London, 1942), 182–183. Standish is named by Marino in *A Quiet American*, page 99, but not by Feuchtwanger. In a version of the escape story told by Mary Jayne Gold, Harry Bingham is the driver of the car. *Crossroads Marseilles, 1940* (Garden City, N.Y., 1980), 188–190.

59   "it isn't cleaner": Hans Sahl, *The Few and the Many*, trans. Richard and Clara Winston (New York, 1962), 305–307. Sahl's meeting with Fry is reprinted in "On Varian Fry," *Hitler's Exiles: Personal Stories of the Flight from Nazi Germany to America*, ed. Mark M. Anderson (New York, 1998), 154–156.

60   "Au revoir": Hertha Pauli, *Break of Time* (New York, 1972), 197–199.

60   "turn others down": Quoted in Sullivan, *Villa Air-Bel*, 205.

61   bawdy conversations: Miriam Davenport, *An Unsentimental Education*, unpublished memoir, http://varianfry.org/ebel_memoir_en.htm.

61   Leon Ball: Fry calls him Dick Ball in *Surrender on Demand*. Others with the
       CAS remembered him as Leon Ball.
62   under a pen name: Marino, *A Quiet American*, 160.
62   station in town: Ibid., 170–171.
63   "exceeding sadness": Quoted in Nigel Hamilton, *The Brothers Mann* (New
       Haven, Conn., 1979), 314.
64   "an American consul": *New York Times*, October 6, 1940, 38.
64   "work in France": "Exiles," *Time*, May 11, 1940, 80.
65   before returning to France: Benjamin's attempted escape and suicide is
       recounted in Marino, *A Quiet American*, 198–200, and Sullivan, *Villa
       Air-Bel*, 1–8. Both follow the account of Benjamin's guide on the escape
       attempt, Lisa Fittko, in *Escape Through the Pyrenees*. Additional details of
       the death are given by a refugee who, also turned back at the Spanish
       border, spent the night in the same Spanish hotel as Benjamin. See Carina
       Burman, "Escape over the Pyrenees," *Quadrant*, 49:10 (October 2005),
       38–43.
65   Koestler accepted: Cesarani, *Arthur Koestler*, 167.
65   speak with them: Fittko, *Escape Through the Pyrenees*, 117ff.
67   They had succeeded: Fry, *Surrender on Demand*, 124. Fry does not relate
       his first meeting with the Fittkos. In a brief account of the escape route
       from Banyuls, pages 122–124, he calls Hans Fittko "Johannes F" and Lisa
       simply his wife.
67   as his word: Fittko, *Escape Through the Pyrenees*, 177.
69   expatriate playgirl: Gold, *Crossroads Marseilles*, 159.
69   paid the rent: For more on Villa Air-Bel and life therein, see ibid, 237ff.
       See also many pages devoted to the villa in Sullivan, *Villa Air-Bel*.
69   steer clear of it: Peggy Guggenheim, *Out of This Century* (New York,
       1979), 228.
69   "shipwrecked continent!": Victor Serge, *Memoirs of a Revolutionary*, trans.
       Peter Sedgwick (New York, 1963), 364.
70   "around Manhattan": Benjamin Harshav, *Marc Chagall and His Times*
       (Stanford, Calif., 2004). 499–500.
70   "whatever we can": Quoted in Isenberg, *A Hero of Our Own*, 221.
71   "go to America!": Ibid., 222–223.
71   "oceanic muck": Walter Mehring, *No Road Back*, trans. S. A. DeWitt
       (New York, 1944), 147.
72   prize of war: This is Fry's explanation in *Surrender on Demand*, page 215,
       for the end of the Martinique route. In *Displaced Doctor* (see note below),
       Richard Berczeller names the ship the *Wyoming* and says the navicert
       granted by the British to allow passage through the blockade was with-
       drawn when Vichy refused to allow the ship to be searched at sea. Yet
       another version has the *Winnipeg* captured by a Dutch gunboat, diverted

to Trinidad, and there delivered to the British, after which all passengers were quarantined and questioned one by one. See Joan Mellen, *Kay Boyle: Author of Herself* (New York, 1994), 252.

72   to New York: Richard Berczeller, *Displaced Doctor* (NewYork, 1964) 100–121. I follow this work for the account below.

74   "25c a package": Quoted in Marino, *A Quiet American*, 313.

75   "hard geometry": Quoted in Isenberg, *A Hero of Our Own*, 218–219.

75   "very stupid policy": *New York Times*, November 3, 1941, 11.

75   "past two months": Ibid. Douglas L. Wheeler suggests that Berthold Jacob may have been turned over to the Gestapo by an agent of the Portuguese secret police in German employ. "In the Service of Order," 11–12. Isenberg in *A Hero of Our Own* says, pages 195–196, that Portuguese police picked up Jacob and passed him along to Spanish police. The Nazis then moved him to Berlin, where he was tortured, starved, and eventually died in a hospital.

76   "That's that": Quoted in Marino, *A Quiet American*, 317.

76   "had to try": In 1996 Fry joined Aristides de Sousa Mendes as one of Israel's Righteous Among the Nations, and in his memory a tree was planted at the Yad Vashem memorial in Jerusalem. In 2000 the U.S. ambassador to France, Felix Rohatyn, dedicated in Marseille a square adjacent to the consulate as Place Varian Fry. In remarks at the time, he noted that his own family, as Polish Jews living in Paris, were refugees in the winter of 1941 and left for Marseille, where they may have been helped by Fry's committee on a journey that took them to Casablanca, Lisbon, and eventually New York.

CHAPTER 4: THE LAST LAP

77   "remaining port": William L. Shirer, *Berlin Diary: The Journal of a Foreign Correspondent, 1934–1941* (New York, 1941), 542.

78   "the writing room": Ibid., 602.

78   "the last lights?": Ibid., 604.

79   "lot of promise": *New York Times*, June 15, 1940, 33. The wartime shipping situation is broadly described in Wyman, *Paper Walls*, 151–154.

80   "concentration camp" conditions: *New York Times*, September 13, 1941, 19.

80   proved to be useless: "Refugee Racket," *Time*, December 30, 1940, 25.

81   "at the earliest": *New York Times*, January 26, 1941, 88.

82   the attack came: A full account of the *Zamzam* affair is given in David Miller, *Mercy Ships* (London, 2008), 47–55.

83   "party or two": *New York Times*, May 29, 1941, 9.

84   the airline offices: Beverley Baxter, "Traveler's Report," *New Horizons*, November 1941, 3. The magazine was a monthly published by Pan American. The report by Baxter, a British MP, was reprinted from Allied Newspapers, a British news syndicate.

84   nominated another airline: Robert Daley, *An American Saga: Juan Trippe and His Pan Am Empire* (New York, 1980), 211.

84   "became the terminus": For more detail about flying boats developed by Boeing and other manufacturers, see ibid., 223–230.

85   running water: The layout of the Clipper and details of the first passenger flight are given in ibid., 243–245.

87   "not myself": George F. Kennan, *Memoirs, 1925–1950* (Boston, 1967), 156.

87   dock workers: Henry J. Taylor, *Time Runs Out* (Garden City, N.Y., 1942), 299–300.

87   sunk in the Atlantic: "Foreign Mail," *The New Yorker*, April 5, 1941, 16.

88   "All aboard, please": *New York Times*, May 18, 1941, XX1.

89   "inside of an airplane": Elmer Rice, *Flight to the West* (New York, 1941), viii.

90   in the lounge: Elmer Rice, *Minority Report: An Autobiography* (New York, 1963), 386.

90   *Lisbon Clipper:* Stanley Cloud and Lynne Olson, *The Murrow Boys* (Boston, 1996), 107.

91   pilot error: Daley, *An American Saga*, 251.

91   "into a boat": *New York Times*, February 25, 1943, 6.

91   on crutches: Froman's rescue, injuries, and relationship with Burn are described in Barbara Seuling, *Say It with Music: The Life and Legacy of Jane Froman* (Princeton, Ill., 2007), 118ff.

92   "seen the stars": Robertson, *I Saw England*, 213.

92   "a war on": Sheilah Graham, *Hollywood Revisited* (New York, 1985), 110.

93   "Still Flying": Marilyn Bender and Selig Altschul, *The Chosen Instrument: Pan Am, Juan Trippe, the Rise and Fall of an American Entrepreneur* (New York, 1982), 345.

93   escorts above: Taylor, *Time Runs Out*, 285–286.

CHAPTER 5: GAIETY, PLENTY, AND BRILLIANT LIGHTS

95   parallel American group: For the formation of the British escape group, see M. R. D. Foot and J. M. Langley, *MI9* (London, 1979). The story of MIS-X is told in Lloyd R. Shoemaker, *The Escape Factory* (New York, 1990).

96   on separate vessels: For Fry's arrangement with the British, see *Surrender on Demand*, 76–78.

97   stirred for duty: Fittko, *Escape Through the Pyrenees*, 159.

97   "the occupied zone": Fry, *Surrender on Demand*, 209.

97   actually at sea: In *Surrender on Demand*, page 109, Fry gives the amount as 225,000 francs. The dollar figure is in Isenberg, *A Hero of Our Own*, 113.

98   "Spanish looked away": Quoted in Persico, *Roosevelt's Secret War*, 321.

98   in North Africa: Hayes, *Wartime Mission in Spain*, 102–103.

99   about two weeks: Ibid., 103–104.

99   east of Bordeaux: Chuck Yeager with Leo Janos, *Yeager: An Autobiography* (New York, 1985), 25–47. I follow this work for the account below.

104   fighting Frenchmen: Hayes, *Wartime Mission in Spain*, 118–119.

104   outside the attention: *Foreign Relations of the United States, 1943*, vol. 2, (Washington, D.C., 1964), 582.

104   "for the duration": Jack Alexander, "The Nazi Offensive in Lisbon," *Saturday Evening Post*, March 6, 1943, 86.

104   was the exception: Jack Ilfrey with Mark S. Copeland, *Happy Jack's Go Buggy: A Fighter Pilot's Story* (Atglen, Pa., 1998), 35–39. I follow this work for the account below.

104   "in my twenties": Saint-Exupéry, *Wartime Writings*, 132.

107   "experienced seamen": *My Three Years with Eisenhower: The Personal Diary of Captain Harry C. Butcher, USNR* (New York, 1946), 194–195.

107   to destroy them: *New York Times*, December 28, 1942, 5.

107   the Spanish frontier: *New York Times*, January 16, 1943, 1.

108   much larger formation: *New York Times*, January 16, 1943, 3.

108   Hanson W. Baldwin: *New York Times*, January 20, 1943, 4.

108   "get home": *Foreign Relations of the United States, 1943*, vol. 2, 582.

109   held in Portugal: Ibid., 583–585.

109   on enemy soil: Reynolds and Eleanor Packard, *Balcony Empire: Fascist Italy at War* (New York, 1942), 311ff. I follow this work for the account below. The Siena confinement is also described in "Back from the Axis," *Time*, June 15, 1942, 69–70.

111   drives about Portugal: *The Reminiscences of Herbert C. Pell*, Columbia University Oral History Collection, 1951, 423ff. Pell's ministerial period in Portugal is also set out in Leonard Baker, *Brahmin in Revolt: A Biography of Herbert C. Pell* (Garden City, N.Y., 1972), 177ff.

112   its own chauffeur: Baker, *Brahmin in Revolt*, 208–213.

112   "fare of Lisbon": Kennan, *Memoirs*, 136–138.

113   Janson wrote: Janson's log, http://384thbombgroup.com/pages/janson .html.

114   "amateur theatricals": Harold Macmillan, *The Blast of War, 1939–1945* (New York, 1968), 312.

115   "to make terms": Quoted in Rick Atkinson, *The Day of Battle: The War in Sicily and Italy, 1943–1944* (New York, 2007), 187.
115   German troops in Italy: Atkinson, *The Day of Battle*, 187–188.
115   unconditional surrender: For the many plot twists on the way to an agreement, see ibid., 187–197. See also Butcher, *My Three Years with Eisenhower*, 391–395, and Macmillan, *The Blast of War*, 296–337.
116   Allied headquarters: Macmillan, *The Blast of War*, 321.
116   unwelcome surprise: The Canaris mission to Italy is recounted in Anthony Cave Brown, *Bodyguard of Lies* (New York, 1975), 305–307.
116   Schwarze Kapelle: For the rise and fall of the Schwarze Kapelle, see ibid., 148ff and 300ff.
117   "hearing in Lisbon": Quoted in Otto John, *Twice Through the Lines: The Autobiography of Otto John*, trans. Richard Barry (New York, 1972), 99. John calls the MI6 agent, mentioned above, Tony Graham-Meingott.
118   peace with Germany: Anthony Cave Brown, *"C": The Secret Life of Sir Stewart Graham Menzies* (New York, 1987), 650.
118   Menzies's agreement: The motive is suggested in Brown, *Bodyguard of Lies*, 314–315.
118   Lisbon Report: Ibid., 314.
118   another nine months: Ibid., 792–793.
118   Lufthansa flight: John, *Twice Through the Lines*, 95ff. I largely follow this work for the account below. See also H. R. Trevor-Roper's introduction to John's memoir and Peter Hoffmann, *The History of the German Resistance, 1933–1945*, trans. Richard Barry (Cambridge, Mass., 1977), 246–248.

CHAPTER 6: LIVING THERE

121   "embark for America": Rougemont, *Journal d'une époque*, 443–444.
122   "never mentioned": Frederic Prokosch, "Landscape—With Figures," *Vogue's First Reader* (New York, 1942), 110. The passage is an edited version of one appearing in the Prokosch novel *The Conspirators* (London, 1943), 8.
122   *The Asiatics*: For a present-day appreciation of Prokosch that concentrates on this novel, see Pico Iyer, "The Perfect Traveler," *New York Review of Books*, November 18, 2004, 50–54.
122   to two years: Frederic Prokosch, *Voices: A Memoir* (New York, 1983), 114–127. I largely follow this work for the account below.
122   in squash: Radcliffe Squires, *Frederic Prokosch* (New York, 1964), 20–21.
125   More substantial: Some reviewers made this point. For example, see Peter Monro Jack, "Lisbon in Wartime," *New York Times Book Review*, January 24, 1943, 6.
125   fine Rolls-Royce: Frederic Prokosch letter to the editor ["Is Hollywood Dying?"], *The New Republic*, November 13, 1944, 627.

125   was newspaper writing: Muir, *European Junction.* I follow this work for the account below.

126   "with embroidery": Alice-Leone Moats, *No Passport for Paris* (New York, 1945), 14.

128   "24 hours nicely": Quoted in Mark Holloway, *Norman Douglas: A Biography* (London, 1976), 448.

128   Lisbon in May: The uncertain nature of the trip is noted in ibid., 449.

128   "A pretty tangle!": Quoted in Nancy Cunard, *Grand Man: Memories of Norman Douglas* (London, 1954), 162. Quotations below also come from this work, pages 163–168.

129   she uncovered: Polly Peabody, *Occupied Territory* (London, 1941). I follow this work for the account below.

130   and the canteen: *New York Times,* March 7, 1940, 10; *New York Times,* March 10, 1940, 5.

133   of refugee flight: Ronald Bodley, *Flight into Portugal* (London, 1941). I follow this work for the account below.

133   "Bodley of Arabia": *The New Yorker,* February 23, 1943, 10.

136   knew from experience: Marya Mannes, *Out of My Time* (Garden City, N.Y., 1971).

137   "Letter from Lisbon": Marya Mannes, "Letter from Lisbon," *The New Yorker,* July 1, 1944, 56–59.

137   second Lisbon Letter: Marya Mannes, "Letter from Lisbon," *The New Yorker,* July 22, 1944, 49–52.

138   "under our noses": Aline [Romanones], Countess of Romanones, *The Spy Wore Red: My Adventures as an Undercover Agent in World War II* (New York, 1987), 63.

138   promised article: Marya Mannes, "In Lisbon—'Dressed for Reaction,'" *Vogue,* September 1, 1944, 140ff.

139   Irish legation: O'Donovan's mission is recounted in Filipe Ribeiro de Meneses, "Investigating Portugal, Salazar and the New State: The Work of the Irish Legation in Lisbon, 1942–1945," *Contemporary European History,* 11:3 (2002), 392–408. I follow this article for the account below.

140   Ireland at the time: For more on Irish attraction to Salazar's Portugal, see Clair Wills, *That Neutral Ireland* (Cambridge, Mass., 2007), 351–352.

CHAPTER 7: CELEBRITÉ DE PASSAGE

144   the side of: Noël Coward, *Future Indefinite* (Garden City, N.Y., 1954), 111–112.

144   work there was: For Coward's amusing account of his undemanding work routine, see ibid., 96ff.

144   "proposition for America": Quoted in ibid., 177.

145   "acme of comfort": Coward, *Future Indefinite*, 152. Quotations below also come from this work, pages 201–202.

146   "is very important": Quoted in Barry Day, ed., *The Letters of Noël Coward* (New York, 2007), 379.

146   "propaganda for peace": Quoted in Philip Ziegler, *King Edward VIII: A Biography* (New York, 1991), 366.

147   "even greater mistake": Quoted in Michael Bloch, *Operation Willi: The Nazi Plot to Kidnap the Duke of Windsor* (Toronto, 1987; orig. pub. 1984), 48.

147   "of the country": Ibid., 82.

148   "an embarrassment": Ibid., 57.

148   neutrality regulations: Ibid., 73.

149   "difficult situation": Quoted in ibid., 79.

149   the pages of: Corkill, "The Double Centenary Commemorations of 1940," 162.

149   "only for you": David Eccles, *By Safe Hand: Letters of Sybil and David Eccles, 1939–1942* (London, 1983), 132.

149   "of the world": Ibid., 139.

150   "quite long enough": Quoted in Bloch, *Operation Willi*, 121.

150   "must be accepted": Ibid., 122.

150   "farewell to Europe": Ibid., 115.

150   "past sailing time": *New York Times*, August 2, 1940, 1ff.

150   a travel trailer: "Mr. and Mrs. Windsor," *Time*, August 12, 1940, 20.

151   "largely American": "Playground Superintendents," *Time*, July 22, 1940, 28,

151   Duke responded: On this point, see Ziegler, *King Edward VIII*, 371. See also John H. Waller, *The Unseen War in Europe: Espionage and Conspiracy in the Second World War* (New York, 1996), 171–173.

151   In memoirs: In an appendix to *Operation Willi*, Bloch examines the authenticity and reliability of Schellenberg's published memoirs. He concludes the work is indeed Schellenberg's and takes serious issue only with matters of chronology.

152   "the dinner-table": Walter Schellenberg, *The Schellenberg Memoirs*, ed. and trans. Louis Hagen (London, 1956), 138.

152   "interests at heart": Ibid., 138–139.

152   "organized at once": Ibid., 139.

152   "to the situation": Ibid., 141.

153   with Germany: The telegram is reproduced in Bloch, *Operation Willi*, 195.

153   "was closed": Schellenberg, *Memoirs*, 142.

154   state valuables: Paul D. Quinlan, *The Playboy King: Carol II of Romania* (Westport, Conn., 1995), 218. I largely follow this work for the account below.

154   wishes of Berlin: Ibid., 226.

154   armed police: *New York Times*, March 6, 1941, 23.

154   "four dogs": *New York Times*, October 15, 1940, 4.

155   "King's fate": Muir, *European Junction*, 93–94.

155   Portuguese soil: *New York Times*, March 6, 1941, 23; "Hohenzollern He-gira," *Time*, March 17, 1941, 32.

155   defying Germany: Quinlan, *The Playboy King*, 227.

155   of the bill: *New York Times*, March 7, 1941, 10.

155   up on them: *New York Times*, March 9, 1941, 16.

155   double her gain: Aline [Romanones], *The Spy Wore Red*, 63–64.

156   Nazi informants: Nettelbeck, *Forever French*, 18.

156   "my own country": *New York Times*, May 3, 1941, 17.

156   "but no more": *New York Times*, May 11, 1941, 30.

157   "in their midst": Muir, *European Junction*, 96.

157   emerged as celebrities: The phrasing, in slightly different form, is applied to Antoine de Saint-Exupéry in Stacy Schiff, *Saint-Exupéry: A Biography* (New York, 1994), 343.

157   "Ah, Mozart!": Neil Baldwin, *Man Ray: American Artist* (New York, 2000), 227. Man Ray gives a slightly different account of the border cross-ing in *Self Portrait* (New York, 1963), 320.

158   "pardoned him": Ray, *Self Portrait*, 322.

158   "know him?": Saint-Exupéry, *Wartime Writings*, 103–105.

158   In his honor: Schiff, *Saint-Exupéry*, 343.

158   "extraordinary anguish": Quoted in ibid.

158   military tactics: *New York Times*, January 1, 1941, 20.

159   "lapis lazuli": Fry, *Surrender on Demand*, 185. In a stunning black-and-white portrait of Boyle by Man Ray, circa 1930, only one of her standard white earrings is visible. See Mellen, *Kay Boyle*, 174–175. Ray had earlier, in 1924, photographed Guggenheim in an exotic evening dress and holding a long cigarette holder. See Guggenheim, *Out of This Century*, 76–77.

159   "to that fiend": Quoted in Mellen, *Kay Boyle*, 253–254.

160   "by Max Ernst": Ibid.

160   took a ship: Sullivan, *Villa Air-Bel*, 339.

160   of the time: Guggenheim, *Out of This Century*, 241.

161   from the premises: Mellen, *Kay Boyle*, 254.

161   "native friend": Guggenheim, *Out of This Century*, 244.

161   "Max loved": Ibid., 242.

162   "doesn't to me": *New York Times Book Review*, August 3, 1941, 2.

162   "if one wished": Cecil Beaton, *Near East* (London, 1943), 140.

162   excursion to Sintra: Cecil Beaton, *The Years Between: Diaries 1939–44* (London, 1965), 198–199.

163   Lisbon studio: Hugh Vickers, *Cecil Beaton: A Biography* (Boston, 1985), 267.

163   "to weep with": Quoted in Jane Emery, *Rose Macaulay: A Writer's Life* (London, 1991), 267. For Macaulay's life and work, see also Sarah Le-Fanu, *Rose Macaulay* (London, 2003).

164   through hints: On this point, see, among other passages devoted to the love affair, Emery, *Rose Macaulay*, 175–179.

164   "begin life again": Quoted in ibid., 272.

164   "without approach": Rose Macaulay, "Looking in on Lisbon," *The Spectator*, July 2, 1943, 8. The article is reprinted in *They Went to Portugal Too*, ed. L. C. Taylor (Manchester, UK, 1990), 305–308.

165   "Setúbal peninsula": Rose Macauley, "Lisbon Day, London Day," *Anglo-Portuguese News*, May 6, 1943, 5.

165   "English in Portugal": Quoted in Emery, *Rose Macaulay*, 278.

166   *was* the star: Susan Lowndes, Introduction to *They Went to Portugal Too*, xxi. The introduction is a primary source of information about Macaulay's time in Lisbon.

167   "doing my best": "The Luftwaffe Intercepts," *Time*, June 14, 1943, 30.

167   "to Bordeaux": Quoted in Chris Goss, *Bloody Biscay*, rev. ed. (Manchester, UK, 2001), 54.

168   "broad daylight": Winston S. Churchill, *The Hinge of Fate* (Boston, 1950), 830.

168   in books by: Ian Colvin, *Flight 777* (London, 1957); Leslie Ruth Howard, *A Quite Remarkable Father* (New York, 1959); Ronald Howard, *In Search of My Father* (London, 1981).

169   "movie star's publicity": Quoted in Aline [Romanones], *The Spy Wore Red*, 60–61.

169   "state of alert": Colvin, *Flight 777*, 198.

169   radio traffic: Ibid., 202–204.

170   "to its doom": Douglas L. Wheeler, "World War II: Leslie Howard May Have Helped Britain Win," *St. Louis Post-Dispatch*, April 5, 2005, 4.

CHAPTER 8: HOLDING OUT HOPES

171   casual inspection: Marino, *A Quiet American*, 89, 345.

171   "was our work": Charles R. Joy, "Lives Were Saved," in *Together We Advance*, ed. Stephen H. Fritchman (Boston, 1947), 23. For more on the USC's wartime work, see Susan Elisabeth Subak, *American Relief Workers Who Defied the Nazis* (Lincoln, Nebr., 2010).

172   German hands: Haim Genizi, "Christian Charity: The Unitarian Service Committee's Relief Activities on Behalf of Refugees from Nazism, 1940–1945," *Holocaust and Genocide Studies*, 2:2 (1987), 265.

172   "off their hands": Quoted in Ghanda Di Figlia, *Roots and Visions: The First Fifty Years of the Unitarian Universalist Service Committee* (Boston, 1990), 27–28.

173   "American Consulate": Ibid., 20–21.

173   for a scoop: Marino, *A Quiet American*, 185–186.

173   to reporters: *New York Times*, October 6, 1940, 38.

174   of her refugees: Ghanda Di Figlia, "Martha Sharp Cogan and Waitstill Hastings Sharp," http://harvardsquarelibrary.org/unitarians/cogan.html.

174   "the war began": *New York Times*, December 24, 1940, 7.

174   officials in Boston: For some detail about the dispute, see Di Figlia, *Roots and Visions*, 28.

174   "friendly gesture": Di Figlia, "Martha Sharp Cogan and Waitstill Hastings Sharp." In *Roots and Visions*, Di Figlia does not mention the Portuguese request to close the Lisbon office.

174   permanent destinations: Martha D. Sharp, "Unitarian Service in the Iberian Peninsula," *Christian Register*, January 1946, 25. In 2005 the Sharps were named Righteous Among the Nations by the Yad Vashem memorial.

175   using the USC: Genizi, "Christian Charity," 264.

175   dedicated Communist: Field's work with the USC and involvement with the Communist party are examined at length in Flora Lewis, *Red Pawn: The Story of Noel Field* (Garden City, N.Y., 1965). See also Stewart Steven, *Operation Splinter Factor* (Philadelphia, 1974), 72–93.

175   sent to Marseille: Brooks, *Prisoners of Hope*, 22.

176   "properly delivered": Ibid., 24.

176   "admired his work": Ibid., x.

176   "working there": Ibid., 282.

176   "return to the States": Fry, *Surrender on Demand*, 220.

176   Vichy authorities: Lewis, *Red Pawn*, 130.

177   American ambassador: Ibid., 141–142. For Dulles's secret work in Bern and his connection with Field, see Peter Grose, *Gentleman Spy: The Life of Allen Dulles* (Boston, 1994).

177   "to make reports": Quoted in Di Figlia, *Roots and Visions*, 29.

178   orders from Moscow: This point is made in Grose, *Gentleman Spy*, 168–169.

178   to OSS attention: The assessment is Lewis's in *Red Pawn*, 143.

178   Communist-front: The charge is made as fact in Steven, *The Splinter Factor*, 88.

178   was eased out: For Field's separation from the USC, see Lewis, *Red Pawn*, 176–180, and Genizi, "Christian Charity," 275 n52.

178   Iron Curtain: For the strange period of Field's life that followed, see Lewis, *Red Pawn*, 198ff.

179   replace a man: Howard Wriggins, *Picking Up the Pieces from Portugal to Palestine: Quaker Refugee Relief in World War II* (Lanham, Md., 2004). I follow this work for the account below.

179   "best I could": Ibid., 22.

180   "over the lip": Ibid.

180   new application: Wyman, *Paper Walls*, 164.

181   "some distinctions": Wriggins, *Picking Up the Pieces*, 27.

182   by a wave: *New York Times*, January 8, 1943, 11.

182   "waits anxiously": Wriggins, *Picking Up the Pieces*, 58.

183   "Nazi victory": Ibid, 54.

183   European headquarters: For further detail about the work of Schwartz and the JDC, see Yehuda Bauer, *American Jewry and the Holocaust: The American Jewish Joint Distribution Committee, 1939–1945* (Detroit, 1981), 45ff. See also Oscar Handlin, *A Continuing Task: The American Jewish Joint Distribution Committee, 1914–1964* (New York, 1964), 74–89.

184   "despair with dignity": Quoted in Bauer, *American Jewry and the Holocaust*, 55.

184   entire wartime period: The figures are given, respectively, in Bauer, *American Jewry and the Holocaust*, 47–48; Handlin, *A Continuing Task*, 87; and Marrus, *The Unwanted*, 264.

185   on their behalf: Bauer, *American Jewry and the Holocaust*, 206–207.

185   as the representative: Differing versions of the creation of the Madrid relief office are given in Bauer, *American Jewry and the Holocaust*, 207; Wriggins, *Picking Up the Pieces*, 51; and Hayes, *Wartime Mission in Spain*, 122–123.

185   moving to France: *New York Times*, February 6, 1941, 3.

185   most of the costs: Wriggins, *Picking Up the Pieces*, 52.

186   his appointment: Bauer, *American Jewry and the Holocaust*, 213–214.

186   From a prosperous: A full account of Israel's life and work is given in Naomi Shepherd, *A Refuge from Darkness: Wilfrid Israel and the Rescue of the Jews* (New York, 1984). I largely follow this work for the account below.

187   "Joint and Hadassah": Quoted in ibid., 177.

188   "save the situation": Ibid., 228.

189   throughout occupied Europe: Shepherd says that while Israel was in Spain "the Agency Executive now . . . had second thoughts" about his mission. She adds that "the organization which had sent him to Portugal and Spain now reined him in." *A Refuge from Darkness*, 248.

189   "played the part": Quoted in Colvin, *Flight 777*, 143.

190   of the journey: Shepherd, *A Refuge from Darkness*, 250–251. For more on the rescue of children from occupied territory, see Bauer, *American Jewry and the Holocaust*, 258ff.

190   bag of largesse: Taylor, *Time Runs Out*, 51–52.
190   "of my ability": *The Times* (London), January 30, 1941, 5.
190   was honored: *The Times* (London), November 24, 1945, 7.
191   prisoners of war: Miller, *Mercy Ships*, 73–81.
191   camps in Germany: *New York Times*, September 7, 1944, 4.

CHAPTER 9: GLORIOUSLY NEUTRAL

193   war's fifth year: *The Times* (London), September 8, 1943, 5.
193   "like the rest": Quoted in ibid.
194   "without blackout": Arthur Koestler, *Arrival and Departure* (New York, 1943), 5. Subsequent quoted passages below are found, respectively, on pages 7, 9, 163, 166, 164, 18.
195   darkened his life: In a comment about the novel, Koestler said that the Nazi brutality Slavek describes was based on real events, including the early period of the Holocaust. Arthur Koestler, *Bricks to Babel* (New York, 1980), 203.
196   "and Subjects": R. E. Vintras, *The Portuguese Connection: The Secret History of the Azores Base* (London, 1974), 111. The texts of both treaties are printed as appendices to the book.
196   "survival as a state": Fernando Rosas, "Portuguese Neutrality in the Second World War," in *European Neutrals and Non-Belligerents During the Second World War*, ed. Neville Wylie (New York, 2002), 269. The essay gives a concise account of Portugal's wartime neutrality. For more on the workings of the Anglo-Portuguese alliance, see, among numerous other works, Glyn Stone, *The Oldest Ally: Britain and the Portuguese Connection, 1936–1941* (London, 1994).
197   bringing from Salazar: Quoted in Kay, *Salazar and Modern Portugal*, 153.
197   "in this determination": *New York Times*, September 3, 1939, 17.
197   to provide it: For more on British views of Portuguese neutrality in the early period of the war, see Stone, *The Oldest Ally*, 131ff.
197   "worst happened": Walford Selby, *Diplomatic Twilight, 1930–1940* (London, 1953), 116–117.
198   "impeccable neutrality": Quoted in Glyn A. Stone, *Spain, Portugal and the Great Powers, 1931–1941* (New York, 2005), 124.
198   any such appeal: Stone, *Spain, Portugal and the Great Powers*, 124.
198   "render assistance": Quoted in ibid.
198   "English Alliance": Ibid., 131.
198   "will be built": *New York Times*, May 30, 1940, 2.
198   a central role: Rosas, "Portuguese Neutrality in the Second World War," 276–277. See also Kay, *Salazar and Modern Portugal*, 122.
198   German submarines: Payne, *Franco and Hitler*, 56–57.

198   for the Axis: For more on the implications of nonbelligerence, see ibid., 63.

199   "Spain's Greece": Ibid., 96.

199   Atlantic coast: For details of the invasion plan, see ibid., 95–98.

199   invade the country: Ibid., 100ff.

200   "Berlin Push": *New York Times*, December 13, 1941, 8.

200   Felix was shelved: For more on Operation Felix, see Waller, *The Unseen War in Europe*, 153–162.

200   Blue Division: For a concise account of the Blue Division, see Payne, *Franco and Hitler*, 146–154.

200   "as in material": William D. Leahy, *I Was There* (New York, 1950), 166.

201   "a living soul": Quoted in Persico, *Roosevelt's Secret War*, 306. The decoded message is reproduced in the book's photo section.

201   swing toward Germany: For more on shifts in Portuguese neutrality, see Rosas, "Portuguese Neutrality in the Second World War," 273–279.

201   to the enemy: The Allied blockade, including the navicert system, is closely examined in *The War and the Neutrals*, ed. Arnold Toynbee and Veronica M. Toynbee (London, 1956), 1–104.

202   duration of the war: Kay, *Salazar and Modern Portugal*, 165. For more on the Timor incident, see Stone, *The Oldest Ally*, 182–199.

202   ending the alliance: Muir, *European Junction*, 146.

202   to its spirit: Kay, *Salazar and Modern Portugal*, 123.

203   "land in Europe": Vernon A. Walters, review of Vintras, *The Portuguese Connection*, http://csi/docs/v18i4a04p_0001.html.

203   "one fine morning": Quoted in Neville Wylie, "'An Amateur Learns His Job'? Special Operations Executive in Portugal, 1940–1942," *Journal of Contemporary History*, 36:3 (2001), 444.

203   "little value": Quoted in Kay, *Salazar and Modern Portugal*, 167. Ambassador Campbell's letter to Salazar invoking the alliance and Salazar's reply are reprinted as appendices in Vintras, *The Portuguese Connection*.

203   news leaked out: Douglas L. Wheeler notes that decoded German-Japanese diplomatic exchanges reveal that Germany had some knowledge of the secret deal. "In the Service of Order," 24 n43.

204   "of British diplomacy": Winston S. Churchill, *Closing the Ring* (Boston, 1951), 165.

204   events and personalities: Kennan, *Memoirs*, 143–145.

204   in Florida: *Anglo-Portuguese News*, July 29, 1943, 2.

204   "smaht for me": Kennan, *Memoirs*, 145.

205   expectation of attack: Ibid., 150. The Azores agreement may have taken Hitler by surprise. A report in the *Saturday Evening Post* had it that the German minister in Lisbon showed Salazar a newspaper with a headline reading "Churchill Announces Azores Bases for Britain," and added that Hitler would surely recall him for failure to prevent the deal. Salazar

proceeded to phone the German foreign office, eventually reached both Ribbentrop and Hitler, and asked that the minister remain in Lisbon. Henry J. Taylor, "Euorpe's Unknown Strong Man," *Saturday Evening Post*, August 19, 1944, 9ff. For a quite different account of the German minister's response to the Azores accord, see Christian Leitz, *Sympathy for the Devil: Neutral Europe and Nazi Germany in World War II* (New York, 2001), 154–155.

205   "was a participant": "Bargain Bases," *Time*, October 25, 1943, 36.

205   calm the storm: "Excitement in Lisbon," *Time*, October 18, 1943, 31.

206   Gibraltar or Lisbon: Hayes, *Wartime Mission in Spain*, 168–169.

206   "by Spain": Quoted in ibid., 170.

206   the two cities: *Foreign Relations of the United States, 1943*, vol. 2, 535–538.

206   "of the inhabitants": Kennan, *Memoirs*, 151.

207   "have to do it": George F. Kennan, *Measures Short of War*, ed. Giles D. Harlow and George C. Maerz (Washington, D.C., 1991), 141. In lectures at the National War College in 1946–1947, collected in this volume, Kennan provided considerable detail about his diplomatic work in Portugal, which would appear in more condensed and formal fashion in his *Memoirs*.

207   "*people* over there": Quoted in Kennan, *Memoirs*, 161. For another version of Kennan's session at the War Department and his meeting with Roosevelt, see his *Measures Short of War*, 145–147.

207   "and great friendship": Roosevelt's letter is reproduced in Kennan, *Measures Short of War*, 147.

208   "meeting the requirements": *Foreign Relations of the United States, 1943*, vol. 2, 571–572.

208   "external appearance": Ibid., 573.

208   and the United States: Kay, *Salazar and Modern Portugal*, 170.

208   "base stealer": Quoted in J. K. Sweeney, *United States' Policy Toward Portugal During the Second World War* (Ph.D. dissertation, Kent State University, 1970), 36.

208   "trading over details": *Foreign Relations of the United States, 1943*, vol. 2, 570.

208   "and little details": Kennan, *Measures Short of War*, 151.

CHAPTER 10: WAR WITHOUT GUNS

209   posting before Lisbon: Selby, *Diplomatic Twilight*, 89.

209   "maximum output": Muir, *European Junction*, 42.

210   "moral cleansing": Quoted in Gallagher, *Portugal*, 101.

210   best for it: Kay, *Salazar and Modern Portugal*, 72.

210 with censorship: Antonio Tabucchi, *Pereira Declares*, trans. Patrick Creagh (New York, 1995). Quotation marks added to dialogue.

211 "to be neutral": Reynolds and Eleanor Packard, *Balcony Empire*, 361–362.

211 up his pace: Shirer, *Berlin Diary*, 603–604.

211 both nations: Leitz, *Sympathy for the Devil*, 150.

212 Axis newsmen: Meneses, *Salazar*, 252.

212 divided attitudes: On this point, see António Costa Pinto, *The Blue Shirts: Portuguese Fascists and the New State* (Boulder, Colo., 2000), 217.

212 for Churchill: Marion Kaplan, *The Portuguese* (New York, 1991), 131–132.

213 other languages: Cole, *Britain and the War of Words in Neutral Europe*, 56.

213 returned home: David Kahn, *Hitler's Spies: German Military Intelligence in World War II* (New York, 1978), 161.

213 double the amount: "What Price News," *Time*, September 27, 1940, 44.

213 off to Berlin: Kahn, *Hitler's Spies*, 161.

213 conquered countries: These and other details of German propaganda in Lisbon are given in Muir, *European Junction*, 42ff.

213 modern art: Beaton, *The Years Between*, 196.

214 of all sorts: *The Times* (London), March 8, 1940, 7.

214 anti-German declarations: Cole, *Britain and the War of Words in Neutral Europe*, 53–54.

215 propaganda triumphs: It would have been a propaganda disaster had the Germans known some details of the Duke's private life, as David Corkill notes in "The Double Centenary Commemorations of 1940," 160–161.

215 "are livid": Quoted in Stone, *Spain, Portugal and the Great Powers*, 186.

215 "paid off": Eccles, *By Safe Hand*, 100.

216 stop to both: Cole, *Britain and the War of Words in Neutral Europe*, 55.

216 nine by Britain: Douglas L. Wheeler, review of António Telo, *Portugal Na Segunda Guerra*, *Luso-Brazilian Review*, 27:1 (Summer 1990), 135–136.

216 blunt title: Cheke served as press attaché of the British embassy in Lisbon from 1938 to 1942, then as first secretary until 1945. His scholarly writing includes *Carlota Joaquina: Queen of Portugal* in 1947.

216 with some care: Cole, *Britain and the War of Words in Neutral Europe*, 91.

216 sacked him: Ibid., 92.

217 hostile isolation: "Dr. Salazar in Doubt," *The Economist*, July 4, 1942, 9.

217 Legion force: Stone, *Spain, Portugal and the Great Powers*, 171–172.

217 was hopeless: Gallagher, *Portugal*, 194. In April 1974 the officer, General António Spínola, became president of Portugal following the overthrow of the dictatorship.

218   and pro-German: *The Times* (London), April 22, 1942, 3.

218   at high rates: *The Times* (London), October 21, 1941, 3.

218   German badges: Cole, *Britain and the War of Words in Neutral Europe*, 70.

218   the pro-German: *New York Times*, December 25, 1940, 19.

218   seen the paper: David E. Walker, *Lunch with a Stranger* (New York, 1957), 160.

219   the same result: Muir, *European Junction*, 49.

219   sea blockade: Cole, *Britain and the War of Words in Neutral Europe*, 111.

219   into Nazi arms: This point is made in ibid., 70.

219   "with both hands": *New York Times*, September 10, 1942, 8.

220   and deadpan no: Jack Alexander, "The Nazi Offensive in Lisbon," *Saturday Evening Post*, March 6, 1943, 86.

220   "has passed away": *The Times* (London), August 13, 1941, 3.

220   in fact he was: David E. Walker recounts his secret work in Lisbon in his memoir *Lunch with a Stranger*, 149–213. I follow this work for the account below. In his study of twentieth-century spying, Phillip Knightley singles out journalists like Walker as among the SOE's better recruits for spreading black propaganda. *The Second Oldest Profession* (New York, 1986), n121.

221   continue the war: Michael Balfour, *Propaganda in War, 1939–1945* (London, 1979), 98.

222   "chief neutrals": "Neutral Nervousness," *Time*, December 29, 1941, 22.

224   the two separate: Cole, *Britain and the War of Words in Neutral Europe*, 105.

225   "on political grounds": Quoted in Ibid., 133.

225   "unpleasant": Ibid.

225   for the Continent: Wallace Carroll, *Persuade or Perish* (Boston, 1948), 190. The post–D-Day figure is given in Clayton D. Laurie, *The Propaganda Warriors: America's Crusade Against Nazi Germany* (Lawrence, Kans., 1996), 126.

225   "by the Nazis": Laurie, *The Propaganda Warriors*, 192. For more on the MO Branch, see this work. See also Mauch, *The Shadow War Against Hitler*, 135–162.

226   hopeful encounters: Laurie, *The Propaganda Warriors*, 196.

226   Goebbels did so: Terry Crowdy, *Deceiving Hitler: Double Cross Deception in World War II* (Oxford, UK, 2008), 217.

226   in the names: Laurie, *The Propaganda Warriors*, 204–205. For more on the MO Branch's use of music, see Mauch, *The Shadow War Against Hitler*, 151–162.

226   directly into Europe: Carroll, *Persuade or Perish*, 127.

226   foreign broadcasts: Ibid., 115.

227   pouch to Madrid: Balfour, *Propaganda in War*, 116–117.

227   "by next December": Quoted in Allan M. Winkler, *The Politics of Propaganda: The Office of War Information, 1942–1945* (New Haven, Conn., 1978), 132.

228   they did so: Winkler, *The Politics of Propaganda*, 136.

228   "in the past": Quoted in Cole, *Britain and the War of Words in Neutral Europe*, 154–155.

229   few restrictions: These and other details about the triumph of Allied propaganda in Portugal are found in Cole, *Britain and the War of Words in Neutral Europe*, 155–158.

229   "he did not!": Quoted in ibid., 157.

CHAPTER 11: THE SEETHING CAULDRON

231   "disentangle things": Kennan, *Measures Short of War*, 131.

231   "seething cauldron": Kennan, *Memoirs*, 143.

231   "or maintained": "Neutral Iberia," *The Economist*, February 21, 1942, 243.

232   "hair-raising": Kennan, *Memoirs*, 143.

232   "my partner": Phillip Knightley, *The Master Spy: The Story of Kim Philby* (New York, 1989), 101-102.

233   "against each other": J. C. Masterman, *The Case of the Four Friends* (London, 1960; orig. pub. 1956), 1961.

233   forty to fifty: Douglas L. Wheeler, "The Archives of Portugal: A Guide to an Intelligence Treasure Trove," *International Journal of Intelligence and Counterintelligence*, 4:4 (1990), 540.

233   "make espionage": Alexander, "The Nazi Offensive in Lisbon," 86.

233   "Portuguese racket": "Enemy Intelligence Activities in Portugal," June–September 1943, 5, 15. National Archives, IRR, File XE 135014.

233   "linking them together": Muir, *European Junction*, 40–41.

234   "gather information": Moats, *No Passport for Paris*, 13.

234   "ones around": Peabody, *Occupied Territory*, 248–250.

234   listening post?: Wriggins, *Picking Up the Pieces*, 34.

235   "top-secret documents": Aline [Romanones], *The Spy Wore Red*, 62.

235   some mail: Wheeler, "In the Service of Order," 12.

235   for delivery: *New York Times*, March 6, 1943, 2.

235   went to prison: *New York Times*, November 20, 1942, 25.

235   German handlers: *New York Times*, September 16, 1943, 15.

235   back of letters: *New York Times*, August 27, 1943, 4; *The Times* (London), October 9, 1943, 3.

236   undercover career: John Beevor, *SOE: Recollections and Reflections, 1940–1945* (London, 1981), 30–43. I largely follow this work in the account below. Beevor's memoir is examined for accuracy in Wylie, "'An Amateur Learns His Job'?," 441–457.

236   in defense of: The discussions are recounted in detail in Gyn Stone, *The Oldest Ally*, 166–181.

237   Beevor's recall: For varying interpretations of Salazar's response to the Beevor case, see Wylie, "'An Amateur Learns His Job'?," 450.

237   in shambles: The failed SOE operation is briefly noted in Wheeler, "In the Service of Order," 8–9.

237   "had the time": Quoted in Wylie, "'An Amateur Learns His Job'?," 455.

237   took action: Wylie, "'An Amateur Learns His Job'?," 455.

238   "bread is buttered": Quoted in Cole, *Britain and the War of Words in Neutral Europe*, 111.

239   to the SOE: Philip Johns, *Within Two Cloaks: Missions with SIS and SOE* (London, 1979), 107–110, 114–115.

239   first OSS operative: Beevor, *SOE*, 132–133.

239   posting to Portugal: Solborg's background is set out in R. Harris Smith, *OSS: The Secret History of America's First Central Intelligence Agency* (Berkeley, Calif., 1972), 41.

239   march into Portugal: Wheeler, "The Price of Neutrality," I, 121–122.

239   of the other: Balfour, *Propaganda in War*, 100.

240   "await orders": Quoted in Smith, *OSS*, 48. For more detail about Solborg's North African mission and his subsequent dismissal by Donovan, see this work, pages 47–51.

240   proceeding smoothly: Solborg's role in the deception scheme is recounted in Thaddeus Holt, *The Deceivers: Allied Military Deception in the Second World War* (New York, 2004), 721–725.

241   "and intemperate": Quoted in Bradley F. Smith, *The Shadow Warriors: O.S.S. and the Origins of the C.I.A.* (New York, 1983), 218.

241   "their judgment": Hayes, *Wartime Mission in Spain*, 77–78.

241   "virtually amateurs": Quoted in Smith, *The Shadow Warriors*, 219.

241   "of the Azores": Kennan, *Memoirs*, 150.

241   "dangerous Fascist": Ibid.

241   trashcan burglary: Accounts of the burglary are given in, among others, Anthony Cave Brown, *The Last Hero: Wild Bill Donovan* (New York, 1982), 305–307, and David Alvarez, "Tempest in an Embassy Trash Can," *World War II*, 22:9 (2008), 54–59.

242   "of the nation": Quoted in Smith, *The Shadow Warriors*, 220–221.

242   who also informed: Alvarez, "Tempest in an Embassy Trash Can," 56.

242   "pick up any": Quoted in Brown, *The Last Hero*, 306.

242   "further activities": Ibid., 306–307.

243   been weakened: On this point, see Brown, *The Last Hero*, 307, and Smith, *The Shadow Warriors*, 221.

243   subagents: Smith, *The Shadow Warriors*, 301.

243   "of their art": J. C. Masterson, *The Double-Cross System in the War of 1939 to 1945* (New Haven, Conn., 1972), 142, 114.

243   Juan Pujol: A primary source of information about Garbo is his memoir: Juan Pujol, with Nigel West, *Operation Garbo: The Personal Story of the Most Successful Double Agent of World War II* (New York, 1985). The book has interspersed chapters by West—the pseudonym of the British intelligence writer Rupert Allason—that add detail and occasionally correct Pujol's account. A necessary addition to, and corrective for, Pujol's memoir is Tomás Harris, *Garbo: The Spy Who Saved D-Day* (Richmond, UK, 2000). Harris wrote his "Summary of the Garbo Case 1941–1945" for internal distribution within MI5. It was published in book form in 2000 under the title indicated above. Among numerous other accounts of Garbo's spy career, see especially Michael Howard, *Strategic Deception in the Second World War* (New York, 1995), 231–241.

245   Pujol went to: This is Pujol's version of contacting an American official. Harris records that initial contact was made by Pujol's wife, who was then living with him in Lisbon, and without her husband's knowledge. Harris, *Garbo*, 62.

246   "direction and example": Norman Holmes Pearson, foreword to Masterman, *The Double-Cross System*, xi. Masterman's book was written in 1945 as a government report. He sought to publish the report in book form in Britain in the 1960s, but it was not until 1972, with the aid of Pearson and permission of the British government, that it was put out by Yale University Press. For further detail on the publication history of the book, see Nigel West, introduction to *The Guy Liddell Diaries*, ed. Nigel West, vol. 1 (London, 2005), 3–4. For more on Pearson's career with the OSS, see Robin W. Winks, *Cloak & Gown: Scholars in the Secret War* (New York, 1987), 247–321.

246   to do so: Nigel West, *A Thread of Deceit: Espionage Myths of World War II* (New York, 1985), 71.

246   controlled the entire: For a skeptical view of the British claim, see Phillip Knightley, *The Second Oldest Profession*, 144ff. For a German assessment that accepts it, see Horst Boog, Gerhard Krebs, and Detlef Vogel, *Germany and the Second World War*, vol. 7 (Oxford, UK, 2006), 493–494. Terry Crowdy writes in *Deceiving Hitler*, page 77, that during the war four German spies in England eluded MI5.

247   his wife: Harris states in *Garbo* that Pujol's wife played an active role in his earlier spy work in Madrid and Lisbon. He also notes that she was highly temperamental and posed many difficulties for MI5. See pages 327–332.

248   diplomatic bag: For a full listing of Pujol's network of notional agents and their activities, see appendices to Harris, *Garbo*.

248   "one-man band": Masterman, *The Double-Cross System*, 142.

248   do and know: The security controls are described by Harris, *Garbo*, 375–377.

248   allowed to keep: Ibid., 335–336.

249   added importance: For Garbo's work in Fortitude, see especially Roger Hesketh, *Fortitude: The D-Day Deception Campaign* (New York, 2000), 131–148.

249   three hours together: Pujol's meeting with the case officer is recounted at length in Harris, *Garbo*, 285–288.

CHAPTER 12: ONE WORLD TO ANOTHER

251   "from the regime": Howard, *Strategic Deception in the Second World War*, 48.

251   "go to war": Quoted in ibid.

251   control from Berlin: F. H. Hinsley and C. A. G. Simkins, *British Intelligence in the Second World War* (New York, 1990), vol. 4, 298.

251   currency transactions: Howard makes these points in *Strategic Deception in the Second World War*, 48–49.

252   "agents at all": Masterman, *The Double-Cross System*, 86n.

252   "was very small": Ibid., 152.

252   driven to France: Jebsen's kidnapping is recounted by Nigel West in Pujol, *Operation Garbo*, 122.

252   from his villa: Dusko Popov, *Spy/Counterspy: The Autobiography of Dusko Popov* (New York, 1974), 300. See also Hesketh, *Fortitude*, 109–110, and Crowdy, *Deceiving Hitler*, 255.

252   agent working on the Continent: Popov's spy career is recounted in his autobiography *Spy/Counterspy* and in Russell Miller, *Codename Tricycle* (London, 2004). I follow both works in the account below.

253   Under the name: To American military intelligence in Lisbon he was known as Albert Von Karsthof.

253   aspects of spying: Miller makes this point in *Codename Tricycle*, 51.

254   (Tar) Robertson: A career Security Service officer, Robertson is credited with being the principal architect of the double-cross system in Nigel West, *A Thread of Deceit*, 71.

255   "emergencies only": Quoted in Popov, *Spy/Counterspy*, 74–77.

255   "went wrong": Quoted in Miller, *Codename Tricycle*, 67.

255   "in the lead": Quoted in Popov, *Spy/Counterspy*, 276.

256   "fondness for": Christopher Andrew, *Defend the Realm: The Authorized History of MI5* (New York, 2009), 253.

258   loan of Tricycle: Holt, *The Deceivers*, 157.

258   "could be made": Masterman, *The Double-Cross System*, 138.

258   deception scheme: Popov credits Jebsen with conceiving the plan. *Spy/Counterspy*, 232.

259   "run me": Quoted in Norman Sherry, *The Life of Graham Greene*, vol. 2

260   intimate contact: This point is strongly emphasized in Miller, *Operation Tricycle*, 211.

261   "contrasts with": Quoted in ibid., 215.

261   "we were saved": Masterman, *The Double-Cross System*, 154.

261   "disclosed nothing": Holt, *The Deceivers*, 564. For more on why Jebsen might have been taken into custody, see Hesketh, *Fortitude*, 110–111.

263   "someone named": A "von Carnap" is identified as Fidrmuc's Abwehr controller in John P. Campbell, "Some Pieces in the Ostro Puzzle," *Intelligence and National Security*, 11:2 (1996), 251. I follow this closely detailed article for much of my account of Fidrmuc. See also a reference to "von Karnap" as Ostro's controller in *The Guy Liddell Diaries*, vol. 2, 154.

263   "to Berlin": Quoted in Popov, *Spy/Counterspy*, 267.

264   in their endeavors: *The Guy Liddell Diaries*, vol. 2, 285.

264   "invented in Lisbon": "Enemy Intelligence Activities in Portugal, June–September 1943," 5, National Archives, IRR. File XE135014.

264   assault took place: Roger Hesketh writes in *Fortitude*, page 356n1, that "on 31 May, 1944, OSTRO gave a correct forecast of the [Normandy] invasion. There is no evidence to show that his message was based on anything more solid than his own imagination." Hesketh goes on to suggest why the Germans discounted the information.

264   none succeeded: Masterman, *The Double-Cross System*, 151.

264   "bump him off": *The Guy Liddell Diaries*, vol. 2, 273.

265   "without trace!": Johns, *Within Two Cloaks*, 111.

265   could be made: Hinsley and Simkins, *British Intelligence in the Second World War*, vol. 4, 279.

265   report on Fidrmuc: National Archives, IRR Personal File, Paul G. Fidrmuc, Box 49A, Folder 2, CI Final Interrogation Report 154.

266   "*fantastically* so": Quoted in C. G. McKay, "MI5 on OSTRO: A New Document from the Archives," *Intelligence and National Security*, 12:3 (1997), 181. Emphasis in the article.

266   "for U-boats": Quoted in Sherry, *The Life of Graham Greene*, vol. 2, 173. Fidrmuc's skill as an oarsman is noted in the Final Interrogation Report indicated above.

266   "leaving London": Quoted in Howard, *Strategic Deception in the Second World War*, 178.

266   She was based: Lily Sergueiev, *Secret Service Rendered* (London, 1968). I follow this work for the account below.

268   in a diary: Passages from the diary appear within Sergueiev's memoir.

268   road accident: This is Sergueiev's report of what happened. Andrew in *Defend the Realm*, page 304, says that the dog died in Portugal.

271   "in Europe!": Masterman, *The Double-Cross System*, 169.

271   "Could be": Popov, *Spy/Counterspy*, 150.

271   "Bond adventure": Ibid.

272   is uncertain: See Andrew Lycett, *Ian Fleming: The Man Behind James Bond* (Atlanta, Ga., 1995), 128.

272   "been exciting": Quoted in ibid., 127.

272   a new post: Greene's work for British intelligence is recounted in two biographies: Michael Shelden, *Graham Greene: The Enemy Within* (New York, 1994), 245–259, and Sherry, *The Life of Graham Greene*, vol. 2, 166–183.

272   clandestine activity: The figures are given in Sherry, *The Life of Graham Greene*, vol. 2, 174.

273   "office job": Quoted in Ibid., 177.

273   "endless files": Graham Greene, *Ways of Escape* (New York, 1980), 307.

273   "of the obvious": Quoted in Sherry, *The Life of Graham Greene*, vol. 2, 168.

273   "work with us": Ibid., 176. For the range of Ustinov's other activities in Lisbon, see *The Guy Liddell Diaries*, vol. 2, 249.

274   "a separate peace": Ibid., 177.

274   "activity in Portugal": Greene, *Ways of Escape*, 246.

275   turns with it: Christopher Hitchens phrases it this way in "Death from a Salesman: Graham Greene's Bottled Ontology," an incisive introduction to the 2007 Penguin edition of *Our Man in Havana*, xviii.

CHAPTER 13: WOLFRAM BY DAY

277   "at night": Hayes, *Wartime Mission in Spain*, 85.

277   coherent replies: Eccles, *By Safe Hand*, 334.

277   "of the nation": Quoted in Douglas L. Wheeler, "The Price of Neutrality: Portugal, the Wolfram Question, and World War II," *Luso-Brazilian Review*, 23:2 (1986), 108. This is the second of a two-part study of the Portuguese wolfram trade. Hereafter cited as "The Price of Neutrality," II.

278   national resource: This point is made in John H. Kemler, *The Struggle for Wolfram in the Iberian Peninsula, June 1942–June 1944* (Ph.D. dissertation, University of Chicago, 1949), 69. The study draws on the author's personal experience of the wolfram trade as a staff member of the United States Commercial Company in Lisbon and Madrid from 1942 to 1946.

278   "had any wolfram": Eccles, *By Safe Hand*, 309.

279   "worth having": Ibid., 98.

279   sent letters: All quotations below come from ibid., pages, respectively, 105, 106, 133, 172, 329, 332, 335, 356.

281   exchanged in Lisbon: Douglas L. Wheeler, "The Price of Neutrality: Portugal, the Wolfram Question, and World War II," *Luso-Brazilian Review*, 23:1 (1986), 112–113. Hereafter cited as "The Price of Neutrality," I. See note above.

281   military equipment: Leitz, *Sympathy for the Devil*, 161.

281   facilitate purchases: *U.S. and Allied Wartime and Postwar Relations and Negotiations with Argentina, Portugal, Spain, Sweden and Turkey on Looted Gold and German External Assets and U.S. Concerns About the Fate of the Wartime Ustasha Treasury*, Supplement to Preliminary Study, coordinated by Stuart E. Eizenstat, prepared by William Slany (Washington, D.C., 1998), 25. Hereafter cited as *Supplementary Eizenstat Report*.

281   offered for sale: *The Times* (London), November 23, 1943, 3.

281   export tax: Payne, *Franco and Hitler*, 239–240.

281   the wolfram business: *Supplementary Eizenstat Report*, 27.

282   "our production": Eccles, *By Safe Hand*, 411–412.

282   for new riches: Wheeler, "The Price of Neutrality," I, 114.

282   to their heads: *Anglo-Portuguese News*, June 15, 1944, 4.

283   favored treatment: For details of the regulatory effort, see Wheeler, "The Price of Neutrality," I, 116–117.

283   severely stressed: For an account of the various agreements, see especially Kemler, *The Struggle for Wolfram in the Iberian Peninsula*, 66–84.

283   "one to do?": Eccles, *By Safe Hand*, 367.

283   "have to carry": Ibid., 415.

283   "present agreement": *Foreign Relations of the United States, 1943*, II, 518.

283   good prices: Wheeler, "The Price of Neutrality," II, 98.

284   in an ally: Kay, *Salazar and Modern Portugal*, 179.

284   "control its flow": *Foreign Relations of the United States, 1943*, vol. 2, 520.

284   Hitler's response: Kay, *Salazar and Modern Portugal*, 179.

284   able to satisfy: Leitz, *Sympathy for the Devil*, 166.

284   "is lying low": *Foreign Relations of the United States, 1944*, vol. 4, 92.

284   among themselves: For details of the disagreement, see J. K. Sweeney, "The Portuguese Wolfram Embargo: A Case Study in Economic Warfare," *Military Affairs*, 38:1 (1974), 23–26. See also *Supplementary Eizenstat Report*, 34–36.

285   in the lead: Wheeler, "The Price of Neutrality," II, 100.

285   lion's share: *New York Times*, January 19, 1944, 8.

285   "of the family": *Foreign Relations of the United States, 1944*, vol. 4, 132.

285   total ban on: The timing, Salazar's response, and Portuguese consideration of the request are closely set out in Wheeler, "The Price of Neutrality," II, 101–104. In his biography of Salazar, Meneses quotes a British source, page 315, that indicates the prime minister hinted to the British that use of the alliance was the only way to end the embargo crisis.

285   earlier announced: *New York Times*, June 8, 1944, 7.

285   "of this mineral": Quoted in Kemler, *The Struggle for Wolfram in the Iberian Peninsula*, 89.

285   great contribution: *The Times* (London), June 8, 1944, 8.

286   "carried the day": *Foreign Relations of the United States, 1944*, vol. 4, 131.

286   "without humiliation": Quoted in Wheeler, "The Price of Neutrality," II, 104.

286   "wartime peak": "Portugal: A Special Survey," *The Economist*, April 17, 1954, 235. For more on the cost to Portugal of ending the wolfram trade, see Wheeler, "The Price of Neutrality," II, 105–106.

286   intelligence activity: Details of the gold-for-escudos transactions were complex, if not mysterious. For some enlightenment see *Supplementary Eizenstat Report*, 40–41.

286   to neutral countries: Tom Bower, *The Paperclip Conspiracy: The Hunt for the Nazi Scientists* (Boston, 1987), 262.

287   sovereign coins: *Preliminary Eizenstat Report*, 130.

287   "to prevent it": Quoted in Bower, *The Paperclip Conspiracy*, 263.

287   all else of value: For a broad study of Nazi looted gold and other valuables, see Arthur L. Smith, Jr., *Hitler's Gold: The Story of the Nazi War Loot* (Oxford, UK, 1989).

287   thriller fiction: Frederick Hazlitt Brennan, *Memo to a Firing Squad* (New York, 1943).

288   "in neutral countries": Samuel Klaus, "Safe Haven Investigation in Europe—August 16 to October 10, 1944," 1. A copy of the report is in the Oscar Cox Papers, Franklin D. Roosevelt Library, Hyde Park, New York.

288   Washington colleagues: Klaus's mission and the start of the Safehaven Program are recounted in Martin Lorenz-Meyer, *Safehaven: The Allied Pursuit of Nazi Assets Abroad* (Columbia, Mo., 2007), 29.

288   "going over for": Quoted in ibid., 45.

288   "marked men": Klaus, "Safe Haven Investigation in Europe," 2.

289   kept secret: *Foreign Relations of the United States, 1944*, vol. 2, 220.

289   "more venal": Klaus, "Safe Haven Investigation in Europe," 10.

290   high irony: The irony is noted both in Bower, *The Paperclip Conspiracy*, 259–274, and Lorenz-Meyer, *Safehaven*, 176–177.

290   which had soared: Gallagher, *Portugal*, 137.

290   gold pool: For the full terms of the agreement involving both monetary gold and German external assets in Portugal, see *Preliminary Eizenstat Report*, 139–140.

291   "on the Sidelines": *New York Times*, January 26, 1997, E1.

291   "World War II": *Preliminary Eizenstat Report*, iii. Until indicated otherwise, all quoted passages below are from the introduction to this volume, iii–xii.

291   "ledger of grief": *Supplementary Eizenstat Report*, xxiv.

292   "the Portuguese people": *New York Times*, August 5, 1999, A8.

CHAPTER 14: WHERE TO SPEND ONE'S HOLIDAY

293   working-class clubs: Soares, *Portugal's Struggle for Liberty*, 32.

294   "sea of people": Ibid., 36.

294   in celebration: Gallagher, *Portugal*, 107–108.
294   "sort of way": Soares, *Portugal's Struggle for Liberty*. 36.
294   snapped up: The D-Day atmosphere in Lisbon is described in Mannes, "Letter from Lisbon," July 1, 1944, 56.
294   was played: *Anglo-Portuguese News*, April 19, 1945, 4.
295   official condolences: *The Times* (London), May 7, 1945, 3.
295   de Valera stood: Wills, *That Neutral Ireland*, 389.
295   had done so: *Foreign Relations of the United States, 1944*, vol. 1, 1,428–1,430.
295   closed immediately: *The Times* (London), May 7, 1945, 4.
295   no longer required: Ibid.
295   of the victors: Kay, *Salazar and Modern Portugal*, 181.
296   "had departed": *The Times* (London), May 19, 1945, 4.
296   dangerous to Portugal: *Foreign Relations of the United States, 1945*, vol. 3 (Washington, D.C., 1968), 800.
296   "in general": Ibid., 800–801.
296   fellow Germans: Letter from General Edwin L. Sibert to Colonel Robert A. Solborg, July 28, 1945, in "German Intelligence in Portugal," National Archives, IRR, File XE135014.
296   "open scandal": *Foreign Relations of the United States, 1945*, vol. 3, 805.
297   X-2 files: *Preliminary Eizenstat Report*, 43.
297   "of protection": Colonel Robert A. Solborg, "Estimate of Situation in Portugal Relative to German Nationals," August 27, 1945, in "German Intelligence in Portugal."
297   Lisbon to Paris: *Foreign Relations of the United States, 1945*, vol. 3, 810.
297   "no further assistance": *Foreign Relations of the United States, 1946*, vol. 5 (Washington, D.C., 1969), 809–810. For the similar struggle to remove Germans from postwar Spain, see Payne, *Franco and Hitler*, 263.
298   mock attack: *The Times* (London), August 21, 1946, 4.
298   cover story: "Portugal: How Bad Is Best?" *Time*, July 22, 1946, 28–33.
298   temporarily added: "A Letter from the Publisher," *Time*, November 4, 1946, 18.
299   "beaten track": *Anglo-Portuguese News*, September 30, 1943, 6. Emphasis in the article.
299   "on a forest": Macaulay, "Lisbon Day, London Day," 5.
299   "across the Channel": Quoted in Emery, *Rose Macaulay*, 280.
300   "inspiration to us": *New York Times*, March 5, 1946, 4.
301   overseas tour: Francis J. Spellman, *Action This Day: Letters from the Fighting Fronts* (New York, 1943), 5–9.
301   passage to Lisbon: Except where noted, I follow Carol's return to Portugal as recounted in Quinlan, *The Playboy King*, 232–238.
301   "and a canary": *New York Times*, October 6, 1947.
302   funeral cars: *New York Times*, April 8, 1953, 20. In 2003 Carol's remains were returned to Romania.

302   Born in Armenia: Ralph Hewins, *Mr Five Per Cent: The Story of Calouste Gulbenkian* (New York, 1985). For the account below I follow this biography and the autobiography of Gulbenkian's son, Nubar Gulbenkian, *Portrait in Oil* (New York, 1965). For added detail, see José de Azeredo Perdigão, *Calouste Gulbenkian, Collector*, trans. Ana Lowndes Marques (Lisbon, 1969). Perdigão was a lawyer in Portugal for Gulbenkian.

303   journeyed back and forth: Gulbenkian, *Portrait in Oil*, 210–211.

303   willingly supplied: Johns, *Within Two Cloaks*, 104–106.

304   stake to $125: John Leggett, *A Daring Young Man: A Biography of William Saroyan* (New York: 2002), 230.

304   eclectic accumulation: For a description of the collection as it was exhibited at the Metropolitan Museum of Art in New York in 1999, see Robert Smith, "A Lifelong Passion for the Best," *New York Times*, November 19, 1999, E35.

SOURCES

Newspaper accounts and archival documents cited in the notes are not included below.

Alexander, Jack. "The Nazi Offensive in Lisbon." *Saturday Evening Post*, March 6, 1943, 15ff.

Aline [Romanones], Countess of Romanones. *The Spy Wore Red: My Adventures as an Undercover Agent in World War II*. New York, 1987.

Alvarez, David. "Tempest in an Embassy Trash Can." *World War II*, 22 (9):54–59.

Anderson, Mark M., ed. *Hitler's Exiles: Personal Stories of the Flight from Nazi Germany to America*. New York, 1998.

Andrew, Christopher. *Defend the Realm: The Authorized History of MI5*. New York, 2009.

Atkinson, Rick. *The Day of Battle: The War in Sicily and Italy, 1943–1944*. New York, 2007.

Baker, Leonard. *Brahmin in Revolt: A Biography of Herbert C. Pell*. Garden City, N.Y., 1972.

Baldwin, Neil. *Man Ray: American Artist*. New York, 2000.

Balfour, Michael. *Propaganda in War, 1939–1945*. London, 1979.

Bauer, Yehuda. *American Jewry and the Holocaust: The American Jewish Joint Distribution Committee, 1939–1945*. Detroit, 1981.

Bayles, William D. "Lisbon: Europe's Bottleneck." *Life*, April 28, 1941, 77ff.

Beaton, Cecil. *Near East*. London, 1943.

———. *The Years Between: Diaries 1939–44*. London, 1965.

Beevor, John. *SOE: Recollections and Reflections, 1940–1945*. London, 1981.

Bender, Marilyn, and Selig Altschul. *The Chosen Instrument: Pan Am, Juan Trippe, the Rise and Fall of an American Entrepreneur*. New York, 1982.

Berczeller, Richard. *Displaced Doctor*. New York, 1964.

Bess, Demaree. "American Strategy Pains Portugal." *Saturday Evening Post*, August 30, 1941, 18ff.

Bloch, Michael. *Operation Willi: The Nazi Plot to Kidnap the Duke of Windsor.* Toronto, 1987; orig. pub. 1984.

Bodley, Ronald. *Flight into Portugal.* London, 1941.

Boog, Horst, Gerhard Krebs, and Detlef Vogel. *Germany and the Second World War.* Vol. 7. Oxford, UK, 2006.

Bower, Tom. *The Paperclip Conspiracy: The Hunt for the Nazi Scientists.* Boston, 1987.

Boyle, Kay. "Les Six Enfants." *Harper's Bazaar,* October 1941, 73ff.

Brennan, Frederick Hazlitt. *Memo to a Firing Squad.* New York, 1943.

Brooks, Howard L. *Prisoners of Hope: Report on a Mission.* New York, 1942.

Brown, Anthony Cave. *Bodyguard of Lies.* New York, 1975.

———. *The Last Hero: Wild Bill Donovan.* New York, 1982.

———. *"C": The Secret Life of Sir Stewart Graham Menzies.* New York, 1987.

Burman, Carina. "Escape over the Pyrenees." *Quadrant,* 49 (4):38–43.

Butcher, Harry C. *My Three Years with Eisenhower: The Personal Diary of Captain Harry C. Butcher, USNR.* New York, 1946.

Campbell, John P. "Some Pieces in the *Ostro* Puzzle." *Intelligence and National Security,* 11 (2):245–263.

Carroll, Wallace. *Persuade or Perish.* Boston, 1948.

Cesarani, David. *Arthur Koestler: The Homeless Mind.* New York, 1998.

Churchill, Winston S. *Closing the Ring.* Boston, 1951.

———. *The Hinge of Fate.* Boston, 1950.

Cloud, Stanley, and Lynne Olson. *The Murrow Boys.* Boston, 1996.

Collier, Richard. *The Freedom Road, 1944–1945.* New York, 1984.

Colvin, Ian. *Flight 777.* London, 1957.

Corkill, David. "The Double Centenary Commemorations of 1940 in the Context of Anglo Portuguese Relations." In *The Portuguese Discoveries in the English Speaking World, 1870–1972,* edited by Teresa Pinto Coelho. Lisbon, 2005.

Coward, Noël. *Future Indefinite.* Garden City, N.Y., 1954.

Crowdy, Terry. *Deceiving Hitler: Double Cross and Deception in World War II.* Oxford, UK, 2008.

Cunard, Nancy. *Grand Man: Memories of Norman Douglas.* London, 1954.

Daley, Robert. *An American Saga: Juan Trippe and His Pan Am Empire.* New York, 1980.

Darling, Donald. *Secret Sunday.* London, 1995.

Davenport, Miriam. *An Unsentimental Education.* Unpublished memoir, http://varianfry.org/ebel_memoir_en.htm.

Day, Barry, ed. *The Letters Noël Coward.* New York, 2007.

Di Figlia, Ghanda. *Roots and Visions: The First Fifty Years of the Unitarian Universalist Service Committee.* Boston, 1990.

———. "Martha Sharp Cogan and Waitstill Hastings Sharp," http://harvardsquarelibrary.org/unitarians/cogan.html.

Diamond, Hanna. *Fleeing Hitler: France 1940.* New York, 2007.

Downing, Rupert. *If I Laugh: The Chronicle of My Strange Adventures in the Great Paris Exodus—June 1940*. London, 1941.

Eccles, David. *By Safe Hand: Letters of Sybil and David Eccles, 1939–1942*. London, 1983.

Eisner, Peter. "Bingham's List." *Smithsonian*, March 2009, 50–57.

Eizenstat, Stuart E., and William Slany. *U.S. and Allied Efforts to Recover and Restore Gold and Other Assets Stolen or Hidden by Germany During World War II*. Preliminary Study. Washington, D.C., 1997.

———. *U.S. and Allied Wartime and Postwar Relations and Negotiations with Argentina, Portugal, Spain, Sweden and Turkey on Looted Gold and German External Assets and U.S. Concerns About the Fate of the Wartime Ustasha Treasury*. Supplement to Preliminary Study. Washington, D.C., 1998.

Emery, Jane. *Rose Macaulay: A Writer's Life*. London, 1991.

Ezratty, Harry. "The Portuguese Consul and the 10,000 Jews." *Jewish Life*, September-October 1964, 17–20.

Feuchtwanger, Lion. *The Devil in France*. Trans. Phyllis Blewitt. London, 1942.

Fischer, Louis. "Lisbon: Europe's Gangplank." *The Nation*, September 6, 1941, 197–199.

Fisher, Clive. *Noël Coward*. New York, 1992.

Fittko, Lisa. *Escape Through the Pyrenees*. Trans. David Koblick. Evanston, Ill., 1991.

Foot, M. R. D., and J. M. Langley. *MI9*. London, 1979.

Fralon, José-Alain. *A Good Man in Evil Times*. Trans. Peter Graham. New York, 2001.

Fry, Varian. *Surrender on Demand*. Boulder, Colo., 1997; orig. pub. 1945.

Gallagher, Tom. *Portugal: A Twentieth-Century Interpretation*. Manchester, UK, 1983.

Gallagher, Wes. ["See You in Lisbon."] In *Free Men Are Fighting: The Story of World War II*, edited by Oliver Gramling. New York, 1942.

Genizi, Haim. "Christian Charity: The Unitarian Service Committee's Relief Activities on Behalf of Refugees from Nazism, 1940–1945." *Holocaust and Genocide Studies* 2 (2):261–276.

Gill, Brendan. "Leslie Howard." *Architectural Digest*. 49 (4):150ff.

Gold, Mary Jayne. *Crossroads Marseilles, 1940*. Garden City, N.Y., 1980.

Goss, Chris. *Bloody Biscay*. Rev. ed. Manchester, UK, 2001.

Graham, Sheilah. *Hollywood Revisited*. New York, 1985.

Greene, Graham. *Ways of Escape*. New York, 1980.

———. *Our Man in Havana*. New York, 2007; orig. pub. 1958.

Grose, Peter. *Gentleman Spy: The Life of Allen Dulles*. Boston, 1994.

Guggenheim, Peggy. *Out of This Century*. New York, 1979.

Gulbenkian, Nubar. *Portrait in Oil: The Autobiography of Nubar Gulbenkian*. New York, 1965.

Hamilton, Nigel. *The Brothers Mann*. New Haven, Conn., 1979.

Handlin, Oscar. *A Continuing Task: The American Jewish Joint Distribution Committee, 1914–1964*. New York, 1964.

Harris, Tomás. *Garbo: The Spy Who Saved D-Day*. Richmond, UK, 2000.

Harshav, Benjamin. *Marc Chagall and His Times*. Stanford, Calif., 2004.

Hawkins, Eric, with Robert N. Sturdevant. *Hawkins of the Paris Herald*. New York, 1963.

Hayes, Carlton J. H. *Wartime Mission in Spain, 1942–1945*. New York, 1946.

Hesketh, Roger. *Fortitude: The D-Day Deception Campaign*. New York, 2000.

Hewins, Ralph. *Mr Five Per Cent*. New York, 1958.

Hinsley, F. H., and C. A. G. Simkins. *British Intelligence in the Second World War*. Vol. 4. New York, 1990.

Hoffmann, Peter. *The History of the German Resistance, 1933–1945*. Trans. Richard Barry. Cambridge, Mass., 1977.

Holloway, Mark. *Norman Douglas: A Biography*. London, 1976.

Holt, Thaddeus. *The Deceivers: Allied Military Deception in the Second World War*. New York, 2004.

Howard, Leslie Ruth. *A Quite Remarkable Father*. New York, 1959.

Howard, Michael. *Strategic Deception in the Second World War*. New York, 1995.

Howard, Ronald. *In Search of My Father*. London, 1981.

Ilfrey, Jack, with Mark S. Copeland. *Happy Jack's Go Buggy: A Fighter Pilot's Story*. Atglen, Pa., 1998.

Isenberg, Sheila. *A Hero of Our Own: The Story of Varian Fry*. New York, 2001.

Janson, Robert. Janson's log, http://384thbombgroup.com/pages/janson.html.

Jeffery, Keith. *The Secret History of MI6*. New York, 2010.

John, Otto. *Twice Through the Lines: The Autobiography of Otto John*. Trans. Richard Barry. New York, 1972.

Johns, Philip. *Within Two Cloaks: Missions with SIS and SOE*. London, 1979.

Joy, Charles R. "Lives Were Saved." In *Together We Advance*, edited by Stephen H. Fritchman. Boston, 1947.

Kahn, David. *Hitler's Spies: German Military Intelligence in World War II*. New York, 1978.

Kaplan, Marion. *The Portuguese*. New York, 1991.

Kay, Hugh. *Salazar and Modern Portugal*. New York, 1970.

Kemler, John H. *The Struggle for Wolfram in the Iberian Peninsula, June 1942–June 1944*. Ph.D. dissertation, University of Chicago, 1949.

Kennan, George F. *Memoirs, 1925–1950*. Boston, 1967.

———. *Measures Short of War*. Eds. Giles D. Harlow and George C. Maerz. Washington, D.C., 1991.

Klemmer, Harvey. "Lisbon—Gateway to Warring Europe." *National Geographic*, August 1941, 259–276.

Knightley, Phillip. *The Second Oldest Profession*. New York, 1986.

———. *The Master Spy: The Story of Kim Philby*. New York, 1989.

Koch, Howard. *Casablanca: Script and Legend*. Woodstock, N.Y., 1973.

Koestler, Arthur. *Scum of the Earth*. New York, 1941.

———. *Arrival and Departure*. New York, 1943.

————. *The Invisible Writing*. New York, 1954.

Laurie, Clayton D. *The Propaganda Warriors: America's Crusade Against Nazi Germany*. Lawrence, Kans., 1996.

Leahy, William D. *I Was There*. New York, 1950.

LeFanu, Sarah. *Rose Macaulay*. London, 2003.

Leggett, John. *A Daring Young Man: A Biography of William Saroyan*. New York, 2002.

Leitz, Christian. *Sympathy for the Devil: Neutral Europe and Nazi Germany in World War II*. New York, 2001.

Lewis, Flora. *Red Pawn: The Story of Noel Field*. Garden City, N.Y., 1965.

Liebling, A. J. "Letter from Lisbon." *The New Yorker*, July 6, 1940, 32–33.

Lorenz-Meyer, Martin. *Safehaven: The Allied Pursuit of Nazi Assets Abroad*. Columbia, Mo., 2007.

Lowndes, Susan. Introduction to *They Went to Portugal Too*, by Rose Macaulay. Manchester, UK, 1990.

Lubell, Samuel. "War by Refugee." *Saturday Evening Post*, March 29, 1941, 12ff.

Lucas, W. E. "Hitler Eyes Portugal." *The Nation*, April 26, 1941, 495–496.

Lukacs, John. *George Kennan*. New Haven, Conn., 2007.

————. *Blood, Toil, Tears, and Sweat*. New York, 2008.

Lycett, Andrew. *Ian Fleming: The Man Behind James Bond*. Atlanta, Ga., 1995.

Macaulay, Rose. "Looking in on Lisbon." *The Spectator*, July 2, 1943, 8.

————. *They Went to Portugal*. London, 1946.

————. *They Went to Portugal Too*. Ed. L. C. Taylor. Manchester, UK, 1990.

Macmillan, Harold. *The Blast of War, 1939–1945*. New York, 1968.

Mannes, Marya. "Letter from Lisbon." *The New Yorker*, July 1, 1944, 56–59.

————. "Letter from Lisbon." *The New Yorker*, July 22, 1944, 49–52.

————. "In Lisbon—'Dressed for Reaction.'" *Vogue*, September 1, 1944, 140ff.

————. *Out of My Time*. Garden City, N.Y., 1971.

Marino, Andy. *A Quiet American: The Secret War of Varian Fry*. New York, 1999.

Marrus, Michael R. *The Unwanted: European Refugees in the Twentieth Century*. New York, 1985.

Masterman, J. C. *The Case of the Four Friends*. London, 1960; orig. pub. 1956.

————. *The Double-Cross System in the War of 1939 to 1945*. New Haven, Conn., 1972.

McKay, C. G. "MI5 on OSTRO: A New Document from the Archives." *Intelligence and National Security*, 12 (3):178–184.

Mehring, Walter. *No Road Back*. Trans. S. A. DeWitt. New York, 1944.

Mellen, Joan. *Kay Boyle: Author of Herself*. New York, 1994.

Meneses, Filipe Ribeiro de. "Investigating Portugal, Salazar and the New State: The Work of the Irish Legation in Lisbon, 1942–1945." *Contemporary European History*, 11 (3):392–408.

————. *Salazar: A Political Biography*. New York, 2009.

Miller, David. *Mercy Ships*. London, 2008.

Miller, Russell. *Codename Tricycle*. London, 2004.

Moats, Alice-Leone. *No Passport for Paris*. New York, 1945.

Mowrer, Edgar Ansel. *Triumph and Turmoil: A Personal History of Our Time*. New York, 1968.

Mowrer, Lilian. "Fiesta in Lisbon." *The New Yorker*, July 20, 1940, 36–42.

Muir, Hugh. *European Junction*. London, 1942.

Neilson, William Allan, ed. *We Escaped: Twelve Personal Narratives of the Flight to America*. New York, 1941.

Nettelbeck, Colin W. *Forever French: Exile in the United States, 1939–1945*. New York, 1991.

Packard, Jerrold M. *Neither Friend Nor Foe: The European Neutrals in World War II*. New York, 1992.

Packard, Reynolds, and Eleanor Packard. *Balcony Empire: Fascist Italy at War*. New York, 1942.

Paldiel, Mordecai. *The Righteous Among the Nations*. New York, 2007.

Pauli, Hertha. *Break of Time*. New York, 1972.

Payne, Stanley G. *Franco and Hitler: Spain, Germany, and World War II*. New Haven, Conn., 2008.

Peabody, Polly. *Occupied Territory*. London, 1941.

Pearson, Norman Holmes. Foreword to J. C. Masterman, *The Double-Cross System in the War of 1939 to 1945*. New Haven, Conn., 1972.

Pell, Herbert C. *The Reminiscences of Herbert C. Pell*. Columbia University Oral History Collection, 1951.

Perdigão, José de Azeredo. *Calouste Gulbenkian, Collector*. Trans. Ana Lowndes Marques. Lisbon, 1969.

Persico, Joseph E. *Roosevelt's Secret War: FDR and World War II Espionage*. New York, 2001.

Pinto, António Costa. *The Blue Shirts: Portuguese Fascists and the New State*. Boulder, Colo., 2000.

Popov, Dusko. *Spy/Counterspy: The Autobiography of Dusko Popov*. New York, 1974.

Prokosch, Frederic. "Landscape—With Figures." *Vogue's First Reader*. New York, 1942.

———. *The Conspirators*. London, 1943.

———. *Voices: A Memoir*. New York, 1983.

Pujol, Juan, with Nigel West. *Operation Garbo: The Personal Story of the Most Successful Double Agent of World War II*. New York, 1985.

Quinlan, Paul D. *The Playboy King: Carol II of Romania*. Westport, Conn., 1995.

Ray, Man. *Self Portrait*. New York, 1963.

Reed, Douglas. *The Prisoner of Ottawa: Otto Strasser*. London, 1953.

Remarque, Erich Maria. *The Night in Lisbon*. Trans. Ralph Manheim. New York, 1964.

Rice, Elmer. *Minority Report: An Autobiography*. New York, 1963.

———. *Flight to the West*. New York, 1941.

Robertson, Ben. *I Saw England.* New York, 1941.

Rosas, Fernando. "Portuguese Neutrality in the Second World War." In *European Neutrals and Non-Belligerents During the Second World War,* edited by Neville Wylie. New York, 2002.

Rougemont, Denis de. *Journal d'une époque, 1926–1946.* Paris, 1968.

Sahl, Hans. *The Few and the Many.* Trans. Richard and Clara Winston. New York, 1962.

Saint-Exupéry, Antoine de. *Wartime Writings, 1939–1944.* Trans. Norah Purcell. San Diego, Calif., 1986.

Sapega, Ellen W. *Consensus and Debate in Salazar's Portugal: Visual and Literary Negotiations of the National Text, 1933–1948.* University Park, Pa., 2008.

Scammell, Michael. *Koestler: The Literary and Political Odyssey of a Twentieth-Century Skeptic.* New York, 2009.

Schellenberg, Walter. *The Schellenberg Memoirs.* Ed. and trans. Louis Hagen. London, 1956.

Schiff, Stacy. *Saint-Exupéry: A Biography.* New York, 1994.

Schoenberner, Franz. *Confessions of a European Intellectual.* New York, 1946.

———. *The Inside Story of an Outsider.* New York, 1949.

Schoonover, Thomas D. *Hitler's Man in Havana: Heinz Lüning and Nazi Espionage in Latin America.* Lexington, Ky., 2008.

Schorer, Mark. "The Little Door." *The New Yorker,* September 20, 1941, 31–33.

Schroth, Raymond A. *The American Journey of Eric Sevareid.* South Royalton, Vt., 1995.

Selby, Walford. *Diplomatic Twilight, 1930–1940.* London, 1953.

Serge, Victor. *Memoirs of a Revolutionary.* Trans. Peter Sedgwick. New York, 1963.

Sergueiev, Lily. *Secret Service Rendered.* London, 1968.

Seuling, Barbara. *Say It with Music: The Life and Legacy of Jane Froman.* Princeton, Ill., 2007.

Sevareid, Eric. "Lisbon—Escape Hatch of Europe." *The Living Age,* January 1941, 408–414.

———. *Not So Wild a Dream.* New York, 1947.

Sharp, Martha D. "Unitarian Service in the Iberian Peninsula." *Christian Register,* January 1946, 24–25.

Shelden, Michael. *Graham Greene: The Enemy Within.* New York, 1994.

Shepherd, Naomi. *A Refuge from Darkness: Wilfrid Israel and the Rescue of the Jews.* New York, 1984.

Sherry, Norman. *The Life of Graham Greene.* Vol. 2. New York, 1995.

Shirer, William L. *Berlin Diary: The Journal of a Foreign Correspondent, 1934–1941.* New York, 1941.

Shoemaker, Lloyd R. *The Escape Factory.* New York, 1990.

Smith, Arthur L., Jr. *Hitler's Gold: The Story of the Nazi War Loot.* Oxford, UK, 1989.

Smith, Bradley F. *The Shadow Warriors: O.S.S. and the Origins of the C.I.A.* New York, 1983.

Smith, R. Harris. *OSS: The Secret History of America's First Central Intelligence Agency.* Berkeley, Calif., 1972.

Soares, Mário. *Portugal's Struggle for Liberty.* Trans. Mary Gawsworth. London, 1975.

Spellman, Francis J. *Action This Day: Letters from the Fighting Fronts.* New York, 1943.

Squires, Radcliffe. *Frederic Prokosch.* New York, 1964.

Stafford, David. *Britain and the European Resistance, 1940–1945.* Toronto, 1980.

Steven, Stewart. *Operation Splinter Factor.* Philadelphia, 1974.

Stone, Glyn. *The Oldest Ally: Britain and the Portuguese Connection.* London, 1994.

———. *Spain, Portugal and the Great Powers, 1931–1941.* New York, 2005.

Strasser, Otto, and Michael Stern. *Flight from Terror.* New York, 1981; orig. pub. 1943.

Subak, Susan Elisabeth. *American Relief Workers Who Defied the Nazis.* Lincoln, Nebr., 2010.

Sullivan, Rosemary. *Villa Air-Bel: World War II, Escape, and a House in Marseille.* New York, 2006.

Sweeney, J. K. *United States' Policy Toward Portugal During the Second World War.* Ph.D. dissertation, Kent State University, 1970.

———. "The Portuguese Wolfram Embargo: A Case Study in Economic Warfare." *Military Affairs,* 38 (1):23–26.

Tabucchi, Antonio. *Pereira Declares.* Trans. Patrick Creagh. New York, 1995.

Taylor, Henry J. *Time Runs Out.* Garden City, N.Y., 1942.

———. "Europe's Unknown Strong Man." *Saturday Evening Post,* August 19, 1944, 9ff.

Toynbee, Arnold, and Veronica M. Toynbee, eds. *The War and the Neutrals.* London, 1956.

Vickers, Hugh. *Cecil Beaton: A Biography.* Boston, 1985.

Vintras, R. E. *The Portuguese Connection: The Secret History of the Azores Base.* London, 1974.

Walker, David E. *Lunch with a Stranger.* New York, 1957.

Waller, John H. *The Unseen War in Europe: Espionage and Conspiracy in the Second World War.* New York, 1996.

Walters, Vernon A. Review of *The Portuguese Connection,* by R. E. Vintras. Online at http://cia.gov/library/center-for-the-study-of-intelligence/kentcsi/docs/v18i4a04p_0001.html.

West, Nigel. *A Thread of Deceit: Espionage Myths of World War II.* New York, 1985.

———, ed. *The Guy Liddell Diaries.* Vols. 1 and 2. London, 2005.

Wheeler, Douglas L. "And Who Is My Neighbor? A World War II Hero or Conscience for Portugal." *Luso-Brazilian Review,* 26 (1):119–139.

———. "In the Service of Order: The Portuguese Political Police and the British, German and Spanish Intelligence." *Journal of Contemporary History,* 18 (1):1–25.

———. "The Price of Neutrality: Portugal, the Wolfram Question, and World War II." *Luso-Brazilian Review,* 23 (1):107–127; 23 (2):97–111.

————. "The Archives of Portugal: A Guide to an Intelligence Treasure Trove." *International Journal of Intelligence and Counterintelligence*, 4 (4):539–550.

Wills, Clair. *That Neutral Ireland*. Cambridge, Mass., 2007.

Winkler, Allan M. *The Politics of Propaganda: The Office of War Information, 1942–1945*. New Haven, Conn., 1978.

Winks, Robin W. *Cloak & Gown: Scholars in the Secret War*. New York, 1987.

Wriggins, Howard. *Picking Up the Pieces from Portugal to Palestine: Quaker Refugee Relief in World War II*. Lanham, Md., 2004.

Wylie, Neville. "'An Amateur Learns His Job'? Special Operations Executive in Portugal, 1940–1942." *Journal of Contemporary History*, 36 (3):441–457.

Wyman, David S. *Paper Walls: America and the Refugee Crisis, 1938–1941*. Amherst, Mass., 1968.

Yeager, Chuck, with Leo Janos. *Yeager: An Autobiography*. New York, 1985.

Ziegler, Philip. *King Edward VIII: A Biography*. New York, 1991.

INDEX

Exposition of the Portuguese World, 27–28, 31, 44; Ben Robertson on, 31; Duke of Kent at, 147, 214–215; opening of, 29–30

Fabled Shore (Macaulay), 299
FBI, 256, 257–258, 271
Ferro, António, 28
Feuchtwanger, Lion, 48–49, 50, 62, 67, 173; discloses escape route, 63–64; escape from internment of 57–58
Fidrmuc, Paul, 263–266, 272; American interrogation of, 265–266; British assessment of, 266; Twenty Committee and, 264–265
Field, Herta, 175, 178
Field, Noel, 175–178; OSS and, 177–178
Fields, Gracie, 143
First of the Few, The, 166
Fischmann, Lena, 6, 97
Fish, Bert, 87, 301; death of, 204; release of downed airmen and, 104; sale of downed aircraft and, 107–109
Fitch, Frederic, 96–98
Fittko, Hans, 65–67, 75, 96–97
Fittko, Lisa, 65–67, 75, 96–97
Flaherty, Robert, 158
Fleming, Ian, 271–272
Flight into Portugal (Bodley), 299
Flight to the West (Rice), 89–90
food rationing, 140–141, 280–281
Foreign Economic Administration (FEA), 288
Foreign Publicity Directorate (FPD), 209, 224
Fortune, 19, 83,
Fraga, Augusto, 219–220
Franckenstein, Joseph, 159
Franco, Francisco, 2, 7, 148, 154, 206; planned attack on Portugal of, 199
Franco-German armistice, 6, 36, 53–54

Franco, Nicolás, 138
Free Men Are Fighting (Gramling), 33
Freiburg University, 253
French Foreign Legion, 40–42, 49
French resistance, 76, 100–102
Froman, Jane, 91
Fry, Varian, 53–76, 157, 159, 171, 172–173, 312n; aids British escapees, 96–98; expelled from France, 74; Hans Sahl on, 59; Lisbon journeys of, 56, 63, 74–75; on Gestapo in Portugal, 75
Fullerton, Hugh, 57, 177

Gallagher, Wes, 32, 33
Garbo. *See* Juan Pujol
Gaymon, Alva E., 5
Gelder, Robert van, 161
Geneva Conventions, 96, 101
Gestapo, 20, 21, 36–37, 46, 67–68, 73, 120, 172; operations in Portugal of, 75, 252, 261; Otto John and, 118–119
Getty, Mrs. Paul, 109–110
Gide, André, 71
Giraudoux, Jean, 144
Gledhill, Cecil, 260
Godfrey, John, 272
Goebbels, Joseph, 54, 209, 233
gold, 286–287, 297; Eizenstat Report and, 291; German payment for wolfram with, 281; Portuguese commission and, 291–292
Gold, Mary Jayne, 68–69
Graham, Sheilah, 92
Grant, Cary, 144
Great Escape, The (Brickhill), 113
Green, Julien, 157
Greene, Graham, 272–275, 277; Nazi agents in Portugal and, 273
Griffith, Aline, 168–169, 235
Guggenheim, Peggy, 69, 159–161
Guggenheim, Solomon R., 70